Monique BREZI

DICTIONNAIRE

DES

PROVERBES

Français - Anglais

DICTIONARY

OF

PROVERBS

French - English

La Maison du Dictionnaire
98, Bld du Montparnasse F-75014 PARIS
Tél : (+33) 1 43 22 12 93 Fax : (+33) 1 43 22 01 77

Hippocrene Books, Inc
171 Madison Avenue, New York, NY, 10016
Tel : (212) 685-4371 Fax : (212) 779-9338

Table des matières

Contents

Contents

PREFACE

Ce dictionnaire de proverbes n'est pas un dictionnaire au sens classique des dictionnaires de langue en ce sens qu'il ne donne pas une traduction littérale ou même littéraire du proverbe recherché. Il donne un proverbe équivalent dans l'autre langue, exprimé la plupart du temps avec une autre image saisissant la même idée. < avoir un chat dans la gorge > en français, c'est < avoir une grenouille dans la gorge > en anglais. L'ouvrage n'a aucune vocation universitaire. Il s'adresse aux hommes et aux femmes d'aujourd'hui, qui voyagent ou travaillent en coopération avec des pays de langue anglophone, aux traducteurs de films ou de livres, à ceux qui utilisent la conversation, opposée à la langue écrite.

Il peut se consulter à titre de simple curiosité même si la pratique de l'anglais n'est pas tout à fait courante. Son grand nombre de proverbes peut servir de liste dans chaque prise séparément.

Amusez-vous bien !

FOREWORD

This dictionary of proverbs is not a usual dictionary, I mean it won't give a literal or literary translation. A foreign equivalent expressed most of the time, with another image will convey the same idea. < To have a frog in the throat > is < avoir un chat dans la gorge > : < to have a cat in the throat >.

The book has on academic purpose. It is targetted for modern travellers or people who work in a cross cultural English French environment, for translators of movies or books, for anybody using conversational language as opposed to written language.

At all language level, it will raise one's curiosity while providing most proverbs of both languages.

Have fun !

PREMIERE

PARTIE

FRANÇAIS
ANGLAIS

PART ONE

FRENCH
ENGLISH

A

abbé
> **il n'est point de plus sage abbé que celui qui a été moine**
> -no man can be a good ruler,unless he has first been ruled

abeille
> **une abeille vaut mieux que mille mouches**
> -it is not how long,but how well we live
> -a little and good fills the trencher

aboi
> **1-être aux abois**
> -to be at your last gasp
>
> **2-l'aboi d'un vieux chien doit-on croire**
> -he the old dog barks,he gives counsel

abondance
> **1-abondance de biens ne nuit pas**
> -you can't get too much of a good thing
> -plenty is not plague
> -store is no sore
>
> **2-abondance engendre fâcherie**
> -he that has lands,has quarrels
>
> **3-la trop grande abondance ne parvient pas à maturité**
> -Jack of all trades,master of none
>
> **4-de l'abondance du coeur la bouche parle**
> -love will go through stone walls
>
> **5-abondance engendre satiété**
> -plenty is no dainty
>
> **6-abondance engendre fâcherie**
> -he that has lands,has quarrels

absence
> **1-en l'absence du valet se connaît le serviteur**
> -a servant is known by his master absence
>
> **2-l'absence est l'ennemie de l'amour**
> -far from eye,far from mind
>
> **3-un peu d'absence fait grand bien**
> -blue are the hills that are far away
> -far folk far best
>
> **4-absent n'est point sans coulpe ni présent sans excuse**
> -the absent are never without fault,nor the present without excuse
>
> **5-les absents ont toujours tort**
> -the absent party is always to blame
> -never were the absent in the right
> -the absent saint gets no candle

acculer
être acculé au mur
-to be driven into a corner

acheter
acheter chat en poche
-to buy a pig in a poke

accorder
accordez-lui long comme un doigt,il en prendra long comme un bras
-give him an inch and he'll take a mile
-if you agree to carry the calf,they'll make you carry the cow
-all lay load on the willing horse

acheter
mieux vaut acheter qu'emprunter
-better buy than borrow
-a trade is better than service

acheteur
1-il y a plus d'acheteurs que de connaisseurs
il y a plus de fols acheteurs que de fols vendeurs
-there are more foolish buyers than foolish sellers

2-que l'acheteur prenne garde
-let the buyer beware
-keep your eye open,a sale is a sale

action
une bonne action ne reste jamais sans récompense
-our own actions are our security,not others'judgments

Adam
1-ne connaître quelqu'un ni d'Eve ni d'Adam
-not to know someone from Adam

2-en tenue d'Adam
-in a birthday suit

admiration
l'admiration est la fille de l'ignorance
-wonder is the daughter of ignorance

advenir
advienne que pourra
-come what may

adversité
1-l'adversité rend sage
-adversity is a good schoolmaster
-adversity makes a man wise,not rich

2-l'adversité est l'épreuve du courage
-adversity is the touchstone of virtue
-sickness shows us what we are

3-adversité est la pierre de touche de l'amitié
-prosperity makes friends,adversity tries them

affaire

1-les affaires du cabri ne sont pas celles du mouton
-keep your breath to cool your porridge

2-affaire à tout le monde,affaire à personne
-what is everybody's business is nobody's business
-a pot that belongs to many is ill stired and worse boiled

3-faire des affaires en or
-to make money hand over fist

4-mon affaire est manquée
l'affaire est dans le lac
-my cake is dough
-all my swans are turned to geese

5-les affaires sont les affaires
-business is business
-a fair exchange is no robbery
-a black dog for a white monkey
-don't mix business with pleasure

6-à nouvelles affaires,nouveaux conseils
-new lords,new laws

7-il n'y a pas de petites affaires
-he will never have a good thing cheap that is afraid to ask the price

8-ceux qui n'ont point d'affaires s'en font
-idleness turns the edge of wit

9-les affaires,c'est l'argent des autres
-trade is the mother of money

affection

affection aveugle raison
-love sees no fault
-love is blind

affiche

tenir l'affiche
-to have a long run

affliction

l'affliction ne guérit pas le mal
-make not two sorrows of one

affronter

1-affronter le fauve dans son antre
-to beard the lion in his den

2-affronter l'orage (figuré)
-to face the music

17

âge

1-chaque âge a ses plaisirs
-to each his own

2-d'âge en âge,on ne fait que changer de folie
-folly is the product of all countries and ages
-if all fools wore feathers we should seem a flock of geese

3-il n'y pas d'âge pour apprendre
-never too old to learn

4-l'âge n'est fait que pour les chevaux
-he who has good health is young;and he is rich who owes nothing

agir

agir dans la colère,c'est s'embarquer durant la tempête
-when a man grows angry,his reason rides out

aggraver

aggraver son cas
-to add insult to injury

agneau

il arrive que l'agneau devienne enragé
-one day the worm will turn

agréer

rien n'agrée sans bonne mine
-a good face is a letter of recommendation

aider

aide toi,le ciel t'aidera
-God helps them that help themselves
-we must not lie down and cry
-for a web begun God sends the thread

aigle

1-l'aigle quand il est malheureux appelle le hibou son frère
-adversity makes strange bedfellows
-while the thunder lasted,two bad men were friends

2-l'aigle n'engendre pas la colombe
-eagles don't breed doves
-as the old cock crows,so does the young one

3-l'aigle d'une maison n'est qu'un sot dans une autre
-a lion at home,a mouse abroad
-a prophet is not without honor except in his own country

4-un aigle ne chasse point aux mouches
-an eagle doen(t hawk at flies

5-qui se frotte à l'aïl ne peut sentir la giroflée
-a herring barrel always smell of fish

18

aile

1-avoir des ailes au talon
-to show a clean pair of heels

2-voler de ses propres ailes
-to stand on one's own two feet
-every tub should stand on its own bottom
-paddle your own canoe

aimer

1-on aime sans raison et sans raison l'on hait
-hatred is blind as well as love

2-qui aime Martin,aime son chien
-qui m'aime,aime mon chien
-les amis de nos amis sont nos amis
-love me,love my dog

3-ce qu'on aime est toujours beau
-beauty is in the eye of the beholder
-if Jack's in love,he's no judge of Jill's beauty
-in the eyes of the lover,pock-marks are dimples
-the owl thinks her own young fairest

4-qui aime bien,châtie bien
-spare the rod and spoil the child

5-quand on aime,ventre affamé n'a pas faim
-in love is no lack

6-si vous n'aimez pas ça,n'en dégoûtez pas les autres
-if you don't like it you may lump it

7-qui aime bien,tard oublie
-love without end has no end

air

1-avoir l'air pensif
-to look deep in thoughts

2-l'air ne fait pas la chanson
-you can't tell a book by its cover
-the fowler's pipe sounds sweet till the bird is caught

aisé

il est bien aisé d'aller à pied quand on tient son cheval par la bride
-a saint in crape is twice a saint in lawn

aller

1-aller à Canossa
-to eat humble pie

2-aller son train de sénateur
-to go at a snail gallop

3-au long aller le fardeau pèse
-in a long journey,straw weighs

aller (suite)
    4-il allait son petit bonhomme de chemin
    -he hit pay dirt (langage minier)
    -to tootle along

    5-l'on ne doit pas aller à la noce sans y être convié
    -who invited you to the roast?

    6-on ne va pas aux noces sans manger
    -they that dance must pay the fiddler

    7-ne pas y aller par quatre chemins
    -not to beat around the bush

    8-il ne faut pas aller par quatre chemins
    -he who hesitates is lost

    9-cela va sans dire
    -it stands to reason

    10-on va de tout vent à un même endroit
    -follow the river and you'll get to the sea

    11-tout va de travers
    -the times are out of joint

    12-cela me va comme un gant
    -that suits me down to the ground

    13-ne pas y aller avec le dos de la cuiller
    -not to put too fine an edge on it

    14-on ne va pas aux mûres sans crochet
    -he who will the end,will the means

    15-qui va doucement,va sûrement
    -fair and soft go far in the day
    -slow but sure wins the race

    16-n'aille au bois qui a peur des feuilles
    -he that fears leaves let him not go into the woods

    17-aller de mal en pis
    -to go from bad to worse

    18-il faut aller selon sa bourse
    -let your purse be your master

    -qui va à la chasse,perd sa place
    -a bleating sheep loses a bite

alouette
    il attend que les alouettes lui tombent toutes rôties dans le bec
    -every day is holiday with sluggards
    -the sluggard's convenient season never comes
    -roasted pigeons don't fly through the air
    -to think that larks will fall into one's mouth ready roasted
    -to lie in bed till meat falls in one's mouth

alouette (suite)
>**il attend que les alouettes lui tombent toutes rôties dans le bec**
>-he that gapes until be fed,well may be gape until he be dead
>-gape long enough,larks will fall into mouth

âme
>**il faut de l'âme pour avoir du goût**
>-to him that has his taste,sweet is sour

amender
>**on ne s'amende pas de vieillir**
>-it early pricks that will be a thorn

ami
>**1-à quoi bon tant d'amis? Un seul suffit quand il vous aime**
>-avoir beaucoup d'amis,c'est n'avoir point d'amis
>-books and friends should be few but good

>**2-mieux vaut ami grondeur que flatteur**
>-better an open enemy than a false friend
>-with friends like that,who needs enemies?

>**3-mieux vaut ami en voie que denier en courroie**
>-a friend in court is better than a penny in purse

>**4-mieux vaut ami en place qu'argent en bourse**
>-a friend in the market is better than a penny in the chest

>**5-les vieux amis et les vieux écus sont les meilleurs**
>-old fish,old oil,and an old friend are the best
>-old friends and old wine and old gold are best

>**6-un ami est long à trouver et prompt à perdre**
>-a friend is not so soon gotten as lost

>**7-qui prête aux amis perd au double**
>**ami au prêter,ennemi au rendre**
>-lend your money and lose your friend
>-when I lent I had a friend,when I asked he was unkind
>-misfortune makes foes of friends

>**8-si ton ami est borgne regarde de profil**
>-love you friend with his fault
>-he that loves the tree loves the branch

>**9-riche homme ne sait qui ami lui est**
>-the rich knows not who is his friend

>**10-la prospérité fait peu d'amis**
>-he that has a full purse never wanted a friend

>**11-les amis de nos amis sont nos amis**
>-love me,love my dog

>**12-dans l'adversité de nos meilleurs amis,nous trouvons quelque chose qui ne nous déplaît pas**
>-love your friend with his fault
>-if you love the boll,you cannot hate the branches

ami (suite)

13-aujourd'hui ami,demain ennemi
-trust not a new friend nor an old enemy

14-amis valent mieux qu'argent
-kind hearts are more than coronets

amitié

sur le chemin de l'amitié,ne laissez pas croître d'herbe
-friendship is a plant which must be often watered

amour

1-filer le parfait amour
-to live like two lovebirds

2-l'amour avidement croit tout ce qu'il souhaite
-when love is in,there is faith

3-l'amour vainc tout sauf coeur de félon
-love will find a way
-love laughs at locksmiths
-love conquers all
-it is love that makes the world go around

4-amour peut moult,argent peut tout
-amour vainc tout,argent fait tout
-love does much ,money does everything

5-il n'y a pas de belles prisons ni de laides amours
-no love is foul,nor prison fair

6-amour apprend aux ânes à danser
-love makes all hearts gentle

7-l'amour ne connaît pas de loi
-love is lawless

8-l'amour et l'amitié s'excluent l'un l'autre
-when love puts in,friendship is gone

9-l'amour est aveugle
-love is blind

10-l'amour fait passer le temps et le temps fait passer l'amour
-love is the fruit of idleness

11-amour,toux,fumée et argent ne se peuvent cacher longtemps
-love and a cough cannot be hid

12-l'amour est souvent le fruit du mariage
-marry first and love will follow

13-amour a de coutume d'entremêler ses plaisisrs d'amertume
the course of true love never did run smooth

an

1-les ans ont beaucoup plus vu que les livres n'en ont connu
-experience without learning is better than learning without experience

2-l'an qui vient est un brave homme
-tomorrow is another day

âne

1-faire l'âne pour avoir du son
-with hankerchief in one hand and sword in the other
-to carry fire in one hand and water in the other

2-un âne ne trébuche pas deux fois sur la même pierre
-it's a silly fish that is caught twice at the same bait
-every failure one meets will add to experience
-trouble brings experience and experience brings wisdom
-he complains wrongfully of the sea that twoce suffered shipwreck

3-d'un âne on ne peut demander de la viande de boeuf
-if you squeeze a cork,you will get but little juice

4-près des ânes,on attrappe des coups de pieds
-they who play bowls must expect to meet with rubbers

5-il y a plus d'un âne à la foire qui s'appelle Martin
-there is more fish for every man
-there are more Jacks than one at the fair
-there are as good fish in the seas as ever came out of it

6-à l'âne,l'âne semble beau
-like begets like
-the owl thinks her own young fairest

7-un âne gratte l'autre
-one fool praises another
-like cures like

8-âne avec le cheval n'attèle
-like blood,like good,and like age make the happiest marriage

9-tous les ânes ne portent pas de sac
-all feet tread not in one shoe
-every shoe fits not every foot
-all meat pleases not all mouths
-no dish pleases not all palates alike

10-qui est un âne et veut être un cerf se connaît au saut du fossé
-the filth under the white snow the sun discovers

11-il n'y a pas d'âne plus mal bâté que celui du commun
-what is everybody's business is nobody's business

ange

qui veut faire l'ange fait la bête
-the bait hides the hook

anguille
>1-il y a anguille sous roche
>-I smell a rat

>2-il fait comme les anguilles de Melun qui crient avant qu'on
>les écorche
>-don't cry before you are hurt

année
>d'un bout de l'année à l'autre
>-from year's end to year's end

aplanir
>aplanir les difficultés
>-to iron out the difficulties

appareil
>dans le plus simple appareil
>-in your birthday suit

appelé
>il y a beaucoup d'appelés mais peu d'élus
>-many are called,but few are chosen

appeler
>-appeler un chat un chat
>-to call a spade a spade

appétit
>l'appétit vient en mangeant
>-the more you have the more you want
>-appetite comes with eating
>-much would have more
>-the appetite grows with what it feeds on

apporter
>1-je n'en apporterai pas la mode
>-I am not the first and I shall not be the last

>2-apporter de l'eau au moulin
>-all's grist to the mill
>-to provide grist for the mill

apprendre
>1-je vais lui apprendre !
>-I will blow him sky high

>2-il faut apprendre de la vie à souffrir la vie
>-life is not all cakes and ale

>3-on apprend à tout âge
>-it is never too late to learn
>-one is never too old to learn

>4-ce qu'on apprend au berceau,dure jusqu'au tombeau
>-who so learns young,forgets not when he is old
>-learning in one's youth is engraving in stone
>-what's learnt in the craddle last till the tomb

-a tree must bent while it is young
-what youth is used to,age remembers

5-on n'apprend pas au singe à faire la grimace
-you can't teach an old dog new tricks
-you cannot teach your grandmother to suck eggs
-never offer fish to swim

apprenti

1-jouer les apprenti-sorciers
-to let the cat out of the bag

2-apprenti n'est pas maître
-experience must be bought

araignée

avoir une araignée dans le plafond
-to have bats in the belfry
-to have your head full of bees
-to have bee in your bonnet

arbre

1-l'arbre ne doit pas nous cacher la forêt
-we cannot see the forest for the trees
-catch not at the shadow and lose the substance
-you cannot see the city for the houses

2-arbre trop souvent transplanté,rarement fait fruit à planter
-a tree often transplanted,bears not much fruit

3-vieil arbre d'un coup ne s'arrache
-custom is a second nature

4-on reconnaît l'arbre à ses fruits
tel arbre,tel fruit
-by their fruits shall you know them
-as the tree,so the fruit

5-quand l'arbre est couché,tout le monde court aux branches
-to kick a man when he is down

arc

1-débander l'arc ne guérit pas la plaie
-to unstring the bow will not heal the wound

2-l'arc ne peut toujours être tendu
-all work and no play makes Jack a dull boy

argent

1-l'argent ne fait pas le sage
-an ass is but an ass,though laden with gold

2-l'argent est le nerf de la guerre
-money is the sinews of war
-money will make the mare go

3-l'argent va à l'argent
-money makes money
-it takes money to make mone
-money begets money

argent (suite)

4-pas d'argent,pas de suisse
-no money,no piper
-no money,no Swiss
-no song,no supper

5-ne jetez pas votre argent par les fenêtres
-don't make ducks and drakes of your money

6-prêter de l'argent fait perdre la mémoire
-creditors have better memories than debtors
-debtors are liars

7-l'argent ne fait pas le bonheur
-money isn't everything

8-argent est serviteur ou maître
-money is a good servant but a bad master

9-argent emprunté porte tristesse
-he that goes a borrowing goes a sorrowing
-he that borrows must pay again with shame and loss

10-l'argent n'a pas d'odeur
-a buck is a buck
-money has no smell
-money is welcome though it comes in a dirty clout
-money never comes out of season

11-qui a de l'argent a des pirouettes
-he who pays the piper calls the tune
you pays your money and you takes your choice

12-argent fait perdre et prendre gens
-evil communications corrupt good manners

13-qui n'a pas d'argent en bourse,qu'il ait du miel en bouche
-he that hath not silver in his purse should have silk in his tongue
-he must stoop that has a low door

14-on fait tout avec de l'argent, excepté les hommes
-rather a man without money than money wuthout a man

arme
les armes sont journalières
-what chances to one man,may happen to all men

arrangement
un mauvais arrangement vaut mieux qu'un bon procès
-to come to an arrangement is better than to going law

arriver
1-arriver après la bataille
-to kiss the hare's foot

2-arriver comme un chien dans un jeu de quille
-better say nothing than not to the purpose

3-il arrive comme les carabiniers
-he acts like a Monday evening quarterback

4-il ne vous arrive pas à la cheville
-he can't hold a candle to you

5-il n'arrive pas à la cheville de son père
-don't name him in the same breath with his father

6-il vaut mieux arriver en retard qu'arriver en corbillard
-it is better to travel hopefully than to arrive
-better be sure than sorry

arrondir
arrondir les angles
-to straighten everything out
-to smooth things over

art
c'est l'enfance de l'art
-it's a lead pipe cinch
-it's all sewed up

artisan
l'artisan vit partout
-an artist lives everywhere

asile
l'asile le plus sûr est le sein de sa mère
-the mother's breast is aye sweet

assassin
l'assassin revient toujours sur le lieu de son crime
-the dog return to its vomit

assiette
ne pas être dans son assiette
-to be out of sorts

asseoir
assieds-toi,ce n'est pas plus cher
-it is as cheap sitting as standing

attendre
il faut attendre à cueillir la poire qu'elle soit mûre
-when the fruit is ripe,it must fall off
-don't try to run before you walk

attraper
on n'attrape pas de lièvres avec un tambour
-silence catches a mouse

auberge
être sorti de l'auberge
-to be out of the woods

audace
payer d'audace
-to put a bolt face on something

autre
vous en êtes un autre
-it takes one to know one

aujourd'hui
1-aujourd'hui en chair,demain en bière
-life is but a long journey to death

2-aujourd'hui roi,demain rien
-today a man,tomorrow a mouse

autant
autant de mariages,autant de ménages
-many men,many minds

autruche
faire la politique de l'autruche
-to burry one's head in the sand

autrui
ne fais pas à autrui ce que tu ne voudrais pas qu'on te fît
-do unto others as you would have them do unto you
-do as you would be done by

avancer
quand on n'avance pas,on recule
-he is not backward in coming forward
-he that looks not before,finds himself behind

avare
1-l'avare crierait famine sur un tas de blé
-beggar's bag is bottomless

2-un avare est toujours gueux
-he is not poor that has little,but he that desires much
-fools live poor to die rich

3-les avares font nécessité de tout
-covetousness is always filling a bottomless vessel
-beggars'bags are bottomless

avarice
l'avarice perd tout en voulant tout gagner
-covetousness bursts the sack

avenir
1-l'avenir appartient à ceux qui se lèvent tôt
-the early bird catches the worm
-he that will thrive must rise at five
-first come (in),first served
-he that rises first,he first dressed
-early to bed and early to rise,makes a man healthy,wealthy and wise
-he that will sleep all the morning may go a begging all the day [2] after

2-nous ne savons pas ce que l'avenir nous réserve
-we don't know what the future has in store for us
-we can't dip into the future

aventurer (s')
qui ne s'aventure pas n'a ni cheval ni mule
-take your venture as many a good ship has done
-nothing venture,nothing have

aveugle
1-au royaume des aveugles le borgne est roi
-among the blind the one eyed man is king
-a big fish in a little pond

2-si un aveugle en conduit un autre,ils tomberont tous les deux
-the blind lead the blind,both shall fall onto the ditch

3-c'est un aveugle qui en conduit un autre
-blind leader of the blind

avis
1-deux avis valent mieux qu'un
-two heads are better than one

2-un bon avis vaut un oeil dans la main
-good advice is beyond price
-good counsel never comes amiss
-if the counsel be good,no matter who gave it

aviser
de tout s'avise à qui pain faut
-necessity is the mother of invention
-poverty i the mother of invention

avocat
bon avocat,mauvais voisin
-a good lawyer makes a bad neighbour

avoir
1-il faut avoir deux cordes à son arc
-although it rain,throw not away your watering pot

2-quand on n'a pas ce que l'on aime,il faut vouloir ce que l'on a
-he that may not as he would,must do as he may
-we must not look for a golden life in an iron age
-one foot is better than two crutches
-half a loaf is better than no bread
-better a louse in the pot than no flesh at all
-better are small fish than an empty dish
-better some of the pudding than none of the pie
-a churl's feast is better than none at all
-half an egg is better than an empty shell
-better a lean jade than an empty halter
-a bad bush is better than the open field
-better a bad foot than none
-better eye sore than be blind altogether
-a man were better to be half blind than both have his eyes out

29

2-quand on n'a pas ce que l'on aime,il faut vouloir ce que l'on a (suite)
-better my hog dirty home than no hog at all
-something is better than nothing
-they that have no other meat,bread and butter are glad
-it is better to sup with a cutty than want a spoon
-a crust is better than no bread
-better a little loss than a long sorrow
-better a finger off than always aching
-better cut the shoe than pinch the foot

3-avoir quelqu'un dans sa poche
to have one on the hip

4-plus on en a,plus on en veut
-qui plus a,plus convoite
-the more one has,the more one desires (wants)
-much would have more

avril

avril,ne te découvre pas d'un fil
mai,mets ce qu'il te plaît
-cast not a clout till May is out

B

baba
> **l'avoir dans le baba** (familier)
> -to get it in the neck

badiner
> **on ne badine pas avec l'amour**
> -do not trifle with love

baguette
> **mener à la baguette**
> -to keep under one's thumb

baigner
> **on ne se baigne jamais deux fois dans le même fleuve**
> -there is nothing permanent except change

bailler
> **bailler à se décrocher la mâchoire**
> -to yawn one's head off

bailleur
> **un bon bailleur en fait bailler sept**
> -if one sheep leaps over the ditch,all the rest will follow

bal
> **donner le bal à quelqu'un**
> -I'll lead you a pretty dance

balayer
> **qu'il balaye d'abord devant sa porte**
> -if each would sweep before his own door,we should have a clean street

barbe
> **1-la barbe ne fait pas l'homme**
> -if the beard were all,the goat might preach
>
> **2-en la grande barbe ne gît pas le savoir**
> -it is not the bear that makes the philosopher

barbier
> **un barbier rase l'autre**
> -like cures like
> -like will to like

bariolé
> **bariolé comme la chandelle des rois**
> -gay as the king's candle

baronie
> **c'est une belle baronie que la santé**
> -health is great riches

barrière
> **1-être du bon (mauvais) côté de la barrière**
> -to be on the right (wrong) side of the hedge

2-là où la barrière est basse,le boeuf enjambe
-cross the stream where it is shallowest

bas

avoir un gros bas de laine
-to have a long stocking

bât

où le bât blesse
-where the shoe pinches

bateau

1-être dans le même bateau
-to be in the same box

2-il m'a monté un bateau
-he lead me up the garden path

bâton

1-mettre des bâtons dans les roues
-to put a spoke in one's wheel

2-du bâton que l'on tient on est souvent battu
-to make a rod for one's own back

battre

1-battre à plates coutures
-to beat the daylight out
-to beat someone black and blue

2-battre le fer pendant qu'il est chaud
-to strike while the iron is hot
-to make hay while the sun shines
-gather ye rosebuds while ye may
-life is short and time si swift

3-battre froid quelqu'un
-to give one the cold shoulder

4-se battre contre des moulins à vent
-it is in vain to cast your net when there is no fish

bavarde

elle est bavarde comme une pie
-a woman's tongue wags like a lamb's tail

bave

la bave du crapaud n'atteint pas la blanche colombe
-sticks and stones may break my bones,but words will never hurt me

beau

il n'est si beau soulier qui ne devienne savate
-beauty is only skin deep

beauté

1-beauté n'est qu'image fardée
-beauty is only skin deep

32

2-la beauté est une fleur éphémère
-beauty is but a blossom
-the fairest flowers soonest fade
-the fairest rose at last is whithered
-prettiness dies first
-grace will last,beauty will blast
-beauty fades like a flower
-the fairest silk is soonest stained

3-beauté ne vaut rien sans bonté
-beauty without bounty avails nought
-goodness is better than beauty

4-il est rare de voir la sagesse alliée à la beauté
-beauty and folly go often in company

5-la beauté ne sale pas la marmite
-many words will not fill a bushel
-praise without profit puts little in the pot
-he who gives fair words feeds you with an empty spoon
-handsome is as handsome does
-beauty won't make the pot boil

6-beauté de femme n'enrichit l'homme
-soft words butter no parsnips

bébé
il ne faut pas jeter le bébé avec l'eau du bain
-don't throw the baby with the bath

belle
belle comme un sous neuf
-fine as five pence

bercer
se bercer d'illusions
-to live in a fool's paradise

besogne
besogne qui plaît est à moitié faite
-not a long day,but a good heart rids work
-it is easy to do what one's own self wills

besoin
1-au besoin l'ami
on connaît le véritable ami dans le besoin
-a friend in need is a friend indeed
-real friendship does not freeze in winter

2-on a toujours besoin d'un plus petit que soi
-the strong prey upon the weak
-a mouse may help a lion
-great fleas have lesser fleas
-a lion may come to be beholden to a mouse
-willows are weak,yet they bind other wood

bête
1-qui bête va à Rome,tel en retourne
-he that is born a fool is never cured
-send a fool to the market and a fool will return again
-if an ass goes a-travelling,he'll not come home a horse
-travellers change climates not conditions
-lead a pig to the Rhine,it remains a pig
-to return home as wise as one went

2-chercher la petite bête
-to nit-pick

3-bête comme ses pieds
-as thick as a door post
-he is a regular flat fish

beurre
1-faire son beurre familier)
-to make one's pile

2-vouloir le beurre et l'argent du beurre
-you cannot eat your cake and have it too
-you cannot have it both ways
-you cannot sell the cow and sup the milk

bien
1-qui fera bien,bien trouvera
-good hand,good hire
-the deed comes back upon the doer
-do well and have well

2-bien au chaud
-as snug as the bug in the rug

3-bien mal acquis ne profite jamais
-ill gotten goods seldom prosper
-ill gotten,ill spent
-what is got over the devil's back is spent under his belly
-money for jam,money for old rope

4-le bien facilement acquis se dépense de même
-light come,easy go

5-tout est bien qui finit bien
-all's well that ends well
-the end crowns the work
-the evening crowns the day
-the ending rounds off the whole

6-qui fera bien,bien trouvera
-do well and have well

7-il est bien dans sa peau
-he is on good footing with the world

8-bien perdu,bien connu
-blessings brighten as they take their flight
-blessings are not valued till they are gone
-a good when lost is valued most
-misfortune tells us what fortune is

9-on fait souvent du bien pour pouvoir impunément faire du mal
-charity covers a multitude of sins

bienfait
1-un bienfait n'est jamais perdu
-a good deed is never lost
-one never loses by doing a good turn

2-les bienfaits s'écrivent sur le sable et les injures sur l'airain
-ten good turns lie dead and one ill deed report abroad   does spread
-old sins cast long shadows
-injuries are written in brass
-injuries don't use to be written on ice
-the evil that man do lives after them,the good is oft
-interred with their bones

3-un bienfait reproché tient lieu d'offense
-money refused loses its brightness

bille
aller bille en tête
-to charge like a bull at the gate

blanc
1-être blanc comme neige
-to be as pure as the driven snow

2-rester blanc comme un navet (ne pas rougir)
-to blush like a blue dog

blanc-bec
c'est un blanc-bec
-he is wet behind the ears
-he's pretty wet
-don't talk wet

blanchir
à vouloir blanchir un nègre,on perd sa lessive
-there is no washing a blackamoor white

blé
1-le bon blé porte bien l'ivraie
-every man has the defects of his own virtues

2-de nuit,le blé semble farine
-all cats are grey in the dark

boeuf
1-le boeuf de la vallée ne connaît pas les souffrances du boeuf de la colline
-it is easy to bear the misfortune of others

2-les grands boeufs ne font pas les grands labours
-there is many a fair thing,full false
-appearances are deceptive
-things are seldom what they seem
-the greatest crabs be not all the best meat
-the greatest calf is not the sweetest veal

3-quand les boeufs vont à deux,le labourage va mieux
-a merry companion is a waggon in the way
-good company on the road is the shortest cut

boire
1-qui a bu boira
-once a thief always a thief
-once a gambler,always a gambler
-he that has done ill once will do it again
-once a knave,always a knave

2-il y a à boire et à manger dans son histoire
-his story is a mixture of fact and fancy

3-boire jusqu'à la lie
-to drink the cup of sorrow

bois
1-le bois tordu fait le feu droit
-crooked logs make straight fires
-a straight stick is crooked in the water
-a straight tree may have crooked roots

**2-bois tordu ne se redresse pas
on ne peut faire de bois tord droite flèche**
-you cannot make a crab walk straight

3-n'aille au bois qui a peur des feuilles
-he that fears leaves,let him not go into the woods

36

4-toucher du bois
-to keep one's fingers crossed

boîte

dans les petites boîtes,les bons onguents
-the best things come in small packages
-the greatest calf is not the sweetest veal
-the greatest crabs be not all the best meat
-an inch is as good as an ell

bon

1-être en bons termes avec quelqu'un
-to be on good footing with somebody

2-les bons pâtissent pour les mauvais
-the worst hog gets the best pear

3-ce qui est bon pour l'un est bon pour l'autre
-what is sauce for the goose is sauce for the gander

4-ce qui est bon à prendre est bon à rendre
-borrowed things will home again

5-qui bon maître a,bon loyer a
-good hand,good hire

6-bon grain périt,paille demeure
-thorns live and roses die

7-bon à tout,propre à rien
-Jack of all trades-master of none
-grasp all,lose all

8-il est bon avoir quelque chose sous le mortier
-lay something for a rainy day

bond

faire faux bond
-to stand someone up

bonheur

tout bonheur que la main n'atteint pas est un rêve
-hope is the dream of a man awake

bonhomme

aller son bonhomme de chemin
-to tootle along

bonnet

1-c'est bonnet blanc et blanc bonnet
-it is six of one and half a dozen of the other

2-que celui à qui le bonnet fait,le mette!
-if the cap fits,wear it

bossu

chacun est bossu quand il se baisse
-he is lifeless that is faultless

boucaut
> **beau boucaut,mauvaise morue**
> -appearances are deceptive
> -fair face,foul heart

bouche
> **1-apprendre par le bouche à oreille**
> -to hear through the grapevine

> **2-bouche en coeur au sage,coeur en bouche au fou**
> -silence never makes any blunder

> **3-la bouche parle de l'abondance du coeur**
> -when the heart is full of lust,the mouth's full of leasings

> **4-dans une bouche close il n'entre point de mouches**
> **dans bouche fermée rien ne rentre**
> -a closed mouth catches no flies

> **5-je le tiens de la bouche du cheval**
> -straight from the horse's mouth

bouchée
> **mettre les bouchées doubles**
> -to work a dead horse

boucherie
> **à la boucherie toutes les vaches sont boeufs, à la tannerie tous**
> **les boeufs sont vaches**
> -after praising the wine,they sell us vinegar

bouclier
> **une levée de bouclier**
> -a chorus of protests

bouder
> **elle boude contre son ventre**
> -to quarrel with your bread and butter

bouée
> **c'est ma bouée de sauvetage**
> -that is my sheet anchor

bouillir
> **faire bouilllir la marmite**
> -to bring home the bacon

boule
> **perdre la boule**
> -to lose one's marbles

boulons
> **il a perdu ses boulons**
> -he has not all his buttons

boulet
> **1-traîner un boulet**
> -to have a millstone around one's neck

2-pour un boulet de canon
-for all the tea in China

bourse
1-selon ta bourse,gouverne ta bouche
-keep no more cats than will catch mice

2-à bourse pleine,amis nombreux
-friends are plenty when the purse is full
-rich folk have many friends
-sucess has many friends
-a rich man's joke is always funny

3-il faut aller selon sa bourse
-cut your coat according to your cloth
-let your purse be your master
-spend as you get
-stretch your arm no further than your sleeve will reach
-everyone streches his legs according to the length of his coverlet
-lay your wame to your winning

bout
1-être poussé à bout
-to be on one's beam ends

2-être au bout du rouleau
-to be at dead lift

boutique
on en peut rester longtemps dans la boutique d'un parfumeur sans en emporter l'odeur
-a herring barrel always smell of fish

bouton
il ne manque pas un bouton de guêtre
-to get one's ducks in a row
-to have something buttoned on

branche
1-il ne faut pas scier la branche sur laquelle on est assis
-never cast dirt into the fountain which you have sometimes drunk
-do not cut the tree that gives you shade
-don't cut the bough you are standing on
-why kick down the ladder by which you have climbed?

2-les branches des arbres trop chargées de fruits rompent
-a shoe too large trips one up

branler
tout ce qui branle ne tombe pas
-all clouds bring not rain
-all that shakes falls not

bras
1-il est mon bras droit
-he is my right hand

bras (suite)
> **2-selon le bras,la saignée**
> lay your wame to your winning

brave
> **il n'y a pas d'heure pour les braves**
> -to a brave and faithful man nothing is difficult
> -to the real hero life is a mere straw

brebis
> **1-quand les brebis enragent,elles sont pires que les loups**
> -a little pot is soon hot
> -short folk are soon angry

> **2-brebis comptées,le loup les mange**
> -the best-laid plans may fall
> -make yourself a lamb and the wolves will eat you

> **3-la brebis bêle toujours d'une même sorte**
> -the leopard cannot change his spots

> **4-une brebis galeuse suffit pour pervertir tout le groupe (infester le troupeau)**
> -one scabbed sheep infests the whole flock
> -a hog that's bemired endeavours to bemire others

> **5-brebis qui bêle perd sa goulée**
> -a bleating sheep loses a bite

> **6-la brebis galeuse**
> -the black sheep

> **7-brebis trop apprivoisée de trop d'agneaux est tétée**
> -a wicked man is his own hell

brillant
> **brillant comme un sou neuf**
> -as bright as a button

briller
> **tout ce qui brille n'est pas d'or**
> -all that glitter is not gold
> -what is sweet in the mouth is often bitter in the stomach
> -all that sizzles may not be meat
> -every light is not the sun
> -he that looks in a man's face knows not what money is in his pocket

bruit
> **1-faire plus de bruit que de mal**
> -to bark worse than one's bite

> **2-beaucoup de bruit pour rien**
> -much ado about nothing
> -much cry and little wool
> -the devil rides on a fiddlestick
> -much smoke,little fire

-a storm in a tea cup
-there is more talk than trouble

brûler

1-il faut quelquefois brûler une chandelle au Diable
-to hold a candle to the devil

2-brûler ses vaisseaux
-to burn one's boats
-to burn one's bridges behind you
-why kick the ladder by which you have climbed?

3-on ne peut brûler la chandelle par les deux bouts
-you cannot burn the candle at both ends

buisson

il n'est si petit buisson qui ne porte son ombre
-little strokes fell great oaks
-there is no little enemy

but

1-de but en blanc
-at the drop of a hat

2-le but n'est pas toujours placé pour être atteint mais pour servir de point de   mire
-hitch your wagon to a star

buse

on ne peut faire d'une buse un épervier
-the leopard cannot change his spots
-you cannot make a silk purse out of a sow's ear
-a carrion kite will never be a good horse
-a booby will never make a hawk

buveur

les buveurs d'eau sont méchants
-water drinkers bring forth nothing good
-Adam's ale is the best brewer

C

cadavre
un cadavre ambulant
-death warmed up
-like an anatomy

cage
la belle cage ne nourrit pas l'oiseau
-he who gives fair words feeds you with an empty spoon

calende
renvoyer aux calendes grecques
-when hell freezes over
-till the ass ascend the ladder
-at later Lammas

calme
1-après le calme,la tempête
-after a storm comes a calm

2-calmer le jeu
-to pour oil on trouble waters

calmer
calmer le jeu
-to pour oil on trouble waters

camelot
quand le camelot a pris son pli,c'est pour toujours
-you can never scare a dog away from a greasy hide

camper
camper sur ses positions
-to stick to one's guns

canard
le vilain petit canard
-the black sheep of the family

caque
la caque sent toujours le hareng
-a herring barrel always smell of fish

caresser
on caresse la vache pour mieux la traire
-the bait hides the hook

carotte
les carottes sont cuites(familier)
-all is over but the shouting
-my goose is cooked
-I'm a dead duck,a dead pigeon

carte
1-les cartes sont truquées
-the dice are loaded

2-donner carte blanche
-to give a blank cheque

casaque
tourner casaque
-to run away from one's own guns

case
avoir une case qui manque (familier)
-to have a tile loose

casse
passez moi la casse(rhubarbe) et je vous passerai le séné
-you scratch my back and I'll scratch yours
-roll my log and I'll roll yours
-ka me,ka thy

casser
1-cela ne casse rien
-it doesn't cut any ice

2-qui casse les verres,les paie
-they that dance must pay the fiddler

3-se casser la tête
-to beat one's brain out

4-casser sa pipe (familier)
-to kick the bucket

5-il faut casser le noyau pour en avoir l'amende
-he that will eat the kernel,must crack the nut

cause
petites causes,grands effets
-a little leak will sink a big ship

cautère
c'est un cautère sur une jambe de bois
-it is just like chip in the porridge

cave
il ne faut pas mettre dans une cave un ivrogne qui a renoncé au vin
-better keep the devil at the door than turn him out of the house

cause
petites causes,grands effets
-a little leak will sink a big ship

cautère
c'est un cautère sur une jambe de bois
-it is like chip in the porridge

cent
1-cent fois sur le métier,remettez votre ouvrage
-if at first you don't succeed,then try,try,and try again
-practice makes perfect
-if it isn't well bobbit we'll bob it again

cent

1-cent fois sur le métier,remettez votre ouvrage (suite)
-custom makes all things easy
-it's dogged that does it
-frequent and regular repetition is the principal factor of success
-seek till you find,and you will not lose your labor
-a work ill done must be done twice
-no man is his craft's master the first day

2-cent livres de mélancolie ne paient pas un sou de dette
-a hundred pounds of sorrow pays not one ounce of debt
-sorrow will pay no debt

certitude

1-mieux vaut une certitude qu'une promesse en l'air
-one thousand probabilities does not make one truth

2-la seule certitude,c'est que rien n'est certain
nothing is certain but the unforeseen

cesser

il ne cesse de brandir l'anathème contre ses ennemis
-he never stops hurling fire and brimstone at his enemies

chacun

1-chacun pour soi et Dieu pour tous
-every man for himself and God for us all
-every man for himself and the devil takes the hindmost
-self preservation is the first law of nature

2-chacun voit midi à sa pendule
-there may be blue and better blue
-every man buckles his belt his ain gate

3-chacun est l'artisan de son sort
-every man is the architect of his own fortune
-every man is the son of his own work
-let every sheep hang by his own shank
-every herring must hang by its own gill
-every tub must stand on its own bottom
-every man should work on his own salvation
-every man buckles his belt his ain gate

4-chacun prend son plaisir où il se trouve
-chacun voit midi à sa pendule
-all things fit not all persons
-there may be blue and better blue
-everyone to his taste
-one man's meat is another man's poison
-all meats to be eaten,all amids to be wed
-if one will not,another will

5-chacun se fait fouetter à sa guise
-let every peddlar carry his own burden
-every man buckles his belt his ain gate
-every man should work out his own salvation

6-chacun son métier et les vaches seront bien gardées
-keep your breath to cool your porridge
-every cobbler sticks to his last

7-chacun aime le sien
-every man likes his own thing best
-he thinks his penny good silver

chagrin
chagrin partagé est moins lourd à porter
-two in distress make sorrow less
-he grieves sore who grieves alone
-grief is lessened when imparted to others
-grief pent up will break the heart
-misery loves company

chair
1-il n'est ni chair ni poisson
-he changes his mind from one day to the next

2-mi-chair,mi-poisson
-neither fish,flesh or fowl
-neither fish,flesh or good herring

3-la chair est faible
-flesh is frail

chameau
il est plus facile à un chameau de passer par le trou d'une aiguille qu'à un riche d'entrer dans le royaume de Dieu
-it is easier for a camel to go through the eye of a needle than for a rich man to enter the kingdom of God

champ
1-le champ est libre
-the coast is clear

2-sur le champ
-on the nail

chance
les chances étaient contre nous
-the odds were against us

chandelle
1-voir trente six chandelles
-to see stars

2-à la chandelle,la chèvre semble demoiselle
-all cats are grey in the dark

3-brûler la chandelle par les deux bouts
-to burn the candle at both ends

4-on ne peut pas brûler la chandelle par les deux bouts
-you cannot burn the candle at both ends

45

---

change
   donner le change
   -to throw you off the scent

changement
   1-changement d'herbage réjouit les veaux
   -change of pasture makes fat calves
   -changing of works is lighting of hearts

   2-changement de corbillon fait trouver le pain bon
   changement de corbillon,appétit de pain béni
   -new meat begets a new appetite

   3-le changement de travail est une espèce de repos
   -a change is as good as a rest

changer
   1-changer et trouver mieux sont deux
   -better the devil you know than the devil you don't know

   2-il ne faut pas changer de cheval au milieu de la rivière
   -don't change horses in midstream

   3-les temps changent et nous changeons avec eux
   -times change and we with them
   -one cannot put back the clock

   4-faire changer de registre à quelqu'un
   -to make someone sing another tune

chanter
   1-il ne faut pas chanter triomphe avant la victoire
   -draw not your bow until your arrow is fixed
   -don't throw your dirty water until you get in fresh
   -don't halloo till you are out of the wood
   -don't triumph before the victory

   2-qui chante ses maux épouvante
   -laugh,and the world laughs with you;weep,and you weep alone

   3-tel chante qui ne rit pas
   -all are not merry that dance lightly

chanterelle
   être sur la chanterelle
   -to be hammering a point home

chapeau
   1-porter le chapeau
   -to carry the cans

   2-travailler du chapeau
   -to be crazy

   3-tirer son chapeau à quelqu'un
   -to take off one's hat to someone

chapon
qui chapon mange,chapon lui vient
-he that has a goose,will get a goose

charbon
être sur des charbons ardents
-to be on tenter hooks

charbonnier
charbonnier est maître chez soi
-a man's home is his castle

charité
charité bien ordonnée commence par soi-même
-charity begins at home

charme
se porter comme un charme
-to be fit as a fiddle

charretier
il n'est si bon charretier qui ne verse
-the best cart overthrows

charrette
vieille charrette crie à chaque tour
-old churches have dim windows

charrue
mettre la charrue avant les boeufs
-to put the cart before the horse
-don't try to run before you walk

chasse
qui va à la chasse perd sa place
-a bleating sheep loses a bite

chasser
**1-chassez le naturel,il revient au galop,
chassez le par la porte,il rentrera par la fenêtre**
-the leopard cannot change his spots
-you can drive out nature with a pitchfork but she keeps coming back
-though you cast nature with a fork,it will still return
-nature will have her course
-it's harder to change human nature than to change rivers and mountains
-bring a cow to the hall and she'll return to the byre

2-qui bien chasse,bien trouve
-busiest men find the most

chat
1-quand le chat n'est pas là,les souris dansent
-when the cat's away,the mice will play

2-nous n'avons pas vu un chat
-we didn't see a soul

___

chat (suite)

    3-un chat de gouttière
    -an alley cat

    4-un chat sur une pelote d'épingles
    -a hen on a hot griddle

    5-à bon chat,bon rat
    -set a thief to catch a thief
    -it's give and take
    -I've got your number
    -an old poacher makes the best keeper
    -diamond cut diamond
    -when Greek meets Greek,then comes the tug of war
    -to a crafty man,a crafty and a half

    6-nous n'avons pas vu la queue d'un chat
    -we didn't see neither hide nor hair of one

    7-le chat d'une aiguille
    -the eye of a needle

    8-n'éveillez pas le chat qui dort
    -let sleeping dogs lie
    -wake not a sleeping lion
    -when sorrow is asleep,wake it not

    9-chat échaudé craint l'eau froide
    -once burned,twice shy
    -wherever an ass falls,there will he never fall again
    -though the wound be healed,yet a scar remains
    -birds once snared fear all bushes
    -he that has been bitten by a serpent,is afraid of a rope
    -whom a serpent has bitten,a lizard alarms
    -a scalded cat fears hot water
    -the escaped mouse ever feels the taste of the bait
    -if a man deceives me once,shame on him;if he deceives me twice, shame on me
    -a burnt child dreads the fire

    10-j'ai d'autres chats à fouetter
    -I have other fish to fry
    -I have my own scissors to grind

    11-avoir un chat dans la gorge
    -to have a frog in one's throat

    12-il n'est si petit chat qui n'égratigne
    -little strokes fell great oaks
    -there is no little enemy

château

    faire des châteaux en Espagne
    -castles in the air
    -castles in Spain
    -to chase rainbows

chatouiller

    on chatouille la truite pour mieux la prendre
    -the bait hides the hook

chaudron

    1-petit chaudron,grandes oreilles
    -little pitchers have great ears

    2-au chaudron des douleurs,chacun porte son écuelle
    -there is a crook in the lot of every one

chauffer

    1-de trop près se chauffe qui se brûle
    -if you play with the fire,you get burnt
    -he that gazes upon the sun,shall at last be blind
    -he lives unsafely that looks too near on things
    -he that touches pitch shall be defiled

    2-tant chauffe-t-on le fer qu'il rougit
    seek till you find,and you will not lose your labor

chemin

    1-il n'y va pas par quatre chemins
    -he makes no bones about it

    2-un grand chemin,une grande rivière et un grand seigneur sont trois mauvais voisins
    -a great man ant a great river are often ill neighbours

    3-tous les chemins mènent à Rome
    -all roads lead to Rome
    -there are many ways of dressing a calf's head
    -there are more ways to the wood than one
    -there is more than one way to skin a cat
    -there are more ways to kill a cat than choking it with cream
    -there are more ways to kill a dog than hang it
    -all rivers run into the sea

    4-il ne faut pas y aller par quatre chemins
    -he who hesitates is lost

    5-trouver sur son chemin
    -to cross one's path

    6-sur le chemin de l'amitié,ne laissez pas croître d'herbe
    -friendship is a plant which must often be watered

    7-à chemin battu il ne croît point d'herbe
    -a pot that belongs to many is ill stired and worse boiled

chemise

    1-la chemise du mort n'a pas de poches
    -shrouds have no pockets

    2-ta chemise ne sache ta guise
    -a hedge between keeps friendship green
    -treat your friend as he might become a foe
    -love your neighbour,yet pull not down your fence

cher

trop cher achète le miel qui le lèche sur les épines
-dear bought is the honey that is licked from the thorn
-they love dancing well that dance among thorns

chercher

1-ce qu'il faut chercher à connaître,c'est le fond du panier
-there is a reason in the roasting of eggs
-what is sweet in the mouth is often bitter in the stomach
-there is many a good cock come out of a tattered bag

2-ne cherchez pas midi à quatorze heure
-don't strain at a gnat and swallow a camel

3-chercher une aiguille dans une meule de foin
-looking for a needle in a bottle of hay,in a haystack
-seeking for a knot in a rush

4-chercher querelle à tout le monde
to have a chip on one's shoulder

chère

1-grande chère,petit testament
-young prodigal in a coach,will be an old beggar barefoot

2-il n'est chère que de vilain
-narrow gathered,widely spent

3-belle chère et coeur arrière
-a fair face may hide a fool heart
-cats hide their claws
-vice is often clothed in virtue's habit
-fair without,false within

cheval

1-c'est son cheval de bataille
-he rides this subject to death

2-ce ne sont pas les chevaux qui tirent le plus fort qui mangent l'avoine
-desert and reward seldom keep company

3-être à cheval sur le règlement
-to go by the book

4-à cheval hargneux,il faut une écurie à part
-when you enter in a house,leave anger ever at the door

5-jamais bon cheval ne devint rosse
-the child is the father of the man
-boys will be men
-it early pricks that will be a thorn
-timely crooks the tree,that good cammock be

6-il n'est si bon cheval qui ne devienne rosse
-old churches have dim windows

7-il n'est si bon cheval qui ne bronche
-it's a good horse that never stumbles

-homer sometimes nods
-a horse stumbles that has four legs
-the best of men may err at times

8-à chevaux maigres vont les mouches
-the poor suffer all the wrong
-the poor man pays for all

9-à cheval donné on ne regarde pas la bride
-don't look a gift horse in the mouth

10-jamais cheval ni méchant homme n'amenda pour aller à Rome
you cannot make people honest by act of Parliament
-to return home as wise as one went

11-tout cheval a besoin d'éperon
a good horse oft needs a good spur

12-celà ne se trouve pas sous le pas d'un cheval
things like that don't grow on trees

13-il vaut mieux être cheval que charrette
-it is better to be the hammer than the anvil

chevalier
tous ne sont pas chevaliers qui à cheval montent
-a man is not always asleep when his eyes are shut
-all are not hunters that blow the horn
-all are not thieves that dogs bark at

cheveu
1-il s'en est fallu d'un cheveu
-he came within a whisker (hair's breath,to a cow's thumb)
-by a nose

2-un cheveu même a son ombre
-no hair so small but has his shadow
-one may see day at a little hole

3-couper les cheveux en quatre
-to split hairs

cheville
1-il n'arrive pas à la cheville de son père
-don't name him in the same breath with his father

2-il a les chevilles qui enflent
-he blows his own trumpet ,horn
-don't take hollyer than thou

chèvre
1-il faut ménager la chèvre et le chou
-run with the hare and hunt with the hounds

2-où la chèvre est liée,il faut qu'elle broute
-when the goat is tied,it must browse

chez-soi

un petit chez-soi vaut mieux qu'un grand chez les autres
-east or west home is best
-there is no place like home

chiche

jamais chiche ne fut riche
-covetousness bursts the sack

chien

1-être comme chien et chat
-to lead a cat and dog life

2-jamais à un bon chien il ne vient un bon os
-desert and reward seldom keep company
-a saint in crape is twice a saint in lawn

3-mauvais chien ne trouve où mordre
-he that cannot beat the ass,beat the saddle

4-à mauvais chien on ne peut montrer le loup
-a bad dog never sees the wolf

5-chien en vie vaut mieux que lion mort
-a live dog is better than a dead lion

6-entre chien et loup
-in the dusk

7-il est comme le chien de Jean de Nivelle il s'en va quand on l'appelle
-he always does everythig backwards
-don't skin an eel by the tail

8-un chien mort ne mord plus
-dead dogs don't bite

9-à méchant chien,court lien
-to a mischievous dog a heavy clog

10-le chien a quatre pattes mais il n'est pas capable de prendre quatre chemins
-one cannot do two things at one time
-one cannot be in two places at once
-one cannot drink and whistle at once

11-le chien du jardinier ne veut ni manger les choux ni permettre au lapin de les manger
-the dog in the manger would neither eat the hay himself nor let the ox eat it

12-les chiens ne font pas de chats
-we may not expect a good whelp from an ill dog
-the toad's bairns are ill to tame
-eagles do not breed doves
-how can the foal amble if the horse and mare trot?
-the litter is like to the sire and dam
-of a thorn springs not a fig
-a booby will never make a hawk

-like breeds like
-as the old cock crows,so does the young one

13-les chiens ne chassent pas ensemble
deux chiens à l'os ne s'accordent
-two cats and a mouse,two wives in a house,two dogs and a bone, never agree in one
-two sparrows on one ear of corn make an ill agreement
-two suns cannot shine in one sphere
-that voyage never has luck where each one has a vote

14-chien qui aboie ne mord pas
-barking dogs seldom bite

15-lavez chien,peignez chien,toutefois n'est chien que chien
-a rose by any other name will still be a rose

16-le chien peureux n'a jamais son soûl de lard
-he who hesitate is lost
-faint heart never won fair lady

17-un chien regarde bien un évêque
-a cat may look at a king

18-chien hargneux a toujours l'oreille déchirée
-a snappish cur is ever in woe

19-un chien est fort à la porte de son maître
-every dog is valiant at its own door
-every dog is a lion at home
-every groom is a king at home

20-bon chien chasse de race
-a well-bred dog hunts by nature

21-le chien attaque toujours celui qui a les pantalons déchirés
-never tell an enemy that your foot aches
-the weaker has the worse
-everyone leaps over the dyke where it is lowest
-where the hedge is lowest,men may soonest over
-the least boy always carries the greatest fiddle
-a low hedge is easily leaped over

22-quand un chien se noie,tout le monde lui offre à boire
-an unhappy man's cart is eith to tumble

23-un chien qui pisse fait pisser l'autre
-if one sheep leaps over the ditch,all the rest will follow

24-le chien détaché traîne encore son lien
-custom is a second nature

25-un chien dans un jeu de quille
-a bull in a china shop

25-qui se couche avec les chiens,se lève avec les puces
-qui hante chien,puces remporte
-if you lie down with dogs,you will get up with fleas
-the shoe will hold with the sole

chinoiserie
abandonner les chinoiseries
-to cut the red tape

choisir
1-ne choisit pas qui emprunte
-beggars shouldn't be choosers

2-qui veut choisir souvent prend le pire
-pick and choose,and take the worst

3-choisis ta femme non à la danse mais à la moisson
-never choose your women or your linen by candlelight
-he who hesitates is lost

chômer
il ne faut pas chômer les fêtes avant qu'elles soient venues
-count not four,except you have them in a wallet

chose
1-une chose en entraîne une autre
-one thing brings up another thing

2-prendre les choses comme elles viennent
-to take the rough with the smooth

3-faire les choses à moitié
-to do a thing by halves

4-en toutes choses il faut considérer la fin
-in every entreprise consider where you would come out
-there is a reason in the roasting of eggs

5-les meilleures choses ont une fin
-all good things must come to an end
-everyday comes night

6-chose accoutumée rarement prisée
-plenty makes dainty
-if there is no clouds,we should not enjoy the sun

7-se sentir "chose"
-to feel under the weather

8-il est bon avoir aucune chose sous le mortier
-to lay something for a rainy day

9-chaque chose en son temps
-everything has its day
-there is a time for everything

10-chose bien commencée est à demi achevée
-well begun is half done
-a good lather is half the shave

11-à chose faite,conseil pris
-counsel is irksome when the matter is past remedy

chou

1-chou pour chou,Aubervilliers vaut bien Paris
-every man has his price

2-faire chou blanc (familier)
-to draw a blank

3-ce n'est pas le tout que des choux,il faut du lard pour les cuire
-a man without a smiling face must not open a shop

ciel

1-ciel rouge le soir,blanc le matin,c'est le souhait du pélerin
-a red sky at night is the sheperd's delight;a red sky in the morning is the pilgrim's warning

2-être au septième ciel
-to be in the ninth heaven
-to be in heaven's heaven

3-ciel pommelé et femme fardée ne sont pas de longue durée
-a woman's mind and a winter wind change oft
-women are as wavering as the wind

4-si le ciel tombait,il y aurait bien des alouettes prises
-roasted pigeons don't fly through the air

ciseaux

il n'est rien comme les vieux ciseaux pour couper la soie
-there is no learning,there is no art
-good broth may be made in an old pot
-years know more than books

citron

se presser le citron (familier)
-to beat one's brain

clair

c'est clair comme deux et deux font quatre
-it's as plain as the nose on your face

clamer

clamer à tous vents
-to cry from the housetop

clé

1-quelque chose à la clé
-more than meets the eye

2-la clé d'or ouvre toutes les portes
-a golden key can open any door
-no lock will hold against the power of gold
-money talks
-an ass laden with gold climbs to the top of the castle
-all things are obedient to money

client

le client a toujours raison
-the customer is always right

clin

faire un clin d'oeil
-to cock your eye

cloche

1-déménager à la cloche de bois
-to do a moonlight flit

2-qui n'entend qu'une cloche,n'entend qu'un son
-one tale is good till another is told
-there are two sides to every question
-it takes two to make a quarrel
-at the end of the game,you'll see the winner
-hear all parties
-it takes two to tango

clocher

Il ne faut pas clocher devant le boiteux
-he that has one of his family hanged,may not say to his neighbour,hang up the fish
-name not a rope where one has hang himself

clou

1-un clou chasse l'autre
-one fire drives out another's burning
-nail drives out nail
-one poison drives out another
-the smell of garlic takes away the smell of onion
-danger itself the best remedy for danger

2-cela ne vaut pas un clou
-not worth a snap of the fingers

clouer

clouer le bec de quelqu'un (familier)
-to settle one's hash

cochon

donner des perles(du pain béni) à des cochons
-to cast pearls before swine

coeur

1-il a du coeur
-his heart is in the right place

2-à coeur vaillant rien d'impossible
-nothing is impossible to a willing mind (heart)

3-le coeur a ses raisons que la raison ignore
-love is without reason
-affection blinds reason
-one cannot love and be wise

4-avoir un coeur d'artichaut
-to wear one's heart upon one's sleeve

5-coeur qui soupire n'a pas ce qu'il désire
-when the heart is a fire,some sparks will fly out of the mouth
-what the heart thinks,the tongue speaks

6-un coeur tranquille est la vie du corps
-next to love, quietness

7-c'est un coeur d'or sous une rude écorce
-he's a diamond in the rough

cogner
à se cogner la tête contre les murs,il ne vient que des bosses
-never abandon oneself to despair

colère
1-la colère est une courte folie
-anger is a short madness

2-quand on est en colère,il ne faut rien dire ni faire avant d'avoir récité l'alphabet
-when angry,count a hundred

3-rien ne gagne à un retardement si ce n'est la colère
-delay is the antidote of anger
-when angry,count a hundred

4-il faut faire coucher la colère à la porte
-when you enter in a house,leave anger ever at the door
-let not the sun go down on your wrath

5-craignez la colère de la colombe
-patience provoked turns to fury

6-colère n'a conseil
-anger and haste hinder good counsel

7-la colère des dieux est lente mais terrible
-murder will out

colique
avoir la colique
-to have butterflies in one's stomach

colombe
à colombe soule,les cerises sont amères
-you can have too much of a good thing

commencement
il faut commencer par le commencement
il faut un commencement à tout
-everything must have a beginning
-step after step the ladder is ascended
-the longest journey starts with a single step
-everything has its seed
-no root,no fruit
-rivers need a spring
-he who climb the ladder must begin at the bottom
-every oak has been an acorn

il faut **commencer** par le commencement
il faut un commencement à tout (suite)
-learn to walk before you run
-all things are difficult before they are easy
-everything has its seed

commencer
celui qui commence et ne parfait sa peine perd
-better never to begin than never to make an end

commerce
le commerce est l'école de la tromperie
-there are tricks in every trade
-keep your eye open a sale is a sale
-the buyer needs a hundred eyes,the seller but one
-ask much to have a little

compagnie
1-mauvaises compagnies corrompent les bonnes moeurs
-corruption of the best becomes the worst
-who trust to rotten boughs,may fall

2-il n'est si bonne compagnie qu'on ne quitte
-the best friends must part

comparaison
comparaison n'est pas raison
-mind and space are not commensurable

compte
1-les bons comptes font les bons amis
à tout bon compte,revenir
-good fences make good neighbours
-even (short) reckoning makes long friends
-love your neighbour but pull nit down thy edge
-honesty is the best policy

2-être laissé pour compte
-to be left in the basket

3-j'ai eu mon compte
-I have had my day

4-les comptes ont été falsifiés
-the books have been cooked

compter
1-compter les ruches à miel porte malheur
-cover yourself with honey and you'll have plenty of flies
-make yourself a lamb and the wolves will eat you

2-il ne faut compter les oeufs dans le derrière de la poule
-don't count your chiken before they are hatched

3-nous ne comptons les heures que lorsqu'elles sont perdues
-pleasant hours fly fast

4-qui compte qans son hôte,compte deux fois
-he that reckons without his host,must reckon again

concert
de concert
-to head together

confiance
confiance est mère de dépit
-in trust is treason
-he who trusts not,is not deceived

confondre
il ne faut pas confondre coco et abricot le coco a de l'eau,l'abricot un noyau
-mind and space are not commensurable

connaître
1-connaître la musique (sens figuré)
-to know a hawk from a handsaw
-to know which side the bread is buttered

2-connaître quelque chose comme sa poche
-to know something like the palm of one's hand

3-je le connais aussi bien que si je l'avais fait
-I know him as well as if I had gone through him with a lighted link

4-pour bien connaître un homme,il faut avoir manger un muid de sel avec lui
-before you make a friend eat a bushel of salt with him

5-on connaît un cerf aux abattues
-a straw shows which way the wind blows

6-connaître quelquechose sur le bout du doigt (dans tous les coins)
-to know something backwards and forwards
-to have it at one's fingers ends

7-connaître sur le bout du doigt
-connaître par coeur
-to have at one's fingers end

8-ne connaître ni d'Eve ni d'Adam
-not to know someone from Adam

conscience
une bonne conscience est un doux oreiller
-a good conscience is a soft pillow
-a good conscience is a sure card
-a good conscience fears no false accusations
-do right and fear no man
-a quiet conscience sleeps in thunder
-a good conscience makes an easy couch
-when one has nothing to reproach oneself with,one laughs at the lies of the wicked

conseil
1-à chose faite,conseil pris
-counsel is irksome,when the matter is past remedy

2-ne donne pas de conseil à moins qu'on t'en prie
-give neither counsel nor salt till you are asked for it
-never answer a question until it is asked
-don't say till you are ask

3-les conseils de l'ennui sont les conseils du diable
-the devil finds works for idle hands to do

4-en conseil écoute le vieil
-it is good sheltering under an old hedge
-if you wish good advice,consult an old man
-if the old dog barks,he gives counsel

conseilleurs
les conseilleurs ne sont pas les payeurs
-advice comes cheap
-the comforter's head never aches

consentir
qui ne dit mot,consent
-silence means consent
-there is a sin of omission as well as of commission

conte
des contes à dormir debout
-cock and bull stories

contenance
faire bonne contenance
-to bottle one's feelings

contentement
contentement passe richesse
-content is more than a kingdom
-a contented mind is a continual feast
-enough is as good as a feast
-enough is enough

contenter
on ne peut contenter tout le monde et son père
-you cannot please everyone
-it's an ill bird that fouls its own nest
-one cannot please everybody and his wife
-not God above gets all men's love

convenance
convenances rompent loi
-circumstances alter cases

coq
1-vivre comme un coq en pâte
-to live like fighting cocks
-to live in clover

2-laisser le coq passer le seuil,vous le verrez bientôt sur le buffet
-if you give him an inch,he'll take a mile
-all lay load on the willing horse

3-un coq est bien fort sur son fumier
-every cock crows on its own dunghill
-every groom is a king at home
-every dog is a lion at home
-every dog is valiant at its own door

coquin

à coquin honteux,plate besace
-nothing venture,nothing have
-nothing stake,nothing draw
-he who hesitates is lost

corbeau

1-jamais un corbeaau n'a fait un canari
-it is hard to make a mutton of a sow

2-de mauvais corbeau,mauvais oeuf
-of an evil crow,an evil egg

corde

1-il s'est passé la corde au cou (il s'est marié)
-he has tied a knot with his tongue that he cannot untie with his teeth

2-avoir plusieurs cordes à son arc
-to have several irons in the fire
-the mouse that hath but one hole is quickly taken
-to have two strings to one's bow

3-il ne vaut pas la corde pour le pendre
-he isn't worth the powder to blow him up with

4-pas dans mes cordes
-not in my beat

cordonnier

les cordonniers sont les plus mal chaussés
-the shoemaker's children never have shoes
-who is worse shod than the shoemaer's wife?
-none is more bare that the shoemaker's wife and the smith's mare

cornemuse

jamais la cornemuse ne dit mot si elle a le ventre plein
-a fully belly neither fights nor flies well

corps

corps et âme
-neck and crop

costume

en costume d'Adam
-naked as he was born

côte

se tenir les côtes
-to shake one's sides

coucher

coucher de poule et lever de corbeau éloignent l'homme du tombeau
-early to bed and early to rise makes a man healthy,wealthy and wise

coucou

les coucous ne font pas les merles
-what can you expect from a pig but a grunt?

coude

au coude à coude
-neck and neck

coudre

coudre la peau du renard à celle du lion
-if the lion's skin cannot,the fox' shall

coup

1-un coup de tonnerre (sens figuré)
-a bolt from the blue

2-un coup de chance
-a bit of fat

3-un coup de dés
-a turn of the wheel

4-tous les coups sont permis
-all is fair in love and war

5-recevoir le coup de fusil
-to be taken to the cleaners

6-par à-coups
-by fits and starts

7-donner un coup de main à quelqu'un
-to give someone a hand

8-ne donnez pas de coups d'épée dans l'eau
-don't hold a candle in the sun

9-jamais coup de pied de jument ne fit mal à un cheval
-the kick of the mare hurts not the colt

coupable

1-celui qui se sait coupable croit toujours qu'on parle de lui
-he that commits a fault thinks everybody speaks of it
-he that has a great nose thinks everybody is speaking of it
-a guilty conscience is a self accuser
-conscience is a thousand witnesses

2-aucun coupable n'est absous devant son propre tribunal
-a guilty conscience needs no accuser

coupe

    1-la coupe est pleine
    -when the pot is full,it will boil over

    2-avoir quelqu'un sous sa coupe
    -to get the drop on someone

    3-être sous la coupe de quelqu'un
    -under the umbrella of so and so

    4-il y a loin de la coupe aux lèvres
    -there's many a slip'twixt the cup and the lip

couper

    1-couper l'herbe sous le pied de quelqu'un
    -to have the ground cut from under one's feet

    2-couper les cheveux en quatre
    -to split the hair

courant

    tenir quelqu'un au courant
    -to put someone in the picture

courber

    ce qui est courbé ne peut être redressé, et ce qui manque ne peut être compté
    -you cannot make a crab walk straight

courir

    1-courir à sa perte
    -to throw good money after bad
    -to shoot a second arrow to find the first

    2-il faut laisser courir le vent par dessus les tuiles
    -we must not look for a golden life in an iron age

    3-rien ne sert de courir,il faut partir à point
    -first creep then walk
    -the short cut is often the longest way around
    -haste makes waste
    -more haste,less speed
    -slow but sure wins the race
    -the snail slides up the tower at last,though the swallow mounteth it sooner
    -it is not enough to run,one must set out intime
    -don't fly in the face of Providence

cousu

    1-cousu de fil blanc
    -as plain as the nose on your face
    -it's all sewed up

    2-c'est du cousu main
    -it is first rate

couteau
>**1-couteau qui ne fait pas le tour du trou n'emporte pas chou**
>-good to begin well,better to end well
>
>**2-être à couteaux tirés avec quelqu'un**
>-to be ready to knife one another
>
>**3-un couteau aiguise l'autre**
>-one kindness is the price of another

couture
>**de forte couture,forte déchirure**
>-the greatest hate springs from the greatest love

couverture
>**tirer la couverture à soi**
>-to take the lion's share

crabe
>**il n'y a pas deux crabes mâles dans un même trou**
>-two suns cannot shine in one sphere

cracher
>**1-cracher le morceau**
>-to spill the bean
>
>**2-quand on crache en l'air,cela vous retombe sur le nez**
>-an arrow shot upright falls on the shooter's head
>-envy shoots at others and wounds herself
>
>**3-qui crache au ciel,il lui retombe sur le visage**
>-he that spits against the wind,spits in his own face

craindre
>**1-qui craint le danger ne doit pas aller en mer**
>-he that is afraid of the wagging of feathers must keep
>from among wild fowl
>-he that is afraid of wounds,must not come nigh a battle
>-he that fears every bush must not go abirding
>-he that fears every grass must not walk in a meadow
>-cowards die many times before their death
>
>**2-craignez la colère de la colombe**
>still waters run deep
>-patience provoked turns to fury

crainte
>**1-qui craint de souffrir,il souffre déjà de ce qu'il craint**
>-who fears to suffer,suffers from fear
>-cowards die many times before their death
>
>**2-la crainte de Dieu est le commencement de la sagesse**
>-the devil sick would be a monk
>-the wind in one's face makes one wise
>-the chamber of sickness is the chapel of devotion
>-danger is next neighbour to security
>-secure is not safe
>-far from Jupiter,far from the thunder

2-la crainte de Dieu est le commencement de la sagesse (suite)
-danger makes men devout
-when it thunders,the thief becomes honest

3-la crainte du gendarme est le commencement de la sagesse
-the stick is the surest pacemaker
-far from Jupiter,far from the thunder

cran

avoir le cran
-to have the cheek

crapaud

qui crapaud aime lunette lui ressemble
-beauty is in the eye of the beholder

crasse

sous la crasse,la beauté s'y cache
-a black plum is as sweet as a white
-all are not thieves that dogs bark at
-the filth under the white snow the sun discovers

crédit

crédit est mort,les mauvais payeurs l'ont tué
-trust is dead,ill payment killed it
-the tapster is undone by chalk

crème

la crème des crèmes
-the very best

crêpe

retourné comme une crêpe
-sing a different tune

crever

cela te crève les yeux
-if it were a bear,it would bite you

crier

1-on crie toujours le loup plus grand qu'il n'est
-a tale never loses in telling
-the devil is not so black as he is painted
-curst cows have curt horns

2-ne criez pas "des moules" avant qu'elles ne soient au bord
-it's ill fishing before the net

3-tant crie-t-on Noël qu'il vient
-long looked for comes at last

4-crier comme un aveugle qui a perdu son bâton
-much smoke,little fire
-much ado about nothing

crin

à tous crins
-dyed in the wool

critique
>   la critique est aisée mais l'art est difficile
>   -criticism is easy and art is difficult

croire
>   1-il se croit quelqu'un
>   il se croit sorti de la cuisse de Jupiter
>   -he thinks he is the cat's whiskers
>   -don't take hollyer than thou
>
>   2-rien n'est cru si fermement que ce que l'on sait le moins
>   -men have greater faith in those things which they do not
>   understand
>
>   3-j'aime mieux le croire que d'y aller voir
>   -belief is better than investigation
>
>   4-chacun croit aisément ce qu'il craint et ce qu'il désire
>   -we soon believe what we soon desire
>
>   5-croyez tout le monde honnête et vivez avec tous comme
>   avec des fripons
>   -select your friend with a silk-gloved hand and hold him with a
>   iron gauntlet
>
>   6-je ne crois que ce que je vois
>   -seeing is believing
>   -I'm from Missouri,you've got to show me
>   -believe nothing of what you hear,and only half of what you see
>
>   7-croyez cela et buvez de l'eau
>   -put that in your pipe and smoke it
>
>   8-il croit au père Noël
>   -he thinks the moon is made of green cheese
>
>   9-on croit parce que l'on croit pouvoir
>   -he can who believes he can

croix
>   1-je n'ai ni croix ni pile
>   -I have neither cross nor pile
>
>   2-vous pouvez faire une croix sur l'argent que vous leur avez
>   prêté
>   -you can kiss the money you lent them goodbye
>
>   3-à chacun sa croix
>   -everyone must bear his own cross

cruche
>   tant va la cruche à l'eau qu'elle se casse
>   -the pitcher goes often to the well but is broken at last
>   -put not the bucket too often in the well
>   -strings high streched either soon crack or quickly grow
>   -when the well is full,it will run over
>   -too-too will in two

cuiller
>**1-ramasser à la petite cuiller**
>-pick us and pieces
>
>**2-en trois coups de cuiller à pot**
>-in two shakes of a lamb's tail
>-in a brace of shakes

cuillerée
>**une cuillerée de goudron gâte un tonneau de miel**
>-one drop of poison infects the whole tun of wine

cuirasse
>**le défaut de la cuirasse**
>-Achilles'heel
>-a chain is no stronger than its weakest link
>-the thread breaks where it is weakest

cul
>**1-péter plus haut que son cul** (familier)
>-to bite off more than one could chew
>-the stream cannot rise above its source
>
>**2-être comme cul et chemise** (familier)
>-to be finger and glove with another

culotte
>**porter la culotte**
>-to rule the roost
>-she is the one who wears the trousers

cygne
>**on ne voit cygne noir ni corbeau blanc**
>**on ne voit cygne noir,ni nulle neige noire**
>-the leopard cannot change his spots

D

damné
> **il n'y a de damnés que les obstinés**
> -to fall into sin is human,to remain in sin is devilish

danger
> **c'est dans les grands dangers qu'on voit un grand courage**
> **au danger on connaît les braves**
> -it is a bold mouse that nestles in the cat's ear

dé
> **1-les dés sont pipés**
> -the dice are loaded
>
> **2-les dés sont jetés**
> -the die is cast
> -the game's a foot

déchirer
> **cela ne vous déchire pas la robe**
> -civility costs nothing

décousu
> **d'une façon décousue**
> -by fits and starts

découvrir
> **plus on se découvre,plus on a froid**
> -the ass that brays most eats least
> -least said,soonsest mended

défendre
> **nous défendre quelque chose,c'est nous en donner envie**
> -forbidden fruit is sweetest

demain
> **1-demain,il fera jour**
> -tomorrow is a new day
> -in every country the sun rises in the morning
> -every day comes night
> -everyday comes night
> -tomorrow is another day
>
> **2-on ne sait pas de quoi demain sera fait**
> -none knows what will happen to him before sunset

demande
> **1-à sotte demande il ne faut point de réponse**
> -a stupid question deserves no answer
>
> **2-demandez et l'on vous donnera**
> -ask and it shall be given to you
>
> **3-qui demande timidement enseigne à refuser**
> -he that asks faintly begs a denial

4-demander des comptes
-to call to account

5-demander la lune
-to cry for the moon
-a pie in the sky

6-qui ne demande rien,n'a rien
-the squeaking wheel gets the grease

demandeur
à bon demandeur bon refuseur
-it is not every question that deserves an answer

déménager
1-sens argotique
-to go off his rocker

2-déménager à la cloche de bois
-to do a moonlight flit

déménagement
trois déménagements valent un incendie
-three removals are as bad as a fire

démordre
il ne voulait pas en démordre
-he wouldn't budge an inch

dénigrer
qui dénigre veut acheter
-he that blames would buy

dent
1-remplir une dent creuse
-to feed a fly

2-dents aigues et ventre plat trouve tout bon qu'est au plat
-hungry dogs will eat dirty pudding
-to the hungry soul every bitter thing is sweet
-hunger makes hard beans sweet

3-bonnes sont les dents qui retiennent la langue
les dents sont bonnes contre la langue
-a closed mouth catches no flies

dentelle
faire de la dentelle
-to cut a feather

descendre
descendre en flèche
-to shoot down in flames

désespoir
le désespoir comble non seulement notre misère,mais notre faiblesse
-despair gives courage to a coward

déshabiller

1-il faut déshabiller un maïs pour voir sa bonté
-there is many a fair thing ,full false

2-il ne faut pas déshabiller Pierre pour habiller Paul
-don't rob Peter to pay Paul

désirer

1-ne désirer que ce qu'on a,c'est avoir tout ce qu'on désire
-he is not poor that has little,but he that desires much
-blessed is who expects nothing, for he shall never be desappointed
-he who is content in his poverty,is wonderfully rich

2-plus on désire une chose,plus elle se fait attendre
-a watched pot never boils
-dearths foreseen come not

dessus

joli dessus,vilaine doublure
-appearances are deceptive
-the filth under the white snow the sun discovers

destin

on ne peut rien changer à son destin
-no flying from fate

deuil

faire son deuil de quelquechose
-to give something up as lost

devoir

1-qui doit,n'a rien à soi
-a man in debt is caught in a net
-he that borrows binds himself with his neighbour's rope

2-ce qui doit être,sera
-what must be,must be

diable

1-au diable vauvert
-at the back of beyond

2-le diable n'est pas toujours à la porte du pauvre
-the lower millstone grounds as well as the upper

3-le diable était beau quand il était jeune
-old wives were aye good maidens

4-il ne faut pas tenter le diable
-an open door may tempt a saint
-the devil dances in an empty pocket

5-à la diable
-anyhow

6-tirer le diable par la queue
-to be hard up
-to live from hand to mouth

7-va au diable
-go to hell
-go to Halifax
-go away and eat coke

8-vous avez le diable dans la peau
-the deuce is in you

9-quand le diable devient vieux,il se fait ermite
-danger makes man devout
-some are atheists only in fair weather

10-c'est le diable qui bat sa femme et marie sa fille
-if it rain when the sun is shining,the devil is beating his wife

11-le diable n'est pas toujours aussi diable qu'il est noir
-the devil is not so black as he is painted

12-avoir le diable au corps
-to be full of the devil

13-le diable parle toujours en l'Evangile
-you would do little for God if the devil were dead

14-le diable s'empare des personnes oisives
-the devil finds work for idle hands to do
-an idle brain is the devil workshop
-an idle person is the devil's cushion
-idleness is the root of all evil
-the devil temptsall,but the idle man tempts the devil
-idle people have the least leisure
-an idle head is a boxe for the wind
-of idleness comes no goodness

15-plus a le diable,plus veut avoir
much would have more

16-le diable chante la grand'messe
-the devil goes up the belfry by the vicar's skirts

Dieu

1-mieux vaut avoir affaire au bon Dieu qu'à ses saints
-always deal with the top man

2-jurer ses grands dieux
-to swear up and down

3-Dieu mesure le froid à la brebis tondue
-God tempers the wind to the short lamb
-heaven suits the back to the burden

4-Dieu donne le froid selon le drap
-Heaven suits the back to the burden

5-Dieu est toujours du côté des gros bataillons
-God is always on the side of the big battalions
-might is right
-God sides with the strongest

6-Dieu nous a tous pétris du même limon
-we are all Adam's children
-homo is a common name to all men
-before God and the bus conductor we are all equal
-in church,in an inn,and in a coffin,all men are equal
-human blood is all of a colour
-all blood is alike ancient
-there is no difference of bloods in a basin

7-Dieu aide à trois personnes aux fous,aux enfants et aux ivrognes
-il y a un Dieu pour les ivrognes
-God forgive sins,otherwise heaven would be empty

8-Dieu lui-même a besoin de cloches
-the squeaking wheel gets the grease

différé
ce qui est différé n'est pas perdu
-if today will not,tomorrow may

difficile
1-cela va être difficile de s'en remettre
-the devil to pay and pitch hot

2-rien n'est plus difficile à écorcher que la queue
-the end crowns the work
-think on the end before you begin

diner
après le diner,la moutarde
-after meat,mustard
-the gods send nuts to those who have no teeth

dire
1-qui ne dit mot consent
-silence gives consent
-no answer is also an answer
-there is a sin of omission as well ac commission

2-quand l'un dit "tue!",l'autre dit "assomme!"
-they went but a pair of shears between them
-they are finger and thumb

3-je ne dis rien mais je n'en pense pas moins
-I say little but I think the more
-one may think that dares not speak

4-il dit cela de bouche mais le coeur n'y touche
-let not thy tongue run away with thy brains
-fine words butter no parsnips

5-dire et faire sont deux
-saying and doing are two things
-saying is one thing and doing is another
-promise is debt
-there is a great difference between words and deeds
-from word to deed is a great space

6-le dire c'est bien mais le faire c'est mieux
-doing is better than saying

7-le beau dire ne dispense pas du bien faire
-it is better to do well than to say well
-promise is debt

8-aussitôt dit,aussitôt fait
-no sooner said than done

9-moins on en dit,mieux on se porte
-least said,soonest mended
-still tongue makes a wise head

10-dis moi qui tu hantes,je te dirai qui tu es
-your friends are your mirror,they show you yourself
-birds of a feather flock together
-a man is known by the company he keeps

11-soit dit en passant
-by and by

12-et le "qu'en dira-t-on?"
-what will mr.Grundy say?
-we are all slaves of opinion

13-qui dit du mal de l'âne le voudrait à la maison
-he that speaks ill of the mare would buy her

discussion
de la discussion jaillit la lumière
-discontent is the first step in progress

diseur
les grands diseurs ne sont pas les grands faiseurs
-the greatest talkers are the least doers

disparaître
disparaître sans laisser de traces
-to vanish into the air

disposition
à ma disposition
-at my fingertips

diversion
faire diversion
-to throw a tub to the whale
-to entertain an angel unaware

---

diviser
diviser pour régner
-divide and rule (conquer)

doigt
1-c'est mon petit doigt qui me l'a dit
-my little finger told me that
-a little bird told me so

2-se fourrer le doigt dans l'oeil jusqu'au coude
-he's off the beam
-to be way out in left field
-you have found an elephant in the moon

3-se faire taper sur les doigts
-to get it in the neck

4-connaître sur le bout du doigt
-to have it at one's fingers end

5-être comme les deux doigts de la main
-to be finger and glove with another
-to be hand and glove with
-between you and me the bedpost

6-avoir les doigts de pieds en éventail (familier)
-to be in clover

7-donnez lui en grand comme le doigt,il en prendra long comme le bras
-if you give him an inch,he'll take a mile
-all lay load on the willing horse

donner
1-s'il me donne des pois,je lui donnerai des fèves
-I'll give him beans

2-qui donne aux pauvres prête à Dieu
-he who gives to the poor lays up a treasure in heaven
-give and spend,and God will send
-the charitable give out at the door and God puts in at the window

3-donner le pied à un nègre,il prend la main
-set a beggar on horseback and he'll ride to the devil

4-donner tard c'est refuser
-to refuse and to give tardily is all the same

5-on lui donnerait le bon Dieu sans confession
-butter wouldn't melt in his mouth

6-il m'a donné du fil à retordre
-it played the deuce with me and my belongings
-he played old gooseberry with me

7-si tu donnes un poisson à un enfant,c'est bien;si tu lui apprends à pécher,c'est mieux
-better untaught than ill taught

tenir
8-mieux vaut donner sans promettre que promettre sans

-one acre of performance,is worth twenty of the land of promise
-doing is better than saying
-it is better to do well than to say well
-deeds are fruit,words are but leaves
-deeds but not words
-a man of words and not of deeds,is like a garden full of weeds

9-on lui donnerai le bon Dieu sans confession
-butter wouldn't melt in his mouth

10-ne donnez pas de coups d'épée dans l'eau!
-don't hold a candle in the sun!

11-donner des perles (du pain béni) à des cochons
-to cast pearls before swine

-12-on ne donne rien si libéralement que des conseils
-the land is never void of counsellors
-nothing is given so freely as advice

13-ne donne point de conseil à moins qu'on ne t'en prie
-don't say till you are asked

14-donner sa chemise
-to give the shirt off one's back

-donner le change
-to throw off the scent

dormir
1-dormir comme un loir,une souche
-to sleep like a log

2-qui dort,dîne
-the sleeping fox catches no poultry
-who sleeps dine
-when a man sleeps,his head is in his stomach
-take it out in sleep

doucement
doucement mais sûrement
-slow but sure wins the race
-the snail slides up the tower at last,though the swallow mounteth it sooner

douceur
plus fait douceur que violence
plus fait douceur que force
-fair and softly goes far in a day
-mildness does better than harshness
-a soft answer turneth away wrath
-soft fire makes sweet malt
-soft pace goes far

douceur
plus fait douceur que violence
plus fait douceur que force (suite)
-wisdom is better than strength
-they also serve who only stand and wait

douleur
1-les grandes douleurs sont muettes
la douleur qui se tait n'en est que plus funeste
-small sorrows speak;great ones are silent
-sorrow makes silent her best orator

2-de toutes les douleurs,on ne peut faire qu'une mort
a man can die but once

doute
1-dans le doute abstiens toi
-when in doubt do nothing

2-le doute est le commencement de la sagesse
-doubt is the key of knowledge

drap
1-on ne peut avoir le drap et l'argent
-you cannot eat your cake and have it too
-you cannot have it both ways
-you cannot sell the cow and sup the milk

2-nous sommes dans de beaux draps
-here's the very devil to pay
-that's a pretty kettle of fish
-to be in sad straits
-to be in deep water

droit
1-bon droit a besoin d'aide
-you cannot make people honest by act of Parliament

2-droit comme un "i"
-as straight as a cedar

duper
on est aisément dupé par ce qu'on aime
-save us from our friends

durer
qui veut durer,doit endurer
-he that will not endure labour in this world,let him not be born

E

eau

1-eau qui court ne porte point d'ordures
-he is not backwards in coming forwards

2-porter l'eau à la rivière
-to carry coal to Newcastle

3-mettre l'eau à la bouche
-to make one's teeth water
-to make one's mouth water

4-l'eau va à la rivière
-it takes money to make money
-money begets money

5-l'eau trouble fait le gain du pêcheur
-it is good fishing in trouble waters

6-il n'est pire eau que l'eau qui dort
-still waters run deep

écart

tenir à l'écart
-to keep at arm's length

échapper

il l'a échappé belle
-he escaped by the skin of his teeth

éclairer

cela éclaire l'affaire sous un nouveau jour
-that puts a new face on the matter

économie

1-faire des économies de bouts de chandelle
-to pinch pennies
-to be penny-wise

2-il n'y a pas de petites économies
-look after the pennies and the pounds will look after themselves
-sparing is a great revenue
-sparing is the first gaining

économiser

il ne faut pas économiser le son et gaspiller la farine
-don't spare the spigot and spill at the bung

écouter

n'écouter que d'une oreille
-to hear as a hog in harvest
-to listen with half an ear

écrire

ce qui est écrit est écrit
-never write what you dare not sign

écrit

écrit noir sur blanc
-put down in black and white

écu

où il y a un écu,il y a le diable
où il n'y en a pas,il y en a deux
-money is the root of all evil
-the love of money is the root of an evil

écurie

l'écurie use plus le cheval que la course
-it is not work that kills but sorrow

effet

1-couper ses effets
-to steal one's thunder

2-il n'y a pas d'effet sans cause
-take away the cause,and the effect must cease

église

1-qui est près de l'église est souvent loin de Dieu
-all are not saints that go to church

2-près de l'église,loin de Dieu
-the nearer the church,the farther from God

3-hors de l'église point de salut
-a monk out of his cloister is like a fish out of water
-money is the only monarch

éléphant

un éléphant dans un magasin de porcelaine
-a bull in a china shop

éloge

l'éloge des absents se fait sans flatterie
-to dead men and absent there are no friend left

embrasser

qui trop embrasse mal étreint
-Jack of all trades-master of none
-all covet,all lose
-grasp all,lose all

empêcher

1-il n'y a point de si empêché que celui qui tient la queue de la poêle
-he who has the frying-pan in his hand turns it at will
-he who holds the thread holds the ball

2-ce qu'on ne peut empêcher,il faut le vouloir
-what can't be cured,must be endured

3-on ne peut empêcher les chiens d'aboyer ni les menteurs de mentir
-what is bred in the bone will come out in the flesh
-it is harder to change human nature than to change rivers and mountains

emporter
autant en emporte le vent
-gone with the wind
-that's all moonshine

emprunter
celui qui emprunte est l'esclave de celui qui prête
-the borrower is the servant of the lender

enclume
à dure enclume,marteau de plume
-he that has patience,has fat thrushes for a farthing
-who has no haste in his business,mountains to him seem valleys

endetter
être endetté jusqu'au cou
-to be up to the ears in debts

enfance
1-l'enfance est le sommeil de la raison
-boys will be men

2-c'est l'enfance de l'art
-it's a lead pipe cinch
-it's all sewed up

enfant
1-être un enfant de l'amour
-to be born on the wrong side of the blanket

2-enfant haï est toujours triste
-fruit ripens not well in the shade

3-petits enfants,petits soucis,grands enfants grands soucis
-a little child weighs on your knee, a big one on your heart
-the fewer his years,the fewer his tears

4-ce que l'enfant dit au foyer est tôt connu jusqu'au moustier
-what children hear at home,soon flies abroad

5-ce ne sont pas des enfants de choeur
-thay are not boyscouts

6-y a p'us d'enfants
-there are no children nowadays

7-c'est l'enfant qui bat sa nourrice
-to bite even the hand that feeds him

8-il vaut mieux laisser un enfant morveux que de lui arracher le nez
-the remedy may be worse than the disease

9-enfant aime moult qui beau l'appelle
-unkissed,unkind
-love begets love
-love is the true reward of love

enfer

l'enfer est pavé de bonnes intentions
-the road to hell is paved with good intentions

enfourner

à mal enfourner,on fait les pains cornus
-such beginning,such end
-an ill beginning,an ill ending

engraisser

on n'engraisse pas les cochons avec de l'eau claire
-nought lay down,nought take up

engrener

qui bien engrène,bien finit
-a good beginning makes a good ending
-no good building without a good foundation

ennemi

1-il n'est nuls petits ennemis
il n'est si petit ennemi qui ne puisse faire tort
-there is no little enemy
-the same knife cuts bread and fingers

2-mieux vaut un sage ennemi qu'un ignorant ami
-better an open enemy than a false friend
-it is better to be stung by a nettle than pricked by a rose

3-de notre ennemi réconcilié,il faut se garder
-if we are bound to forgive an enemy,we are not bound to trust him

4-chacun est l'ennemi de soi-même
-every man is his own worst enemy

ennui

1-l'ennui naquit un jour de l'uniformité
-variety is the spice of life
-all work and no play make Jack a dull boy

2-l'ennui est une maladie dont le travail est le remède
-if you are bored,work,it is the only remedy for this terrible evil

enseigne

à la même enseigne
-in the same boat

enseigner

en enseignant,on apprend
-he who teaches,learns

entendeur
à bon entendeur,salut
à bon entendeur demi-mot suffit
-a word to the wise is enough

entendre
1-ils s'entendent comme larrons en foire
-they are thick as thieves

2-qui n'entend qu'une cloche,n'entend qu'un son
-it takes two to tango
-at the end of the game,you'll see the winner
-there are two sides to every question

entretenir
il faut entretenir la vigueur du corps pour conserver celle de l'esprit
-the soul needs few things,the body many

entrer
qui entre en nef n'a pas vent à gré
-the greatest step is that out of doors

envelopper
envelopper dans du papier de soie
to wrap up in clean linen

envoyer
1-être envoyer dans l'autre monde
-to be called to one's account

2-il les a envoyés paître,se promener,sur les roses
-he sends the pests packing
-to send one to the right about
-to send one packing

épargner
qui épargne,gagne
-a penny saved is a penny earned
-waste not,want not

épervier
on ne peut faire d'un épervier un busard
-the frog cannot out of her bog

épargne
l'épargne est un grand revenu
sparing is a great revenue

épée
l'épée est la meilleure langue pour répondre à l'outrage
-fight fire with fire

épine
1-tirer une épine du pied
-to take a load off one's minds

2-une épine dans le pied
-a thorn in the flesh

3-l'épine en naissant va la pointe en avant
-the thorn comes forth with the point forward

épingle
tiré à quatre épingles
-dressed up like a dog's dinner

épouser
1-qui épouse la femme,épouse les dettes
-it is too late to husband when all is spent

2-épouser le bonheur ou le malheur d'un autre
-to cast in one's lot

épouseur
épouseur à toutes mains,épouseur du genre humain
-who gives to all,denies all

erreur
1-erreur n'est pas compte
-two blacks do not make a white
-two wrongs do not make a right

2-l'erreur est humaine
-homer sometimes nod
-no man is wise at all times
-he is lifeless that is faultless
-to fall into sin is human,to remain in sin is devilish

3-l'erreur est humaine,le pardon divin
-to err is human,to forgive divine

espérance
1-l'espérance est le pain des malheureux
-hope is the poor man's bread
-hope is the bread of the unhappy

2-l'espérance est le songe d'un homme éveillé
-hope is the dream of those that wake

espoir
1-l'espoir a la vie dure
-hope springs eternal in the human breast

2-l'espoir fait vivre
-man lives by hope
-hope keeps man alive
-if it were no hope,the heart would break
-expectation is better than realization
-none so old,that he hopes not for a year of life

3-espoir de gain diminue la peine
-great gain makes work easy
-bode good and get it
-pain is forgotten where gain follows
-everyone fastens where there is gain

4-l'espoir différé rend le coeur malade, mais le désir accompli est un arbre de vie
-hope deferred makes the heart sick
-hope is a good breakfast but a bad supper

esprit

1-avoir l'esprit mal tourné
-to have a mind like a cesspool

2-un esprit sain dans un corps sain
-a sound mind in a sound body

3-la plus universelle qualité des esprits est la diversité
-variety is the spice of life

4-une once d'esprit vaut mieux qu'une livre de science
-learning makes a good man better and an ill man worse
-knowledge without practice makes but half an artist
-experience without learning is better than learning without experience

5-les grands esprits se rencontrent
-great minds think alike

estomac

avoir l'estomac dans les talons
-to be hungry enough to eat a horse

étable

il ne faut pas faire l'étable au veau avant qu'il soit né
-don't build the sty before the litter comes

étalage

faire étalage
-to shoot one's linen

étincelle

c'est l'étincelle qui a mis le feu aux poudres
-il suffit d'une étincelle pour allumer un incendie
-a single spark can start a prairie fire

étouffer

étouffer l'affaire dans l'oeuf
-to nip the brair in the bud

étoile

il est sous une bonne étoile
-he's in clover

étourneaux

les étourneaux sont maigres parce qu'ils vont en troupe
-many hands make little work
-too many cooks spoil the broth
-two is company but three is none

étouffer

étouffer l'affaire dans l'oeuf
-to nip the brair in the bud

être

être et paraître sont deux
-never judge from appearances
-appearances are deceptive
-things are not always what they seem
-they that are booted are not always ready
-all Stuarts are not sib to the king

évènement

l'évènement à venir projette son ombre
-coming events cast their shadow before them
-a little straw shows which way the wind blows
-what goes around,comes around

exactitude

l'exactitude est la politesse des rois
-punctuality is the politness of kings

exagérer

tout ce qui est exagéré est insignifiant
-from the sublime to the ridiculous is only one step

exception

l'exception confirme la règle
-the exception proves the rule

excès

1-l'excès en tout nuit
-take not a musket to kill a butterfly
-too much pudding will choke a dog
-too much honey cloys the stomach
-if in excess,even nectar is poison
-burn not your house to rid it of the mouse
-one must draw a line somewhere
-too much of ought is good for nought

2-l'excès d'un très grand bien devient un mal très grand
-too much of ought is good for nought
-more than enough is too much

excuser

qui s'excuse,s'accuse
-he who excuses himself,accuses himself

expédient

vivre d'expédients
-to live a hand-to-mouth existence

expérience

expérience est mère de science
-every failure one meets with adds to one's experience
-lightning never strikes twice at the same place
-it's a silly fish that is caught twice with the same bait
-adversity comes with instruction in its hand
-trouble brings experience and experience brings wisdom
-he gains enough whom fortune loses

-whenever an ass falls,there will he never fall again
-he complains wrongfully of the sea that twice suffered shipwreck
-an old fox is not easily snared
-if a man deceives me once,shame on him;if he deceives me twice,shame on me

extrême
les extrêmes se touchent
-extremes meet
-too far east is west
-the longer east,the shorter west

F

fable

    la fable est la soeur aînée de l'histoire
    -many a true word is spoken in jest

face

    face d'homme porte vertu
    -fair face,foul heart
    -truth has a good face,but bad clothes

facile

    1-plus facile à dire qu'à faire
    -easier said than done
    -saying is one thing and doing another

    2-c'est facile comme bonjour
    -it's a piece of cake
    -it's apple pie

    3-il est plus facile de descendre que de monter
    -it is easier to descend than to ascend
    -one may sooner fall than rise
    -it is easier to pull down than to build
    -a good name is sooner lost than won

façon

    la façon de donner vaut mieux que ce qu'on donne
    -he that gives thee a bone,would have not thee die

fagot

    il y a fagots et fagots
    -we must separate the sheep from the goat

faim

    1-à qui a faim,tout est pain
    -hungry dogs will eat dirty pudding
    -good appetite needs no sauce
    -hunger is good kitchen meat
    -hunger makes hard beans sweet
    -to a hungry soul every bitter thing is sweet

    2-rester sur sa faim
    -to leave off with an appetite

    3-j'ai une faim de loup
    -I could eat a horse
    -I'm as hungry as a bear

    4-lorsque la faim est à la porte,l'amour s'en va par la fenêtre
    -when poverty comes in at the door,love flies out at the window
    -when the wolf comes at the door,love creeps out of the window
    -first thrive then wive
    -love lasts as long as money endures

    5-la faim est mauvaise conseillère
    -an empty belly bears no body

6-la faim fait sortir le loup du bois
-hunger will break through stone walls
-hunger drives the wolf out of the wood

faire

1-fais ce que je dis et non ce que je fais
-do as I say,not as I do
-the friar preached against stealing and had a goose in his sleeve
-practice what you preach

2-ce qui se fait de nuit paraît au grand jour
-truth will come to light

3-faire avec les moyens du bord
-to make brick without straw

4-fais du bien à un cochon et il viendra chier sur ton balcon
-all is lost that is put into a riven dish

5-il n'y a que ceux qui ne font rien qui ne se trompent pas
-he is lifeless that is faultless
-he who makes no mistakes,makes nothing
-he that never climbed,never fell

6-ne pas s'en faire pour
-to make no bones about

7-ce qui est fait, est fait
-what is done cannot be undone
-don't cry over spilt milk

8-fais ce que tu dois, advienne que pourra
-do your duty,come what may

9-faites vous miel, les mouches vous mangeront
-cover yourself with honey and you'll have plenty of flies

10-comme on fait son lit, on se couche
-as you make your bed,so you must lie upon it

11-ne pas faire long feu
-to run through quickly

12-qui fait un panier fait bien une hotte
-whatever man has done man may do

13-fais ce que tu fais
-don't try to do two things at once

14-faire plus que ce que l'on a promis
-to be better that one's words

15-ne fais pas à autrui ce que tu ne voudrais pas qu'on te fît
-do onto others as you would have them do unto you
-do as you would be done by

16-qui fera bien,bien trouvera
-good hand,good hire

faire (suite)
-17-il ne s'en fait pas
-he makes no bones about it

18-ça ne fait rien
-it makes no odds

19-vous devriez vous faire une raison
-you should come to your senses

20-ne vous en faites pas pour si peu
-for a tint thing,care not

fait
1-venez en au fait
-get down to brass tack,to nitty-gritty

2-les faits sont là
-facts are stubborn things
-the effect speaks,the tongue need not

3-le fait juge l'homme
-the proof of the pudding is in the eating

familiarité
la familiarité engendre le mépris
-familiarity breeds contempt
-an englishman's house is his castle
-a hedge between keeps friendship green
-respect is better from a distance
-manners know distance

farine
1-tout fait farine à bon moulin
-all is fish that comes to the net

2-farine du daible retourne en son
-thieves'handsel ever unlucky
-ill gotten goods seldom prosper

faucher
être fauché comme les blés (familier)
-to be poor as a rat

faute
1-qui fait la faute la boit
-every sin brings its punishment with it
-who swims in sin shall sink in sorrow
-they that dance must pay the fiddler

2-faute d'un point,Martin perdit son âne
-one false move may lose the game
-a little fire burns up a great deal of corn
-of a small spark,a great fire
-a small leak will sink a great ship
-a little stone in the way overturns a great wain
-a miss is as good as a mile
-for want of a nail,the shoe was lost

3-rarement de sa faute on aime le témoin
-the cat shuts his eyes when stealing cream
-he that does ill hates the light

4-ce n'est pas de sa faute siles grenouilles n'ont pas de queue
-how can the cat help it,if the maid is a fool?

5-faute de souliers, on va nu-pieds
-take the goods God provide

6-qui fait la faute,aussi la boive
-they that dance must pay the fiddler

fauteuil
il est arrivé dans un fauteuil
il y est arrivé haut la main
-he won hands down

femme
1-contre femme point ne débattre
-he that has a wife has a master

2-il y a bien de la différence entre une femme et un fagot
-one tongue is enough for a woman

3-à femme avare, galant escroc
-niggard father,spendthrift son

4-souvent femme varie,bien fol est qui s'y fie
-women are fickle
-a woman is a weathercock
-a woman's mind and a winter wind change oft
-women are as wavering as the wind

5-les femmes sont comme les omelettes, elles ne sont jamais assez battues
-a woman,a dog,and a walnut tree,the more you beat them the better they be

6-ce que femme veut,Dieu le veut
-once a woman's mind is made up,there's no changing it
-women will have their will
-swine,women,and bees cannot be turned

7-à une femme et une vieille maison,il y a toujours à refaire
-a woman and a ship ever want mending

8-une femme honnête et jolie est deux fois honnête
-who has a fair wife,needs more than two eyes

9-femme sait un art avant le diable
-no devil so load as a she-devil

10-les femmes font et défont les maisons
-the wife is the key of the house

11-femme rit quand elle peut et pleure quand elle veut
-women laugh when they can and weep when they will

12-la femme de César ne doit pas être soupçonnée
-Caesar's wife must be above suspicion

13-il faut chercher une femme avec les oreilles plutôt qu'avec les yeux
-marriage is a lotery

fermer

qui ferme la bouche ne montre pas les dents
-the face is not the index to the heart
-he that looks in a man's face knows not what money is his purse
-when angry,count a hundred
-a closed mouth catches no flies

ferveur

ferveur de novice ne dure pas longtemps
-what is new cannot be true
-variety takes away satiety

festin

il n'est festin que de gens chiches
-narrow gathered,widely spent

fête

1-à la fête des rois,le jour croît d'un pas de roi
-at Twelfth Day the days are lengthened a cock-stride

2-la fête passée,adieu le saint
-the river passed and God forgotten
-eaten bread is soon forgotten

3-il n'y a pas de bonne fête sans lendemain
-God send joy,for sorrow will come fast enough

feu

1-le feu le plus couvert est le plus ardent
-the stream stopped swells the higher
-fire that's closest kept burns most of all

2-un feu de paille
-a flash in the pan
-a wonder lasts but nine days

3-ses derniers feux
-his last hurrah

4-il n'est feu que de bois vert
-green wood makes a hot fire
-young colts will canter

5-se méfier du feu qui couve
-just because there's snow on the roof doesn't mean there's no fire in the heart
-there's snow on the roof but there is fire in the furnace
-beware of a silent dog and still waves

fiançailles
> **fiançailles vont en selle et repentailles en croupe**
> -marry in haste,repent at leisure

fiancer
> **tel fiance qui n'épouse point**
> -many fair promises in marriage making,but few in totcher paying

fiel
> **un peu de fiel gâte beaucoup de miel**
> -one ill weed mars a whole pot of pottage

fier
> **1-il est fier comme Artaban**
> -he is as proud as a peacock
>
> **2-il ne faut pas se fier à qui entend deux messes**
> -all are not saint that go to church
> -to keep two faces under one hood
> -to be doubled-faced (or two faced)
>
> **3-ne vous fiez pas aux apparences**
> -don't take things at their face value

fil
> **1-donner du fil à retordre**
> -to lead somebody a merry chase
> -it played the deuce with me and my belongings
> -he played old gooseberry with me
>
> **2-il a un fil à la patte**
> -his hands are tied

filer
> **filer le parfait amour**
> -to live like two love birds

filet
> **attraper dans ses filets**
> -to lure into one's web

fille
> **1-la plus belle fille du monde ne peut donner que ce qu'elle a**
> -you can't take the breeks of a Highlander
> -you can't get blood out of a turnip
> -there comes nought out of the sack but what was there
> -you cannot make a silk purse out of a sow's ear
> -the frog cannot out of her bog
> -you cannot make a crab walk straight
> -fire cannot be hidden in flax
> -nature and the sin of Adam can ill be concealed by fig leaves
> -what can you have of a cat but her skin?
> -we may not expect a good whelp from an ill dog
> -he that comes of a hen,must scrape
> -one cannot gather grapes of thorns or figs of thistles
> -what is bred in the bone will come out in the flesh
> -blood will tell
> -you cannot get water out of a stone

fille (suite)
> **1-la plus belle fille du monde ne peut donner que ce qu'elle a**
> -to ask pear from an elm tree
> -every man cannot be a master
> -out of nothing one can get nothing
> -of nought comes nought
> -you cannot make a horn of a pig's tail
> -it is hard to make mutton of a sow
> -if you squeeze a cork,you will get but little juice
>
> **2-fille et ville qui parlementent sont à demi rendues**
> -a city (woman) that parleys is half gotten
> -a maid that laughs is half taken
> -a woman kissed is half won
> -women resist in order to be conquered
> -nineteen nay-says of a maiden are half a grant
> -maids say "nay" and take it
>
> **3-une fille sans ami est un printemps sans rose**
> -he that does not love a woman,suked a saw
>
> **4-quand ma fille est mariée,tout le monde la demande**
> -the gods send nuts to those who have no teeth

filer
> **filer à l'anglaise**
> -to take a French leave

fin
> **1-à la fin saura-t-on qui a mangé le lard**
> -the ending rounds off the whole
>
> **2-qui veut la fin,veut les moyens**
> -he who will the end,will the means
> -you can't make an omelet without breaking eggs
> -he who would catch the fish mustn't mind getting wet
>
> **3-nul si fin que femme n'assote**
> -man is the head,but woman turns it
> -love is blind
>
> **4-la fin justifie les moyens**
> -the end justifies the means

finir
> **on n'a jamais fini de faire son devoir**
> -work expands to fill the time available

flambeau
> **porter le flambeau**
> -to bear the bell

flatteur
> **tout flatteur vit aux dépens de celui qui l'écoute**
> -no foes to a flatterer
> -every ass likes to hear himself bray

flèche
> la flèche d'un sot file vite
> -a fool's bolt is soon shot

fleur

> 1-ni fleurs,ni couronnes
> -no flowers by request

> 2-celà s'est passé comme une fleur
> -it worked like a charm

flûte
> ce qui vient de la flute,s'en va par le tambour
> -light come,light go

flux

> après le flux,le reflux
> -a flow will have an ebb

foi

> 1-rien n'est si dangereux que trop de bonne foi
> -he who follows truth too closely will have dirt kicked in his face

> 2-il n'y a que la foi qui sauve
> -faith is everything
> -bear with evil and expect good

> 3-la foi transporte les montagnes
> -faith will move mountains

foin
> quand le foin manque au ratelier,les chevaux se battent
> -want makes a strife between man and wife
> -spread the table and contention will cease
> -when meat is in,anger is out

fois

> 1-une fois en mauvais renom,jamais puits n'a été estimé bon
> -a good name is sooner lost than won

> 2-on le lui a dit trente six fois
> -they told him dozens of times

> 3-je le lui ai répété vingt fois
> -I repeated it to him hundreds of times

> 4-une fois n'est pas coutume
> -one sparrow doesn't make a summer
> -once does not make a habit
> -once is no rule

fol

> 1-qui fol envoie,fol attend
> -send a fool to the market and a fool he will return again

> 2-fol semble sage quand il se tait
> -a straight stick is crooked in the water
> -a fool should never hold a bauble in his hand
> -fools are wise as long as silent

3-fol et avoir ne se peuvent entr'avoir
-fools live poor to die rich

4-de fol folie,de cuir courroie
it is a foolish bird that soils its own nest
-it is a foolish sheep that makes the woolf his confessor
-he is a fool who makes his physician his heir
-it is a blind goose that comes to the fox's sermon

folie

1-quand la folie est faite,le conseil en est pris
-when a thing is done,advice comes too late

2-il n'est pas si grande folie que de sage homme
-no man can play the fool so well as the wise man

3-c'est folie de vanner les plumes au vent
standing pools gather filth

fond

1-au fin fond de soi-même
-in one's heart of heart

2-il a un bon fond
-his heart is in the right place

fondement

de méchant fondement,jamais bon bâtiment
-no good building without a good foundation
-a bad beginning makes a bad ending

fondre

fondre comme neige au soleil
-to melt like butter before the sun

fontaine

il ne faut pas dire "fontaine,je ne boirai pas de ton eau"
-never say never
-never is a long day

force

1-à force de choisir on prend le pire
-he who hesitates is lost

2-à force de coups on abat le chêne
-little strokes fell great oaks
-constant dripping wears away the stone
-spit on a stone,and it will be wet at the last
-a mouse in time may bite in two a cable

3-la force prime le droit
-might makes right
-much law,but little justice

4-nous avons tous assez de force pour supporter les maux d'autrui
-it is easy to bear the misfortune of others

forcer
> **ne forcez pas votre talent**
> -stretch your arm no further than your sleeve will reach

forger
> **c'est en forgeant qu'on devient forgeron cf doing**
> -by dint of doing blacksmith work,one becomes blacksmith
> -in doing we learn

fort
> **quand on n'est pas le plus fort il faut être le plus fin**
> -little fishes slip through net,but great ones are taken

fortune
> **1-la fortune vient en dormant**
> -the net of the sleeper catches fish
>
> **2-faire contre mauvaise fortune bon coeur**
> -to find a silver lining in every cloud
> -keep a stiff upper lip
> -the show must go on
> -you must make the best of a bad bargain
> -to put a bold or a good face on the matter
> -you must put a good face on a bad business
> -you must make the best of a bad job
>
> **3-la fortune est aveugle**
> -fortune is blind
>
> **4-la fortune est de verre;au moment où elle brille le plus,elle se brise**
> -fortune is made of glass
>
> **5-la fortune tourne à l'avantage de ceux qu'elle favorise**
> -fortune to one is mother,to another is stepmother
>
> **6-la fortune sourit aux audacieux**
> -fortune favours brave
> -a cat in gloves catches no mice
> -adventures are to the adventurous
> -fortune favours the bold
>
> **7-de la fortune nul n'est content**
> -no man is content with his lot

fou
> **1-tête de fou ne blanchit pas**
> -he that is born a fool is never cured
> -fools will be fools still
>
> **2-il est fou à lier**
> -he is as nutty as a fruitcake
>
> **3-il vaut mieux être fou avec tous que sage tout seul**
> -it's often better to swim with the stream
>
> **4-fou est le prêtre qui blâme ses reliques**
> -lovers are mad men

5-il y a plus de fous que de sages
-folly is the product of all countries and ages

6-fou qui se tait passe pour sage
-fools are wise as long as silent
-if the fool knew how to be silent he could sit amongst the wise

7-rendre fou
-to go nut,onion
-to go off one's head
-to drive someone up the wall
-to go round the bend
-to be driven round the bend

8-les vieux fous sont plus fous que les jeunes
-there's no fool like an old fool

9-qui ne sait être fou n'est pas sage
-every man is a fool sometimes and none at all times

10-un fou avise bien un sage
-a fool may give a wise man counsel
-fool rush in where angels fear to tread
-a wise man can learn from a fool

11-à chaque fou sa marotte
-to each his own

12-les fous inventent les modes et les sages les suivent
-ce sont les fous qui troublent l'eau et ce sont les sages qui pêchent
-les fols font les banquets et les sages les mangent
-a wise man can learn from a fool

13-il n'y a que les fous qui ne changent pas d'avis
-fools bite one another,but wise men agree
-a wise man changes his mind,a fool never

14-plus on est de fous,plus on rit
-the more,the merrier
-the company makes the feast

15-fou est qui s'oublie
-don't cut your nose to spite your face

foudre

la foudre ne tombe pas toutes les fois qu'il tonne
-all threats are not carried out
-all is not lost that is in danger
-all clouds bring not rain

four

on ne peut être au four et au moulin
-one cannot be in two places at one time
-one cannot do two things at once
-one cannot drink and whistle at once

fourmi

1-quand les ailes poussent à la fourmi,c'est pour sa perte
-the ant had wings to her hurt
-the highest branch is not the safest roost
-uneasy lies the head that wears a crown

2-avoir des fourmis dans les jambes
-to have pins and needles in one's legs

frais

aux frais de la princesse
-to her Majesty's expense

fraise

aller aux fraises
-to shoe the goose

frapper

1-frapper à la mauvaise porte
-to bark up the wrong tree
-to come to the wrong shop

2-on frappe sur le sac pour que l'âne le sente
-the worst hog often gets the best pear

3-frapper les trois coups
-to ring up the curtain

fréquenter

dis moi qui tu fréquentes,je te dirai qui tu es
-a man is known by the company he keeps
-a man is known by his friends
-tell me with whom thou goest,and I'll tell thee what thou doest
-as a man is,so is his company

frère

être comme deux frères
-between you and me the bedpost
-to agree like the fiddle and the stick
-to agree like two cats in a gutter
-they are finger and thumb
-as near as bark to tree
-to be hand and glove with

froid

un froid de canard
-brass monkey weather

froide

froides mains,chaudes amours
-cold hands,warm heart

frotter

1-qui s'y frotte,s'y pique
-meddle and smart for it
-the fly that plays too long in the candle,singes his wings at last

1-qui s'y frotte,s'y pique (suite)
-you may play with a bull till you get his horn in your eye
-he that steals honey,should beware of the sting
-don't go near the water until you know how to swim
-he that touches pitch shall be defiled

2-qui se frotte à l'aïl ne peut sentir la giroflée
-a herring barrel always smell of fish

fruit

1-bon fruit vient de bonne semence
-as the tree is bent,so is the tree inclined

2-il n'est si dur fruit et acerbe qui ne mûrisse
-ill weeds grow apace

fumée

1-la fumée s'attache au blanc
-no wool is so white than a dyer cannot blacken it

2-pas de fumée sans feu
-those who play at bowls must look for rubbers
-no smoke without fire
-where there are reeds,there is water
-there was aye some water where the stirk drowned
-where there is a secret,there must be something wrong

fumer

fumer comme un pompier
-to smoke like a chimney

fusil

il a changé son fusil d'épaule
-he changed his tune
-he tried another tack

G

gâcher
>**il a tout gâché**
>-he upset the applecart

gagner
>**1-gagne assez qui sort de procès**
>-to come to an arrangement is better than to going law

>**2-on ne gagne pas beaucoup à courir le monde**
>-much spends the traveller more than the abider

>**3-il a gagné le gros lot**
>-he has found the bean in the cake

>**4-on ne peut pas toujours gagner**
>-you can't win them all
>-win a few,lose a few

>**5-rien ne gagne à un retardement que la colère**
>-delay is the antidote of anger

>**6-j'ai gagné ma journée!**
>-I've gone and done it

gai
>**gai comme un pinson**
>-merry as a cricket
>-as merry as a lark
>-merry as a pie

gaine
>**en une belle gaine d'or,couteau de plomb gît et dort**
>-fair without,false within
>-poison is poison though it comes in a golden cup
>-they that have honey in their mouths have stings in their tales

gaité
>**la gaité,la santé changent l'hiver en été**
>-health and wealth create beauty
>-a blithe heart makes a blooming visage
>-the joy of the heart makes the fair face

gale
>**il est mauvais comme la gale**
>-he's rotten to the core

gallerie
>**pour la gallerie**
>-all his goods in the window
>-window dressing

galoper
>**qui ne peut galoper,qu'il trotte**
>-no one is expected to do the impossible

garçon
c'est un garçon manqué
-she is a tomboy

garde
1-tenez-vous sur vos gardes
-mind your "P,s" and "Q,s"

2-il sait se tenir sur ses gardes
-if he be angry,he knows how to turn his girdle
-to rid with the beard on the shoulder

garder
1-il a gardé un atout dans sa manche
-he kept an ace up his sleeve

2-gardez-vous d'un homme qui ne connaît qu'un livre
-there is no blindness like ignorance

3-garder une poire pour la soif
-to lay something for a rainy day
-although it rain,throw not away your watering pot

gardien
je ne suis pas le gardien de mon frère
-each man is his brother's keeper

gâteau
c'est du gâteau
-it's as easy as pie

gêne
où il y a de la gêne,il n'ay a pas de plaisir
-fingers were made before forks

génie
1-le génie commence les beaux ouvrages mais le travail les achèvent
-to finish Aladdin's window

2-le génie est une longue patience
-genius is an infinite capacity for taking pains

genre
ce n'est pas mon genre
-it's not my cup of tea

gens
gens de lettres, gens de peine
-ninety percent of inspiration is perspiration

gentilhomme
le gentilhomme croit sincèrement que la chasse est un plaisir royal, mais son piqueur n'est pas de ce sentiment
-serve a great man and you will know what sorrow is

gibet
> **le gibet ne perd jamais ses droits**
> -truth will out
> -time is the father of truth

gland
> **d'un petit gland sourd un grand chêne**
> -mighty oaks from little acorns grow
> -every oak must be an acorn

glisser
> **glisser entre les doigts**
> -to slip through one's finger

glouton
> **deux gloutons ne s'accordent pas à une même assiette**
> two cats and a mouse,two wives in a house,two dogs and a bone,never agree in one

go
> **tout de go**
> -at the drop of a hat

gond
> **sortir de ses gond**
> -to make one's hackles rise
> -to blow one's top

goujat
> **mieux vaut goujat debout qu'empereur enterré**
> -a live dog is better than a dead lion
>
> **2-d'un goujat on ne peut faire un gentilhomme**
> -what is bred in the bone will come out in the flesh

gourmand
> **le gourmand creuse sa fosse avec ses dents**
> -the glutton commits suicide with his fork

gourmandise
> **la gourmandise tue plus de monde que l'épée**
> -gluttony kills more than the sword
> -whatsoever was the father of the disease,an ill diet was the mother
> -many dishes make many diseases
> -much meat,much malady

goût
> **1-tous les goûts sont dans la nature ; à chacun son goût**
> -to each his own
> -there is no accounting for tastes
> -everyone to his taste
> -all meat pleases not all mouths
> -no dish pleases all palates alike
> -all feet tread not in one shoe
>
> **2-des goûts et des couleurs on ne discute pas**
> -there is no disputing about tastes

goutte

1-goutte à goutte,l'eau creuse la pierre
-constant dropping wears away a stone
-the falling drops hollow the stone

2-c'est la goutte d'eau qui fait déborder le vase
-the pitcher went once too often to the wall
-that's the last straw
-that's the straw that broke the camel's back
-the last drop makes the cup run over
-the cord breaks at last by the weakest point
-more than enough is too much

3-ils se ressemblent comme deux gouttes d'eau
-they are as alike as peas in a pod

gouverner

1-quand on veut gouverner les hommes,il ne faut pas les chasser devant soi,il faut les suivre
-who drive fat oxen shall himself be fat

2-gouverner,c'est prévoir
-providing is preventing

grace

être dans les bonnes graces de quelqu'un
-to be in somebody's good graces

grain

1-le bon grain finit toujours par lever
-sooner or later merit will come to the front

2-parer au grain
-to batten down the hatches

3-chaque grain a sa paille
-every bean has its black

4-grain à grain la poule remplit son ventre
-many sands will sink a ship

5-veiller au grain
-to keep one's eyes peeled
-to keep one's weather eye open for trouble

6-bon grain périt,paille demeure
-thorns live and roses die

graisse

c'est la graisse du cochon qui a cuit le cochon
-don't make a rod for your own back

graisser

graissez les bottes d'un vilain,il dira qu'on les lui brûle
-set a beggar on horseback and he will ride to the devil
-if you give him an inch,he'll take a mile

grand
1-il n'y a pas de grand homme pour son valet de chambre
-no man is a hero to his valet

2-les grands esprits se rencontrent
-great minds think alike

3-pour être grand,il faut avoir été petit
-he that cannot obey cannot command
-it needs more skill than I can tell to play the second fiddle well
-through obedience learn to command

gratter
1-il faut gratter les gens où il leur démange
-imitation is the sincerest form of flattery

2-grattez le russe et vous trouverez le tartare
-scratch a Russian and you find a Tartar

grenouille
1-la grenouille veut se faire aussi grosse que le boeuf
-the bear wants a tail and cannot be a lion

2-il n'est pas de grenouille qui ne trouve son crapaud
-if the shoe fits,wear it

3-une grenouille de bénitier
-a church mouse

griffe
à la griffe on reconnaît le lion
-the workman is known by his work

grimace
faire une grimace
-to pull a face

grimper
cela me fait grimper aux arbres
-it drives me up the wall
-it rouses my bile

grive
faute de grives on se contente de merles
-half a loaf is better than no bread
-something is better than nothing
-one foot is better than two crutches
-better a bare foot than none
-better eye sore than all blind
-better a mouse in the pot than no flesh at all
-better are small fish than an empty dish
-a crust is better than no bread
-better a louse in the pot than no flesh at all
-better some of a pudding than none of a pie
-a churl's feast is better than none at all
-half an egg is better than an empty shell
-they that have no other meat,bread and butter are glad to eat
-it is better to sup with a cutty than want a spoon

grive

faute de grives on se contente de merles (suite)
-better a lean jade than an empty halter
-a bad bush is better than the open field
-better my hog dirty than no hog at all

gros

en gros
-by and large

guerre

1-à la guerre comme à la guerre
-we shall have to rough it,that's all
-all is fair in love and war
-however things are,we must accept them as they are

2-nul ne sait ce qu'est la guerre s'il n'y a son fils
-war is sweet to them that know it not

gueule

1-elle a une gueule de raie
-she has a face that would stop a clock

2-se jeter dans la gueule du loup
-to put one's head in the lion's mouth
-to take the bear by the tooth
-to beard the lion in his den

H

habit

1-l'habit fait l'homme
-the tailor makes the man
-finding's keeping

2-l'habit ne fait pas le moine
-it's not the hood that makes the monk
-it is not the gay coat that makes the gentleman
-fine clothes don't make a gentleman
-you can't tell a book by its cover
-a black plum is as sweet as a white
-all are not maiden that wear bare hair
-things are seldom what they seem

3-habit de velours,ventre de son
-don't be penny wise and pound foolish

4-l'habit volé ne va pas au voleur
-borrowed garments never fit well
-ill gotten goods seldom prosper

habitude

l'habitude est une seconde nature
-you can never scare a dog away from a greasy hide
-custom is a second nature
-use is a second nature

hacher

il se ferait hacher plutôt que d'avouer
-wild horses cannot make him admit
-nobody ever admits they are to blame

haine

la haine,c'est la colère des faibles
-wiles help weak people

haïr

1-on a peine à haïr ce qu'on a bien aimé
-save us from our friends

2-homme haï est demi-mort
-seldom does the hated man ends well

hanter

qui hante chien,puces remporte
-the shoe will hold xith the sole

hasarder

qui ne hasarde rien,n'a rien
-nothing venture,nothing have

hâter

1-qui trop se hâtent,s'empêchent
-hasty climbers have sudden falls

2-qui trop se hâte reste en chemin
-a minute gained,a lifetime lost
-he that leaves the highway to cut short,commonly goes about

3-plus me hâte et plus me gâte
-good and quickly seldom meet

hâter

1-hâtez-vous lentement
-make haste slowly
-haste makes waste
-a soft fire makes sweet malt
-nothing must be done hastily but killing of fleas

2-qui trop se hâte reste en chemin
-he that leaves the highway to cut short,commonly goes about

haut

1-haut les coeurs!
-keep your pecker up!

2-il y a des hauts et des bas dans la vie
-there is a tide in the affairs of men

hauteur

se montrer à la hauteur des circonstances
-to rally to the occasion

herbe

1-l'herbe est toujours plus verte dans le pré du voisin
-the grass is always greener on the other side of the fence
-the apples on the other side of the wall are the sweetest
-our neighbour's cow yields better milk than ours

herbe

2-mauvaise herbe croît soudain
les mauvaises herbes poussent toujours
-ill weeds grow apace
-weeds want no sowing

herbe

3-couper l'herbe sous le pied
-to take the wind out of one's sails
-to pull the rug out from under someone
-to cut the grass from under a person's feet

heur

tout n'est qu'heur et malheur
-one man's loss is another man's gain

heure

1-à toute heure chien pisse et femme pleure
-trust not a woman when she weeps

2-à l'heure juste
-dead on the hour

3-avant l'heure,c'est pas l'heure;après l'heure c'est plus l'heure
-though you rise early,yet the day comes at his time,and not till then
-soon enough is well enough

4-il n'y a pas d'heure pour les braves
-to a brave and faithful man nothing is difficult
-to a real hero life is a mere straw

5-sentir sa dernière heure arriver
-to feel that the hour for the upturning of one's glass was at hand

heureux
1-pour vivre heureux vivons cachés
-the quiet life is the happy life
-let's stay out of the limelight

2-heureux au jeu,malheureux en amour
-lucky at cards,unlucky in love

3-heureux les pauvres d'esprit,le royaume des cieux leur appartient
-blessed are the poor in spirit

hic
voilà le hic!
-that's the rock you split on
-here is the rub

hirondelle
une hirondelle ne fait pas le printemps
-a robin doesn't make spring
-one sparrow doesn't make summer

histoire
1-l'histoire est un perpétuel recommencement
-history repeats itself

2-c'est l'histoire du corbeau et du renard
-it was the story of the dog and the shadow

3-faire toute une histoire,une affaire d'Etat
-to make a federal case

hiver
au plus fort de l'hiver
-in the dead of winter

homme
1-un homme averti en vaut deux
-forewarned is forearmed
-one volunteer is worth two pressed men

2-l'homme arrive novice à chaque âge de la vie
-live and learn

3-l'homme est un loup pour l'homme
-man is wolf to man

4-un homme mort n'a ni parents ni amis
-to dead men and absent there are no friend left

5-l'homme donne sa mesure dans l'adversité
-adversity makes men,prosperity monsters

6-l'homme propose et Dieu dispose
-when heavens appoints,man must obey

7-homme rusé,tard abusé
-too much cunning undoes
-at length the fox is brought to the furrier
-though the fox run,the chicken has wings
-cheats never prosper
-falsehood never made a fair hinder end

8-l'homme naquit pour travailler comme l'oiseau pour voler
-work expands as to fill the time available

9-tant vaut l'homme,tant vaut la terre
-the workman is known by his work
-a good farmer makes a good farm

10-homme aime quand il veut et femme quand elle peut
-a man is as old as he feels and a woman as old as she looks

11-homme seul est viande à loups
-the lone sheep is in danger of the wolf

12-l'homme est un apprenti et la douleur est son maître
-calamity is man's true touchstone

13-d'un petit homme souvent grand ombre
-a little body often harbours a great soul
-there is no little enemy

14-il n'y a pas de grand homme pour son valet de chambre
-no man is a hero to his valet

15-l'homme ne vit pas seulement de pain
-man cannot live by bread alone

16-l'homme noble c'est l'homme vertueux
-virtue is the only true nobility

honni

honni soit qui mal y pense
-evil to him that evil thinks
-shame to him
-he that shames,shall be shent

honte

nous aurions souvent honte de nos plus belles actions si le monde voyait tous les motifs qui les produisent
a straight tree may have crooked roots

honteux
> **jamais honteux n'eut belle amie**
> -none but the brave deserve the lady
> -faint heart never won fair lady
> -fortune favours the bold

hôpital
> **c'est l'hôpital qui se moque de la charité**
> -every man's censure is first moulded in his own nature
> -ill may the kiln call the oven burnt-house

hôte
> **l'hôte et la pluie après trois jours ennuient**
> -do not wear out your welcome
> -a constant guest is never welcome

huile
> **1-c'est une huile,un ponte une grosse légume**
> -he's a big wheel,a V.I.P.
>
> **2-jeter de l'huile sur le feu**
> -to poke fire with a sword
> -to fan the flames
> -to add fuel to the fire

huis
> **se réunir à huis clos**
> -to meet behind closed doors

hurler
> **il faut hurler avec les loups**
> -never wear a brown hat in Friesland
> -it's often better to swim with the stream
> -who keeps company with a wolf will learn to howl
> -one must howl with the wolves
> -it is ill shaving against the wool
> -it is ill striving against the stream
> -do as must men do,then most men will speak well of you
> -there is safety in numbers
> -the beaten road is the safest
> -the longest way round is the nearest way home
> -he who goes against the fashion is himself its slave
> -he that follows Nature is never out of his way
> -you must do as others do
> -better be out of the world than out of the fashion

hypocrisie
> **l'hypocrisie est un hommage que le vice rend à la vertu**
> -hypocrisy is a homage that vice pays to virtue

I

ignorance

1-l'ignorance est toujours prête à admirer
-wonders will never cease

2-c'est la profonde ignorance qui inspire le ton dogmatique
-cracked pipkins are discovered by their sound

3-l'ignorance et l'incuriosité font un doux oreiller
-ignorance and incuriosity are two very soft pillows

ignorer

-nul n'est censé ignorer la loi
-ignorance of the law excuses no man

imbécile

il n'y a que les imbéciles qui ne changent pas d'avis
il n'y a de damnés que les obstinés
-a wise man changes his mind, a fool never will

impossible

à l'impossible nul n'est tenu
-no one is expected to do the impossible
-no one is bound to do impossibilities
-no living man all things can
-it's no use trying to put a quart into a pint pot
-the best of men are but men at best
-only an elephant can bear an elephant's load
-a man cannot do more than he can
-take no more on you than you are able to bear

individu

c'est un individu sans feu ni lieu
-he is a footloose and fancy free

infortune

l'infortune est la sage femme du génie
-poverty is the mother of all arts
-poverty is the mother of invention

infortuné

il n'y a rien de si infortuné qu'un homme qui n'a jamais
souffert
-calamity is man's true touchstone

innocent

aux innocents les mains pleines
-if you are born to be hanged then you'll never be drowned
-beginner's luck
-fortune favours fools
-lucky men need no counsel

intelligence

accusé d'intelligences avec l'ennemi
-accused to give aid and comfort to the enemy

intention

1-c'est l'intention qui compte
-every deed is to be judged by the doer's intention
-the good intention excuses the bad action

2-l'intention vaut le fait
-take the will for the deed

inventer

il n'a pas inventé le fil à couper le beurre
il n'a pas inventé la poudre
-he won't set the world on fire

ivre

ivres et forcenés disent toute leur pensée
-children and fools tell the truth

ivrogne

il ne faut pas mettre dans la cave un ivrogne qui a renoncé au
-vin the righteous man sins before an open chest
-an open door may tempt a saint
-at open doors dogs come in

J

jalousie

> la jalousie est la soeur de l'amour comme le diable est le frère des anges
> -love is never without jealousy

jamais

1-jamais deux sans trois
-of one ill come many
-if at first you don't succed the try,try,and try again
-a work ill done must be done twice
-misfortune never comes singly

2-jamais grand nez ne gâta beau visage
-God has a great share in a little house

3-il n'est jamais trop tard pour bien faire
-it is never too late to learn

4-jamais deux orgueilleux ne chevaucheront bien un âne
-if two ride a horse,one must ride behind
-don't speak to the man at the wheel

jambe

1-traiter par dessus la jambe
-to treat like dirt

2-tenir la jambe
-to bend one's ear
-to talk the hind leg off a donkey

3-n'étend les jambes qu'à la longueur du tapis
-stretch your arm no further than your sleeve will reach
-never bite unless you make your teeth meet

4-il a des jambes de coq
-his calves are gone to grass
-veal will be dear,because there are no calves

jardin

jardin entamé n'est plus respecté
-a maid oft seen and a gown oft worn,are desestemed and held in scorn

jeu

le jeu n'en vaut pas la chandelle
-the game is not worth the candle
-business will not quite cost
-to give a lark to catch a kite

jeter

1-ne jetez pas votre argent par les fenêtres
-don't throw good money after bad
-give her bells and let her fly
-don't make ducks and drakes of your money

2-être jeté dehors tambour battant
-to be drummed out

3-jeter l'éponge
-to throw the towel

4-jeter de la poudre aux yeux
-to through dust(speck) in his eyes

5-jeter le manche après la cognée
-to send (throw)the axe after the helve
-to throw the rope after the bucket
-to throw the helve after the hatchet
-never say die
-keep your pecker up

6-jeter un pavé dans la mare
-to drop a brick
-to set the cat among the pigeons

7-on ne jette pas le coffre au feu parce que la clef en est perdue
-burn not your house to get rid of the mouse
-widows are always rich

8-jeter de l'huile sur le feu
-the fat is in the fire

9-on ne jette de pierres qu'à l'arbre chargé de fruits
-it is only at the tree loaded with fruit,that people throw stones
-he that has lands, has quarrels
-abundance of things engenders disdainfulness

10-il ne faut pas jeter le bébé avec l'eau du bain
-don't throw the baby with the bath

jeu

1-à mauvais jeu,bonne mine
-the object of words is to conceal thoughts

2-le jeu ne vaut pas la chandelle
-the game is not worth the candle
-business will not quite cost
-to give a lark to catch a kite

jeune

de jeune avocat,héritage perdu
-experience is the best teacher

jeunesse

1-il faut que jeunesse se passe
-youth will have its swing
-a ragged colt may make a good horse
-wanton kittens make sober cats
-naughty boys sometimes make good men
-royet lads make sober men
-you must take allowance for youth
-youth must be served

2-si jeunesse savait,si vieillesse pouvait
-if youth but knew,if age but could
-if youth knew what age would crave,it would both get and save
-if the young man would,and the old man could,there would be nothing

3-jeunesse oiseuse,viellesse disetteuse
-an idle youth,a needy age
-idleness is the key of beggary
-if you lie upon roses when young,you'll lie upon thorns when old

joindre

joindre l'utile à l'agréble
-combine business with pleasure,the useful with the agreeable

joli

joli dessus,vilaine doublure
-a whore in a fine dress is like an clean entry to a durty house

jouer

1-on ne joue pas avec le feu
-don't play with matches
-it is dangerous to play with edged tools
-if you play with the fire,you get burnt
-he that touches pitch will be defiled
-it is ill jesting with edged tools

2-jouer quelque chose sur un coup de dés
-to put all one's eggs in one basket
-to put one's shirt
-to bet one's bottom dollar
-to stake everything on a single cast of dice

3-jouer au chat et à la souris
-to play cat and mouse

4-jouer sa dernière carte
-to play one's last trump

joueur

au bon joueur la balle
-good hand,good hire
-the deed comes back upon the doer

jouir

qui veut jouir d'aile,il lui faut lever la cuisse
-nothing ventured,nothing gained

jour

1-elles sont comme le jour et la nuit
-they are poles apart

2-les jours se suivent et ne se ressemblent pas
-tomorrow is another day
-sadness and gladness succcd each other

3-bon jour,bonne oeuvre
-the better the day,the better the deed

4-à chaque jour suffit sa peine
-sufficient unto the day is the evil thereof

5-marquer ce jour d'une pierre blanche,noire
-to call that a red ,black letter day
-to mark with a white stone

6-paraître sous son meilleur jour
-best foot foremost
-to put your best foot forward

7-Paris ne s'est pas fait en un jour
-Rome wasn't built in a day
-a strong town is not won in one hour

8-ses jours sont comptés
-he lives on borrowed time

9-ce n'est pas tous les jours fête (Dimanche)
-Christmas comes but once a year

10-les jours se suivent mais ne se ressemblent pas
-sadness and gladness succeed each other
-after Chritmas comes Lent

11-un jour ou l'autre
-sooner or later

12-passé le jour,passé la fête
-after Christmas comes Lent

journée
rouge au soir,blanc au matin,c'est la journée du pélerin
-evening red and morning grey sets the traveller on his way
-red sky at night,sheperd's delight
-red sky in the morning,sheperd's warning

juge
1-juge hâtif est périlleux
-one must not condemn without hearing

2-on ne peut être juge et partie
-a fox shouldn't be one of the jury at a goose's trial

3-de fou juge,brève sentence
-from a foolish judge,a quick sentence

juger
on ne peut juger le sac à l'étiquette
-il ne faut juger un paquet d'après ses ficelles
-you can't tell a book by its cover
-never judge from appearances
-none can guess the jewel by the casket
-you cannot judge a tree (a dog) to its bark

jument
> **quand la jument est sortie,il n'est plus temps de fermer l'étable**
> -don't cry over the spilt milk
> -it si too late to lock the stable when the horse has been stolen

jupe
> **être dans les jupes de sa mère**
> -tied to one's mother's apron strings

jurer
> **1-il ne faut jurer de rien**
> -nothing is certain
> -never is a long day
> -never say never
>
> **2-jurer comme un charretier**
> -to swear like a trooper

jus
> **c'est jus vert et vert jus**
> -it is tweedledum and twedledee

juste
> **1-le juste pèche sept fois par jour**
> -no man is wise at all times
>
> **2-c'est juste de te rendre la pareille**
> -turn about is fair play

L

là
là où l'on est bien,là est la patrie
-where it is well with me,there is my country
-wise men esteem every place

labeur
labeurs sans soin,labeurs de rien
-a work ill done must be done twice
-if a thing is worth doing,it's worth doing well

laboure
celui qui laboure le champ le mange
-plough deep,while sluggards smeep;and you will have corn to sell and to keep
-he that will eat the kernel,must crack the nut
-he that would have the fruit,must climb the tree
-if you put nothing into your purse,you can take nothing out
-if you won't work,you shan't eat

lac
un lac réfléchit mieux les étoiles qu'une rivière
-lookers-on see more than players

lâcher l
lâcher la proie pour l'ombre
-to give up the substance for the shadow
-wrangle for an ass shadow
-the devil catch the hindmost
-gone to the bad for the shadow of an ass

laisser
1-cela se laisse manger
-that doesn't taste half bad

2-il faut laisser courir le vent par dessus les tuiles
il faut laisser couler l'eau
-don't throw straws against the wind
-don't try to sweep back the Atlantic with a besom
-we must not look for a golden life in an iron age

3-être laissé pour compte
-to be left in the basket

lait
nul lait noir,nul corbeau blanc
-the leopard cannot change his spots

lame
la lame use le fourreau
-the blade wears out the scabbard

lampe
il ne faut pas mettre la lampe sous le boisseau
-tell the truth and shame the devil
-don't hide your lamp under a bushel
-what is the good of a sundial in the shade?

lance

la lance d'Achille blesse et guérit
-the greater grief drives out the less

lange

le lange l'a apporté,le linceul l'emportera
-life is but a long journey to death
-the first breath is the beginning of death

langue

1-il vaut mieux se mordre la langue avant de parler qu'après avoir parlé
-a closed mouth catches no flies

2-la langue est un bon bâton
-the tongue is not steel,yet it cuts
-a word spoken is an arrow let fly
-the tongue is sharper than any word

3-un coup de langue est pire qu'un coup de lance
-the tongue is sharper than any word
-the tongue is mightier than any sword

4-donner sa langue au chat
-to give up

5-longue langue,courte main
-a long tongue is a sign of short hand
-he that promises too much means nothing
-better deny at once than promise long

6-la langue des femmes est leur épée,elles ne la laissent pas rouiller
-a woman's sword is her tongue,and she does not let it rust

7-tourner sept fois sa langue dans sa bouche
-to count to ten
-don't get the wrong saw by the ear
-don't get the wrong end of the stick
-think twice before you speak
-it's often better to bite one's tongue
-be swift to hear,slow to speak
-a word spoken is past recalling
-first think,then speak
-a word and a stone let go cannot be recalled
-better the foot slip than the tongue trip
-second thoughts are best
-let not thy tongue run away with thy brains
-little can a long tongue lein
-let not your tongue run at rover
-score twice before you cut once

8-avoir la langue bien pendue
-to have a long tongue

9-avoir quelque chose sur le bout de la langue
-to have something on the tip of one's tongue

10-retrouver sa langue,ses esprits
-to find one's tongue

11-de quoi ne pas avoir sa langue dans sa poche
-enough to make a cat speak

12-la langue va où la dent fait mal
-the foot knows where the foot pinches

13-un coup de langue est pire qu'un coup de lance
-the tongue is mightier than the sword

larme
pleurer des larmes de crocodile
-to weep millstones

larron
à gros larron,grosse corde
-give a thief a rope and he'll hang himself

laurier
dormir sur ses lauriers
-to rest on one's oars

laver
1-à laver la tête d'un âne,on y perd sa lessive
-to carry water to the river
-to carry water to Newcastle

2-il faut laver son linge sale en famille
-one does not wash one's dirty clothes in public
-it is an ill bird that fouls its own nest
-no names,no packdrill

3-lavez chien,peignez chien,toutefois n'est chien que chien
-a rose by any other name would still be a rose

lendemain
1-le lendemain s'instruit aux leçons de la veille
-custom makes things easy
-no man is his craft's master the first day
-all things are difficult before they are easy
-practice makes perfect

2-le plus beau lendemain ne nous rend pas la veille
-things past cannot be recalled
-it is too late to call back yesterday
-the mill cannot grind with the water that is past

léopard
un léopard change-t-il ses taches?
-a leopard cannot change his spots

lever

1-il a beau se lever tard qui a bruit de se lever matin
-a good name is better than a golden girdle
-a good fame is better than a good face

2-tu t'es levé du pied gauche
-you got out of the bed the wrong way,on the wrong side,with the left leg foremost

3-ne pas lever le petit doigt
-not to lift a finger

4- les uns lèvent le lièvre,les autres le tuent
-one may steal a horse while another may not look over a hedge
-two dogs fight for a bone and a third one runs away with it
-one beats the bush,another takes the bird
-little dogs start the hare but great dogs catch it

5-à qui se lève matin,Dieu aide et prête la main
-he that comes first to the hill,may sit where he will

lèvre

accepter du bout des lèvres
-to pay lip service

liberté

liberté et pain cuit
-a lean liberty is better than fat slavery

libre

être libre comme l'air
-to be free as a bird

lien

le lien ne fait pas le fagot
-it's not the cowl that makes the friar
-none can tell the jewel by the casket

lierre

le lierre meurt où il s'attache
-the lover is not where he lives but where he loves
-faithfulness is a sister of love
-sound love is not soon forgotten

lieue

être à cent lieues de...
-to be a far cry from

lièvre

1-il ne faut pas courir deux lièvres à la fois
-to try to do two things at once
-he that follows two hares at a time is sure to catch neither
-don't have too many irons in the fire
-he who begins many things,finishes but few
-one cannot be in two places at once
-the moon is not seen when the sun shines

120

2-il ne faut pas mettre le lièvre en sauce avant de l'avoir attrapé
-make not your sauce,before you have caught the fish

3-le lièvre retourne toujours au lancer
-the dog return to its vomit

4-soulever un lièvre
-to stir up a hornet's nest

5-lièvre qui court n'est pas mort
-first catch your hare

6-faire le lièvre
-win at first and lose at last

7-un lièvre va toujours mourir au gîte
-the bird loves her nest

lime

au long aller,la lime mange le fer
-a mouse in time may bite in two a cable

limite

il y a limite à tout
-one must draw a line somewhere

livre

1-un gros livre est un grand mal
-a great book is a great evil

2-les bons livres font les bons clercs
-a great book is a great evil

loi

1-nul n'est censé ignorer la loi
-ignorance of the law is no excuse

2-la loi dit ce que le roi veut
-the king can do no wrong

loin

il y a loin de la coupe aux lèvres
-a promise is a promise
-there is many a slip'twixt the cup and the lip

louer

1-celui là seul sait louer,qui loue avec restriction
-don't paint the lily

2-loue le beau jour au soir,et la vie à ta mort
-at the game's end,we shall see who gains

3-qui se loue s'emboue
-he that praises himself,patters himself

loup

1-à chair de loup,sauce de chien
-it is an ill dog that deserves not a crust

2-c'est connu comme le loup blanc
-it is believed on all hands

3-c'est un loup déguisé en brebis
-it is a wolf in sheep's clothing

4-introduire le loup dans la bergerie
-to put the cat among the pigeons
-to set the fox to mind the geese

5-les loups ne se mangent pas entre eux
-there is honor among thieves
-dog doesn't eat dog
-crow does not pick crow's eye

6-quiconque est loup agisse en loup
-you cannot make a silk purse out of a sow's ear
-you cannot make a horn of a pig's tail
-you cannot make a mercury out of every log
-what can you expect from a hog but a grunt?

7-le loup change de poil mais non de naturel
-the wolf may lose his teeth,but never his nature

8-quand le loup est pris,tous les chiens lui lardent les fesses
-to kick a man when he is down
-the poor man pays for all

9-avec les loups,on apprend à hurler
-he that dwells next door to a cripple,will learn to halt

lueur

une lueur d'espoir
-a ray of hope

lumière

il y a des lumières que l'on éteint en les plaçant sur des chandeliers
-high places have their precipices
-sit in your place and none can make you rise

lune

1-demander la lune
-to cry for the moon

2-être dans la lune
-to be a John-a dreams
-to be wool gathering

3-la lune est à l'abri des loups
-money is the only monarch

lunettes

bonjour lunettes,adieu fillettes
lunettes et cheveux gris sont quittance d'amour
-when bees are old,they yield no honey

-old cattle breed not
-grey hairs are death's blossoms

lutter

lutter jusqu'à la dernière extrêmité
-to die in the last ditch
-a last ditch struggle
-to fight up to the last ditch

M

mâcher
> **ne pas mâcher ses mots**
> -not to mince one's words

maçon
> **1-il n'est bon maçon qui pierre refuse**
> -every salesman boats of his own wares

> **2-c'est au pied du mur qu'on reconnaît le maçon**
> -office will show the man

Mahomet
> **si tu ne vas pas à Mahomet,Mahomet viendra à toi**
> -if the moutain will not come to Mahomet,Mahomet must go to the mountain
> -you never know what you can do till you try

maille
> **1-maille à maille est fait le haubergeon**
> -by one and one the spindles are made

> **2-je ne veux pas avoir maille à partir avec vous**
> -I'm not going to bandy words with you

> **3-avoir maille à partir avec quelqu'un**
> -to have a bone to pick with someone

main
> **1-la main qui caresse est souvent la main qui tue**
> -all are not friends that speak us fair

> **2-main morte**
> -to give the gun

> **3-avoir la main verte**
> -to have a green thumb

> **4-mains blanches sont assez lavées**
> -a clean hand wants no washing
> -a clean conscience laughs at false accusations

> **5-mettre sa main au feu**
> -to swear on a stack of bibles

> **6-mettre la dernière main**
> -give it another brush

> **7-en un tour de main**
> -before you can say Jack Robinson

> **8-si on met la main à la pâte,il en reste toujours aux doigts**
> -if the ball does not stick to the wall,it will at least leave a mark
> -he that has to do with a fool,never comes away clean
> -he that touches pitch sall be defiled

9-être pris la main dans le sac
-to be caught red-handed

10-jeu de mains,jeu de vilains
-no horseplay

11-les mains noires font manger le pain blanc
-busiest men find the most leisure time
-no gain without pain
-there is no pleasure without pain
-through hardship to the stars
-no cross,no crown
-take a pain for a pleasure all wise men can
-if you don't work,you shan't eat

12-que ta main gauche ignore ce que fait ta main droite
-the right hand does not know what the left hand does

13-j'en mettrais ma main au feu (a main à couper)
-if not,I'm a Dutchman
-may this piece of bread choke me if what I say is not true

14-une main lave l'autre
-one hand washes the other
-real friendship does not freeze in winter

15-mains froides ,coeur chaud
-mains froides,chaudes amours
-cold hands,warm heart
-in the coldest flint there is hot fire

16-main serrée,coeur étroit
-a miser has no friends

17-de longue main
-for ages
-for a long time(past)

18-il n'y a que la main d'un ami qui arrache l'épine du coeur
-when friends meet,hearts warm

19-les mains sont faites avant les couteaux
-fingers were made before forks

20-une main de fer dans un gant de velours
-the iron fist (hand) in the velvet glove

maison
1-grande maison se fait par petite cuisine
-a high building,a low foundation

2-la maison close
-the cat's house

3-à la maison acheter,au marché vendre
-buy at a fair,but sell at home

maître

1-un maître familier nourrit un valet impertinent
-better to have a dog fawn on you than bite you

2-les bons maîtres font les bons valets
-Jack's as good as his master

3-pour devenir le maître,il faut agir en esclave
-one must be a servant before one can be a master

4-qui bon maître a,bon loyer a
-good hand,good hire

5-il vaut mieux être maître,on est valet quand on veut
-it is better to be the hammer than the anvil

mal

1-mal sur mal n'est pas santé
-sore upon sore is not salve

2-ne faites pas de mal par excès de zèle
-don't throw the baby out with the bath

3-nous avons tous assez de force pour supporter les maux d'autrui
le mal d'autrui est un songe
-it is easy to bear the misfortunes of others
-the stone that lies not in your gate breaks not your toes

4-mal passé n'est que songe
-eaten bread is soon forgotten

5-mal passé,adieu le saint
-the river passed and God forgotten

6-en mal fait ne gît qu'amendes
-every sin brings its punishment with it

7-entre deux maux,il faut choisir le moindre
-of two evils,choose the less
-where bad's the best,bad must be the choice
-there is small choice in rotten apples
-no choice among stinking fish
-make the best of a bad bargain

8-qui mal cherche,mal trouve
-qui veut mal,mal lui vient
-he that mischief hatches mischief catches
-he that seeks trouble,never misses

9-mal est caché à qui l'on voit le dos
-many would be cowards if they had courage enough

10-qui veut mal,mal lui tourne
-he that seeks trouble never misses

11-aux grands maux les grands remèdes
-desperate diseases must have desperate remedies
-a fog cannot be dispelled with a fan

12-c'est le mal joli il n'est pas plutôt fini qu'on en rit (pour parler de la femme qui a accouché)
-the danger past and God forgotten

13-mal fait qui ne parfait
-let not your wits go wool-gathering
-if a thing is worth doing,it's worth doing well
-well is that well done

14-le mal arrive d'un seul coup et se retire par parcelles
-misfortune arrives on horseback but departs on foot

malade
malade comme un chien
-sick as a cat

maladie
les maladies viennent à cheval et s'en retournent à pied
-agues come on horseback but go away on foot
-mischief comes by the pound and goes away by the ounce
-ill comes in ells and goes out by inches

maladroit
maladroit
-butterfingers
-his fingers are all thumbs

malheur
1-c'est dans le malheur qu'on connaît ses vrais amis
-a friend in need is a friend indeed
-prosperity makes friends,adversity tries them

2-un malheur n'arrive jamais seul
-misfortune never comes singly
-an unhappy man's cart is easy to tumble
-it never rains,it pours
-of one ill come many
-ill come often on the back of worse
-one funeral makes many
-ill news comes often on the back of worse

3-quand le malheur entre dans la maison,faut lui donner une chaise
-when the going gets tough,the tough gets going
-good news goes on crutches,bad news travel quickly,ill news travel apace

4-à quelque chose malheur est bon
-evil does not always come to injure
-there is no great loss without some gain
-good counsil never comes amiss
-bitter pills may have wholesome effects

4-à quelque chose malheur est bon (suite)
-ill luck is good for something
-sweet are the uses of adversity
-nothing but is good for something

5-le malheur des uns fait le bonheur des autres
-one man's loss is another man'gain
-the folly of one man is the fortune of another
-one man's meat is another man's poison
-if one will not,another will

6-plus le malheur est grand,plus il est grand de vivre
-calamity is man's true touchstone

7-le malheur n'est pas toujours à la porte du pauvre
-the lower millstone grounds as well as the upper

malheureux
1-les malheureux sont seuls au monde
-loneliness is the ultimate poverty
laugh,and the world laughs with you;weep,and you weep alone

2-il est plus malheureux de commettre une injustice que de la souffrir
-it is better to suffer wrong than do it

malin
1-malin comme un singe
-a clever little devil

2-à malin,malin et demi
-set a thief to catch a thief
-to a crafty man,a crafty and a half
-an old poacher makes the best keeper

3-il est malin comme un singe
-he is as tricky as they come

maman
une maman est un bon bol à couvercle
-every mother's child is handsome
-the owl thinks her young fairest
-there is only one pretty child in the world,and every mother has it

manche
1-il ne faut pas jeter la manche après la cognée
-never say die
-don't venture the saddle after the horse
-don't throw the helve after the hatchet

2-c'est une autre paire de manches
-that is a horse of another color
-that is another pair of shoes
-that's another cup of tea

manger
1-il faut manger pour vivre et non vivre pour manger
-eat to live, not live to eat

2-manger à plusieurs rateliers
-to have a foot in several camps

3-se manger la laine sur le dos
-to quarrel one's over bishop's cope,over goat's wool

4-si tu manges ton pain blanc le premier,tu manges ton pain noir plus tard
-it is a good thing to eat your brown bread first
-if you don't work,you shan't eat
-idleness must thank itself if it go barefoot

5-mange bien des mouches qui n'y voit pas
-a nod is as good as a wink to a blind horse

6-mangeant du foin,vous sentirez l'âne
-they who play bowls must expect to meet rubbers

7-manger de la vache enragée
-to have a hard time

8-qui a mangé le lard,ronge l'os
-conscience does make coward of us all
-he that commits a fault thinks everyone speaks of it

9-à manger avec le diable,la fourchette n'est jamais trop longue
-he who sups with the devil should have a long spoon

10-il y a longtemps qu'il mange les pissenlits par la racine
-he's been pushing up the daisies for a long time
-to be food for worms

11-il mange toujours son blé en herbe
-money burns a hole in his pocket

12-quand on mange la vache du roi,à cent ans de là en paye les os
-one cannot do a foolish thing once in one's life but turns-lie dead,ten good
-do wrong once and you'll never hear the end of it

13-on mange bien des perdrix sans oranges
-we must not look for a golden life in an iron age

14-il mange comme quatre
-he eats like a horse

manier
1-ne maniez pas le pavé de l'ours
-don't throw the baby out with the bath

2-on ne manie pas le beurre sans se graisser les doigts
-muck and money go together
-where there is muck there is brass

manière

1-la manière de donner vaut mieux que ce que l'on donne
-it's not the gift,it's the giver

2-la manière fait tout
-manners make the man

manquer

il ne manque pas un bouton de guêtre
-to have something buttoned up
-to get one's ducks in a row

marchand

1-marchand qui perd ne peut rire
-a merchant that gains not loses

2-n'est pas marchand qui toujours gagne
-he that cannot abide a bad market,deserves not a good one

3-le marchand de sable est passé
-the sandman is about
-the dustman has arrived

marché

1-on n'a jamais bon marché de mauvaises marchandises
-ill ware never cheap

2-bon marché fait argent débourser
-many have been ruined by buying good pennyworths
-a good bargain is a pick-purse
-good cheap is dear
-ill ware is never cheap

3-bon marché vide le panier mais n'emplit pas la bourse
-light cheap,lither yield

marcher

1-marche ou crève
-sink or swim
-it's do or die
-it is neck or nothing

2-marcher du pied gauche dans la merde,ça porte bonheur
-shitten luck is good luck

3-faire marcher à la baguette
-to rule someone with a rod of iron

4-marcher droit,au pas
-to toe the line,the mark

5-marcher à quatre pattes
-to go on all four

6-il faut marcher quand le diable est aux trousses
-needs must when the devil drives

mari

1-la crème des maris
un mari en or
-a prince of a husband

2-vieux mari et jeune épouse font rarement un heureux
mariage
-a december and may marriage is seldom a happy one

mariage
1-les mariages sont écrits dans le ciel
-marriages are made in heaven
-hanging and wiving go by destiny

2-mariage de gueux,la faim épouse la soif
-first thrive,then wive

3-autant de mariages,autant de ménages
-every couple is not a pair

4-au mariage et à la mort,le diable fait son effort
-at marriages and funerals,friends are discerned from kinsfolk

5-le mariage est une loterie
-marriage is a lotery
-hanging and wiving go by destiny
-wedlock is padlock
-many men,many minds

marier
1-qui trop loin va se marier sera trompé ou veut tromper
-better wed over the mixen than over the moor

2-marie ton fils quand tu voudras et ta fille quand tu pourras
-marry your son when you will,your daughter when you can

3-l'on se marie promptement et puis l'on se repend à loisir
-marry in haste,repent at leisure
-sudden friendship,sudden repentance

4-qui se marie par amour a de bonnes nuits et de mauvais
jours
-who marries for love without money,has good nights and sorry
days

5-qui se marie à la hâte se repent à loisir
-short acquaintance brings repentance
-sudden friendship,sudden repentance

marmite
1-c'est dans les vielles marmites qu'on fait les meilleures
soupes
-good broth may be made in an old pot

2-la marmite dit au chaudron "tu as le derrière noir!"
-the kettle calls the pot burnt-arse

ron

marron

1-tirer les marrons du feu
-to put up to the prank
-to pull the chesnuts out of the fire

2-être marron
-to be done brown

Mars

quand Mars entre comme un mouton,il sort comme un lion
si Mars commence en courroux,il finira tout doux,tout doux
-March comes in like a lion and goes out like a lamb

marteau

mieux vaut être marteau qu'enclume
-when you are an anvil,hold you still;when you are a hammer
strike your fill

Martin

on ne dit guère Martin qu'il n'y ait d'âne
-where there is smoke there is fire
-the fire is never without heat

matamore

il fait le matamore
-he is the boast of England
-don't take hollyer than thou

matin

un de ces quatre matins
-one of these days
-one day or another

mâtine

mâtines bien sonnées sont à demi chantées
-a beard well lathered is half shaved
-a good beginning makes a good ending

mauvais

mauvaise tête mais bon coeur
-truth has a good face but bad clothes

méchanceté

méchanceté porte sa peine
-like fault,like punishment
-the biter is sometimes bit

méchant

1-les méchants portent leur enfer en eux
-the deed comes back upon the doer

2-il n'y a que le méchant qui soit seul
-a solitary man is either a beast or an angel

3-il n'est si méchant pot qui ne trouve son couvercle
-if the shoe fits,wear it

médaille
toute médaille a son revers
-every medal has its reverse
-every medal has two sides
-every cloud has a silver lining
-every light has its shadow
-every commodity has its discommodity
-there is no joy without alloy
-of all wars,peace is the end
-every bean has its black

médecin
1-médecin,guéris toi toi-même
-bachelors'wives and maids'children are well taught
-he that has no children brings them up well
-he that has no wife,beats her oft

2-les médecins font les cimetières bossus
-physicians kill more than they cure
-a young physician fattens the churchyard

médire
chacun médit du tiers comme du quart
-everybody slanders everybody else

méfier
méfiez-vous de l'eau qui dort
-the still sow eats up all the draff

meilleur
1-les meilleurs partent les premiers
-whom the gods love die young
-the good die young
-the gods send nuts to those who have no teeth

2-les meilleures choses ont une fin
-all good things must come to an end
-every day comes night
-everything has an end

3-le meilleur est toujours le moins cher
-best is best cheap
-best is cheapest

mélanger
il ne faut pas mélanger les torchons et les serviettes
-we must separate the sheep from the goats

mêler
1-mêlez-vous de ce qui vous regarde
-this is none of your business
-keep your breath to cool your porridge

2-ne vous mêlez pas de ce qui ne vous regarde pas
-if each would sweep before his own door,we should have a clean street

133

mémoire
>**mémoire du bien tantôt passe**
>-eaten bread is soon forgotten

menacer
>**tel menace qui a grand peur**
>-a bully is always a coward

ménage
>**1-faire du ménage**
>-to make a clean sweep
>
>**2-autant de ménages,autant de mariages**
>-many men,many minds
>
>**3-le ménage va mal quand la poule chante plus haut que le coq**
>-it is a sad house where the then crows louder than the cock

ménager
>**on ne peut ménager la chèvre et le chou**
>-you can't please everyone
>-to sit on tne fence
>-run with the hare and hunt with the hounds

mener
>**1-elle le menait par le bₒut du nez**
>-he was putty in her hands
>-to lead one by the ear (nose)
>
>**2-mener une vie de bâton de chaise**
>-to shake a loose leg
>
>**3-mener quelqu'un à la baguette**
>-to keep someone under one's thumb
>
>**4-on a beau mené le boeuf à l'eau, s'il n'a pas soif**
>-you can take a horse to the water but you cannot make him drink
>-one man may lead an ass to the pond's brink but twenty men cannot make him drink

mensonge
>**1-beaux mensonges aident**
>-better a lie than heals than a truth that wounds
>
>**2-à beau mensonge,longue mémoire**
>-give a lie a twenty four hours'start,and you can never overtake it
>-a liar ought to have a good memory
>
>**3-qui dit un mensonge en dit cent**
>-a lie has no legs

menteur
>**1-il faut qu'un menteur ait une bonne mémoire**
>-a liar ought to have a good memory
>-one lie makes many

2-les menteurs sont les enfants du diable
-the liar and the murderer are children of the same village

3-on attrappe plus vite un menteur qu'un voleur
-the liar is sooner caught than the cripple

mentir
    1-mentir comme un arracheur de dents
    -to lie in one's throat

    2-à beau mentir qui vient de loin
    -a traveller may lie with authority
    -travellers tell fine tales

    3-il ne ment jamais s'il n'ouvre la bouche
    -a closed mouth catches no flies

mépris
    il n'est point de dette si tôt payée que le mépris
    -contempt will sooner kill an injury than revenge

mer
    1-si la mer bouillait,il y aurait des poissons cuits
    -if wishes were horses beggars would ride

    2-ce que la mer apporte en montant,elle le remporte en descendant
    -money is round,and rolls away

merci
    1-avoir quelqu'un à sa merci
    -to have someone over a barrel
    -to make one's beard

    2-être à la merci de quelqu'un
    -to serve someone hand and foot

mercier
    1-à petit mercier,petit panier
    -don't bite off more than you can chew
    -strech your arm no further that your sleeve will reach

    2-chaque mercier prise ses aiguilles et son panier
    -every potter praises his own pot

mérite
    1-le mérite se cache,il faut l'aller trouver
    -first deserve,then desire

    2-à chacun selon ses mérites
    -to each let it be given according to his deserts

merle
    1-les merles ne chantent pas comme les grives
    -sadness and gladness succeed each other

2-on ne prend pas les vieux merles à la pipée
-an old bird is not to be caught with chaff

messager
  on ne trouve jamais meilleur messager que soi-même
  -the miller got never better moulter than he took with his own hands
  -if you want a thing well done,do it yourself

mesurer
  1-ne mesurez pas autrui à votre aulne
  -to measure other people's corn by one's own bushel

  1-ne mesurez pas autrui à votre aulne (suite)
  -no one should be judge in his own cause
  -don't measure other's feet by your own last

  2-on vous mesurera avec la mesure dont vous vous serez servi
  -things present are judged by things past

  3-on ne mesure pas les hommes à la toise
  -men are not to be measure by inches

méticuleux
  être méticuleux
  -to dot the "i"s and cross the "t"s

métier
  1-il n'y a pas de sot métier ,il n'y a que de sottes gens
  -all work is honorable
  -it is no sin for a man to labour in his vocation

  2-il n'est si petit métier qui ne nourrice son maître
  -a little labour,much health

  3-qui a métier a rente
  -no pains,no gains

  4-à chacun son métier,les en sont mieux gardées
  -every cobbler sticks to his last
  -keep your breath to cool your porridge

mettre
  1-mettre du sien
  -to put one's shoulder to the wheel
  -to shake a leg
  -to pull one's weight

  2-en mettre plein la vue
  -to shoot a line

  3-mettre en question
  -to call in question

  4-mettre une question sur le tapis
  -to bring a question on the carpet

5-mettez-ça dans votre poche et votre mouchoir par-dessus
-put that in your pipe and smoke it

6-quand on met la main à la pâte,il en reste toujours aux doigts
-he that touches rouge will be red
-throw plenty of dirt some will sure to stick

7-se mettre la tête sous l'oreiller
-to bury one's head in the sand

8-mettre des bâtons dans les roues
-to throw a spanner in the works

9-mettre les points sur les "i"
-to dot the "i"s and cross the "t"s

10-mettre de l'eau dans son vin
-to draw in one's horns

11-mettre de l'huile sur le feu
-to add fuel to the fire
-to fan the flames

12-il ne faut pas mettre le doigt entre l'arbre et l'écorce
-put not thy hand between the bark and the tree

13-mettre quelqu'un au pied du mur
-to have someone with his back to the wall
-to back someone into a corner

14-se mettre en quatre
-to give the shirt off one's back

miel

1-miel sur la bouche,fiel dans le coeur
-bees that have honey in their mouths have stings in their tales
-a honeyed tongue,a heart of gall
-he has honey in his mouth,and a razor at the girdle

2-qui manie le miel s'en lèche les doigts
-honey catches more flies than vinegar
-the rough net is not the best catcher of birds

3-faites vous miel,les mouches vous mangeront
-make yourself all honey and the flies will eat you
-don't make yourself a mouse,or the cat will eat you
-he that make himself a sheep,shall be eaten by the wolf
-make yourself a lamb and the wolves will eat you

mieux

1-mieux vaut plus tôt que plus tard
-an hour in the morning is worth two in the evening

2-tout est pour le mieux dans le meilleur des mondes
-all's for the best in the best of all possible worlds

137

3-le mieux est l'ennemi du bien
-the good is the enemy of the best
-striving the better oft we mar what's well
-let well enough alone
-nothing is worse than care

4-il vaut mieux être qu'avoir été
-better say "here it is",than,"here it was"

5-mieux vaut user des souliers que des draps
-'tis better to wear out shoes than sheets
-better to wear out than to rust out

6-il vaut mieux aller au moulin qu'au médecin
-a little labour,much health
-keep your shop and your shop will keep you
-the mill gets by going

7-mieux vaut tard que jamais
-better late than never

8-il vaut mieux arriver en retard qu'arriver en corbillard
-better late than never
-expectation is better than realization

9-il vaut mieux tenir que courir
-a bird in the hand is worth two in the bush
-possession is better than expectation

10-mieux vaut moineau en cage que poule d'eau qui nage
-better a good cow than a cow of a good kind
-half is more than the whole

11-mieux vaut mourir selon les règles que de réchapper contre les règles
-better to die in glory than live in dishonor

12-mieux vaut ta propre morue que le dindon des autres
-dry bread at home is better than roast meat abroad
-he who depends on another dines ill and sups worse

13-il vaut mieux tendre la main que le cou
-better bend the neck than bruise the forehead

14-il vaut mieux se dédire que se détruire
-discretion is the better part of valour
-he that fights and run away may live to fight another day
-one pair of heels is often worth two pairs of hands
-mieux vaut se dédire que se détruire

15-mieux vaut faire envie que pitié
-better be envied than pitied

16-il vaut mieux aller au moulin qu'au médecin
-better be sure than sorry

17-mieux vaut être premier dans son village que second à Rome
-better be the head of a yeomanry than the tail of a gentry
-better be the head of an ass than the tail of a horse
-better to reign in Hell than serve in Heaven
-better be the head of a pike than the tail of a sturgeon
-better be the head of a dog than the tail of a lion

18-il vaut mieux être le premier de sa race que le dernier
-the early man never borrows from the late man

19-mieux vaut moins mais mieux
-a little and good fills the trencher
-it is not how long,but how well we live

mille
donner en mille
-to guess in a thousand years

mire
il a pris l'homme de tête en point de mire
-he got a bead on the man in the lead

misère
1-la misère du boeuf n'est pas une peine pour le cheval
-it is easy to bear the misfortune of others

2-misère et pauvreté font mauvais ménage
-more belongs to marriage than four bare legs in a bed

modération
la modération est la santé de l'âme
-measure is medicine

moëlle
pour avoir la moëlle,il faut briser l'os
-he that would have the fruit,must climb the tree
-you don't get something for nothing

moeurs
les mauvaises moeurs engendrent les bonnes lois
-of ill manners good laws

moine
1-pour un moine,l'abbaye ne se perd pas
-take not a musket to kill a butterfly

2-le moine répond comme l'abbé chante
-a good master, a good scholar

moineau
le moineau dans la main vaut mieux que la grue qui vole
-one bird in the net is worth a hundred flying

moins
1-il y a moins de mal à perdre sa vigne qu'à la plaider
-to come to an arrangment is better than to going law

2-en moins de deux
before you can say Jack Robinson

moisson
moisson d'autrui plus belle que la sienne
-our neighbour's ground yields better corn than ours

monde
1-le monde est bossu quand il se baisse
-don't cry stinking fish

2-la moitié du monde ne sait comment l'autre vit
-one half of the world does not know how the other lives

3-il faut de tout pour faire un monde
-it takes all sorts to make a world
-there's nowt so queer as folk
-there may be blue and better blue

4-il faut que tout le monde vive
-live and let live

5-vieux comme le monde
-as old as the hills

6-le monde est un spectacle à regarder et non un problème à résoudre
-let the world wag

Monsieur
Monsieur je-sais-tout
-he is a know-it-all

montagne
1-seules les montagnes ne se rencontrent jamais
-it's a small world

2-la montagne a accouché d'une souris
-the mountain has brought forth a mouse

3-en faire une montagne
-to make a mountain out of a molehill
-to break a butterfly on a wheel
-to use an elephant to crack a nut

4-il n'y a pas de montagne sans vallée
-in the coldest flint there is a hot fire
-every cloud has a silver lining

montée
de grande montée,grande chute
-the bigger they are,the harder they fall
-the highest tree has the greatest fall

monter

>**monter sur ses grands chevaux**
>-to ride the high horse
>-to be on one's high horse

montre

>**belle montre,peu de rapport**
>-appearances are deceptive

montrer

>**1-se montrer sous son vrai jour**
>-to come out in one's true colours
>
>**2-montrer patte blanche**
>-to show your credentials
>
>**3-il veut montrer à son père à faire des enfants**
>-you can't teach an old dog new tricks
>-you can't teach an old dog new tricks
>-never offer to teach fish to swim

moquer

>**1-se moquer du tiers comme du quart**
>-not to give a rap about anything
>
>**2-s'en moquer comme de l'an quarante**
>**s'en moquer comme de sa première chemise**
>-not to care two hoots,a tinker's cuss,a tinker's damn
>-to be at sixes and sevens

morceau

>**1-remporter le morceau**
>-to take the cake
>
>**2-faire trois morceaux d'une cerise**
>-to make two bites of a cherry
>
>**3-morceau avalé n'a plus de goût**
>-eaten bread is soon forgotten

mordre

>**1-autant vaut être mordu d'un chien que d'une chienne**
>-where bad's the best,bad must be choice
>
>**2-il ne mord pas à l'hameçon**
>-it's an old rat that won't eat cheese

mors

>**mors doré ne rend pas le cheval meillleur**
>-an ape is an pae,a varlet is a varlet though be clad in silk or scarlet

mort

>**1-mort et enterré**
>**raide mort**
>-dead as a dodo
>-dead as a door nail

2-plus mort que vif
-half dead with fright

3-quand nous serons morts,fouira la vigne qui pourra
-do what you ought,and come what can
-the wagon must go whither the horses draw it

4-après la mort,le médecin
-after death,doctor

5-contre la mort,pont de remède
-there is remedy for everything but death
-nothing is certain but death abd taxes
-every door may be shut but death's door
-they that live longest must die at last
-diing is as natural as living
-no man knows when he shall die,although he knows he must die
-he that is once born,once must die

6-la mort est un moissonneur qui ne fait pas la sieste
-there is a reaper whose name is death

7-au mort et à l'absent,injure ni tourment
-far folk fare best
-they are aye good that are away
-earth is the best shelter
-death pays all debts

morte
1-c'est la morte qui se moque de la décapitée
-every man's censure is first moulded in his own nature
2-morte la bête,morte le venin
-dead dogs don't bite
-dead man tell no tales

mortier
le mortier sent toujours l'ail
-a herring barrel always smell of fish

morveux
qui se sent morveux,qu'il se mouche
-when all men say you are an ass,it is time to bray
-if one,two,or three tell you you are an ass,put on a bridle

mot
1-pas un mot plus haut que l'autre
-without striking a blow

2-ce ne sont pas les mots qui comptent mais les actions
-action speaks louder than words
-handsome is as handsome does
-the proof of the pudding is in the eating
-deeds are fruits,words are but leaves
-a man of words and not of deeds is like a garden full of weeds
-doing is better than saying

-good words without deeds are like rushes and reeds
-fine words butter no parsnips
-deeds not words
-the effect speaks,the tongue needs not
-a little help is worth a great deal of pity
-an ounce of practice is worth a pound of theory

3-un mot dit à l'oreille est entendu de loin
-all that is said in the kitchen should not be heard in the hall

4-en deux mots
-the long and the short of the matter

mouche
1-faire mouche
-to hit the axe on the helve
-to hit the bull'seye

2-être une fine mouche
-to be sly minx

3-on n'attrape pas les mouches avec du vinaigre
-an old bird is not to be caught with chaff

4-on prend plus de mouches avec du miel qu'avec du vinaigre
-mildness does better than harshness

5-faire la mouche du coche
-to be made the cat's paw of
-to be busybody
-to be the fly on the coachwheel

6-prendre la mouche
-to get the needle
-to get the spike
-to get huffy

7-écrire des pattes de mouche
-hen scratching

8-la mouche se brûle à la chandelle
-la mouche va si souvent au lait qu'elle y demeure
-too much curiosity lost paradise
-listeners(eavesdroppers) never hear any good of themselves
-the fish will soon be caught that nibbles at every bait
-he who peeps through a hole may see what will vex him

9-faire d'une mouche un éléphant
-to change a fly into an elephant
-to make a storm in a tea cup

moucher
il ne se mouche pas du pied (familier)
-he thinks no small beer of himself

moulin
1-qui entre dans un moulin,il convient de nécessité qu'il enfarine
-who keeps company with a wolf will learn to howl

143

2-va bien au moulin qui y envoie son âne
-the stone that lies not in your gate breaks not your toes

mourir
1-on ne meurt qu'une fois
-he that dies this year is excused for the next
-he that died half a year ago is as dead asAdam
-a man can die but once

2-mourir debout
-to die with one's boots on
-to die in harness
-to die in one's shoes

3-autant meurt veau que vache
-death is the great leveller
-as long lives a merry man as a sad
-death combs us all with the same comb

4-on ne sait ni qui meurt ni qui vit
-death keeps no calendar
-there is but one way to enter this life but the gates of death are without number

5-mourir à petit feu
-to die by inches

6-mieux vaut mourir selon les règles que de réchapper contre les règles
-better to die in glory than live in dishonor

mouvement
en deux temps trois mouvements
-in two shakes of a lamb's tail

mouton
revenons à nos moutons
-let's get down to brasstacks
-to hit the nail on the head

mule
la mule du pape garde sept ans son coup de pied
-as savage as a bear with a sorehead

mur
1-raser les murs
-to be hangdog

2-mettre quelqu'un au pied du mur
-to have someone with his back to the wall
-to back someone into a corner
-to nail down someone

3-les murs ont des oreilles
-walls have ears
-asses as well as pitchers have ears
-fields have eyes,and woods have ears

mûre
>   **aller aux mûres sans crochet**
>   -to go up the creak wihtout a paddle

musique
>   **-la musique est le plus cher de tous les bruits**
>   -music is the eye of the ear

myope
>   **myope comme une taupe**
>   -blind as a bat(or beetle,mole,owl)

N

nager
>**il est plus facile de nager quand on vous tient le menton**
>-he must need help,that is held by the chin

nageur
>**bons nageurs sont à la fin noyés**
>-good swimmers at length are drowned

nain
>**un nain sur les épaules d'un géant voit plus loin que celui qui le porte**
>-a dwarf on a giant's shoulders sees the farthest of the two

naissance
>**la naissance n'est rien où la vertu n'est pas**
>-virtue is the only true nobility

naître
>**1-né coiffé**
>-born with a silver spoon in one's mouth
>
>**2-né sous one bonne étoile**
>-born under a lucky star
>
>**3-qui naquit chat court après les souris**
>-the nature of a fish is to swim
>
>**4-on naît poète,artiste**
>-poets are born not made
>
>**5-qui naît poule,aime à gratter**
>-he that comes of a hen must scrape
>
>**6-quand tu es né rond,tu ne meurs pas pointu**
>-he that is born a fool is never cured
>
>**7-il n'est pas né de la dernière pluie** (familier)
>-you can't teach an old dog new tricks

nature
>**1-la nature a horreur du vide**
>-nature abhors a vacuum
>
>**2-nature ne peut mentir**
>-nature will have her course
>-you can drive out nature with a pitchfork but she keeps coming back
>
>**3-la nature fait bien les choses**
>-nature is no botcher
>
>**4-la nature nous a donné deux oreilles et seulement une**
>**-langue afin de pouvoir écouter davantage et parler moins**
>-be swift to hear,slow to speak

5-la nature fait le mérite et la fortune le met en oeuvre
-first deserve,then desire

6-on ne commande à la nature qu'en lui obéissant
-nature is conquered by obeying her

7-la nature se contente de peu
-nature is content with a little

naturel
    le naturel de la grenouille est qu'elle boit et souvent gazouille
    -the frog cannot out of her bog

navire
    à navire brisé,tous vents sont contraires
    -when the going gets tough,the tough gets going

nécessité
    1-nécessité fait loi
    -necessity knows no laws

    2-nécessité n'a pas de loi
    -nécessité n'a pas de loi

    3-nécessité est de raison la moitié
    -any port in a storm

    4-nécessité n'a pas de jour férié
    -necessity has no holiday

    5-nécessité fait du timide un brave
    -necessity and opportunity may make a coward valiant

    6-nécessité fait trotter les vieilles
    -need makes the old wife trot
    -need makes the naked man run
    -a moneyless man goes fast through the market

    7-nécessité est mère d'industrie
    -discontent is the first step in progress
    -necessity is the mother of invention

    8-il faut faire de nécessité vertu
    -he that may not do as he would,must do as he may

négligence
    petite négligence accouche d'un grand mal
    -standing pools gather filth
    -he that repairs not a part,builds all
    -he that repairs not his gutters,repairs his whole house
    -who lives by hope,will die by hunger

neiger
    quand il neige dans les montagnes,il fait froid dans les vallées
    -poverty and wealth are twin sisters
    -grey hairs are dead blossoms

netteté
> **netteté nourrit santé**
> -wash your hands often,your feet seldom,and your head never

nez
> **1-faire un pied de nez**
> -to thumb your nose
> -to cock a snook

> **2-celà se voit comme le nez au milieu de la figure**
> -it is as plain as the nose on your face

> **3-mettre son nez partout**
> -to have a finger in every pie

> **4-si on lui pressait le nez il en sortirait encore du lait**
> -he is wet behind the ears

noblesse
> **noblesse oblige**
> -true blue will never stain
> -breed will tell

noeud
> **faire un noeud à son mouchoir**
> -to put a string on your finger

nord
> **perdre le nord**
> -to lose one's bearings

nourriture
> **nourriture passe nature**
> -when meat is in,anger is out
> -spread the table,and contention will cease
> -nature passes nurture

nouveau
> **tout nouveau,tout beau**
> **-de nouveau tout m'est beau**
> -novelty always appears handsome
> -a new broom sweeps clean
> -everything new is fine
> -anything for a change
> -new things are fair

nouvelle
> **1-pas de nouvelles,bonnes nouvelles**
> -no news is good news

> **2-à nouvelles affaires,nouveaux conseils**
> -new lords,new laws
> -of a new prince,new bondage

> **3-les bonnes nouvelles sont toujours retardées et les mauvaises ont des ailes**
> -good news goes on crutches,bad news travel quickly,ill news travel apace

noyau

1-il faut casser le noyau pour avoir l'amende
-he who would eat the nut must first crack the shell
-he that will eat the kernel,must crack the nut

2-beau noyau gît sous piètre écorce
-the toad,ugly and venomous,wears yet a precious jewel in his head
-you cannot judge a tree by its bark
-sweet is the nut,but bitter is the shell

noyé

un noyé s'accroche à un brin d'herbe
-a drowning man will catch a straw
-self preservation is the first law of nature

noyer

1-qui veut noyer son chien,l'accuse de la rage
-give a dog a bad name and hang him
-he that would hang his dog,gives out first that he is mad
-if you want a pretence to whip a dog,say he ate the frying pan
-any stick will do to beat a dog with
-there are more ways of killing a cat than by choking it with cream
-he who has in mind to beat his dog will easily find a stick

2-noyer le poisson (familier)
-a triton among the minnows
-driving a red herring across the path
-to draw a red herring across the track

3-se noyer dans un verre d'eau
-to make heavy weather of something

nu

nu comme un ver
-naked as my nail
-naked as a frog
-naked as a needle
-naked as a worm
-naked as a robin

nuit

1-la nuit tous les chats sont gris
-de nuit,le blé semble farine
-all cats are grey in the dark
-when candles are away,all cats are grey
-the fair and the foul by dark are like store

2-que la nuit nous porte conseille
-advise with your pillow
-sleep on it
-night is the mother of counsel

3-c'est la nuit qu'il est beau de croire à la lumière
-never was cat or dog drowned,that could but see the shore

nul

1-nul ne naît appris et instruit
-no man is born wise or learned
-the best horse needs breaking and the aptest child needs training
-there is no royal road to learning

2-nul n'est censé ignorer la loi
-ignorance of the law excuses no man

O

obéir

1-obéir au doigt et à l'oeil
-to be at one's beck and call

2-il faut apprendre à obéir pour savoir commander
-through obedience learn to command

obéissance

l'obéissance est un métier bien rude
-it needs more skill than I can tell to play the second fiddle well

obliger

qui oblige promptement,oblige doublement
-he that gives quickly,gives twice

occasion

1-une occasion perdue ne se rattape jamais
-opportunity never knocks twice
-he that will not when he may,when he will he shall have nay
-it is too late to grieve when the chance is past
-it is no use crying over spilt milk
-for a tint thing,care not
-the tide must be taken when it comes
-it is best to sit near the fire when the chimney smokes
-when fortune smiles,embrace her
-it's too late to come back yesterday

2-l'occasion est chauve
-il faut saisir l'occasion aux cheveux
-l'occasion n'a qu'un cheveu
-never refuse a good offer
-life is short and time is swift
-we must take time by the forelock
-no time like the present

3-l'occasion fait le larron
-opportunity makes the thief
-a fair booty makes many a thief

4-occasion trouve qui son chat bat
-he who has a mind to beat his dog will easily find a stick

occuper

occupe-toi de tes affaires
-keep (save) your breath to cool your porridge

odeur

être en odeur de sainteté
-être dans les bonnes graces de quelqu'un
-to be in somebody's good graces

oeil

1-un oeil suffit au marchand,l'acheteur en a besoin de cent
-the buyer needs a hundres eyes,the buyer but one

œil (suite)
    2-oeil un autre oeil voit mais pas le sien
    -l'oeil porte en soi l'image laquelle il ne voit
    -he can't see the beam he has in his own eye
    -men are blind in their own cause
    -he that is his own lawyer has a fool for a client
    -the camel never sees its own hump,but sees his companion's
    -the eye that sees all things else sees not itself
    -every man is his own worst enemy

    3-ne pas fermer l'oeil de la nuit
    -not to sleep a wink

    4-oeil pour oeil,dent pour dent
    -an eye for an eye,a tooth for a tooth
    -a goat's hide buys a goat's hide and a gourd a gourd
    -revenge is sweet
    -a goat's hide buys a gaot's hids and a gourd a gourd
    -revenge is sweet

    5-voir du même oeil
    -to see eye to eye

    6-mon oeil!
    -and did you ever see an oyster walk upstairs?
    -tongue and cheek
    -I'm from Missouri
    -all my eye and Betty Martin

    7-l'oeil du maître engraisse le cheval
    -the master's eye makes the horse fat

    8-à oeil malade,la lumière nuit
    -he bears misery best that hides it most

oeuf
    1-étouffer le complot dans l'oeuf
    -to nip the plot in the bud

    2-tuer dans l'oeuf
    -to nip in the bud
    -to check in the bud

    3-un oeuf aujourd'hui vaut mieux qu'un poulet pour demain
    -better an egg to day than a hen tomorrow

    4-j'ai des oeufs sur le feu
    -I have eggs on the spit

    5-il ne faut pas mettre tous ses oeufs dans le même panier
    -don't put all your eggs in one basket
    -never venture all in one bottom
    -the mouse that has but one hole is quickly taken

5-il ne faut pas mettre tous ses oeufs dans le même panier (suite)
-I'll not hang all my bells on one horse

6-un oeuf clair
-a wind egg

oeuvre
à l'oeuvre on connaît l'artisan
-the workman is known by his work
-office will show the man

oie
1-les oies sont perchées
-beans are in flower

2-oie blanche
-a naive young girl

oignon
1-ce ne sont pas mes oignons
-that's no skin off my nose

2-se mettre en rang d'oignon
-to line up all in a row

oindre
oignez vilain,il vous poindra
-all is lost that is put into a riven dish

oiseau
1-l'oiseau sur la branche
-a rolling stone

2-être comme l'oiseau sur la branche
-to lie at rack and manger

3-l'oiseau ne peut voler sans ailes
-no flying without wings

4-petit à petit,l'oiseau fait son nid
-little and often fill the purse
-feather by feather,the goose is plucked
-grain by grain,and then the hen fills her belly
-step by step the ladder is ascended
-spit on a stone,and it will be wet at the last
-hair by hair you will pull out the horse's tail
-slow but sure wins the race
-the tortoise wins the race while the hare is sleeping

5-juge l'oiseau à la plume et au chant et au parler l'homme bon ou méchant
-speech is the picture of the mind

6-c'est un vilain oiseau qui salit son nid
-it's an ill bird that fouls its own nest
-no names,no pack drill
-don't tell tales out of school
-birds in their little nest agree

7-à chaque oiseau son nid est beau
-a small bird wants a small nest
-there is no place like home

8-selon l'oiseau le nid,selon la femme le logis
-men make houses,women make homes
-such bird,such nest

9-l'oiseau doit beaucoup à son plumage
-finding's keeping
-the tailor makes the man

10-on ne prend pas les oiseaux à la tarterelle
-an old bird is not to be caught with chaff

oisiveté

l'oisiveté est la mère de tous les vices
-the devil finds work for idle hands to do
-an idle brain is the devil workshop
-idle people have the least leisure
-an idle person is the devil's cushion
-the devil tempts all,but the idle man tempts the devil
-he that is busy is tempted by but one devil;he that is idle,by a legion
-idleness is the root of all evil
-busiest men find the most
-an idle head is a box for the wind
-of idleness comes no goodness

oison

les oisons mènent paître les oies
-blind leader of the blind

ombre

1-avoir peur de son ombre
-to be afraid of one's shadow

2-il y a une ombre au tableau
-there's a fly in the ointment

omelette

on ne peut faire d'omelette sans casser des oeufs
-you can't make bricks without straws
-give us the tools and we will finish the job
-what is a workman without his tools?

oncle

il est mon oncle qui mon ventre me comble
-when meat is in,anger is out
-every man bows to the bush he gets bield of
-every one speaks well of the bridge which carries him over
-cast no dirt into the well that has given you water

ongle

à l'ongle,on connaît le lion
-a man is not a horse because he was born in a stable

or

1-pas pour tout l'or du monde
-not on your life
-not for all the tea in China

2-nul or sans écume
-much coin,much care

3-l'or s'épure au feu,l'homme s'éprouve au creuset du malheur
-calamity is the touchstone of a brave mind
-misfortune makes foes of friends

4-rouler sur l'or
-to be rolling in money

oreille

1-avoir les oreilles qui chauffent
-to get hot under the collar
-his ears mist be burning

2-ses oreilles doivent lui siffler
-if your ears glow,someone is talking of you
-his ears must be burning

3-dormir sur ses deux oreilles
-not to worry

4-il a les deux oreilles et la queue
-he has gotten the boot and the better horse

5-se faire tirer l'oreille
-to take a lot of coaxing

6-une oreille coupée a toujours son conduit
-you cannot judge of a dog by its bark

7-entré par une oreille,sorti par l'autre
-in one ear and out of the other
-to hear like a hog in harvest

8-par dessus les oreilles
-over head and ears,up to the ears

9-avoir les oreilles qui traînent
-to have one's ear to the ground
-to have one's nose to the grindstone

10-faire la sourde oreille
-to turn a deaf ear

11-dresser l'oreille
-to prick up one's ears

orgueil

1-il n'est orgueil que de pauvre enrichi
-plenty breeds pride

2-quand orgueil chevauche devant,honte et dommage suivent de près
-pride goes before and shame follows after

ormeau

l'ormeau ne peut donner des poires
-to ask pear from an elm tree

os

les os sont pour les absents
-far from court,far from care
-the absent saint gets no candle

oui

un béni oui-oui
-a yes-man

ourdir

il ne faut pas ourdir plus qu'on ne peut tisser
-stretch your arm no further than your sleeve will reach

ours

c'est un ours mal léché
-he has a lot of rough edges

ouvrier

mauvais ouvrier ne trouve jamais bon outil
-a bad workman blames his tool
-as is the workman so is the work
-a bad shearer never had a good sickle

P

paie

cela fait une paie,un bail
-in dog's age

paille

1-avec la paille et le temps,se mûrissent les nèfles et les glands
-long looked for comes at last

2-il y a plus de paille que de grain
-the weeds overgrow the corn

pain

1-avoir du pain sur la planche
-to have the work cut out for

2-le pain d'autrui est amer
-he who depends on another dines ill and sups worse
-dry bread at home is better than roast meet abroad

3-il a mangé son pain blanc le premier
-he's found out that life isn't just a bowl of cherries

4-celà se vend comme des petits pains
-it's selling like hot cakes

5-je l'ai eu pour un morceau de pain
-I got it for a song

6-nul pain sans peine
-no reward without toil
-he that gapes until he be fed,well may he gape until he be dead
-no gain without pain
-no pains,no gains
-if you don't work,you shan't eat

7-tel pain,telle soupe
-if the mother trot,how can the daughter amble?

paire

les deux font la paire
-they are made for one another

2-c'est une autre paire de manches
-that's another cup of tea
-that's another pair of shoes

paix

1-si tu veux la paix prépare la guerre
-attack is the best form of defense
-hope for the best and prepare the worst
-in fair weather,prepare for foul
-if you want peace,prepare for war

2-une méchante paix est pire que la guerre
-a just war is better than an unjust peace

pâle

se faire porter pâle
-to report sick

panier

1-ils sont tous à mettre dans le même panier
-they are all tared with the same brush

2-qui a fait un panier fera bien une hotte
-he that has done ill once will do it again

3-c'est un panier percé
-money burns a hole in his pocket
-he that has but four and spends five,has no need of a purse
-he has a large mouth and a small girdle

4-adieu paniers,les vendanges sont faites
-now,it's all over
-now,it's too late

5-faire le panier à deux anses
-an ass with two panniers

pape

tel entre pape au conclave qui en sort cardinal
-many go out for wool and come home shorn

papier

1-le papier souffre tout
-the calf,the goose,the bee the world is ruled by these three

2-réglé comme du papier à musique
-like clockwork

3-être dans les petits papiers de quelqu'un
-to be in somebody's good books

papillon

le plus beau papillon n'est qu'une chenille habillée
-beauty is only skin deep

pardon

"pardon" ne guérit pas la bosse
-forebearance is no acquittance
-past shame,past amendment
-a bad excuse is better than none

pardonner

1-on ne pardonne point à qui nous fait rougir
-who is a cuckold and conceals it,carries coals in his bosom
-past shame,past amendment

2-on pardonne tant que l'on aime
-fautes are thick when love is thin

pareil
1-c'est du pareil au même
-it is much of a muchness

paresseux
1-au paresseux,le poil lui pousse dans la main
-standing pools gather filth
-every day is holiday with sluggards

parler
1-qui parle sème,qui écoute récolte
-there is a time to speak and a time to be silent
-speech is silver but silence is golden
-from hearing,comes wisdom;from speaking repentance

2-on sait ce que parler veut dire
-in many words,the truth goes by

3-à beau parler qui n'a cure de bien faire
-action speaks louder than words
-an ounce of practice is worth a pound of theory
-doing is better than saying
-example is better than precept
-better to do well than to say well
-a good example is the best sermon

4-parler de quelque chose comme un aveugle des couleurs
-flow of words is not always flow of wisdom

5-parler comme une mitraillette
-to talk nineteen to the dozen

6-quand on parle du loup,on en voit la queue
quand on parle du soleil,on en voit les rayons
-talk of the devil and he is sure to appear
-talk of the angels and you will hear the flutter of their wings

7-ne me parlez pas de mes dettes à moins que vous ne vouliez les payer
-speak not of my debts unless you mean to pay them

8-au parler ange,au faire change
-from word to deed is a great space
-saying and doing are two things

9-beau parler n'écorche pas la langue
-education begins a gentleman,education completes him
-civility costs nothing

10-il ne faut pas parler de corde dans la maison d'un pendu
il ne faut pas parler latin devant les cordeliers
-name not a rope where one has hang himself

11-moins on parle,mieux cela vaut
trop parler nuit
-much babbling is not without offense
-least said,soonest mended

12-c'est trop parler qui a fait que le crabe n'a pas de tête
-the ass that brays most eats least

13-il est bon de parler et meilleur de se taire
-an ounce of discretion is worth a pound of wit
-more have repented speech than silence
-from hearing comes wisdom,from speaking repentance

14-on ne parle pas de corde dans la maison d'un pendu
-he that one of his family hanged,may not say to his neighbour,hang up your fish

paroi

parois blanches,parois fendues
-you can't tell a book by its cover

parole

1-donner sa parole
-to give or pass one's word

2-parole d'honneur
-upon my word

3-être de parole
-as good as one's promise
-as good as one's word

4-méchante parole jetée va partout à la volée
-words are but wind,but blows unkind

5-prendre des paroles pour argent comptant
-paroles d'évangile
-to take words for gospel

6-la parole est d'argent mais le silence est d'or
-speech is silver but silence is golden
-some things are better left unsaid
-he cannot speak well that cannot hold his tongue
-there is a time to speak and a time to be silent
-a fool's tongue is long enough to cut his own throat

7-il n'a qu'une parole
-he is as good as his word

8-mesurer ses paroles
-tourner sa langue dans sa bouche
-to curb one's tongue

9-les belles paroles ne donnent pas à manger
-talking pays no toll

10-les paroles s'envolent mais les écrits restent
-words fly,writings remain
-never write what you dare not sign

11-les paroles des grands ne tombent jamais à terre
les paroles des grands sont des sentences
-a rich man's joke is always funny

part

1-prendre la part du lion
-to take the lion's share

2-avoir sa part du gâteau
-to be given a fair crack of the whip
-to have a finger in the pie

3-il faut faire la part des choses
-you must make allowance for things

parti

à parti pris,point de conseil
-counsel is no command
-when a thing is done, advice comes too late

partie

c'est partie remise
-you'll get a rain check

partir

partir c'est mourir un peu
-one cannot leave one's country without a tug

pas

1-c'est le premier pas qui coûte
-it's the first step that is difficult
-every beginning is hard
-the first step is the hardest
-the greatest step is that out of the door
-things thought difficult and hard usually become quite simple when faced

2-ce n'est pas pour un mauvais pas qu'on tue un boeuf
-homer sometimes nod

3-pas du tout
-as the devil loves holy water

4-être dans un mauvais pas
-to be in deep water

passer

1-passer sous les fourches caudines
-to pass under the yoke

2-passer l'arme à gauche (familier)
-to kick the bucket
-to go west

3-passez votre chemin!
-don't dare to darken my door again!

4-passer au crible
passer au peigne fin
-to canvas a subject

5-il passera bien de l'eau sous le pont
-it will all be the same in a hundred year s hence

passer (suite)
    6-on passe la haie par où elle est la plus basse
    -men leap where the hedge is lowest
    -cross the stream where it is shallowest

    7-se passer la corde au cou (familièrement se marier)
    -wedlock is padlock

    8-tout passera sauf le bien que tu as fait
    -virtue never grows old

patience
    1-la patience vient à bout de tout
    -patience and time run through the longest day
    -a mouse in time may bite in two a cable
    -patience is a plaster for all sores
    -patience drives a snail to Jerusalem

    2-patience et longueur de temps font plus que force et rage
    -fair and softly goes far in a day
    -mildness does better than harshness

    3-la patience est la vertu des ânes
    -patience is a virtue
    -they also serve who only stand and wait

    4-la patience est amère mais son fruit est doux
    -he that has patience,has fat thrushes for a farthing
    -long looked for comes at last
    -they also serve who only stand and wait

pâtir
    tel en pâtit qui n'en peut mais
    -les bons pâtissent pour les mauvais
    -the worst hog often gets the best pear

patte
    1-faire patte de velours
    -to handle with kid gloves

    2-les pattes d'oie (rides)
    -the crow's feet

pauvre
    1-au pauvre la besace
    -the weaker has the worse

    2-être pauvre comme Job
    -not to have a penny to bless oneself with
    -to be as poor as Job's turkey
    -to be poor as a rat
    -to be as poor as a church mouse
    -to carry off meat from the graves

    3-à pauvres,enfants sont richesse
    -children are poor men's riches

4-pauvre homme n'a point d'amis
-in time of prosperity,friends will be plenty;in time of
-adversity not one amongst twenty
-poverty parts fellowship

pauvreté
1-la pauvreté n'est pas un péché,mieux vaut cependant la cacher
pauvreté n'est pas vice
-poverty is no crime

2-en grande pauvreté ne gît pas grande loyauté
-there is no virtue that poverty destroys not

pavé
jeter un pavé dans la mare cf baby
-to throw the baby out with the bath

pavillon
le pavillon couvre la marchandise
-the flag protects the cargo

payer
1-payer rubis sur l'ongle
-to pay cash on the nail
-to pay on the barrelhead

2-payer les pots cassés
-to face the music

3-payer en monnaie de singe
-to pay in promises

4-payer en espèces sonnantes et trébuchantes
-to pay in cold hard cash

5-qui paye ses dettes s'enrichit
-out of debt,out of danger

6-qui paie les violons choisit la musique
-he who pays the piper calls the tune

7-payer d'audace
-to put a blot face on something

pays
1-pays de Cocagne
-never never land
-a land of milk and honey

2-autant de pays,autant de guises
-so many countries,so may customs
-every country has its customs
-every land has its own law

3-bon pays,mauvais chemin
-he that has land has trouble at hand

peau

1-la peau est plus proche que la chemise
-close sits my shirt,but closer my skin

2-il n'y eut jamais peau de lion à bon marché
-at a good bargain,think twice

3-dans sa peau mourra le loup
en la peau où le loup est il meurt
en sa peau mourra le renard
sous la peau est l'âne
-the fox may grow grey but never good
-a bad penny always turns up
-sous la peau est l'âne
-the wolf may lose his teeth but never his nature

4-vous y laisserez votre peau si ...
-it'll be curtain for you if ...

5-il n'y eut jamais peau de lion bon marché
point de pigeon pour une obole
-that thing which is rare is dear

6-sur la peau d'une brebis,on écrit ce que l'on veut
-the calf,the goose,the bee the world is ruled by these three

péché

1-à tout péché miséricorde
-there is no such thing as unforgiveable sin
-forgive and forget
-no sin but should find mercy
-let bygones be bygones
-let the dead bury the dead

2-le péché pénètre entre la vente et l'achat
-two of a trade never agree

3-péché avoué est à demi pardonné
-a fault confessed is half redressed
-open confession is good for the soul

4-vieux péché fait nouvelle honte
-old sins cast long shadows

pécher

1-que celui qui n'a jamais pêché jette la première pierre
-it is a wicked world and we make part of it

2-autant pèche celui qui tient le sac que celui qui l'emplit
-if you steal for others,you shall be hang for yourself
-the receiver is as bad as the thief

3-toujours pèche qui en prend un
-he that will steal a pin,will steal a better thing

peigner
> **on ne peut peigner un diable qui n'a pas de cheveu**
> -you cannot get blood out of a stone

peindre
> **qui peint la fleur,n'en peut peindre l'odeur**
> -the face is not index to the heart

peine
> **1-toute peine mérite salaire**
> -the labourer is worthy of his hire
> -the dog must be bad indeed that is not worth a bone
> -a good dog deserves a good bone
>
> **2-ce qui vaut la peine d'être fait vaut la peine d'être bien**
> -if a thing is worth doing,it's worth doing,it's worth doing well

pélerin
> **pélerin qui chante,larron épouvante**
> -a beggar may sing before a pickpocket
> -he that is down needs fear no fall

pelle
> **1-c'est la pelle qui se moque du fourgon**
> -the frying pan said to the kettle,"avaunt,black brows"
> -it is the pot calling the kettle black
> -it' Satan rebuking sin
> -ill may the kiln call the oven burnt-house
>
> **2-on en trouve à la pelle** (familier)
> -they are a dime a dozen (familier)

pelote
> **1-faire sa pelote**
> -to feather one's nest
>
> **2-sur une pelote d'épingles**
> -like a cat on hot bricks

pencher
> **faire pencher la balance**
> -to type the scales

pendule
> **1-avoir une pendule dans le ventre**
> -the belly is the truest clock
>
> **2-remettre les pendules à l'heure**
> -to put the clock back
>
> **3-en faire une pendule (familier)**
> -to make a mountain out of a molehill

pensée
> **1-la pensée est libre**
> -thought is free

2-les pensées ne paient point de douane
the rope has never been made that binds thoughts

penser
ce que pense l'âne,ne pense l'ânier
-the donkey means one thing and the driver another

perdre
1-on ne perd pas à attendre
on ne perd pas son temps quand on aiguise ses outils
-patient waiters are no losers

2-ce que vous avez perdu dans le feu,vous le retrouverez dans la cendre
-when one door shuts,another opens
-he that falls today may rise tomorrow

3-on ne peut perdre ce que l'on n'a jamais eu
-you cannot lose what you never had

4-il faut perdre un vairon pour gagner un saumon
-better a finger off than always aching
-better hazard once than always in fear
-better to light one candle than to curse the darkness
-a hook's well lost to catch a salmon
-venture a small fish to catch a great one

4-il faut perdre un vairon pour gagner un saumon (suite)
-throw out a sprat to catch a mackerel
-better a little lost than a long sorrow
-better eye out than always ache
-lose a leg rather than a life

5-qui perd sa matinée,perd les trois quarts de sa journée
-an hour in the morning is worth two in the evening

6-on a perdu une bataille mais on n'a pas perdu la guerre
-when one door shuts,another opens
-all is not lost that is in danger
-the tortoise wins the race while the hare is sleeping

7-qui perd le sien perd le sens
qui perd son bien,perd son sang
he that is not sensible to his loss has lost nothing

8-il y a moins de mal à perdre sa vigne qu'à la plaider
-to come to an arrangement is better than to going law

9-quand on n'a rien à perdre,on peut tout risquer
-better hazard once than be always ib fear

perdu
1-perdu corps et biens
-lost with all hands

2-ce n'est pas perdu pour tout le monde
-one man's loss is another man's gain

3-je suis perdu
-I'm a dead duck,a dead pigeon

4-un de perdu,dix de retrouvés
-there are as good fish in the seas as ever came out of it
-remember you are but a man

5-il a perdu ses boulons (familier)
-he has not all his buttons

père

1-à père avare,fils prodigue
-niggard father,spendthrift son
-if a man is a miser,he will certainly have a prodigal son

2-tel père,tel fils
-like mother,like daughter
-she is the apple of her father's eye
-he is a chip of the old block
-the apple never falls far from the tree
-like father,like son
-what is bred in the bone will never come out of the flesh
-like hen,like chicken
-if the mother trot,how can the daughter amble?
-how can the foal amble if the horse and the mare trot?
-of an evil crow,an evil egg
-of evil grain,no good seed can come
-the shoe will hold with the sole

3-il veut montrer à son père à faire des enfants
-you can't teach an old do new tricks

perfection

la perfection n'est pas de ce monde
-there are lees to everyone

persévérance

la persévérance vient à bout de tout
perseverance kills the game

personne

1-personne n'est parfait
-none is without his faults

2-personne ne veut attacher la sonnette au cou du chat
-the greatest step is that out of doors

3-personne n'est irremplaçable
-no man is indispensable
-there is as good fish in the sea as ever came out of it
-there is more fish where that came from

peser
> **pesez vos paroles**
> -second thoughts are best

peste
> **entre la peste et le choléra**
> -between the devil and the deep blue sea

péter
> **1-il vaut mieux péter en compagnie que crever seul**
> -adversity makes strange bedfellows
> -woes unite foes
> -while the thunder lasted two bad men were friends
>
> **2-on ne saurait péter plus haut que son cul** (familier)
> -stretch your arm no further than your sleeve will reach

petit
> **1-d'un petit homme souvent grand ombre**
> -a little body often harbours a great soul
>
> **2-petit à petit,l'oiseau fait son nid**
> -hair by hair you will pull out the horse's tail
> -every little helps
>
> **3-il n'y a pas de petit chez-soi**
> **-un petit chez-soi vaut mieux qu'un grand chez les autres**
> -there is no place like home
> -a man's home is his castle
>
> **4-il n'y a pas de petites économies**
> **-il n'y a pas de petit profit**
> -every little helps
> -many a little makes a muckle
> -many small make a great
> -little gains make a heavy
> -one grain fills not a sack,but helps his fellow
>
> **5-de tout temps,les petits ont pâti des sottises des grands**
> -the dainties of the great are the tears of the poor
> -the pleasures of the mighty are the tears of the poor
>
> **6-en petite maison la part de Dieu est grande**
> -God oft has a good share in a little house

petit-fils
> **le petit-fils revient aux sabots que le grand-père avaient quittés**
> -clogs to clogs is only three generations
> -twice clogs,once boots

peur
> **1-elle a une peur bleue**
> -she is scared to death

2-elle est verte de peur
-she is white with fear

3-avoir la peur au ventre
-his heart sank in his boots

4-avoir peur de son ombre
-to be afraid of one's shadow

5-la peur ne guérit de rien
-all fear is bondage

6-la peur a bon pas
la peur donne des ailes
-fear gives wings

7-plus de peur que de mal
-the noise is greater than the nuts
-there is more talk than trouble

peut-être
"peut-être" garde les gens de mentir
-every maybe has a may not be

pet
cela ne vaut pas un pet de lapin (familier)
-not worth a snap of the fingers

pic
à pic
-in the nick of time

pie
ils espéraient trouver la pie au nid
-they hope to catch the fox in his den

pied
1-se défendre pied à pied
-to fight tooth and nail

2-bon pied,bon oeil
-sharp eye and steady hand
-up and running
-to be fit as a fiddle

3-mettre un pied à l'étrier
-to be off to a good start
-to give somebody a leg up

4-perdre pied
-to lose one's grip

5-ne pas savoir sur quel pied danser
-not to know on which foot a man halts

pied (suite)
7-six pieds de terre suffisent au plus grand homme
-a piece of churchyard fits everybody
-six feet of earth make all men equal
-death combs us all with the same comb
-death is a great leveller

8-celui qui n'a pas bon pied,part avant
-to put the best foot foremost

9-pied à pied
-back and edge
-tooth and nail

10-c'est au pied du mur qu'on reconnaît le maçon
-office will show the man

11-faire des pieds et des mains
-to leave no stone unturned

pierre
1-la pierre va toujours au tas
-he that have plenty of goods shall have more

2-c'est une pierre dans votre jardin
-that dig was meant for you

3-pierre qui roule n'amasse pas mousse
-a rolling stone gathers no moss

4-faire d'une pierre deux coups
-to kill two birds with one stone
-to fall two dogs with one stone
-to kill two flies with one flap

pifomètre
aller au pifomètre
-to play it by ear

pigeon
point de pigeon pour une obole
-nought lay down,nought take up
-that thing which is rare is dear

pile
pile ou face
-heads or tails

pilule
avaler la pilule
-to pay the piper
-a bitter pill to swallow

pince
un pince sans rire
-a straight faced man

170

piquer
    trop piquer le cheval le fait rétif
    -don't spur the willing horse

pire
    1-le pire n'est pas toujours sûr
    -the lower millstone grounds as well as the upper

    2-cela aurait pu être pire
    -nothing so bad but might have been worse

pisser
    1-pisser dans un violon (familier)
    -to whistle down the wind

    2-à pisser contre le vent on mouille sa chemise
    -piss not against the stream

piste
    nous ne sommes pas sur la bonne piste
    -we are not yet on the right scent

place
    1-il n'y a pas de place pour se retourner
    -there is no room to swing a cat

    2-une place pour chaque chose et chaque chose à sa place
    -a time for everything and everything in its proper place

    3-être à la place de quelqu'un
    -to be in somebody's shoes

    4-je ne suis pas à ma place
    -I have got into the wrong box

placement
    placement de père de famille
    -to invest in blue chip stock

plaie
    plaie d'argent n'est pas mortelle
    -money isn't everything1

plaindre
    chacun se plaint que son grenier n'est pas plein
    -every horse thinks his own pack heaviest

plaire
    1-on doit plaire par moeurs et non par robe de couleur
    -a whore in a fine dress is like a clean entry to a durty house

    2-si cela ne vous plaît pas,n'en dégoûtez pas les autres
    -if you don't like it,you may lump it

plaisanterie
    les plaisanteries les plus courtes sont les meilleures
    -don't carry a joke too far
    -let your jest when it is at the best
    -leave off when the play is good
    -long jesting was never good

plaisir

1-pour un plaisir,mille douleurs
-short pleasure,long lament

2-chacun prend son plaisir où il se trouve
-one man's meat is another man's poison

planche
c'était ma planche de salut
-that was my sheet anchor

plaquer
plaquer un amoureux
-to give one the mitten

plat
1-elle avait mis les petits plats dans les grands
-she put on a big spread

2-le plat le plus bas est toujours vide
-where the water is shallow,no vessel will ride

plate-bande
marcher sur les plates-bandes de quelqu'un
-to poach on other people's territory

pleurer
il ne faut pas pleurer avant d'être battu
-sufficient unto the day is the evil thereof
-don't cry before you are hurt
-sorrow is soon enough when it comes
-let your trouble tarry till its own day comes
-don't meet troubles half-way
-never trouble trouble till trouble troubles you
-let the morn come,and the meat with it
-never ask pardon before you are accused
-what's the odds so long as you are happy?

pleuvoir
1-qu'il pleuve ou qu'il vente
-come hell or high water
-come rain or shine

2-il pleut des cordes
il pleut des hallebardes
-it is raining cats and dogs

3-s'il pleut à la Saint-Médard,il pleut quarante jours plus tard
-if it rains on St Swithin's day (15 July),there will be rain for forty days

4-il pleut à tout vent
-the unexpected always happens

172

5-il ne pleut que sur la vendange
-nature is no botcher

6-il ne pleut pas comme quand il tonne
barking dogs seldom bite

plomb
  avoir du plomb dans l'aile
  -to have a broken feather in one's wing
  -better bend the neck than bruise the forehead

ployer
  mieux vaut ployer que rompre
  -better bow than break

pluie
  1-pluie matinale n'est pas journale
  -rain before seven,fine before eleven

  2-petite pluie abat grand vent
  -small rain lays great dust

  3-toute la pluie n'enlève pas la force d'un piment
  -black will take no other hue

  4-après la pluie,le beau temps
  -when bale is highest boot is nighest
  -it's a long lane that has no turning
  -the darkest hour is that before dawn
  -in the end things will mend
  -cloudy mornings turn to clear evenings
  -when things are the worst they begin to mend
  -after black clouds,clear weather
  -a foul morning may turn to a fair day
  -we must abide better times
  -the longest day has an end
  -the longest night will have an end
  -every day comes night
  -most things have two handles
  -heaven suits the back to the burden
  -of all wars,peace is in the end

  5-pluie du matin n'arrête pas le pélerin
  -to a brave and faithful man nothing is difficult

  6-ce sont de petites pluies qui gâtent les grands chemins
  -there is no little enemy

plume
  1-c'est la plume qui fait l'oiseau
  -fine feathers make fine birds

  2-il n'y a pas de plume tombée sans oiseau plumé
  -where there is smoke there is fire
  -where there is reek,there is heart

plus
1-plus on en a,plus on en veut
-the more one has,the more one desires

2-qui plus a ,plus convoite
-much would have more

3-plus a le diable,plus veut avoir
-he that serves God for money,will serve the devil for better wages

poche
1-se remplir les poches
-to line one's pockets

2-avoir quelqu'un dans sa poche
-to have one on the hip

poids
il n'y a pas deux poids,deux mesures
-you must not make fish of one and flesh of the other

poil
1-il a un poil dans la main
-to be bone idle
-a bear sucking his paws

2-un poil fait ombre
-little strokes fell great oaks
-there is no little enemy

3-les poils du chien guérissent la morsure du chien
-one poison drives out another

point
un point de désaccord
-a bone of contention

poire
1-quand la poire est mûre,il faut qu'elle tombe
-il faut attendre à cueillir la poire qu'elle soit mûre
-when the fruit is ripe,it must fall off

2-il a gardé une poire pour la soif
-he put something by for a rainy day
-don't have your cloak to make when it begins to rain
-keep something for the sorefoot
-although it rain,throw not away your watering pot
-although the sun shine,leave not your cloak at home
-nothing is as good as it seems before hand

3-il a une bonne poire(familier)
-he looks a bit of a mug

pois
s'il me donne des pois je lui donnerai des fèves
-I'll give him beans
-tit for tat

174

pois (suite)
-a roland for an oliver

poisson
1-un poisson d'avril
-an april fool's joke

2-être comme un poisson dans l'eau
-to swim like a cork
-to swim like a fish
-to swim like a duck

3-les meilleurs poissons nagent près du fond
-the best fish swim near the bottom

4-les gros poissons mangent les petits
-great fish eat up the small

poix
ceux qui touchent la poix se souillent les doigts
-the finger that touches rouge will be red
-one who lies down with dogs,must rise with fleas
-one cannot touch pitch without being defiled
-they who play bowls must expect to meet with rubbers
-he that deals in dirt has aye foul fingers
-he that has to do with what is foul,never comes away clean
-keep not ill men company,lest you increase the number
-who keeps company with the wolf,will learn to howl
-he who lives with cats will get a taste of mice
-he who goes into a mill comes out powdered

politesse
la politesse ne coûte rien
-one never loses anything by politeness
-civility costs nothing
-there is nothing that costs less than civility

poltron
il vaut mieux être poltron et vivre plus longtemps
-it is better to be coward for a minute than dead for the rest of
your life

pomme
1-pomme de discorde
-bone of contention

2-la pomme ne tombe jamais loin de l'arbre
-the apple never falls far from the tree

3-il suffit d'une pomme pourrie pour gâter le tas
-a rotten apple injures its neighbours
-one scabbed sheep infests a whole flock
-the unrighteous penny corrupts the righteous pound
-one ill weed mars a whole pot of pottage
-one drop of poison infects the whole tun of wine
-a hog that's bemired endeavours to bemire others

pont

faire un pont d'or
-to offer the sun and the moon,the king ransom
-to shower money
-to give a silver bullet (pour se débarrasser de quelqu'un)

porte

1-entrer par la petite porte
-to sneak in through the back door

2-fermer la porte au nez de quelqu'un
-to shut the door to someone's face

3-il faut qu'une porte soit ouverte ou fermée
-the door must be either shut or open

porter

1-porter au pinacle
-to praise to the skies

2-être porté au pinacle
être porté aux nues
-to be lionized

3-porter la ceinture et les bretelles
-to butter one's bread on both sides
-to make assurance doubly sure

4-se porter comme le Pont Neuf
-fit as a fiddle

5-elle porte la culotte
-she wears the breeches
-the grey mare is the better horse
-the woman wears the trousers

6-porter le flambeau
-to bear the bell

7-porter le chapeau
-to hold the bag

position

1-rester sur ses positions
-to stick to one's guns

2-être en position difficile
-to be on a sticky wicket

possession

en fait de meuble la possession vaut titre
-possession is nine points of the law

pot

1-payer les pots cassés
-to hold the bag

2-les pots félés sont ceux qui durent le plus
-a creaking gate hangs long
-an ill stack stands longest

3-à tel pot,telle cuiller
-il n'est si méchant pot qui ne trouve son couvercle
-if the shoe fits,wear it

4-le pot de terre contre le pot de fer
-the earthen pot must keep clear of the brass kettle
-whether the pitcher strikes the stone,or the stone the pitcher,it is bad for the pitcher

potier
   le potier au potier porte envie
   one potter envies another

pouce
   1-pouce!
   -time out!

   2-se tenir les pouces
   -to keep one's fingers crossed

poulailler
   poulailler (au théâtre)
   -peanut galery

poulain
   1-ce que le poulain prend en jeunesse,il le continue en vieillesse
   -a tree must bent while it is young
   -what's learnt in the craddle lasts till the tomb
   -learning in one's youth is engraving in stone
   -whoso learns young,forgets not when he is old

   2-méchant poulain peut devenir bon cheval
   -some do amend when they cannot go worse

poule
   1-une poule noire pond un oeuf blanc
   -a black hen lays a white egg
   -white silver draws black lines

   2-ce n'est pas à la poule de chanter devant le coq
   -it is a sorry flock where the ewe bears the bell

   3-comme une poule qui a trouvé un couteau
   -as fussy as a hen with one chick

   4-être une poule mouillée
   -to be chicken

   5-quand les poules auront des dents
   -when the cat can lick her ear
   -when the pigs have wings
   -when the moon turns blue
   -not until the cows come home

5-quand les poules auront des dents (suite)
-when the devil is blind
-when Hell freezes over
-at later Lammas

6-une poule n'y retrouverait pas ses poussins
-to throw the house out of the window

7-les poules qui gloussent le plus fort ne sont pas les meilleures pondeuses
-avoid a questionner,for he is also a tattler

8-chaque poule vit de ce qu'elle gratte
-if you don't work,you shan't eat

9-qui suit les poules,apprend à gratter
-who keeps company with a wolf will learn to howl

10-quand on tient la poule,il faut la plumer
-when fortune smiles,embrace her

11-poule égarée est bonne pour le renard
-the lone sheep is in danger of the wolf

pourquoi
1-pourquoi faire simple quand on peut faire compliqué?
-why buy a cow when the milk is so cheap?

2-et voilà pourquoi votre fille est muette
-that accounts for the milk in the coconut

pourri
1-il y a quelque chose de pourri au royaume des cieux
-something is rotten in the state of Denmark

2-il est pourri jusqu'à la racine
-he's rotten to the core

pousser
1-pousser quelqu'un dans la tombe
-to drive a nail into one's coffin

2-être poussé à bout
-to be on one's beam ends

poussière
et poussière,tu retourneras en poussière
-ashes to ashes, dust to dust

poussin
poussin chante comme le coq lui apprend
-soft wax will taake any impression

pouvoir
1-qui peut le plus peut le moins
-whatever man has done man may do

2-on peut parce que l'on croit pouvoir
-he can who believes he can

3-tu ne peux pas me faire ça
-you can't cod me

4-on ne peut faire d'une buse un épervier
-you cannot make a silk purse out of a sow's ear
-you cannot make a horn of a pig's tail
-you cannot make a Mercury of every log
-a booby will never make a hawk
-what can you expect from a hog but a grunt?

5-qui peut et empêche,pêche
-every tub must stand on its own bottom
-score twice before you cut once
-let every sheep hang on its own shank

précaution
deux précautions valent mieux qu'une
it is best to be on the safe side

précepte
nous avons d'assez bons préceptes mais peu de maîtres
-example is better than precept
-practice what you preach

prêcher
1-prêcher le faux pour savoir le vrai
-with hankerchief on one hand and sword in the other
-the bait hides the hook
-to carry fire in one hand and water in the other

2-prêcher pour son saint
-to have an ax to grind

3-prêcher dans le désert
-to waste one's breath talking

4-a beau precher qui n'a cure de bien faire
-practice what you preach

premier
1-le premier venu engrène
premier levé,premier chaussé
-first in,first served

2-il vaut mieux être le premier de sa race que le dernier
-the early man never borrows from the late man

première
c'est la première impression qui compte
-the first blow is half the battle

prendre
1-quand on prend du galon,on n'en saurait trop prendre
-the more one has,the more one desires

2-prendre les choses comme elles viennent
-to take things as they come

3-tel est pris qui croyait prendre
-the tables are turned
-it's a case of bitter bit
-he that mischief hatches mischief catches

4-prendre le taureau par les cornes
-to take the bull by the horns

5-prendre les enfants du Bon Dieu pour des canards sauvages
-to take eggs for money

6-c'est à prendre ou à laisser
-do or die

7-elle l'a bien pris
-she took it like a lamb

8-prendre le mal à la racine
-to nip the brair in the bud

9-à tout prendre on ne gagne ni ne perd
-what you gain on the swings,you lose on the roundabouts

10-il se prend pour un puits de science
-he thinks he is a know-it-all
-don't take hollyer than thou

11-prendre la balle au bond
-to take the ball before the bound

12-qui va en prendre le risque?
-who is to bell the cat?

13-prendre le taureau par les cornes
-to take the bull by the horns

prépare
qu'est_ce qui se prépare?
-what's cooking?

près
il est près de ses sous
-he is close-fisted

présent
1-à petit présent,petit merci
-throw no gift again at the giver's head

2-les petits présents entretiennent l'amitié
-give flowers make friends

3-petit présent trop attendu n'est point donné mais bien vendu
-he loses his thanks who promises and delays
-long tarrying takes all the thanks away

presse
>**à la presse vont les fous**
>-a fool always rushes to the fore

presser
>**1-si on lui presse le nez,il en sort du lait**
>-he's not even dry behind the ears
>-he is wet behind the ears
>
>**2-se presser le citron** (familier)
>-to beat one's brain out

pression
>**à la pression (pour la bière)**
>-drawn from the wood

prêt
>**soyez fin prêts**
>-keep your powder dry

prêté
>**c'est un prêté pour un rendu**
>-tit for tat

prêter
>**1-prêter argent fait perdre la mémoire**
>-creditors have better memories than debtors
>
>**2-on ne prête qu'aux riches**
>-every man bastes the fat dog
>
>**3-chose divine est prêter,devoir est vertu héroïque**
>-not so good to borrow as be able to lent

prévenir
>**mieux vaut prévenir que guérir**
>-an ounce of prevention is worth a pound of cure
>-prevention is better than cure

prier
>**qui ne prie ne prend**
>-the squeaking wheel gets the grease

pris
>**tel est pris qui croyait prendre**
>-it's a case of bitter bit

prison
>**il n'y a pas de belles prisons ni de laides amours**
>-no love is foul,nor prison fair

prix
>**1-à quelque prix que ce soit**
>-for love nor money
>
>**2-les prix montent en flèche**
>-prices have been skyrocketing

procession
on ne fait pas de procession pour tailler les vignes
-every tub must stand on its own bottom
-let every peddlar carry his own burden

profit
1-il n'y a pas de petit profit
-all is fish that comes to my net
-light gains make a heavy purse

2-je fais profit de tout
-all's grist that comes to my mill

3-trop de profit crève la poche
-a shoe too large trips one up

promettre
1-qui tout promet,rien ne promet
-who gives all,denies all
-he that promise too much,means nothing

2-entre promettre et donner,doit-on sa fille marier?
-between promising and performing,a man may marry his daughter

3-promettre et tenir sont deux
-promises are pie-crust,made to be broken
-between promising and performing,a man may marry his daughter

promise
chose promise,chose due
-a promise is a promise

prophète
nul n'est prophète en son pays
-a prophet is not without honor except in his own country

propos
1-fort à propos
-in the nick of time

2-les longs propos font les courts jours
-don't take your harp to the party
-harp not for ever on the same string
-it is useless to flog a dead horse
-not good is to harp on the frayed string

propre
qui est propre à tout n'est propre à rien
-Jack of all trades,master of none

propriétaire
faire le tour du propriétaire
-to give the Cook's tour

prospérité
la prospérité fait peu d'amis
-he that has a full purse never wanted a friend

prouver
qui prouve trop,ne prouve rien
-that which proves too much,proves nothing

provision
provision,profusion
-it is not too late to spare when the bottom is bare

provisoire
il n'y a que le provisoire qui dure
-once a use,ever a custom

prudence
prudence est mère de sureté
-a stitch in time saves nine
-safe bind,safe find
-diligence is the mother of good fortune(sucess)
-it is no use spoiling the ship for a ha'p'orth of tar
-the way to be safe is never to be secure

prunelle
j'y tiens comme à la prunelle de mes yeux
-he is the apple of my eye

puce
1-mettre la puce à l'oreille
-to smell a rat

2-puce en l'oreille,l'homme réveille
-fast bind,fast find
-it is better to fear than to trust too far

puiser
il faut puiser quand la corde est au puits
-the tide must be taken when it comes

puissant
selon que vous serez puissant ou misérable, les jugements de cour vous rendront blanc ou noir
-there's one law for the rich,and another one for the poor

puits
quand le puits est à sec,on sait ce que vaut l'eau
-you never miss the water till the well runs dry
-fools never know when they are well off
-fortune is good to him who know to make use of her
-blessings are not valued till they are gone
-the cow knows not the worth of her tail till she loses it
-no man better knows what good is than he who endured evil
-water is a boon in the desert but the drowning man curses it
-we never know the worth of water till the well is dry
-of small account is a fly till it gets into the eye

183

puits (suite)
    -a good when lost is valued most
    -health is not valued till sickness comes
    -goods are theirs that enjoy them
    -blessings brighten as they take their flight
    -misfortune tells us what fortune is

punir
    on est souvent puni par où l'on a péché
    -who swims in sin shall sink in sorrow

punition
    la punition boîte mais elle arrive
    -if today will not,to morrow may

pur
    tout est pur aux purs
    -to the pure all things are pure

Q

qualité
> **la plus universelle qualité des esprits est la diversité**
> -vairiety is the spice of life
> -all work and no play makes Jack a dull boy

quatre
> **se mettre en quatre**
> -to give the shirt off one's back

querelle
> **les querelles ne dureraient pas si longtemps,si le tort n'était que d'un côté**
> -quarrels would not last so long if the fault was only on one side
> -it takes two to make a quarrel

question
> **1-mettre une question sur le tapis**
> -to bring a question on the carpet
>
> **2-à question abstruse,abstruse réponse**
> -like question,like answer
> -ask a silly question and you'll get a silly answer

queue
> **1-à la queue gît la difficulté**
> -the end crowns the work
> -think of the end before you begin
>
> **2-en la queue et en la fin gît de coutume le venin**
> -the sting is in the tail
> -the venom is in the tail

qui
> **pour qui me prenez-vous?**
> -do you see any green in my eye?
> -do I look greenhorn?

quiconque
> **quiconque se sert de l'épée périra par l'épée**
> -he who lives by the sword dies by the sword
> -he that strikes wiith the sword,shall be beaten with the scabbard

quitte
> **quitte ou double**
> -double or quits
> -I will win the horse or lose the saddle

quitter
> **qui quitte la partie,la perd**
> -a bleating sheep loses a bite

R

rabattre
> **rabattre le caquet**
> -to settle one's hash

rafraichir
> **se rafraichir les idées**
> -to blow away the cobwebb

rage
> **1-la rage d'amour fait passer le mal de dents**
> -love covers many infirmities
>
> **2-rage d'amour est pire que le mal de dents**
> -no herb will cure love
> -fire cannot be hidden in flax

rail
> **être sur les rails**
> -to be on the beam

raillerie
> **la raillerie ne doit point passer le jeu**
> long jesting was never good

raisin
> **1-mi- figue mi-raisin**
> -neither fish nor fowl
>
> **2-de beaux raisins parfois pauvre vin**
> -the fowler's pipe sounds sweet till the bird is caught

raison
> **1-la raison qui s'emporte a le sort de l'erreur**
> -the bear and the tea kettle
> -when a man grows angry,his reason rides out
> -when wrath speaks,wisdom veils her face
> -anger punishes itself
>
> **2-la raison du plus fort est toujours la meilleure**
> -might makes right
>
> **3-la raison n'est pas ce qui règle l'amour**
> -love is without reason
>
> **4-c'est raison que chacun soit maître en son logis**
> -one master in a house is enough
> -one bad general is better than two good ones
> -where every man is a master,the world goes to wrack
> -there is no good accord,where every man would be a lord

rappeler
> **cela me rappelle quelque chose**
> -that rings a bell

ras
> **être au ras des pâquerettes**
> -not to have a soul above buttons

raser
> **raser les murs**
> -to be hangdog

rat
> **les rats désertent le navire qui coule**
> -a rat leaving a sinking ship

recevoir
> **recevoir une gifle**
> -to get a thick ear

réchauffer
> **réchauffer le coeur de quelqu'un**
> -to warm the cockles of one's heart

récolter
> **on récolte ce que l'on a semé**
> -as you sow,so you shall reap
> -he that sows thorns must not expect corn
> -the wheel has come full circle
> -good seed makes a good crop
> -cast thy bread upon the water,for thou shalt find it after many days

reconnaissance
> **ne pas avoir la reconnaissance du ventre**
> -to bite even the hand that feeds him

reculer
> **il faut reculer pour mieux sauter**
> -one must draw back in order to leap better
> -look before you leap
> -lookers-on see most of the game

réfléchir
> **réfléchissez avant de parler**
> -first think,then speak

refroidir
> **refroidir quelqu'un**(sens figuré)
> -to throw cold water on a scheme

refuser
> **tel refuse qui après muse**
> -he who hesitates is lost
> -he that will not when he may,when he will he shall have nay

regard
> **avoir un droit de regard**
> -to have a finger in the pie

regarder

1-y regarder de plus près
-to think better of the matter

2-qui trop regarde quel vent vente jamais ne sème ni ne plante
-nothing venture,nothing have
-better hazard once than be always in fear

3-quand on regarde quelqu'un,on n'en voit que la moitié
-he that looks in man's face knows not what money is in his purse
-they that are booted are not always ready
-handsome is as handsome does
-the face is no index to the heart

4-il ne faut pas regarder la saleté d'un cochon pour en manger
-there is many a good cock come out of a tattered bag

5-il ne faut pas regarder derrière soi
-it is too late to call back yesterday

6-il faut regarder à ses mains plutôt qu'à ses pieds
-take heed of the snake in the grass

registre

faire changer de registre à quelqu'un
-to make someone sing another tune

règle

il n'est règle qui ne faille,on peut violer sans qu'elle crie
-every law has a loophole

religion

1-une religion peu à peu emporte une autre
"pater noster' built churches,and 'our father' pulls them down

2-la religion ne nous fait pas bons,mais elle nous empêche de devenir mauvais
-a man without religion is like a horse without a bridle

remède

1-une femme comme çà,c'est un remède contre l'amour
-she is as homely as a mud fence

2-le remède est parfois pire que le mal
-the remedy may be worse than the disease

3-quand il n'y a pas de remède,il faut se résigner
-what can't be cured,must be endured
-don't kick against the pricks

remettre

il ne faut jamais remettre à plus tard ce que l'on peut faire le jour même
-by the street of by and by one arrives at the house of never
-never put off till tomorrow what you can do today

-procrastination is the thief of time
-time and tide wait for no man
-one of these days is none of these days
-what may be done at any time may be done at no time
-tomorrow never comes
-one hour today is worth two tomorrow
-one today is worth two tomorrows
-no time like the present
-don't use the swing-it-till-Monday basket
-"tomorrow"leads to the dead end of "never"
-for the diligent the week has seven days,for the slothful seven tomorrows

remuer

1-remuer le fer dans la plaie
-to wake the sleeping dog

2-remuer ciel et terre
-to leave no stone unturned
-to move heaven and earth
-as best as one can

3-plus on remue la boue,plus elle pue
-one is not smelt where all stink
-corruption of the best becomes the worst
-the more you stir,the more it stinks

renard

1-un bon renard ne mange jamais les poules de son voisin
-a wise fox will never rob his neighbour's henroost

2-un renard ne se laisse pas prendre deux fois à un piège
-trouble brings experience and experience brings wisdom

3-renard qui dort la matinée n'a plus la gueule emplumée
-the sleepy fox has seldom feathered breakfasts
-the cow that's first up,gets the first of the dew

4-quand le renard pèche,veillez sur vos oies
-when the fox preaches,then beware your geese
-it is an ill sign to see a fox lick a lamb

5-le renard cache sa queue
-a crafty knave needs no broker

rendre

1-il faut rendre à César ce qui est à César
-render unto Caesar the things which are Caesar's

2-rendre la monnaie de sa pièce
-to pay in one's own coin
-a dose of one's medicine
-answer a fool according to his folly
-to return like for like
-to pay with the same dish you borrow

renom
> une fois en mauvais renom,jamais un puits n'a été estimé bon
> -a good name is sooner lost than won

renommée
> bonne renommée vaut mieux que ceinture dorée
> -a good name is better than a golden girdle
> -a good fame is better than a good face

repentir
> notre repentir n'est pas tant un regret du mal que nous avons
> fait qu'une crainte de celui qui nous en peut arriver
> -the thief is sorry to be hanged but not that he is a thief

répondre
> répondre à ses espérances
> -to fall short of one's expectations

réputation
> mauvaise réputation va jusqu'à la mer;bonne réputation
> reste au seuil de la maison
> -ten good turns lie dead and one ill deed report abroad does
> spread

ressembler
> 1-qui se ressemble,s'assemble
> -birds of a feather flock together
>
> 2-on se ressemble de plus loin
> -like breeds like

retirer
> se retirer sous sa tente
> -to sulk in one's tent

rétro
> être rétro
> -to be a back number

réunir
> se réunir à huis clos
> -to meet behind closed doors

réussir
> 1-rien ne réussit comme le succès
> -nothing succeeds like success
> -more worship the rising man than the setting sun
>
> 2-c'est réussi!
> -I've gone and done it

revanche
> à charge de revanche
> -one good turn deserves another
> -claw me and I'll claw thee
> -give and take

revenir
>**1-on revient toujours à ses premières amours**
>-old love will not be forgotten
>-no love like the first love
>-let's get down to the brasstacks
>-first impressions are the most lasting

>**2-revenons à nos moutons!**
>-let's pick up the threads
>-cut the cackle and come to the "osses"
>-cut it short!

révolution
>**on ne fait pas les révolutions avec de l'eau de rose**
>-revolutions are not made with rosewater

rhubarbe
>**passe moi la rhubarbe et je te passerai le séné**
>-one good turn deserves another
>-you scratch my back and I'll scratch yours
>-ka me,ka thy
>-roll my log and I'll roll yours

riche
>**1-il vaut mieux être riche et bien portant que pauvre et malade**
>-it is better to be born lucky than rich

>**2-je suis riche des biens dont je sais me passer**
>-the greatest wealth is content with a little
>-he is rich that has few wants
>-he who desires but little has no need for much

>**3-le plus riche en mourrant n'emporte qu'un drap**
>-death combs us all with the same comb
>-death is a great leveller
>-we shall lie all alike in our graves
>-all our pomp the earth covers
>-on the turf all men are equal-and under it
>-the end makes all equal

>**4-riche homme ne sait qui ami lui est**
>-friends are plenty when the purse is full
>-the rich knows not who is his friend

richesse
>**richesse donne hardiesse**
>-money makes a man free everywhere
>-plenty breeds pride

rien
>**1-il n'y a rien de nouveau sous le soleil**
>-there is nothing new under the sun

>**2-qui rien ne sait de rien ne doute**
>-he that knows nothing,doubts nothing
>-ignorance is bliss
>-ignorance is the peace of life

3-on n'a rien pour rien
-there is no such a thing as a free lunch

4-on n'a rien sans rien
-it takes a sprat to catch a mackerel
-nothing seek,nothing find
-no sweat without sweat
-ninety percent of inspiration is perspiration
-genius is an infinite capacity for taking pains
-no pains,no gains
-you don't get something from nothing
-the race is got by running
-think of ease,but work on

5-où il n'y a rien,le roi perd ses droits
-of nought comes nought

rire

1-rira bien qui rira le dernier
-he laughs best who laughs last
-at the end of the game you'll see the winner
-the opera isn't over till the fat lady sings

2-tel qui rit vendredi,dimanche pleurera
-he who laughs on Friday will weep on Sunday
-laugh before breakfast,you'll cry before supper
-if you sing before breakfast,you'll cry before night
-laugh at leisure,you may greet ere night
-joy and sorrow are next door neighbour
-God send you joy,for sorrow will come fast enough

3-rire jaune
-to laugh on the wrong side

4-rire sous cape
-to laugh on one's sleeve

5-rire à gorge déployée
-to laugh one's head off

6-le rire est le propre de l'homme
-laughter is natural to man

7-trop rire fait pleurer
joy and sorrow are next door neighbours

risque

qui ne risque rien n'a rien
-nothing ventured,nothing gained
-if you will not take pains,pains will take you
-no sweet without sweat
-no pains,no gains
-he who would catch fish must not mind getting wet
-all cats love fish but fear to wet their paws

-the cat wanted fish but dared not wet her feet in the stream
-if you would enjoy the fire,you must put up with the smoke
-nothing stake,nothing draw
-nought lay down,nought take up
-he that stays in the valley,shall never get over the hill

rivière
1-les rivières ne deviennent jamais grosses qu'il n'y entre de l'eau
-every why has a wherefore

2-les rivières retournent à la mer
-money makes money

3-la rivière ne grossit pas sans trouble
he that will be rich before night,may be hanged before noon

robe
1-la robe ne fait pas le médecin
-it's not the hood that makes the monk
-it's not the cowl that makes the friar

2-c'est la robe qu'on salue
-the tailor makes the man

Robin
toujours il souvient à Robin de ses flûtes
-the dog return to its vomit
-the bird loves hes nest
-bring a cow to the hall and she'll return to the byre
-the hare always returns to her form

roi
1-tel roi,telle loi
-new lords,new laws

2-le roi n'est pas servi sans qu'il parle
-the squeaking wheel gets the grease

3-le roi n'est pas son cousin
-I wouldn't call the king my cousin
-he is the emperor of China

4-les rois et les juges n'ont point de parents
-love and lordship like no fellowship

Rome
à Rome,il faut vivre comme à Rome
-when in Rome,do as Romans do

rose
1-nulle rose sans épines
-no rose without a thorn
-we must take the bad with the good
-there is a crook in every lot
-every sweet has its sour

rose (suite)
-no garden without its weeds
-honey is sweet but the bee stings
-every family has a skeleton in the cupboard
-there are spots even in the sun
-no silver without its dross
-there is no pack of cards without a knave
-every light has its shadow
-no sun without a shadow
-no day so clear but has dark clouds
-no summer,but has its winter
-there was never a good town but has a mire at one end of it
-no larder but has its mice
-every path has a puddle
-there's a black sheep in every flock

2-il n'est si belle rose qui ne se flétrisse
-the fairest rose at last is withered

3-il n'est si belle rose qui ne devienne gratte-cul
-beauty fades like a flower
-beauty won't make the pot boil

4-tout n'a pas été rose dans sa vie
-his life was not a bed of roses

rossignol
quand le rossignol a vu ses petits,il cesse de chanter
-he that has children,all his morsels arez not his own

roue
1-il n'est que la cinquième roue du carosse
-his word carries no weight

2-la plus mauvaise roue d'un chariot fait toujours le plus de bruit
-they brag most who can do the least

route
faire fausse route
-to be on the wrong track

royaliste
il ne faut pas être plus royaliste que le roi
-stretch your arm no further than your sleeve will reach

Rubicon
franchir le Rubicon
-to reach the point of no return

ruer
il rue dans les brancards
-he's kicking over the traces

ruisseau
les petits ruisseaux font les grandes rivières
-many drops make an ocean
-many drops make a shower
-little brooks make great rivers
-thrift is a great revenue

S

sac

1-sac vide ne tient pas debout
-empty sacks will never stand upright
-bread is the staff of life

2-d'un sac à charbon on ne peut sortir blanche farine
il ne sort du sac que ce qu'il y a
-there comes nought of the sack but what was there

3-sac plein fait dresser l'oreille
-plenty breeds pride
-a full purse makes the mouth speaks

4-il faut lier le sac avant qu'il soit plein
-you can't have too much of a good thing
-safety lies in the middle course
-enough is enough

5-il ne sort du sac que ce qu'il y a
-he that has no money needs no purse

sage

1-il n'est si sage qui ne foloie
-every man a little beyond himself is a fool

2-il est sage comme une image
-he is as good as gold
-as wise as an owl
-as quiet as a mouse

3-tout le monde sait être sage après coup
-it is easy to be wise after the event

4-les sages ont la bouche dans le coeur et les fous le coeur dans la bouche
-the ass waggeth his ears

5-c'est être sage que de savoir feindre la folie
-no man can play the foll so well as the wise man

sagesse

1-toute la sagesse n'est pas enfermée dans une tête
-hear all parties

2-il est rare de voir la sagesse alliée à la beauté
-beauty and folly go often in company

saint

1-à quel saint se vouer
-which way to turn
-at one's wits'end

2-à la saint Glinglin
-once in a blue moon

3-être un vrai Saint-Bernard
-to be Johnny-on-the-spot

saison
de saison tout est bon
-everything is good in its season

salir
on n'est jamais sali que par la boue
-slander leaves a sore behind

salive
1-je n'ai plus de salive
-I am dry with talking

2-salive d'homme tous serpents dompte
-the tongue is the rudder of our ship

sang
1-c'est dans le sang
-it runs in the blood

2-bon sang ne peut mentir
-blood will tell
-breed will tell
-a good anvil does not fear the hammer

3-mon n'a fait qu'un tour
-it makes my blood boil

4-pur sang
-dyed in the wool

santé
1-celui qui a la santé est riche
qui a la santé a tout,qui n'a pas la santé n'a rien
-health is better than wealth

2-une santé délicate est quelquefois un brevet de longue vie
-an ill stack stands longest

sauce
1-il n'est sauce que d'appétit
-good appetite needs no sauce
-hunger is the best sauce
-hunger is good kitchen meat

2-la sauce vaut mieux que le poisson
-the sauce was better than the fish

sauter
sauter du coq à l'âne
-to skip from one subject to another

sauver
> **il y en a toujours qui aimeront mieux se sauver que passer les seaux**
> -look to thyself when thy neighbour's house is on fire
> -whenever Skiddaw hath a cap,Scruffel wots full well of that

savoir
> **1-savoir ce que vaut l'aune**
> -to know a hawk from a handsaw
> -to know the difference between chalk and cheese
> -to know which side one's bread is buttered
>
> **2-il faut savoir s'arrêter**
> -one must draw the line somewhere
>
> **3-savoir c'est pouvoir**
> -knowledge is power
>
> **4-on sait ce que l'on perd,on ne sait pas ce que l'on gagne**
> -better the devil you know than the devil you don't know
> -possession is better than expectation
> -a bird in the hand is worth two in the bush
>
> **5-on sait ce que parler veut dire**
> -one end is sure to be boned
> -he knows how many beans make five
>
> **6-il sait trop de chasse qui a été veneur**
> -he knows the water best who has waded through it
> -I have lived too near a wood to be frightened by owls
>
> **7-on ne sait ni qui vit,ni qui meurt**
> -none knows what will happen to him before sunset
> -the time to come is no more that the time past
> -the time to come is no more than the time past
> -there is but one way to enter this life but the gates of death are without number
>
> **8-nul ne sait ce qu'il peut faire avant d'avoir essayé**
> -you never what you can do till you try
>
> **9-nul ne sait ce qu'est la guerre s'il n'y a son fils**
> -war is sweet to them that knows it not
>
> **10-on ne sait pas de quoi demain sera fait**
> -never speak ill of the year till it be past
>
> **11-qui ne sait rien, de rien ne doute**
> the more one knows,the less one believes
> he that knows nothing ,doubts nothing

savon
> **passer un savon**
> -to give a dressing down

science

science sans conscience n'est que ruine de l'âme
-study without thought is vain,thought without study is dangerous
-a little learning is a dangerous thing
-a little knowledge is a dangerous thing
-there is no royal road to learning
-zeal without knowledge is a runaway horse

scier

il ne faut pas scier la branche sur laquelle on est assis
-never cast dirt into the fountain which you have sometimes drunk
-do nut cut the tree that gives you shade
-don't cut the bough you are standing on
-why kick down the ladder by which you have climbed?

sécher

rien ne sèche aussi vite que les larmes
-nothing dries sooner than tears
-a bellowing cow soon forgets her calf

seconde

à la seconde
-in a crack
-in two shakes of a lamb's tail
-in a brace of shakes

secouer

se secouer
-to pull oneself together

secret

1-secret de trois,secret de tous
-when three people know,the whole world knows
-a secret is too little for one,enough for two,too much for three
-three may keep a secret if two of them are dead

2-sous le sceau du secret
-under the rose

seigneur

1-tant vaut le seigneur,tant vaut la terre
-well goes the case when wisdom counsels

2-à tout seigneur,tout honneur
-give the devil his due
-honor to whom honor is due
-give credit where credit is due

sein

les seins ne sont jamais trop lourds pour la poitrine
-nature is the true law
-nature does nothing in vain

semaine
> **la semaine des quatre jeudis**
> -when two Fridays come together

sembler
> **tel vous semble applaudir,qui vous raille et vous joue**
> -full of courtesy,full of craft
> -many kiss the hand they wish to cut off

semer
> **1-l'un sème,l'autre récolte**
> -one man sows and another reaps
> -one beat the bush and another caught the hare
>
> **2-qui sème,récolte**
> -no root,no fruit
> -no bees,no honey
>
> **3-qui sème le vent,récolte la tempête**
> -people who live in glass houses shouldn't throw stones
>
> **4-il ne faut pas laisser de semer par crainte des pigeons**
> -he who hesitates is lost
> -nothing venture,nothing have
>
> **5-qui sème en pleurs recueille en heur**
> -keep your shop open and your shop will keep you
> -the mill gets by going
> -a going foot is aye getting
> -he that labours and thrives,spins gold
> -the diligent spinner has a large shift
>
> **6-il faut semer pour récolter**
> **-il faut semer pour recueillir**
> **-il faut semer qui veut moissonner**
> -no sweet without sweat

sens
> **sens dessus dessous**
> -topsy turvy

séparer
> **il faut séparer le bon grain de l'ivraie**
> -to separate the wheat from the chaff
> -we must separate the sheep from the goats

sermon
> **le sermon édifie,l'exemple détruit**
> -a good example is the best sermon

serpent
> **1-nourrir un serpent dans son sein**
> -to cherish a serpent in your bosom

2-serpent qui change de peau est toujours serpent
-fair wihtout,false within
-bees that have honey in their mouths,have sting in their tails
-don't take things at their face value
-poison is poison,though it comes in a golden cup
-a rose by any other name would still be a rose

serré

la lutte était si serrée qu'on ne savait pas qui allait gagner
-it was nip and tuck as to which would win

serrer

quand on serre trop l'anguille,on la laisse partir
-too much of ought is good for nought

service

service d'autrui n'est pas héritage
-service is no inheritance

serviette

serviette damassée devient torchon de cuisine
-beauty fades like a flower
-old churches have dim windows

servir

1-l'on ne peut servir ensemble et Dieu et le Diable
-you cannot serve God and Mammon
-there is no leaping from Deliah's lap into Abraham'bosom

2-il ne sert à rien de montrer les dents lorsqu'on est édenté
-if you cannot bite,never show your teeth
-never make threats you cannot carry out
-two things a man should never be angry at what he can help,and what he cannot help
-never grieve for that you cannot help

3-on n'est jamais aussi bien servi que par soi-même
-if you want to be well served,serve yourself
-if you want a thing done well,do it yourself
-why keep a dog and bark yourself?
-the miller got never better moulter than he took with his own hands
-he who wants a mule without fault,must walk on foot

4-nul ne peut servir deux maîtres
-no man can serve two masters

seul

1-mieux vaut être seul que mal accompagné
-better be alone than in bad company
-solitude is often the best society

2-je ne suis jamais moins seul que dans la solitude(Cicéron)
-a wise man is never less alone than when he is alone

seul

    quand on est seul,on devient nécessaire
    -tradesmen live upon lack

si

    avec des si et des mais on mettrait Paris dans une bouteille
    -if wishes were horses beggars would ride
    -if ifs and ands were pots and pans,there'd be no work for tinkers'hand
    -pigs might fly
    -mere wishes are silly fishes
    -if wishes were butter-cakes,beggars might bite
    -if wishes were thrushes,then beggars would eat birds
    -if he were as long as he is lither,he might thatch a house without a ladder

siège

    entre deux sièges on tombe à terre
    -he who hesitates is lost

sifflet

    si vous n'avez pas d'autre sifflet,votre chien est perdu
    -that fish will soon be caught that nibbles at every bait

sillon

    le sillon n'est pas le champ
    -good to begin well,better to end well
    -a good salad may be the prologue to a bad supper

singe

    1-plus le singe monte,plus on lui voit la queue
    -the higher the ape goes,the more he shows his tail
    -the higher the monkey climbs,the more he shows his tail

    2-payer en monnaie de singe
    -to pay with wooden nickels

    3-un singe vêtu de pourpre est toujours un singe
    -an ape is an ape,a varlet is a varlet,though be clad in silk or scarlet
    -vice is often clothed in virtue'habit
    -poison is poison though it comes in a golden cup
    -cut off a dog's tail and he will be a dog still

sobre

    sobre comme un chameau
    -sober as a judge

soin

    il était aux petits soins pour elle
    -he catered to her every whim

soldat

    tout soldat a dans son sac un bâton de maréchal
    -there's always room at the top

soleil

le soleil luit pour tout le monde
-the sun belongs to everyone
-the sun loses nothing by shining into a puddle
-man is a man to God

sommeil

le sommeil est l'enfance de la raison
-in sleep all passes away

songe

tous songes sont mensonges
-dreams are lies

sonner

1-on ne peut sonner les cloches et aller à la procession
-one cannot do two things at one time
-one cannot be in two places at once
-one cannot drink and whistle at once

2-sonner le glas d'une affaire
-to ring down the curtain

sort

1-le sort fait les parents,le choix fait les amis
-wheresoever you see your kindred,make much of your friend
-a near neighbour is better than a far dwelling kinsman

sortir

1-être sorti de l'auberge
-to be out of the woods

2-sortir du pétrin
-to get off the hook

3-sortir de ses gonds
-to fly off the handle

sot

1-il est des sots de tout pays
-the world is full of fools
-folly is the product of all countries and ages

2-à sot compliment,point de réponse
-neglect will kill injuries sooner than revenge

sottise

les sottises des grands sont des sentences
-a rich man's joke is always funny

sou

1-un sou amène l'autre
-put two pennies in a purse and they will draw together
-money would be gotten if there were money to get it with
-take care of the pence and the pounds will take care of themselves
-penny and penny laid up will be many
-a pin a day is a groat a year
-thrift is a great revenue

2-il n'a pas un sou vaillant
-he has not a penny to bless himself with

souffler
1-sans souffler mot
-without striking a blow

2-on ne peut soufffler et humer ensemble
-one cannot drink and whistle at once

3-il ne faut pas souffler le chaud et le froid
-one must not blow hot and cold

souffrir
il faut souffrir ce qu'on ne peut empêcher
il faut souffrir patiemment ce qu'on ne peut amender sainement
-what can't be cured,must be endured
-don't kick against the pricks
-he that may not do as he would,must do as he may
-the goat must browse where she is tied
-a man must plough with such oxen he has
-you must grin and bear it
-what must be,must be

souhait
1-si souhaits fussent vrais,pastoureaux seraient rois
-if wishes were horses,beggars would ride

2-oncques souhait n'emplit le sac
-wishes never can fill a sack

soûler
soûler quelqu'un de paroles
-to talk a person's head off

soulier
1-il est dans ses petits souliers
-he feels like a fish out of water
-he quakes in his boots
-he is ill at ease

2-en attendant les souliers des morts,on peut aller longtemps à pied
qui court après les souliers d'un mort risque souvent d'aller nu-pieds
-he that waits for a dead man's shoes is in danger of going barefoot

3-il n'est si beau soulier qui ne devienne savate
-beauty is but a blossom
-old churches have dim windows
-the fairest rose at last is withered
-the fairest silk is soonest stained

soupçonner
> **il est soupçonné**
> -he is under a cloud

soupe
> **1-la soupe fait le soldat**
> -there is nothing like plain food
>
> **2-une soupe maigre**
> -a tea-kettle broth
>
> **3-on fait de bonne soupe dans un vieux pot**
> -good broth may be made in an old pot

source
> **une source salée ne peut donner d'eau douce**
> -of a thorn springs not a fig
> -eagles do not breed doves
> -of evil grain,no good seed can come

sourd
> **1-sourd comme un pot**
> -deaf as a white cat
> -deaf as a post
>
> **2-il n'y a de pire sourd que celui qui ne veut pas entendre**
> -none so deaf as those who won't hear
> -none so blind as those who won't see

souris
> **souris qui n'a qu'un trou est bientôt prise**
> -that fish will soon be caught that nibbles at every bait

souvenir
> **-toujours il souvient à Robin de ses flûtes**
> -the dog return to its vomit

style
> **le style,c'est l'homme**
> -the style is the man

succès
> **le succès fut toujours un enfant de l'audace**
> -all cats love fish but fear to wet their paws
> -nothing venture,nothing have
> -it is better to be a has been than a never was

suer
> **il vaut mieux suer que grelotter**
> -better to wear out than to rust out

suffisance
> **1-qui n'a suffisance,n'a rien**
> -he freezes who does not burn
>
> **2-suffisance fait richesse et convoitise fait pauvresse**
> -he who is content in his poverty,is wonderfully rich
> -he has nothing that is not contented

sûr
>
> **aussi sûr que deux et deux font quatre**
> -as sure as eggs is eggs

surplus
>
> **le surplus rompt le couvercle**
> -too much of ought is good for nought
> -too much pudding will choke a dog
> -too much honey cloys the stomach
> -if in excess even nectar is poison
> -mirth without measure is madness
> -a little wind kindles,much puts out the fire
> -too much money makes one mad
> -too much water drowned the miller
> -more than enough is too much

sursomme
>
> **la sursomme abat l'âne**
> *-cf le surplus rompt le couvercle*

T

table
>la table est l'entremetteuse de l'amitié
>-spread the table,and contention will cease
>-all griefs with bread are less

tableau
>il mise sur les deux tableaux
>-he keeps a foot in both camps
>-he lays odds both ways

taille
>de toutes tailles bon lévrier
>-an inch is as good as an ell

tailler
>1-se tailler la part du lion
>-to eat high off the hog
>-the lion's share

>2-il faut tailler son manteau selon son drap
>-make not the gate wider than the city

taillis
>au fond du taillis sont les mûres
>-you don't get something for nothing
>-he that would have the fruit,must climb the tree

talon
>1-être toujours sur les talons de quelqu'un
>-to dog someone footsteps

>2-c'est son talon d'Achille
>-a chain is no stronger than its weakest link
>-the thread breaks where it is weakest

tambour
>1-tambour lointain n'a pas de son
>-out of office,out of danger
>-the danger past, and God forgotten
>-far shooting never killed birds

>2-tambour battant
>-in two shakes of a lamb's tail

taper
>1-taper sur les nerfs de quelqu'un
>-to get in one's hair
>-to get my goat

>2-taper dans le mille
>-to hit the bull's eye
>-to hit the nail on the head
>-to hit the axe on the helve

taper (suite)
    3-se faire taper sur les doigts
    -to get it in the neck

tapisserie
    faire tapisserie
    -to be a wallflower

tard
    1-il n'est jamais trop tard pour bien faire
    -it's never too late to mend
    -never too late to do well

    2-mieux vaut tard que jamais
    -better late than never
    -it is not lost that comes at last

tartine
    une tartine de sirop chez nous est parfois meilleure qu'un banquet ailleurs
    -dry bread at home is better than roast meat abroad

tartuffe
    être un tartuffe
    -to keep two faces under one hood
    -to be doubled-faced

témoin
    un seul témoin oculaire en vaut dix qui ont entendu
    -one eye-witness is better than ten ear-witness

temps
    1-il est temps d'être sérieux
    -it is time to lay our nuts aside

    2-il faut prendre le temps comme il vient,les gens pour ce qu'ils sont, l'argent pour ce qu'il vaut
    -all things in their being are good for something

    3-il est bien près du temps des cerises,le temps des cyprès
    -life is but a span

    4-après bon temps,on se repent
    -remorse is lust's dessert

    5-le temps perdu ne se rattrape jamais
    -lost time is never found again
    -you cannot put back the clock

    6-autres temps,autres moeurs
    -other times,other ways
    -other days,other ways
    -that which is now shall not abide for ever
    -time changes and we with them

6-autres temps,autres moeurs (suite)
-there is nothing permanent except change
-other times,other manners

7-le temps,c'est de l'argent
-time is money

8-le temps fait des merveilles
-time works wonders

9-le temps est le meilleur remède
-time with his balm heals all wounds
-time is a great healer

10-le temps passe
-time flies

11-qui a temps,a vie
-he that has time,has life

12-le temps est un grand maître
-use makes mastery

13-le temps dévore tout
-time devours all things
-time is a file that wears and makes no noise

14-il n'y a rien qui aille aussi vite que le temps
-life is short and time is swift
-time slips away when one is busy

15-en deux temps,trois mouvements
-I'll do it in a brace of shakes
-in two shakes of a lamb's tail

16-c'est un temps à ne pas mettre un chien dehors
-the weather is so foul,not even a Caper would venture out

17-le temps passé est toujours le meilleur
-the golden age was never the present age
-jam tomorrow and jam yesterday but never jam today
-the remembrance of past sorrow is joyful

18-le temps est comme l'argent,n'en perdez pas et vous en aurez assez
-those that make the best thing of their time,have none to spare

19-avec le temps et la paille,les nèfles mûrissent
-all things come to those who wait

20-le temps fuit sans retour
-one cannot put back the clock

21-ça n'a qu'un temps
-it is but honeymoon

temps (suite)

> **22-les temps changent et nous changeons avec eux**
> -times change and we with them
>
> **23-il y a un temps pour tout**
> -there is a time for all things

tendre

> **1-il faut toujours tendre un ver pour avoir une truite**
> -a hook's well lost to catch a salmon
>
> **2-il vaut mieux tendre la main que le cou**
> -better bend the neck than bruise the forehead
> -discretion is the better part of valour

tenir

> **1-tenir par un fil**
> -to hand on by the eyelids
>
> **2-tenir quelqu'un à distance**
> **-tenir quelqu'un à l'écart**
> -to keep someone at arm's length
> -to put someone in the picture
>
> **3-cela ne tient pas la route** (familier)
> -that won't hold water
>
> **4-un tiens vaut mieux que deux tu l'auras**
> **-il vaut mieux tenir que courir**
> -a bird in the hand is worth two in the bush
> -a pound in the purse is worth two in the book
> -possession is better than expectation
>
> **5-il faut se tenir au gros de l'arbre**
> -you must do as others do
>
> **6-il vaut mieux tenir que courir**
> -better the devil you know than the devil you don't know
>
> **7-se tenir les pouces**
> -to keep one's fingers crossed
>
> **8-se tenir les côtes**
> -to shake one's sides

tentation

> **tout est tentation à qui la craint**
> -all temptations are found in hope or fear

tenter

> **il ne faut pas tenter le diable**
> -the devil dances in an empty pocket
> -an open door may tempt a saint

terre
> qui terre a,guerre a
> de grasse terre,méchant chemin
> bonne terre,mauvais chemin
> -he that has land,has trouble at hand
> -he taht has land,has quarrels

tesson
> aux tessons,on sait ce que fut le pot
> -the carpenter is known by his chips
> -how can the foal amble if the horse and the mare trot?

tête
> 1-ce qui n'a pas de tête ne va pas;ce qui a deux têtes va moins bien encore
> -where every man is a master,the world goes to wrack
>
> 2-belle tête,peu de sens;belle bourse,peu d'argent
> -appearances are deceptive
>
> 3-mauvaise tête mais bon coeur
> -quick tempered but his heart is in the right place
> -the toad,ugly and venomenous,wears yet a precious jewel in his head
>
> 4-autant de têtes,autant d'avis
> -many men,many minds
>
> 5-être la tête de turc
> -to be the scapegoat
>
> 6-une tête bien faite est mieux qu'une tête bien pleine
> -a little and good fills the trencher
> -little things please little minds
>
> 7-il a la tête sur les épaules
> -his head is screwed on the right way
>
> 8-quand on n'a pas de tête,il faut avoir des jambes
> -who has not a heart,let him have legs
>
> 9-faire sa tête de cochon
> -to show the bull-horn
>
> 10-en petite tête gît grand sens
> -a little body often harbours a great soul
>
> 11-c'est par la tête que le poison commence à sentir
> -fish begins to stink at the head
>
> 12-grosse tête,peu de sens
> -great trees are good for nothing but shades
> -things are seldom what they seem

têter
> il tête encore sa mère
> -he's not even dry behind the ears

têtu
> **être têtu comme un âne**
> -to ride the black donkey

tiens
> **un "tiens" vaut mieux que deux "tu l'auras"**
> -a thousand probabilities do not make one truth
> -you may go farther and far worse

tierce
> **tierce fois c'est droit**
> -all things thrive at thrice
> -third time's lucky
> -there is luck in odd numbers

tirer
> **1-on a tiré un beau feu d'artifice à sa naissance**
> -what can you expect from a pig but a grunt?
>
> **2-on tirerait plutôt de l'huile d'un mur**
> -you cannot get water out of a stone
>
> **3-on tirerait plutôt un pet d'un âne mort qu'un sou de sa bourse**
> -an ass laden with gold still eats thistles
>
> **4-il ne faut pas trop tirer sur la corde**
> -to strain a rope to breaking point
>
> **5-tirer à la courte paille**
> -to draw straws
>
> **6-tirer sur les ficelles**
> -to pull the strings

titre
> **c'est un titre de gloire**
> -it's a feather in his cap

toi
> **si ce n'est toi,c'est donc ton frère**
> -if not Bran,it's Bran's brother

toile
> **à toile ourdie,Dieu envoie le fil**
> -God helps them that help themselves
> -for a web begun God sends the thread

toilette
> **une toilette de chat**
> -a lick and a promise

tombe
> **muet comme une tombe**
> **muet comme une carpe**
> -mute as a fish

212

tombe (suite)
-mute as a mackerel
-as silent as a grave
-as close as an oyster

tomber
1-tomber à l'eau
-to go by the board

2-tout ce qui tombe,arrive
-what goes around,comes around

3-c'est tombé du ciel
-it fell off the back of a lorry
-to fall on one's lap

4-laisser tomber quelqu'un
-to sweep someone under the rug

5-tomber de Charybde en Scylla
-between Scylla and Charybdis
-to be caught between the devil and the deep blue sea
-to go from bad to worse
-to jump from the frying pan into the fire
-shunning the smoke they fall into the fire

6-tout ce qui tombe dans le fossé est pour le soldat
-finders,keepers;loosers weepers
-findings is keepings

ton
c'est le ton qui fait la chanson
-the voice is the best music

tondre
1-il faut tondre ses brebis et non pas les écorcher
-a man cannot do more than he can

2-tondre un oeuf
-to skin a flint

3-on ne peut pas tondre un oeuf
-it is very hard to shave an egg

tonneau
1-c'est le tonneau des Danaïdes
-don't draw water with a sieve

2-au tonneau(pour le vin)
-drawn from the wood

3-ce sont les tonneaux vides qui font le plus de bruit
-empty vessels make the greatest sound

tonner
1-quand il tonne,le voleur devient honnête
-when it thunders,the thief becomes honest

tonner (suite)
    2-toutes les fois qu'il tonne,le tonnerre ne tombe pas
    -all clouds bring not rain

tonnerre
    1-un coup de tonnerre
    -a bolt from the blue

    2-contre le tonnerre ne pète
    -it's often better to swim with the stream

torchon
    le torchon brûle
    -they go at it hammer and tongue

torturer
    se torturer l'esprit
    -to beat one's brain out

tôt
    le plus tôt sera le mieux
    -the sooner,the better

touche
    touche-à-tout
    -to have a finger in every pie

toucher
    1-vous avez touché son point faible
    -you came on his blind side

    2-toucher du bois
    -to knock on wood

    3-ceux qui touchent la poix,se souillent les doigts
    -low company taints the mind

toupet
    avoir le toupet
    -to have the cheek

tour
    1-il a plus d'un tour dans son sac
    -he has more than one trick up his sleeve

    2-les tours les plus hautes font les plus hautes chutes
    -the higher the mountain the greater descent
    -he sits not sure that sits too high

tourner
    1-cesser de tourner et de virer
    -no more shilly-shallying
    -stop hemming and hawing

    2-tourner autour du pot
    -to beat around the bush

3-il faut tourner le moulin lorsque souffle le vent
-gather ye rosebuds while ye may
-hoist your sail when the wind is fair
-life is short and time is swift
-an ounce of good fortune is worth a pound of forecast
-to make hay while the sun shines

4-se tourner les pouces
-to twiddle one's thumbs

5-tourner côté en peine
-to turn cat-in-pan

tout
tout ou rien
-the whole tree or not a cherry on it

trahir
on n'est jamais trahi que par les siens
-may God defend me from my friends;I can defend myself from my enemies

train
prendre le train en marche
-to climb on the bandwagon

tranchant
trop tranchant ne coupe pas,trop pointu ne perce pas
-if in excess,even nectar is poison

tranquille
tranquille comme Baptiste
-as snug as the bug in a rug

travail
1-avoir du travail par dessus la tête
-to be up to the eyes in work

2-le travail est souvent le père du plaisir
-busiest men find the most leisure
-those who make the best use of their time,have none to spare
-work expands to fill the time available

3-qui fuit la meule fuit la farine
-the mill gets by going
-God gives the milk,but not the pail
-footprints on the sands of time are not made by sitting down
-the higher the plum-tree,the riper the plum the richer thecobbler,the blacker his thumb

travailler
1-travailler pour des prunes (familier)
-to sow beans in the wind
-to work for peanuts

2-travailler pour la gloire,pour le grand turc,pour le roi de Prusse
-to be a fool for one's pains

3-travailler sans se soustraire à la tâche
-to work tooth and nail

4-travailler à sa propre perte
-to cut one's throat
-don't cut off your nose to spite your face

5-tu travailles du chapeau
-you are talking through your hat

6-travailler au coude à coude
-to work shoulder to shoulder

trébucher
qui trébuche et ne tombe pas,avance son chemin
-trouble brings experience and experience brings wisdom
-experience is good if not bought too dear

treize
treize à la douzaine
-by the baker's dozen

trembler
1-trembler comme une feuille
-trembler dans sa culotte(familier)
-to shake in one's shoes

2-il ne faut jamais trembler qu'on ne voit sa tête à ses pieds
-don't cry before you are hurt

trente-six
1-il n'y a pas trente-six façons de le faire
-there are no two ways of doing it

2-le trente-six du mois
-once in a blue moon
-not until the cows come home
-before the cat can lick her ear
-when the pigs have wings
-when the moon turns blue
-when the devil is blind
-when hell freezes over
-when two Fridays come together
-till the ass ascend the ladder
-at later Lammas

trente sixième
il est dans le trente-sixième dessous
-he is in a very bad situation

tripe
>**rendre tripes et boyaux**
>-to shoot the cat

triste
>**être triste comme un bonnet de nuit**
>-to be as cheerful as a grave

tromper
>**1-se tromper est humain,persister dans son erreur est diabolique**
>-to fall into sin is human,to remain in sin is devilish
>-it is a shame to steal but worse to carry home
>
>**2-il est permis de se tromper**
>-the best of men may err at times

trompeur
>**à trompeur,trompeur et demi**
>-if you deal wit a fox,think of his tricks

trop
>**trop et trop peu n'est pas mesure**
>**il y a deux sortes de trop le trop et le trop peu**
>**-entre trop et trop peu est la juste mesure**
>-the mean is the best
>-golden mean is best
>-measure is a merry man
>-measure is treasure
>-there is measure in all things
>-moderation in all things
>-keep the golden mean
>-more than enough is too much
>-not too high for the pie,not too low for the crow
>-the truth is between the two
>-enough is as good as a feast
>-enough is enough
>-safety lies in the middle course

troquer
>**troquer son cheval borgne pour un aveugle**
>-shunning the smoke they fall into the fire
>-to jump from the frying pan into the fire

trou
>**1-autant de trous,autant de chevilles**
>-when one door shuts,another opens
>-God's in heaven;all's right with the world
>
>**2-à petit trou,petite cheville**
>-don't try to put a square peg in a round hole
>-it's no use trying to put a quart into a pint pot

trouver
>**1-il a trouvé plus fort que lui**
>-he met his match

trouver (suite)

2-on ne trouve jamais meilleur messager que soi-même
-if you want to be well served,serve yourself

3-trouver chaussure à son pied
-if the shoe fits,wear it

truie

la truie ne pense pas qu'elle est de la fange
-the ass waggeth his ears
-a man who is his own lawyer has a fool for his client

tuer

1-il a tué la poule aux oeufs d'or
tuer le veau gras
-he killed the goose that laid the golden eggs
-quey calves are dead veal

2-se tuer à le dire
-to talk until you are blue in the face

3-mieux vaut tuer le diable que le diable ne nous tue
-attack is the best method of defense

U

union
> **l'union fait la force**
> -union is strength
> -united we stand,divided we fall
> -a house divided against itself cannot stand
> -there is safety in numbers
> -many hands make light work
> -in unity there is strength

unique
> **il n'est pas unique au monde**
> -no man so good,but another may be as good as he

usage
> **1-usage rend maître**
> -use makes mastery
>
> **2-l'usage est le tyran des langues**
> -words bind men

V

vache

1-il vient un temps où les vaches ont besoin de leur queue
-the cow knows not the worth of her tail till she loses it
-all things in their being are good for something
-it is a poor dog that is not worth the whistling
-willows are weak,yet they bind other wood
-there is no tree but bears some fruit

2-une peau de vache
-a tough customer

3-connaître des périodes de vaches maigres et de vaches grasses
-to know downs and ups

4-on dirait une vache qui regarde passer un train
-to stare like a stuck pig

5-vache qui vient de loin a gros pis
-far fowls have fair feathers

vaillant

à vaillant homme,courte épée
-the weapon of the brave is in his heart

vaincre

qui se vainc une fois peut se vaincre toujours
-he gets a double victory,who conquers himself

vairon

il faut perdre un vairon pour gagner un saumon
-what you lose on the swings you gain on the roundabouts

valet

autant de valets,autant d'ennemis
-so many servants,so many enemies

valoir

1-c'est proprement ne valoir rien que de n'être utile à personne
-nothing so bad as not to be good for something
-it is more pain to do nothing than something

2-tant vaut l'homme,tant vaut la terre
-a good farmer makes a good farm

3-il vaut mieux être maître,on est valet quand on veut
-it is better to be the hammer than the anvil

4-tant vaut la chose comme elle peut être vendue
-the worth of a thing is what it will bring

5-il vaudrait mieux le tuer que le nourrir
-to eat someone out of house and home

6-il vaut mieux être cheval que charrette
-it is better to be the hammer than the anvil

7-cela ne vaut pas un sous
-no worth a rap

8-cela ne vaut pas un clou
-cela ne vaut pas un pet de lapin (familier)
-not worth a snap of the fingers

vanité
la vanité n'a pas de plus grand ennemi que la vanité
-self praise stinks

vanteur
de grands vanteurs,petits faiseurs
-the greatest talkers are the least doers

veau
1-autant meurt veau que vache
-young men may die,but old men must die

2-d'un veau on espère une boeuf et d'une poule un oeuf
-don't use a sprat to catch a mackerel

vendre
1-il vendrait père et mère
-he would steal from his own grandmother

2-ce n'est pas tout de vendre,il faut livrer
-promise is debt

3-vendre la mèche
-to spill the bean

4-il ne faut pas vendre la peau de l'ours avant de l'avoir tué
-don't sell the skin before you have caught the bear
-don't count your chicken before they are hatched
-never spend your money until you have it
-boil not the pap until the child is born
-don't spread the cloth till the pot begins to boil
-gut no fish till you get them
-to eat the calf in the coco's belly
-first catch your hare
-don't cry (or halloo) till you are out of the wood
-say no ill of the year till it be past
-set not your loaf in till your oven is hot

veneur
c'est le bon veneur qui fait la bonne meute
-a good master, a good scholar

vengeance
1-la vengeance est un plat qui se mange froid
-the mills of God grind slowly
-vengeance does not spoil with keeping
-Heaven's vengeance is slow but sure
-revenge is a dish that can be eaten cold
-revenge of a hundred year has still its sucking teeth

vengeance (suite)
    2-la vengeance est plus douce que le miel
    -revenge is sweet

venir
    1-vienne qui plante
    -come what may

    2-ce qui vient du Diable retourne au Diable
    ce qui vient de la flûte retourne au tambour
    d'où vient l'agneau,là retourne la peau
    celà va,celà vient
    ce qui vient de fric,s'en va de frac
    -ill gotten goods seldom prosper
    -what is got over the devil's back is spent under his belly
    -soon ripe,soon rotten
    -lightly come,lighty go
    -easy come,easy go
    -a fool and his money are soon parted
    -soon learnt,soon forgotten
    -soon gotten,soon spent
    -soon hot,soon cold
    -soon up,soon down

    3-ce qui vient avec le béguin,s'en retourne avec le suaire
    -life is but a long journey to death

    4-tout vient à point à qui sait attendre
    -all things come to those who wait
    -every dog has his day
    -fortune knocks once at least at every man's gate
    -the worse luck now,the better another time

    5-il vient un temps où les vaches ont besoin de leur queue
    -the cow knows not the worth of her tail till she loses it
    -keep a thing seven years and you'll always find a use for it

vent
    1-selon le vent,la voile
    -trim your sails to the wind
    -vows made in storms are forgotten in calms

    2-qui sème le vent récolte la tempête
    -he who sows the wind reaps the whirlwind

    3-le vent de prospérité change bien souvent de côté
    -what chances to one man,may happen to all men

    4-il faut que le vent soit bien mauvais pour n'être bon à personne
    -one man's meat is another man's poison

    5-voir de quel côté le vent souffle
    prendre le vent
    -to see which way the cat jumps
    -to see how the land lies
    -to see how the wind blows

6-contre vents et marées
-through thick and thin
-to the horns of the altar
-come hell or high water

7-vent au visage rend l'homme sage
-the wind in one's face makes one wise
-adversity is a good schoolmaster

8-c'est un mauvais vent
-it's an ill wind that blows no good

ventre

1-à ventre soûl,cerises amères
-wine-is a turncoat

2-ventre affamé n'a point d'oreilles
-a hungry man,an angry man
-the belly has no ears
-a hungry man will not listen to reason
-the way to man's heart is through his stomach

3-tout fait ventre
-hungry dogs will eat dirty pudding

4-ventre plein donne de l'assurance
-a merry man makes a cheerful countenance
-plenty breeds pride

vêpres

après vêpres,complies
-there is a time and a place for everything
-a time for everything and everything in its proper place

vérité

1-il n'y a pas de prescrption contre la vérité les erreurs pour être vieilles n'en sont pas meilleures
-wrong never comes right

2-la vérité comme l'huile vient au dessus
-truth and oil are ever above
-truth is time's daughter
-time is the father of truth
-it will all come out in the wash
-nothing comes sooner to light than that has been long hid

3-la vérité est cachée au fond du puits
-truth lies at the bottom of the well

4-à dire vérités et mensonges,les vérités seront les dernières crues
-a liar is not believed when he speaks the truth

5-je lui ai dit ses quatre vérités
-I told him off straight to his face
-I talk to him like a Dutch uncle

vérité (suite)
6-toute vérité n'est pas bonne à dire
-many a true word is spoken in jest
-some truths are better left unsaid
-all truths are not to be told
-better a lie that heals that a truth that wounds

7-il n'y a que la vérité qui blesse
-nothing hurts like the truth
-the greater the truth,the greater the libel
-the sharper the point,the better the needle
-the sting of a reproach is the truth of it

8-la vérité est un fruit qui ne doit être cueilli que s'il est tout à fait mûr
-what is new is not true and what is true is not new

9-la vérité sort de la bouche des enfants
-children and fools tell the truth

10-à vouloir connaître la vérité à tout prix,on risque de se bruler soi-même
-truth and roses have thorns about them

vertu
la vertu est sa propre récompense
la vertu a cela d'heureux qu'elle se suffit à elle-même
-virtue is its own reward

vessie
prendre des vessies pour des lanternes
-to believe that the moon is made of green cheese

veste
1-ramasser une veste
-to take a licking

2-tourner sa veste
-turning one's coat for luck

viande
1-c'est viande mal prête que lièvre en buisson
-it's ill prizing of green barley

2-il n'y a pas de viande sans os
-no land without stones,or meat without bones

vide
vides chambres font dames folles
-a house well-furnished makes a woman wise

vider
je lui ai vider mon sac
-I talk to him like a Ditch uncle

vie
1-tant qu'il y a de la vie,il y a de l'espoir
-while there is life there is hope

-nothing so bad but might have been worse
-in the land of hope,there is never any winter
-the bees suck honey out of the bitterest flowers

2-la vie est courte,l'art est long
-art is long,life is short

3-la vie est un songe
-life is but a span

4-il faut apprendre de la vie à souffrir la vie
la vie est un panier de rats
la vie n'est pas toujours facile
-life is not beer and skittles
-life is not all cakes and ale
-the life of man is a winter's day and a winter's way

5-il est entre la vie et la mort
-he is hovering between heaven and earth

6-de telle vie,telle fin
-as we live,so shall we end
-as a tree falls,so shall it lie
-a good life makes a good death
-they die well that live well
-an ill life,an ill end
-he dies like a beast who has done no good while he lived
-such a life,such a death
-he that live wickedly can hardly die honestly
-he that does evil,never was good

7-vie de cochon,courte et bonne
-he that lives most,dies most
-the more light a torch gives,the shorter it lasts

vieillesse
la vieillesse nous attache plus de rides en l'esprit qu'au visage
-men's years and their faults are always more than they are willing to own

vieillir
1-l'on ne s'amende pas de vieillir
-old age does not protect from folly

2-il faut viellir ou mourir jeune
-old be,or young die
-if you would not live to be old,you must be hanged when you are young

vieux
c'est vieux comme Erode
-Queen Ann is dead

2-le vieux n'y voit pas assez pour marteler la faux et le jeune ne sait pas l'affiler
-young folks think old folks to be fools but old folks know young folks to be fools

vieux (suite)
    3-c'est un vieux de la vieille
    -he is from the old guard

vin
    1-vin versé n'est pas avalé
    -sorrow is soon enough when it comes

    2-bon vin,mauvaise tête
    le vin entre et la raison sort
    -a drunken man is a mad man
    -wine is a turncoat
    -what soberness conceals,drunkenness reveals

    3-chaque vin a sa lie
    -there are lees to every wine
    -every path has its puddle
    -there is a black sheep in every flock

    4-toujours le vin sent son terroir
    -the frog cannot out of her bog
    -a kindly aver will never make a good horse
    -of an evil crow,an evil egg
    -no good apple in a sour stock
    -of evil grain,no good seed can come
    -what can you expect of a pig but a grunt?

    5-le vin est le lait des viellards
    -wine is old men's milk

    6-quand le vin est tiré,il faut le boire
    -in for a penny,in for a pound
    -when the wine is drawn,one has to drink it
    -as well be hanged for a sheep as for a lamb
    -as you brew so you shall bake
    -over shoes,over boots
    -he who rides a tiger is afraid to dismount
    -if you have swallowed the devil,you may swallow his horns

    7-on ne connaît pas le vin au cercle
    -you cannot know the wine by the barrel

    8-de bon vin,bon vinaigre
    -from the sweetest wine,the tartest vinegar

    9-à bon vin point d'enseigne
    -good wine needs no bush

    10-au vin qui se vend bien,ne faut point de lierre
    -quality speaks for itself

    11-un bon verre de vin enlève l'écu au médecin
    -after supper walk a mile

12-in vino veritas
-la vérité est dans le vin
-there is truth in wine
-what soberness conceals,drunkenness reveals

13-vin au tonneau
-wine drawn from the wood

violence
les oeuvres de la violence ne sont pas durables
-nothing that is violent is permanet
-the sharper the storm,the sooner it's over
-all that is sharp,is short

violon
envoyer au violon (familier)
-to send up the river

virage
prendre un virage sur les chapeaux de roues
-to screech round the corner

vis
serrer la vis à quelqu'un
-to sit on somebody

visage
un beau visage est le plus beau de tous les spectacles
-beauty is eloquent even when silent

vivre
1-quand on n'a pas su vivre,on doit encore moins savoir mourir
-a good life makes a good death
-he that live wickedly can hardly die honestly

2-pour vivre heureux,vivons cachés
-he that talk much of his happiness summons grief

3-qui vit à compte,vit à honte
-neither a borrower nor a lender be

4-il fait bon vivre et ne rien savoir
-what you don't know can't hurt you
-ignorance is the peace if life

5-qui vivra verra
-time will tell
-live and learn

6-vivre au jour le jour
-to live from hand to mouth
-to lie at arck and manger

7-qui veut vivre à Rome ne doit pas se quereller avec le Pape
-it is ill sitting at Rome and striving against the Pope

8-vivre d'amour et d'eau fraîche
-to live on a shoestring

227

9-vivre sur un grand pied
-to live high off the hog
-to live like fighting cocks

10-vivre sur la corde raide
-to live on knife's edge

11-vivre comme un oiseau sur la branche
vivre au jour le jour
-to lie at rack and manger

12-vivre au crochet de quelqu'un
-to sponge on someone

13-qui vit en espérance danse sans tambourin
-who that lives in hope dances to an ill tune
-in the land of hope,there is never any winter
-the bees suck honey out of the bitterest flowers

voie

1-mieux vaut la vieille voie que le nouveau sentier
-when a new book appears,read an old one

2-les voies du seigneur sont impénétrables
-God works in mysterious ways

3-être sur la bonne voie
-to be on the right track

voir

1-qui voit ses veines,voit ses peines
-grey hairs are death's blossoms

2-ne pas voir plus loin que le bout de son nez
-to follow one's nose
-to see an inch before his nose

3-cela se voit comme le nez au milieu de la figure
-it's as plain as the nose on your face
-if it were a bear it would bite you

4-voir les choses en noir
-to look through blue glasses

5-voir tout en rose
-all his geese are swans

6-il voit la paille dans l'oeil du voisin mais pas la paille dans le sien
-he can't see the beam he has in his own eye

7-chacun voit avec ses lunettes
-so many men,so many opinions

8-il n'est pour voir que l'oeil du maître
-the eye of the master will do more work than both his hands
-one eye of the master sees more than ten of the servants

9-voir du même oeil que quelqu'un
-to see eye to eye with someone

10-chacun voit midi à sa pendule
-every man buckles his belt his ain gate

11-voir de quel côté le vent souffle
-to see which way the cat jumps
-to see how the wind blows
-prendre le vent

12-voir trente-six chandelles
-to see stars

voisin

1-qui a bon voisin a bon matin
-a good neighbour,a good morrow

2-il n'est voisin qui ne voisine
-no one is rich enough to do without his neighbours
-we can live without our friends,but not without our neighbours

voix

1-la voix du peuple est la voix de Dieu
-it must be truth what all man say

2-c'est la voix du sang qui parle
-blood is thicker than water

vol

à vol d'oiseau
-as the crow flies

volée

toute la haute volée était venue
-everyone who was anyone was there

voler

1-qui vole un oeuf vole un boeuf
-he that steal an egg,will steal an ox
-he that steal a pin,will steal a pound
-he that steal a pin,will steal a better thing
-sin plucks on sin
-he that has done ill once,will do it again

2-voler dans les plumes de quelqu'un (familier)
-to fly in one's face
-to make the feathers fly

3-volez de vos propres ailes
-paddle your own canoe

voleur

les grands voleurs pendent les petits
-little thieves are hanged,but great ones escape
-great fish eat up the small

volonté

à bonne volonté ne vaut faculté
-you can't make an omelet without breaking eggs
-he who would catch the fish mustn't mind getting wet

vouloir

1-faire ce que l'on veut de quelqu'un
-to twist someone around one's little finger

2-veux-tu des oeufs,souffre le caquetage des poules
-he that would have the fruit,must climb the tree
-he that would have eggs must endure the cackling of hens
-you don't get something for nothing

3-si tu veux la paix,prépare la guerre
-hope for the best and prepare the worst

4-qui veut mal,mal lui vient
-he that mischief hatches,mischeif catches

5-vouloir c'est pouvoir
quand on veut,on peut
-where there is a will,there is a way
-a wilful man will have his way
-when your will is ready,your feet are light

6-il ne voulait pas en démordre
-he wouldn't budge an inch

7-il ne voulait pas qu'on entrave sa liberté
-he didn't want anyone to fence him in

8-qui veut la fin,veut les moyens
-he who will the end,will the means

voyage

les voyages forment la jeunesse
-he that travel far knows much
-travel broaders the mind

voyager

qui veut voyager loin,ménage sa monture
-fair and softly goes far in the day
-don't ride your horse to death
-the best horse needs breaking and the aptest child training

vrai

le vrai peut quelquefois n'être pas vraisemblable
-truth is stranger than fiction

Y

yeux

1-avoir des yeux de lynx
-to have eyes like a hawk

2-avoir les yeux plus gros que le ventre
-he bite off more than he could chew
-eyes are bigger than the belly
-make not the gate wider than the city

3-quatre yeux voient mieux que deux
-four eyes see more than two

4-loin des yeux loin du coeur
-out of sight out of mind
-far from eye far from heart
-far from eye,far from mind
-seldom seen,soon forgotten
-a prophet is not without honor,save in his own country,and in his own house
-absence diminishes little passions and increases great ones
-salt water and absence wash away love
-unminded,unmoaned
-unseen,unrued
-long absent,soon forgotten
-far from court,far from care
-absence is the mother of desillusion
-the absent saint gets one candle
-long absence changes a friend
-out of sight,out of languor
-seldom seen,seldom heard

5-loin des yeux,près du coeur
-absence makes the heart grow fonder
-far folk far best
-they are aye good that are away
-blue are the hills that are far away
-distance leads enchantment to the view
-friends agree best at distance
-separation secures manifest friendship
-the best of a thing is best known by the want of it
-the soul is not where it lives,but where it loves
-though lost to sight,to memory dear
-men are best loved furthest off

6-coûter les yeux de la tête
-to cost a mint
-to pay through the nose

7-cela saute aux yeux
-it's as plain as the nose on your face
-if it were a bear it would bite you

---

yeux (suite)
    8-les yeux sont le miroir de l'âme
    -the eye is the window of the heart(mind)
    -in the forehead and the eye,the lecture of the mind doth lie

    9-tel a de beaux qui ne voit goutte
    -the peacock has fair feathers but foul feet
    -things are seldom what they seem

    10-ce que les yeux ne voient pas ne fait pas mal au coeur
    -what the eye doesn't see,the heart doesn't grieve over
    -where ignorance is bliss,'tis folly to be wise
    -the light is naught for sore eye
    -much science,much sorrow
    -what you don't know can't hurt you
    -he that never ate flesh,thinks a pudding a dainty
    -acorns were good till bread was found

Z

zouave
> **faire le zouave**
> -to fool about

DEUXIEME PARTIE

ANGLAIS
FRANÇAIS

PART TWO

ENGLISH
FRENCH

A

abandon
> **never abandon oneself to despair**
> -à se cogner la tête contre les murs,il ne vient que des bosses

abide
> **1-he that cannot abide a bad market,deserves not a good one**
> -n'est pas marchand qui toujours gagne

> **2-we must abide better times**
> -après la pluie,le beau temps

absence
> **1-absence is the mother of desillusion**
> **-long absence changes a friend**
> **-absence diminishes little passions and increases great ones**
> -loin des yeux,loin du coeur

> **2-absence makes the heart grow fonder**
> -loin des yeux,près du coeur

absent
> **1-the absent are always wrong**
> **the absent party is always to blame**
> **never were the absent in the right**
> -les absents ont toujours tort

> **2-the absent are never without fault nor the present without excuse**
> -absent n'est point sans coulpe ni présent sans excuse

> **3-long absent,soon forgotten**
> **-the absent saint gets one candle**
> -loin des yeux,loin du coeur

> **4-the absent saint gets no candle**
> -les os sont pour les absents

abundance
> **abundance of things engenders disdainfulness**
> -on ne jette de pierres qu'à l'arbre chargé de fruits

accord
> **there is no good accord where every man would be a lord**
> -c'est raison que chacun soit maître en son logis

account
> **1-that accounts for the milk in the cocoa-nut**
> -et voilà pourquoi votre fille est muette

> **2-of small account is a fly till it gets into the eye**
> -quand le puits est à sec,on sait ce que vaut l'eau

accounting
> **there is no accounting for tastes**
> -des goûts et des couleurs, on ne discute pas
> -à chacun son goût
> -à chaque fou sa marotte

accuse
> **accused to give aid and comfort to the enemy**
> -accusé d'intelligence avec l'ennemi

ace
> **he kept an ace up his sleeve**
> -il a gardé un atout en réserve
> -il a plus d'un tour dans son sac

acorn
> **acorns were good till bread was found**
> -ce que les yeux ne voient pas ne fait pas mal au coeur

acre
> **one acre of performance is worth twenty of the land of promise**
> -mieux vaut donner sans promettre que promettre sans tenir

acquaintance
> **short acquaintance brings repentance**
> -qui se marie à le hâte,se repent à loisir

act
> **he acts like a Monday evening quarterback**
> -il arrive comme les carabiniers

action
> **1-action speaks louder than words**
> -ce ne sont pas les mots qui comptent mais les actions
> -à beau parler qui n'a cure de bien faire
>
> **2-our own actions are our security,not others judgments**
> -une bonne action ne reste jamais sans récompense

Adam
> **1-Adam's ale is the best brewer**
> -les buveurs d'eau sont méchants
>
> **2-we are all Adam's children**
> -Dieu nous a tous pétris du même limon

add
> **1-to add insult to injury**
> -aggraver son cas
>
> **2-to add fuel to the fire**
> -mettre de l'huile sur le feu

ado
> **much ado about nothing**
> -beaucoup de bruit pour rien12/08/19970

adversity
> **1-adversity comes with instruction in its hand**
> -experience est mère de science
>
> **2-adversity makes men;prosperity monsters**
> -l'homme donne sa mesure dans l'adversité

3-adversity is a good schoolmaster
-vent au visage rend l'homme sage
-l'adversité rend sage

4-adversity makes strange bedfellows
-l'aigle quand il est malheureux,appelle le hibou son frère
-il vaut mieux péter en compagnie que crever seul

5-adversity is the touchstone of virtue
-l'adversité est l'épreuve du courage

6-adversity makes a man wise ,not rich
-l'adversité rend sage

advice
1-good advice is beyond price
-un bon avis vaut un oeil dans la main

2-nothing is given so freely as advice
-on ne donne rien si libéralement que des conseils

3-if you wish good advice,consult an old man
-en conseil écoute le vieil

4-advice comes cheap
-les conseilleurs ne sont pas les payeurs

advise
advise with your pillow
-la nuit porte conseille

affection
affection blinds reason
-le coeur a ses raisons que la raison ignore

afraid
1-he that is afraid of the wagging of feathers must keep from among wild fowl
he that is afraid of wounds,must not come nigh a battle
-qui craint le danger ne doit pas aller en mer

2-to be afraid of one's shadow
-avoir peur de son ombre

age
1-for ages
-de longue main

2-old age doesn't protect from folly
-l'on ne s'amende pas de vieillir

agree
1-if you agree to carry the calf,they'll make you carry the cow
-accordez-lui long comme un doigt,il en prendra long comme un bras

2-to agree like the fiddle and the stick
-to agree like the fiddle and the stick
-être comme deux frères
-être comme les deux doigts de la main

agues

-**agues come on horseback but go away on foot**
-les maladies viennent à cheval et s'en retournent à pied

alike

they are as alike as peas in a pod
-ils se ressemblent comme deux gouttes d'eau

all

1-all's well that ends well
-tout est bien qui finit bien

2-it takes all sorts to make a world
-il faut de tout pour faire un monde

3-all things come to those who wait
-tout vient à point à qui sait attendre

4-all is over but the shouting
les carottes sont cuites (*familier*)

5-all's for the best in the best of all possible worlds
-tout est pour le mieux dans le meilleur des mondes

allowance

1-you must make allowance for youth
-il faut que jeunesse se passe

2-you must make allowance for things
-il faut faire la part des choses

alone

better be alone than in bad company
-mieux vaut être seul que mal accompagné

amend

some do amend when they cannot go worse
-méchant poulain peut devenir bon cheval

anatomy

he was like an anatomy
-c'était un cadavre ambulant

anchor

this is my sheet anchor
-c'est ma bouée de sauvetage

anger

1-anger is the short madness
-la colère est une courte folie

2-anger punishes itself
-la raison qui s'emporte a le sort de l'erreur

3-anger and haste hinder good counsel
-colère n'a conseil

angry

1-two things a man should never be angry at what he can help,and what he cannot help
-il ne sert à rien de montrer les dents lorsqu'on est édenté

2-when angry,count a hundred
-qui ferme la bouche,ne montre pas les dents
-quand on est en colère il ne faut rien dire ni rien faire avant d'avoir récité l'alphabet
-rien ne gagne à un retardement si ce n'est la colère

3-when a man grows angry,his reason rides out
-la raison qui s'emporte a le sort de l'erreur
-agir dans la colère,c'est s'embarquer dans la tempête

4-if he be angry,he knows how to turn his girdle
-il sait se tenir sur ses gardes

answer

1-never answer a question until it is asked
-ne donne pas de conseil à moins qu'on ne t'en prie

2-answer a fool according to his folly
-rendre la monnaie de sa pièce

3-a soft answer turns away wrath
-plus fait douceur que violence

4-no answer is also an answer
-qui ne dit mot consent

ant

the ant had wings to her hurt
-quand les ailes poussent à la fourmi,c'est pour sa perte

anvil

1-a good anvil does not fear the hammer
-bon sang ne peut mentir

2-when you are an anvil,hold you still,when you are a hammer,strike your fill
-mieux vaut être marteau qu'enclume

anything

anything for a change
-tout nouveau,tout beau

ape

an ape is an ape,a varlet is a varlet though they be clad in silk or scarlet
-un singe vêtu de pourpre est toujours un singe
-mors doré ne rend pas le cheval meilleur

appearance

appearances are deceptive
-belle tête peu de sens,belle bourse,peu d'argent
-l'air ne fait pas la chanson
-joli dessus,vilaine doublure
-belle montre et peu de rapport

appearances are deceptive (suite)
-les grands boeufs ne font pas les grands labours
-beau boucaut,mauvaise morue
-être et paraître sont deux

appetite
1-good appetite needs no sauce
-il n'est sauce que d'appétit
-à qui a faim tout est pain

2-appetite comes with eating
the appetite grows with what it feeds on
-l'appétit vient en mangeant

apple
1-a rotten apple injures its neighbours
-il suffit d'une pomme pourrie pour gâter tout le tas

2-no good apple in a sour stock
-toujours le vin sent son terroir

3-she is the apple of her father's eye
-the apple never falls far from the tree
-tel père,tel fils
-la pomme ne tombe jamais loin de l'arbre

4-it's apple pie
-c'est facile comme bonjour

5-the apples on the other side of the wall are the sweetest
-l'herbe est toujours plus verte dans le pré du voisin

6-she is the apple of my eye
-j'y tiens comme à la prunelle de mes yeux

applecart
he upset the applecart
-il a tout gâché

April
an April fool's joke
-un poisson d'avril

arm
1-to keep at arm's length
-tenir quelqu'un à distance

2-stretch your arm no further than your sleeve will reach
-n'étend les jambes qu'à la longueur du tapis
-ne forcez pas votre talent
-il ne faut pas être plus royaliste que le roi

arrangement
to come to an arrangement is better than to going law
-un mauvais arrangement vaut mieux qu'un bon procès
-il y a moins de mal à perdre sa vigne qu'à la plaider
-gagne assez qui sort de procès

arrow

an arrow shot upright falls on the shooter's head
-quand on crache en l'air,cela vous retombe sur le nez

art

art is long,life is short
-la vie est courte,l'art est long

artist

an artist lives everywhere
-l'artisan vit partout

ash

ashes to ashes,dust to dust
-et poussière,tu retourneras en poussière

ask

1-ask and it shall be given to you
-demandez et l'on vous donnera

2-he that asks faintly begs a denial
-qui demande timidement enseigne à refuser

3-ask much to have a little
le commerce est l'école de la tromperie

4-to ask pear from an elm tree
-l'ormeau ne peut donner des poires
-la plus belle fille du monde ne peut donner que ce qu'elle a

5-never ask pardon before you are accused
-il ne faut pas pleurer avant d'être battu

6-ask a silly queton and you'll get a silly answer
-à question abstruse,abstruse réponse

ass

1-whenever an ass falls,there will he never fall again
-chat échaudé craint l'eau froide
-expérience est mère de science

2-if an ass goes a travelling,he'll not come home a horse
-qui bête va à Rome,tel en retourne

3-an ass is but an ass,though laden with gold
-l'argent ne fait pas le sage

4-the ass that brays most eats least
-plus on se découvre,plus on a froid
-c'est trop parler qui a fait que le crabe n'a pas de tête

5-an ass with two panniers
-faire le panier à deux anses

6-till the ass ascend the ladder
-renvoyer aux calendes grecques
-le trente-six du mois

7-the ass laden with gold still eats thistles
-on tirerait plutôt un pet d'un âne mort qu'un sou de sa bourse

8-an ass laden with gold climbs to the top of the castle
-la clé d'or ouvre toutes les portes

9-asses as well as pitchers have ears
-les murs ont des oreilles

10-every ass likes to hear himself bray
-tout flatteur vit aux dépens de celui qui l'écoute

11-an ass with two panniers
-faire le panier à deux anses

12-the ass waggeth his ears
-les sages ont la bouche dans le coeur et les fous le coeur dans la bouche
-la truie ne pense pas qu'elle est de la fange

assurance
 to make assurance doubly sure
 -porter la ceinture et les bretelles

atheist
 some are atheists only in fair wheather
 -quand le diable devient vieux,il se fait ermite

attack
 attack is the best method of defense
 -mieux vaut tuer le diable que le diable ne nous tue

aver
 a kindly aver will never make a good horse
 -on ne peut faire d'une buse un épervier

avoid
 avoid a questionnner,for he is also a tattler
 -les poules qui gloussent le plus fort ne sont pas les meilleures pondeuses

ax
 to have an ax to grind
 -prêcher pour son saint

axe
 to send the axe after the helve
 -jeter le manche après la cognée

B

babble
> **much babbling is not without offense**
> -moins on parle,mieux cela vaut
> -trop parler nuit

baby
> **don't throw the baby out with the bath**
> -ne maniez pas le pavé de l'ours
> -ne faites pas de mal par excès de zèle
> -il ne faut pas jeter le bébé avec l'eau du bain

bachelor
> **bachelors'wives and maids'children are well taught**
> -médecin,guéris-toi toi-même

back
> **1-at the back of beyond**
> -au diable vauvert
>
> **2-to be a back number**
> -être rétro
>
> **3-back and edge**
> -entièrement,pied à pied
>
> **4-to have someone with his back to the wall**
> **to back someone into a corner**
> -mettre quelqu'un au pied du mur

backward
> **he is not backward in coming forward**
> -eau qui court ne porte point d'ordures
> -qui n'avance pas recule

backwards
> **1-he always does everything backwards**
> -il est comme le chien de Jean de Nivelle il s'en va quand on l'appelle
>
> **2-to know something backwards and forwards**
> -connaître quelque chose dans tous les coins
> -connaître quelque chose sur le bout des doigts

bad
> **1-that doesn't taste half bad**
> -cela se laisse manger
>
> **2-nothing so bad as not to be good for something**
> -c'est proprement ne valoir rien que de n'être utile à personne
>
> **3-where bad's the best,bad must be choice**
> -autant vaut être mordu d'un chien que d'une chienne
> -entre deux maux,il faut choisir le moindre
>
> **4-nothing so bad but might have been worse**
> -cela aurait pu être pire
> -tant qu'il y a de la vie,il y a de l'espoir

5-we must take the bad with the good
-nulle rose sans épines

bait

the bait hides the hook
-en une belle gaine d'or,couteau de plomb gît et dort
-on caresse la vache pour mieux la traire
-qui veut faire l'ange,fait la bête
-on chatouille la truite pour mieux la prendre
-prêcher le faux pour savoir le vrai

baker

by the baker's dozen
-treize à la douzaine

bale

when bale is highest boot is nighest
-après la pluie,le beau temps

ball

1-to take the ball before the bound
-prendre la balle au rebond

2-if the ball does not stick to the wall,it will at least leave a mark
-si on met la main à la pâte,il en reste toujours aux doigts

bandy

I'm not going to bandy words with you
-je ne veux pas avoir maille à partir avec vous

bargain

1-at a good bargain,think twice
-que l'acheteur prenne garde

2-a good bargain is a pick-purse
-bon marché fait argent débourser

bark

1-barking dogs seldom bite
-chien qui aboie ne mord pas

2-his bark is worse than his bite
-il fait plus de bruit que de mal

3-to bark up the wrong tree
-frapper à la mauvaise porte

barrel

a herring barrel always smell of fish
-la caque sent toujours le hareng
-le mortier sent toujours l'ail
-on ne peut rester longtemps dans la boutique d'un parfumeur sans en emporter l'odeur
-qui se frotte à l'ail ne peut sentir la giroflée

basket

to be left in the basket
-être laissé pour compte

246

bat
>**to have bats in the belfry**
>-avoir des araignées dans le plafond

batten
>**to batten down the hatches**
>-parer au grain

be
>**1-to be on a sticky wicket**
>-être en position difficile
>
>**2-one cannot be in two places at once**
>-on ne peut être à la fois au four et au moulin
>-on ne peut sonner les cloches et être à la procession
>-on ne peut souffler et humer ensemble
>-le chien a quatre pattes mais il n'est pas capable de prendre quatre chemins
>
>**3-to be way out in left field**
>-se fourrer le doigt dans l'oeil jusqu'au coude (familier)
>
>**4-better be out of the world than out of the fashion**
>-il faut hurler avec les loups
>
>**5-to be at one's beck and call**
>-obéir au doigt et à l'oeil
>
>**6-to be in somebody's good graces**
>-être dans les bonnes graces de quelqu'un
>-être en odeur de sainteté
>
>**7-to be in somebody's good books**
>être dans les petits papiers de quelqu'un
>
>**8-to be off to a good start**
>-mettre un pied à l'étrier
>
>**9-to be in somebody's shoes**
>être à la place de quelqu'un
>
>**10-to be out of the woods**
>-être sorti de l'auberge
>
>**11-to be up to the eyes in work**
>-avoir du travail par dessus la tête
>
>**12-to be on the right track**
>-être sur la bonne voie

beam
>**1-to be on the beam**
>-être sur les rails
>
>**2-to be off the beam**
>-se fourrer le doigt dans l'oeil jusqu'au coude (familier)
>
>**3-to be on one's beam ends**
>-être poussé à bout

247

4-he can't see the beam he has in his own eye
-il voit la paille dans l'oeil du voisin mais pas la paille dans le sien
-oeil un autre oeil voit mais pas le sien

bean

1-beans are in flower
-les oies sont perchées

2-he has found the bean in the cake
-il a gagné le gros lot

3-I'll give him beans
-s'il me donne des pois,je lui donnerai des fèves

4-to spill the bean
-cracher le morceau
-vendre la mèche

5-every bean has its black
-chaque médaille a son revers
-chaque grain a sa paille

bear

1-a bear sucking his paws
-il a un poil dans la main

2-if it were a bear,it would bite you
-cela te crève les yeux
-cela saute aux yeux
-cela se voit comme le nez au milieu de la figure

3-the bear wants a tail and cannot be a lion
-la grenouille veut se faire aussi grosse que le boeuf

4-he bears misery best that hides it most
-à oeil malade,la lumière nuit

5-bear with evil and expect good
-il n'y a que la foi qui sauve

6-everyone must bear his own cross
-à chacun sa croix

7-it is not the bear that makes the philosopher
-en la grande barbe ne gît pas le savoir

8-to bear the bell
-porter le flambeau

9-the bear and the tea kettle
-la raison qui s'emporte a le sort de l'erreur

beard

1-to make one's beard
-avoir quelqu'un à sa merci

2-to beard the lion in his den
-affronter le fauve dans son antre
-se jeter dans la gueule du loup

3-it's not the beard that makes the philosopher
-en la grande barbe ne gît pas le savoir

4-if the beard were all, the goat might preach
-la barbe ne fait pas l'homme

5-a beard well lathered is half shaved
-mâtines sonnées sont à demi chantées

beat

1-to beat one's brain out
-se casser la tête
-se presser le citron (*familier*)
-se torturer l'esprit

2-not in my beat
-pas dans mes cordes

3-to beat the daylights out
to beat someone black and blue
-battre à plates coutures

4-to beat around the bush
-tourner autour du pot

5-not to beat around the bush
-ne pas y aller par quatre chemins

6-he that cannot beat the ass, beat the saddle
-mauvais chien ne trouve où mordre

7-the beaten road is the safest
-il faut hurler avec les loups

beauty

1-beauty is but a blossom
beauty fades like a flower
-la beauté est une fleur éphémère

2-beauty is eloquent even whe silent
-un beau visage est le plus beau de tous les spectacles

3-beauty and folly go often in company
-il est rare de voir la sagesse alliée à la beauté

4-beauty is only skin deep
-beauté n'est qu'image fardée
-il n'est si beau soulier qui ne devienne savate
-le plus beau papillon n'est qu'une chenille habillée
-serviette damassée devient torchon de cuisine

5-beauty is in the eye of the beholder
-ce qu'on aime est toujours beau
-qui crapaud aime lunette lui ressemble

6-beauty without bounty avails nought
-beauté ne vaut rien sans bonté

7-beauty won't make the pot boil
-la beauté ne sale pas la marmite
-beauté n'est qu'image fardée
-il n'est si belle rose qui ne devienne gratte-cul

bed

you got out of bed the wrong way,onthe wrong side,with the left leg foremost
-tu t'es levé du pied gauche

bee

1-bees that have honey in their mouths have stings in their tales
-en une belle gaine d'or,couteau de plomb gît et dort
-miel sur la bouche,fiel dans le coeur
-serpent qui change de peau est toujours serpent

2-to have bee in your bonnet
to have your head full of bees
-avoir des araignées dans le plafond

3-the bees suck honey out of the bitterest flowers
-qui vit en espérance danse en tambourin
-tant qu'il y a de la vie,il y a de l'espoir

4-when bees are old,they yield no honey
-lunettes et cheveux gris sont quittance d'amour

5-no bees,no honey
-qui sème,récolte

beer

life is not all beer and skittles
-la vie n'est pas toujours facile

before

before you can say Jack Robinson
-en moins de deux
-en un tour de main

beggar

1-a beggar may sing before a pickpocket
-pélerin qui chante,larron épouvante

2-beggars shouldn't be choosers
-ne choisit pas qui emprunte

3-set a beggar on horseback and he will ride to the devil
-graissez les bottes d'un vilain,il dira qu'on les lui brûle
-donnez le pied à un nègre,il prend la main

4-beggar's bag is bottomless
-l'avare crierait famine sur un tas de blé
-les avares font nécessité de tout
-un avare est toujours gueux

begin

1-better never to begin than never to make an end
-celui qui commence et ne parfait sa peine perd

2-good to begin well,better to end well
-le sillon n'est pas le champ
-couteau qui ne fait pas le tour du trou n'emporte pas le chou

3-he who begins many things finishes but few
-il ne faut pas courir deux lièvres à la fois

beginner
beginner's luck
-aux innocents les mains pleines cf innocent

beginning
1-a good beginnng makes a good ending
-such beginning,such end
-qui bien engrène,bien finit
-le bon commencement attrait la bonne fin
-mâtines bien sonnées sont à demi chantées

2-everything must have a beginning
-il faut commencer par le commencement
-il faut un commencement à tout

3-an ill beginning,an ill ending
-à mal enfourner ,on fait les pains cornus

4-every beginning is hard
-c'est le premier pas qui coûte

begun
well begun is half done
-chose bien commencée est à demi achevée

belief
belief is better than investigation
-j'aime mieux le croire que d'y aller voir

believe
1-we soon believe what we desire
-chacun croit aisément ce qu'il craint et ce qu'il désire

2-believe nothing of what you hear,and only half of what you see
-je ne crois que ce que je vois

3-it is believed on all hands
-c'est connu comme le loup blanc

4-to believe that the moon is made of green cheese
-prendre des vessies pour des lanternes

bell
1-who is to bell the cat?
-qui va en prendre le risque?

2-to bear the bell
-porter le flambeau

3-that rings a bell
-cela me rappelle quelque chose

belly

1-the belly has no ears
-ventre affamé n'a pas d'oreille

2-the belly is the truest clock
-avoir une pendule dans le ventre

3-never a fully belly neither fights nor flies well
-jamais la cornemuse ne dit mot si elle a le ventre plein

4-an empty belly bears nobody
-la faim est mauvaise conseillère

belong

more belongs to marriage than four bare legs in a bed
-misère et pauvreté font mauvais ménage
-qui se marie par amour,a de bonnes nuits et de mauvais jours

bend

to go round the bend,to be driven round the bend
-rendu fou

2-better bend the neck than bruise the forehead
-mieux vaut ployer que rompre
-il vaut mieux tendre la main que le cou
-il vaut mieux se dédire que se détruire
3-to bend one's ear
-tenir la jambe

best

1-the best things come in small packages
-dans les petites boîtes,les bons onguents

2-all's for the best in the best of all possible worlds
-tout est pour le mieux dans le meilleur des mondes

3-the very best
-la crème des crèmes

4-best is best cheap
best is cheapest
-le meilleur est toujours le moins cher

5-the best of men may err at times
-il est permis de se tromper

6-as best as one can
-remuer ciel et terre

7-the best of a thing is best known by the want of it
-loin des yeux,près du coeur

bet

-to bet one's bottom dollar
-jouer quelque chose sur un coup de dés

better

1-better be sure than sorry
-il vaut mieux aller au moulin qu'au médecin

2-better be envied than pitied
-mieux vaut faire envie que pitié

3-it is better to be a has been than a never was
-le succès fut toujours un enfant de l'audace

4-better a louse in the pot than no flesh at all
-better are small fish than an empty dish
-better some of the pudding than none of the pie
-better a lean jade than an empty halter
-better a bare foot than none
-better eye sore than be blind altogether
-it is better to sup with a cutty than with a spoon
-better a mouse in the pot than no flesh at all
-better my hog dirty than no hog at all
-better a little loss than a long sorrow
-faute de grives on se contente de merles
-quand on n'a pas ce que l'on aime,il faut vouloir ce que l'on a

5-better hazard once than be always in fear
-better to light one candle than to curse the darkness
-better a little lost than a long sorrow
-better eye out than always ache
-better a finger off than always aching
-better cut the shoe that pinch the foot
-quand on n'a rien à perdre,on peut bien tout risquer
-qui trop regarde quel vent vente,jaùais ne sème ni ne plante
-quand on n'a pas ce que l'on aime,il faut vouloir ce que l'on a
-il faut perdre un vairon pour gagner un saumon

6-better untaught than ill taught
-si tu donnes un poisson à un enfant,c'est bien;si tu lui apprends à pécher,c'est mieux

7-it is better to do well than to say well
-le beau dire ne dispense pas du bien faire
-mieux vaut donner sans promettre que promettre sans tenir

8-to think better of the matter
-y regarder de plus près

9-to be better than one's word
-faire plus que ce que l'on a promis

10-better late than never
-mieux vaut tard que jamais
-il vaut mieux arriver en retard qu'arriver en corbillard

11-the better the day,the better the deed
-bon jour,bonne oeuvre

12-better be the head of a yeomanry than the tail of a gentry
-better be the head of an ass than the tail of a horse
-better to reign in Hell than serve in Heaven
-better be the head of a pike than the tail of a sturgeon
-better be the head od a dog than the tail of a lion
-mieux vaut être premier dans son village que second à Rome

between

    1-between Scylla and Charybdis
    -tomber de Charybde en Scylla

    2-between hay and grass
    -trop tôt ou trop tard

    3-between you and me the bedpost
    -être come les deux doigts de la main
    -être comme deux frères

beware

    beware of a silent dog and still waves
    -se méfier du feu qui couve

big

    the bigger they are,the harder they fall
    -de grande montée,grande chute

bile

    it rouses my bile
    -cela me fait grimper aux arbres

bind

    1-if we are bound to forgive an enemy,we are not bound to trust him
    -de notre ennemi réconcilié,il faut se garder

    2-no one is bound to do impossibilities
    -à l'impossible,nul n'est tenu

    3-fast bind,fast find
    -puce en l'oereille,l'homme réveille

bird

    1-the early bird catches the worm
    -l'avenir appartient à ceux qui se lèvent tôt

    2-a bird in the hand is worth two in the bush
    -un tiens vaut mieux que deux tu l'auras
    -il vaut mieux tenir que courir
    on sait ce que l'on perd,on ne sait pas ce que l'on gagne

    3-a little bird told me so
    -c'est mon petit doigt qui me l'a dit

    4-birds once snared fear all bushes
    -chat échaudé craint l'eau froide

    5-birds of a feather flock together
    -qui se ressemble s'assemble
    -dis moi qui tu hantes je te dirai qui tu es

    6-it's an ill bird that fouls its own nest
    -birds in their little nest agree
    -c'est un vilain oiseau qui salit son nid
    -on ne peut contenter tout le monde et son père

    7-such bird,such nest
    -selon l'oiseau le nid,selon la femme le logis

8-birds once snared fear all bushes
-chat échaudé craint l'eau froide

9-the bird loves her nest
-un lièvre va toujours mourir au gîte
-tuojours il souvient à Robin de ses flûtes

10-an old bird is not to be caught with chaff
-on ne prend pas les vieux merles à la pipée
-on n'attrappe pas les mouches avec du vinaigre
-on n'attrappe pas les oiseaux à la tarterelle

11-one bird in the net is worth a hundred flying
-le moineau dans la main vaut mieux que la grue qui vole

birthday
in a birthday suit
-en tenue d'Adam
-dans le plus simple appareil

bit
1-once bit,twice shy
-chat échaudé craint l'eau froide

2-a bit of fat
-un coup de chance

3-he that has been bitten by a serpent,is afraid of a rope
-chat échaudé craint l'eau froide

bite
1-if you cannot bite never show your teeth
-il ne sert à rien de montrer les dents lorsqu'on est édenté

2-don't bite off more than you can chew
-à petit mercier,petit panier
-il ne faut péter plus haut que son cul (familier)
-il ne faut pas avoir les yeux plus gros que le ventre

3-to make two bites of a cherry
-faire trois morceaux d'une cerise

4-to bite even the hand that feedds him
-c'est l'enfant qui bat sa nourrice
-ne pas avoir la reconnaissance du ventre

5-never bite unless you make your teeth meet
-n'étend les jambes qu'à la longueur du tapis

biter
the biter is sometimes bit
-méchanceté porte sa peine

black
1-black will take no other hue
-toute la pluie n'enlève pas la force d'un piment

2-two blacks do not make a white
-erreur n'est pas compte

255

blade
>**the blade wears out the scabbard**
>-la lame use le fourreau

blame
>**he that blames would buy**
>-qui dénigre veut acheter

blank
>**to give a blank cheque**
>-donner carte blanche

bless
>**1-blessed are the poor in spirit**
>-heureux les pauvres d'esprit,le royaume des cieux leur appartient
>
>**2-he has not a penny to bless himself with**
>-il n'a pas un sou vaillant
>
>**3-blessed is who expects nothing,for he shallnever be desappointed**
>-ne désirer que ce qu'on a,c'est avoir tout ce qu'on desire

blessing
>**blessings brighten as they take their flight**
>**blessings are not valued till they are gone**
>-quand le puits est à sec,on sait ce que vaut l'eau
>-bien perdu,bien connu

blind
>**1-blind as a bat (or beetle or mole or owl)**
>-myope comme une taupe
>
>**2-among the blind,the one eyed man is king**
>-au royaume des aveugles le borgne et roi
>
>**3-blind leader of the blind**
>-c'est un aveugle qui en conduit un autre
>-les oisons mènent paître les oies
>
>**4-the blind lead the blind,boh shall fall onto the ditch**
>-si un aveugle en conduit un autre,ils tomberont tous les deux
>
>**5-none so blind as those who won't see**
>-il n'est pire sourd que celui qui ne veut entendre
>
>**6-it is a blind goose that comes to the fox's sermon**
>de fol folie,de cuir courroie

blindness
>**there is no blindness like ignorance**
>-gardez-vous d'un homme qui ne connaît qu'un livre

blithe
>**a blithe heart makes the fair face**
>-la gaité,la santé changent l'hiver en été

blood
>**1-it runs in the blood**
>-c'est dans le sang

2-blood is thicker than water
-c'est la voix du sang qui parle

3-blood will tell
-bon sang ne peut mentir
-noblesse oblige

4-it makes one's blood boil
-mon sang n'a fait qu'un tour

**5-all blood is alike ancient
human blood is all of a colour**
-Dieu nous a tous pétris du même limon

6-like blood,like good,and like age make the happiest marriage
-âne avec le cheval n'attèle

blow

1-I will blow him sky high
-je vais lui apprendre!

2-without striking a blow
-sans souffler mot
-pas un mot plus haut que l'autre

3-one must not blow hot and cold
-il ne faut pas souffler le chaud et le froid

**4-to blow one's own trumpet
to blow one's own horn**
-crâner
-avoir les chevilles qui enflent (*familier*)

5-to blow one's top
-sortir de ses gonds

6-the first blow is half the battle
-c'est la première impression qui compte

7-to blow away the cobwebb
-se rafraîchir les idées

blue

1-true blue will never stain
-bon sang ne peut mentir
-noblesse oblige

2-there may be blue and better blue
-chacun prend son plaisir où il se trouve
-chacun voit midi à sa pendule
-il faut de tout pour faire un monde

3-once in a blue moon
-le trent-six du mois

4-blue are the hills that are far away
-un peu d'absence fait grand bien
-loin des yeux,près du coeur

blush

> **to blush like a blue dog**
> -rester blanc comme un navet (ne pas rougir)

board

> **to go by the board**
> -tomber à l'eau

boast

> **he is the boast of England**
> -il fait le matamore

bobbit

> **if it isn't well bobbit we'll bob it again**
> -cent fois sur le métier remettez votre ouvrage

bode

> **bode good and get it**
> -espoir de gain diminue la peine

body

> **a little body often harbours a great soul**
> -d'un petit homme souvent grand ombre
> -en petite tête gît grand sens

bolt

> **1-a bolt from the blue**
> -un coup de tonnerre (*sens figuré*)

> **2-to put a blot face on something**
> -payer d'audace

> **3-it's like a bolt from the blue**
> -c'est comme un coup de tonnerre

bone

> **1-to be bone idle**
> -avoir un poil dans la main

> **2-bone of contention**
> -point de désaccord

> **3-to have a bone to pick with someone**
> -avoir maille à partir avec quelqu'un

> **4-to make no bones about**
> -ne pas s'en faire pour

booby

> **a booby will never make a hawk**
> -on ne peut faire d'une buse un épervier

book

> **1-books and friends should be few but good**
> -à quoi bon tant d'amis?un seul suffit quand il vous aime
> -avoir beaucoup d'amis,c'est n'avoir point d'amis

> **2-a great book is a great evil**
> -un gros livre est un grand mal
> -les bons livres font les bons clercs

3-when a new book appears,read an old one
-mieux vaut la vieille voie que le nouveau sentier

boot

1-the boot is on the other foot
-les circonstances ont changé

2-he has gotten the boot and the better horse
-il a les deux oreilles et la queue

3-they that are booted are not always ready
-être et paraître sont deux
-quand on regarde quelqu'un,on n'en voit que la moitié

booty

a fair booty makes many a thief
-l'occasion fait le larron

bored

if you are bored,work,it is the only remedy for this terrible evil
-l'ennui est une maladie dont le travail est le remède

born

1-born with a silver spoon in one's mouth
-né coiffé

2-born under a lucky star
-né sous une bonne étoile

3-he that is born a fool is never cured
-qui bête va à Rome, tel en retourne
-tête de fou ne blanchit pas
-quand tu es né rond,tu ne meurs pas carré

4-poets are born not made
-on naît poète, artiste...

5-to be born on the wrong side of the blanket
-être un enfant de l'amour

6-if you are born to be hanged then you'll never be drowned
-aux innocents les mains pleines

7-he that is once born,once must die
-contre la mort, point de remède

8-it is better to be bo n lucky than rich
-il vaut mieux être riche et bien portant que pauvre et malade

borrow

1-he that goes a borrowing goes a sorrowing
-he that borrows must pay again with shame and loss
-argent emprunté porte tristesse

2-borrowed things will home again
-ce qui est bon à prendre est bon à rendre

3-he that borrows bind himself with his neighbour's rope
-qui doit n'a rien à soi

4-borrowed garments never fit well
-l'habit volé ne va pas au voleur

5-not so good to borrow as be able to lend
-chose divivne est prêter,devoir est vertu héroïque

borrower
1-neither a borrower nor a lender be
-qui vit à compte vit à honte

2-the borrower is the servant of the lender
-celui qui emprunte est l'esclave de celui qui prête

bottle
1-bottled moonshine
-utopie

2-looking for a needle in a bottle of hay,in a haystack
-chercher une aiguille dans une meule de foin

3-to bottle one's feelings
-faire bonne contenance

bow
1-he has two strings to his bow
-il a plus d'une corde à son arc

2-better bow than break
-mieux vaut ployer que rompre

box
1-I have got into the wrong box
-je ne suis pas à ma place

2-to be in the same box
-être dans le même bateau

boy
1-the least boy always carries the greatest fiddle
-le chien attaque toujours celui qui a les pantalons déchirés
-au pauvre la besace

2-they are not boyscouts
-ce ne sont pas des enfants de choeur

3-boys will be men
-jamais bon cheval ne devient rosse
-il faut que jeunesse se passe
-l'enfance est le sommeil de la raison

4-naughty boys sometimes make good men
-il faut que jeunesse se passe

brag
they brag most who can do the least
-la plus mauvaise roue d'un chariot fait toujours plus de bruit

Bran
if not Bran,it's Bran's brother
-si ce n'est toi,c'est donc ton frère

brass
> **brass monkey weather**
> -un froid de canard

brasstacks
> **let's get down to the brasstacks**
> -revenons à nos moutons

brave
> **1-to a brave and faithful man nothing is difficult**
> -il n'y a pas d'heure pour les braves
>
> **2-none but the brave deserve the lady**
> -jamais honteux n'eut belle amie
> -le chien peureux n'a jamais son saoûl de lard

bread
> **1-eaten bread is soon forgotten**
> -mémoire du bien tantôt passe
> -morceau avalé n'a plus de goût
> -mal passé n'est que songe
> -la fête passée,adieu le saint
>
> **2-it is a good thing to eat your brown bread first**
> -si tu manges ton pain blanc le permier,tu manges ton pain noir plus tard
>
> **3-dry bread at home is better than roast abroad**
> -le pain d'autrui est amer
> -mieux vaut ta propre morue que le dindon des autres
> -une tartine de sirop chez nous est parfois meilleure qu'un banquet ailleurs
>
> **4-bread is the staff of life**
> -sac vide ne tient pas debout

break
> **to break a butterfly on the wheel**
> -en faire une montagne
> -se noyer dans un verre d'eau
> -faire d'une mouche un éléphant

breath
> **keep your breath to cool your porridge**
> -chacun son métier et les vaches seront bien gardées
> **keep your breath to cool your porridge (suite)**
> -mêlez-vous de ce qui vous regarde
> -les affaires du cabri ne sont pas celles du mouton

bred
> **what is bred in the bones will come out in the flesh**
> -quand tu es né rond,tu ne meurs pas pointu
> -tel père,tel fils
> -tel pain,tel soupe
> -on ne peut empêcher les chiens d'aboyer ni les menteurs de mentir
> -d'un goujat on ne peut faire un gentilhomme

breeches
> **she wears the breeches**
> -elle porte la culotte

breed

breed will tell
-bon sang ne peut mentir
-noblesse oblige

brew

as you brew,you shall bake
-quand le vin est tiré,il faut le boire
-comme on fait son lit,on se couche

briar

to nip the brair in the bud
-prendre le mal à la racine
-étouffer l'affaire dans l'oeuf

brick

1-to drop a brick
-jeter un pavé dans la mare

2-to make brick without straw
-faire avec les moyens du bord

3-you can't make bricks without straw
-on ne peut faire d'omelette sans casser des oeufs

bright

as bright as a button
-brillant comme un sou neuf

bring

1-to bring home the bacon
-faire bouillir la marmite

2-to bring a question on the carpet
-mettre une question sur le tapis

3-bring a cow to the hall and she'll return to the byre
-toujours il souvient à Robin de ses flutes

brook

little brooks make great rivers
-les petits ruisseaux font les grandes rivières

broom

a new broom sweeps clean
-tout nouveau,tout beau

broth

good broth may be made in an old pot
-c'est dans les vieilles marmites qu'on fait les meilleures soupes
-on fait de bonne soupe dans un vieux pot
-il n'est rien comme les vieux ciseaux pour couper la soie
-l'aboi d'un vieux chien doit on croire

brown

to be done brown
-être marron

262

brush
> **give it another brush**
> -donnez-y encore une petite touche

buck
> **a buck is a buck**
> -l'argent n'a pas d'odeur

bucket
> **1-to kick the bucket**
> -passer l'arme à gauche
> -casser sa pipe
>
> **2-put not the bucket too often to the well**
> -tant va la cruche à l'eau qu'elle se casse

budge
> **he wouldn't budge an inch**
> -il ne voulait pas en démordre

bug
> **as snug as the bug in a rug**
> -tranquille comme Baptiste
> -bien au chaud

build
> **don't build the sty before the litter comes**
> -il ne faut pas faire l'étable au veau avant qu'il soit né

building
> **1-no good building without a good foundatin**
> -de méchant fondement jamais bon bâtiment
>
> **2-a high building,a low foundation**
> -grande maison se fait par petite cuisine

bull
> **1-a bull in a china shop**
> -un éléphant dans un magasin de porcelaine
> -un chien dans un jeu de quilles
>
> **2-to hit the bull's eye**
> -taper dans le mille
> -faire mouche
>
> **3-to take the bull by the horns**
> -prendre le taureau par les cornes

bully
> **a bully is always a coward**
> -tel menace qui a grand peur

burn
> **1-his money burns a hole in his pocket**
> -c'est un panier percé
>
> **2-burn not your house to rid it of the mouse**
> -on ne jette pas le coffre au feu parce que la clef en est perdue
> -pour un moine,l'abbaye ne se perd pas
> -l'excès en tout nuit

3-to burn one's boats
to burn one's bridges behind you
-brûler ses vaisseaux

4-you cannot burn the candle at both ends
-on ne peut pas brûler la chandelle par les deux bouts

5-once burned,twice shy
-chat échaudé craint l'eau froide

burnt

a burnt child dreads the fire
-chat échaudé craint l'eau froide

burry

to burry one's head in the sand
-faire la politique de l'autruche
-se mettre la tête sous l'oreiller

bush

1-a bad bush is better than an open field
-quand on n'a pas ce que l'on aime,il faut aimer ce que l'on a

2-one beat the bush and another caught the hare
-l'un sème,l'autre récolte

business

1-combine business with pleasure,the useful with the agreeable
-joignez l'utile à l'agréable

2-what is everybody's business is nobody's business
-il n'y a pas d'âne plus mal bâté que celui du commun
-affaire à tout le monde,affaire à personne

3-business is business
don't mix business with pleasure
-les affaires sont les affaires

4-this is none of your business
-mêlez-vous de ce qui vous regarde

5-business will not quite cost
-le jeu n'en vaut pas la chandelle

6-this is none of your business
-mêlez-vous de ce qui vous regarde

busy

1-he that is busy is tempted but by one devil;he that is idle,by a legion
-le diable s'empare de personnes oisives
-l'oisiveté est la mère de tous les vices

2-busiest men find the most
-qui bien chasse bien trouve

3-busiest men find the most leisure time
-les mains noires font manger le pain blanc
-le travail est souvent le père du plaisir

4-to be busybody
-faire la mouche du coche

butter
butter wouldn't melt in his mouth
-on lui donnerai le bon Dieu sans confession

butterfingers
-maladroit

butterfly
to have butterflies in one's stomach
-avoir la colique

button
1-to have a soul above buttons
-ne pas être au ras des pâquerettes

2-he has not all his buttons
-il a perdu ses boulons (*familier*)

3-to have something buttoned on
-il ne manque pas un bouton de guêtre

buy
1-many have been ruined by buying good pennyworths
-bon marché fait argent débourser
-bon marché vide le panier mais n'emplit pas la bourse

2-to buy a pig in a poke
-acheter chat en poche

3-buy at a fair,but sell at home
-à la maison acheter.au marché vendre

4-better buy than borrow
-mieux vaut acheter qu'emprunter

5-why buy a cow when the milk is so cheap?
-pourquoi faire simple quand on peut faire compliqué

buyer
1-let the buyer beware
-que l'acheteur prenne garde

2-the buyer needs a hundred eyes,the seller but one
-un oeil suffit au marchand,l'acheteur en a besoin de cent

3-there are more foolish buyers than foolish sellers
-il y a plus d'acheteurs que de connaisseurs
-il y a plus de fols acheteurs que de fols vendeurs

by
1-by and by
-soit dit en passant

2-by and large
-en gros

bygone
let bygones be bygones
-à tout péché miséricorde

C

Caesar
>**Caesar's wife must be above suspicion**
>-la femme de César ne doit pas même être soupçonnée

cake
>**1-it's a piece of cake**
>-c'est facile comme bonjour
>
>**2-my cake is dough**
>-l'affaire est dans le lac
>
>**3-you cannot eat your cake and have it too**
>-vouloir le beurre et l'argent du beurre
>-on ne peut avoir le drap et l'argent
>
>**4-to take the cake**
>-remporter le morceau

calamity
>**1-calamity is man's true touchtone**
>-il n'y a rien de si infortuné qu'un homme qui n'a jamais souffert
>-plus le malheur est grand,plus il est grand de vivre
>-l'homme est un apprenti et la douleur est son maître
>
>**2-calamity is the touchstone of a brave man**
>-l'or s'épure au feu,l'homme s'éprouve au creuset du malheur

calf
>**1-his calves are gone to grass**
>-il a des jambes de coq
>
>**2-the greatest calf is not the sweetest veal**
>-dans les petites boîtes,les bons onguents
>
>**3-the calf,the goose,the bee,the world is ruled by these three**
>-le papier souffre tout
>-sur la peau d'une brebis,on écrit ce que l'on veut
>
>**4-quey calves are dead veal**
>-il a tué la poule aux oeufs d'or

call
>**1-many are called,but few are chosen**
>-il y a beaucoup d'appelés mais peu d'élus
>
>**2-to call a spade a spade**
>-appeler un chat un chat
>
>**3-to call in question**
>-mettre en question
>
>**4-to call to account**
>-demander des comptes
>
>**5-to be called to one's account**
>-être envoyé dans l'autre monde

6-to call that a red,black letter day
-marquer ce jour d'une pierre blanche,noire

7-I wouldn't call the king my cousin
-le roi n'est pas mon cousin

camel

1-it is easier for a camel to go through the eye of a needle,than for a rich man to enter in the kingdom of God
-il est plus facile à un chameau de passer par le trou d'une aiguille qu'à un riche d'entrer dans le royaume de Dieu

2-the camel never sees its own hump,but sees his companion's
-oeil un autre oeil voit mais pas le sien

camp

to have a foot in several camps
-manger à plusieurs rateliers

can

he can who believes he can
-on croit parce que l'on croit pouvoir

candle

1-gay as the king's candle
-bariolé comme la chandelle des rois

2-to hold a candle to the devil
-il faut quelquefois brûler une chandelle au Diable

3-don't hold a candle in the sun!
-ne donnez pas de coups d'épées dans l'eau!

4-when candles are away,all the cats are grey
-la nuit,tous les chats sont gris

canvas

to canvas a subject
-passer au crible
-passer au peigne fin

cap

if the cap fits,wear it !
-que celui à qui le bonnet fait, le mette !

care

1-not to care two hoots,a tinker's cuss,a tinker's damn
-s'en moquer comme de l'an quarante
-s'en moquer comme de sa première chemise

2-take care of the pence and the pounds will take care of themselves
-un sou amène l'autre

carpenter

the carpenter is known by his chips
à l'oeuvre on connaît l'artisan
-aux tessons,on sait ce que fut le pot

carpet
>**to bring a question on the carpet**
>-mettre une question sur le tapis

carrion
>**a carrion kite will never be a good hawk**
>-on ne peut faire d'une buse un épervier

carry
>**1-to carry the cans**
>-porter le chapeau

>**2-to carry water to the river**
>**to carry coal to Newcastle**
>-à laver la tête d'un âne,on y perd sa salive
>-porter l'eau à la rivière

>**3-to carry fire in one hand and water in the other**
>-prêcher le faux pour savoir le vrai
>-faire l'âne pour avoir du son
>-qui veut faire l'ange fait la bête

>**4-to carry off meat from the graves**
>-être pauvre comme Job

>**5-don't carry a joke too far**
>-les plaisanteries les plus courtes sont les meilleures

cart
>**1-to put the cart before the horse**
>-mettre la charrue avant les boeufs

>**2-the best cart overthrows**
>-il n'est si bon charretier qui ne verse

case
>**-it's a case of bitter bit**
>-tel est pris qui croyait prendre

cash
>**to pay cash on the nail**
>-payer rubis sur l'ongle

cast
>**1-though you cast on nature with a fork,it will still return**
>-chassez le naturel,il revient au galop

>**2-to cast in one's lot**
>-épouser le bonheur ou le malheur d'un autre

>**3-cast not a clout till May is out**
>-Avril ne te découvre pas d'un fil
>-Mai,mets ce qu'il te plaît

>**4-it is in vain to cast your net when there is no fish**
>-se battre contre des moulins à vent

>**5-never cast dirt into the fountain whoich you have sometimes drunk**
>-il ne faut pas scier la branche sur laquelle on est assis

6-to cast pearls before swine
-donner des perles (du pain béni) à des cochons

7-cast no dirt into the well that has given you water
-il est mon oncle qui mon ventre me comble

8-cast thy bread upon the water,for thou shalt find it after many days
-on récolte ce que l'on a semé

castle

castles in the air
castles in Spain
-faire des châteaux en Espagne

cat

1-an alley cat
-un chat de gouttière

2-a scalded cat fears hot water
-chat échaudé craint l'eau froide

3-the cat's house
-la maison close

4-a cat may look at a king
-un chien regarde bien un évêque

5-to turn cat-in-pan
-tourner côté en peine

6-like a cat on hot bricks
-sur une pelote d'épingles

7-when the cat's away,the mice will play
-quand le chat n'est pas là,les souris dansent

8-before the cat can lick her ear
-quand les poules auront des dents
-renvoyer aux calendes grecques
-le trente-six du mois

9-how can the cat help it,if the maid is a fool?
-ce n'est pas de sa faute si les grenouilles n'ont pas de queue

10-sick as a cat
-malade comme un chien

11-to lead a cat and dog life
-être comme chien et chat

12-to play cat and mouse
-jouer au chat et à la souris

13-to put (set) the cat among the pigeons
-mettre le loup dans la bergerie

14-to let the cat out of the bag
-jouer les apprenti-sorciers

15-two cats and a mouse,two wives in a house,two dogs and a bone,never agree in one
-deux chiens à l'os ne s'accordent

16-there is no room to swing a cat
-il n'y a pas de place pour se retourner

17-cats hide their claws
-belle chère et coeur arrière

18-all cats are grey in the dark
-la nuit,tous les chats sont gris
-de nuit,le blé semble farine
-à la chandelle,la chèvre semble demoiselle

19-a cat in gloves catches no mice
-la fortune sourit aux audacieux

20-the cat shuts his eyes when stealing the cream
-rarement de sa faute on aime le témoin

21-what can you have of a cat but her skin?
-la plus belle fille du monde ne peut donner que ce qu'elle a

22-to be made the cat's paw of
-faire la mouche du coche

23-never was cat or dog drowned,that could but see the shore
-c'est la nuit qu'il est beau de croire à la lumière

24-the cat loves fish but fears to wet his paws
-the cat wanted fish but dared not to wet her feet in the stream
-qui ne risque rien,n'a rien
-le succès est toujours un enfant de l'audace

catch

1-catch not at the shadow and lose the substance
-l'arbre ne doit pas nous cacher la forêt

2-to be caught between the devil and the devil blue sea
-c'est la peste ou le choléra

3-first catch your hare
-lièvre qui court n'est pas mort
-il ne faut pas vendre la peau de l'ours avant de l'avoir tué

4-he who would catch the fisn mustn't mind getting wet
-la fin justifie les moyens
-on ne peut faire d'omelette sans casser les oeufs

5-to be caught red-handed
être pris la main dans le sac

cater

he catered to her every whim
-il est aux petits soins pour elle

cattle
>**old cattle breed not**
>-bonjour lunettes,adieu fillettes
>-lunettes et cheveux gris sont quittance d'amour

cause
>**take away the cause,and the effect must cease**
>-il n'y a pas d'effet sans cause

censure
>**every man's censure is first moulded in his own nature**
>-c'est l'hôpital qui se moque de la charité

cesspool
>**to have a mind like a cesspool**
>-avoir l'esprit mal tourné

chain
>**a chain is no stronger than its weakest link**
>-c'est le talon d'Achille
>-c'est le défaut de la cuirasse

chamber
>**the chamber of sickness is the chapel of devotion**
>-la crainte de Dieu est le commencement de la sagesse

chance
>**what chances to one man,may happen to all men**
>-les armes sont journalières
>-le vent de la prospérité change bien souvent de côté

change
>**1-change of pasture makes fat calves**
>**changing of work is lighting of hearts**
>-changement d'herbage réjouit les veaux
>
>**2-a change is as good as a rest**
>-le changement de travail est une espèce de repos
>
>**3-he changes his mind from one day to another**
>-il n'est ni chair ni poisson
>
>**4-don't change horses in midstream**
>-il ne faut pas changer de cheval au milieu de la rivière
>
>**5-to change a fly into an elephant**
>-faire d'une mouche un éléphant
>
>**6-he changed his tune**
>il a changé son fusil d'épaule

charge
>**to charge like a bull at the gate**
>-aller bille en tête

charitable
>**the charitable gives out at the door and God puts in at the window**
>-qui donne aux pauvres,prête à Dieu

charity

>**1-charity covers a multitude of sins**
>-on fait souvent du bien pour pouvoir impunément faire du mal
>
>**2-charity begins at home**
>-charité bien ordonnée commence par soi-même

chase

>**to chase rainbows**
>-faire des châteaux en Espagne

cheap

>**1-it is as cheap sitting as standing**
>-assieds-toi,ce n'est pas plus cher
>
>**2-he will never have a good thing cheap that is afraid of asking the price**
>-il n'y a pas de petites affaires
>
>**3-good cheap is dear**
>-bon marché fait argent débourser
>
>**4-light cheap,lither yield**
>-bon marché vide le panier mais n'emplit pas la bourse

cheat

>**cheats never prosper**
>-homme rusé,tard abusé

check

>**to check in the bud**
>-tuer dans l'oeuf

cheek

>**to have the cheek**
>-avoir le cran,avoir le toupet

cheerful

>**to be as cheerful as a grave**
>-être triste comme un bonnet de nuit

cherish

>**to cherish a serpent in your bosom**
>-nourrir un serpent dans son sein

cherry

>**the whole tree or not a cherry on it**
>-tout ou rien

chicken

>**1-chickens always come home to roost**
>-quand on crache en l'air,celà vous retombe sur le nez
>
>**2-to be no chicken**
>-ne pas être une poule mouillée

child

>**1-the child is the father of the man**
>-jamais bon cheval ne devint rosse

2-children and fools tell the truth
-la vérité sort de la bouche des enfants
-ivres et forcenés disent toute leur pensée

3-children are poor men's riches
-à pauvres,enfants sont richesse

4-a little child weighs on your knee,abig one on your heart
-petits enfants, petits soucis,grands enfants,grands soucis

5-there is only one pretty child in the world,and every mother has it
-une maman est un bon bol à couvercle

6-there are no children nowadays
-y a p'us d'enfants!

7-he that has no children brings them upwell
-médecin,guéris-toi toi-même

8-what children hear at home,soon flies abroad
-ce que l'enfant dit au foyer est tôt connu jusqu'au moustier

9-children are poor men's riches
-à pauvres, enfants sont richesses

10-he that has children,all his morsels are not his own
-quand le rossignol a vu ses petits,il cesse de chanter

chip

1-he has a chip on his shoulder
-il cherche querelle à tout le monde

2-it is just like chip in the porridge
-c'est un cautère sur une jambe de bois
-pisser dans un violon (*familier*)

3-he is a chip of the old block
-tel père,tel fils
-tel pain,telle soupe

choice

there is small choice in rotten apples
-no choice among stinking fish
-entre deux maux il faut choisir le moindre

choose

never choose your women or your linen by candlelight
-choisis ta femme non à la danse mais à la moisson

chorus

a chorus of protests
-une levée de boucliers

Christmas

1-Christmas comes but once a year
-ce n'est pas tous les jours fête (dimanche)

2-after Christmas comes Lent
-les jours se suivent mais ne se ressemblent pas
-passé le jour,passé la fête

church

1-in church,in an inn,and in a coffin,all men are equal
-Dieu nous a tous pétris du même limon

2-the nearer from church,the farther from God
-près de l'église, loin de Dieu

3-old churches have dim windows
-vieille charrette crie à chaque tour
-il n'est si bon cheval qui ne devienne rosse

4-a church mouse
-une grenouille de bénitier

churchyard

a piece of churchyard fits everybody
-six pied de terre suffisent au plus grand homme

churl

a churl's feast is better than none at all
-quand n'a pas ce que l'on aime,il faut aimer ce que l'on a

circumstance

circumstances alter cases
-convenances rompent loi

city

1-you cannot see the city for the houses
-l'arbre ne doit pas nous cacher la forêt

2-a city that parleys is half gotten
-fille et ville qui parlementent sont à demi rendues

civility

civility costs nothing
-cela ne vous déchire pas la robe
-beau parler n'écorche pas la langue
-la politesse ne coûte rien

claw

claw me,I'll claw thee
-à charge de revanche

clean

1-to make a clean sweep
-faire du ménage

2-a clean hand wants no washing
-mains blanches sont assez lavées

clever

a clever little devil
-malin comme un singe

climb

> **1-to climb on the bandwagon**
> -prendre le train en marche
> -se mettre dans le mouvement

> **2-he who climbs the ladder must begin at the bottom**
> -il faut commencer par le commencement

> **3-he that never climbed,never fell**
> -il n'y a que ceux qui ne font rien qui ne se trompent pas

climber

> **hasty climbers have sudden falls**
> -qui trop se hâtent, s'empêchent

cloak

> **don't have your cloak to make when it begins to rain**
> -il faut garder une poire pour la soif

clock

> **1-to put the clock back**
> -remettre les pendules à l'heure

> **2-you cannot put back the clock**
> -le temps perdu ne se rattrappe jamais

> **3-like clockwork**
> -réglé comme du papier à musique

clog

> **clogs to clogs is only three generations**
> **twice clogs,once boots**
> -le petit-fils revient aux sabots que l'aïeul avait quittés

close

> **1-close sits my shirt,but closer my skin**
> -la peau est plus proche que la chemise

> **2-as close as an oyster**
> -fermé comme une huître
> -muet comme une carpe

closed

> **a closed mouth catches no flies**
> -bonnes sont les dents qui retiennent la langue

clothes

> **fine clothes don't make a gentleman**
> -l'habit ne fait pas le moine

cloud

> **1-if there is no clouds,we should not enjoy the sun**
> -chose accoutumée,rarement prisée
> -si tu veux la paix,prépare la guerre

> **2-all clouds bring not rain**
> -tout ce qui branle ne tombe pas
> -toutes les fois qu'il tonne,le tonnerre ne tombe pas

3-every cloud has a silver lining
-toute médaille a son revers
-il n'y a pas de montagnes sans vallée

4-he's under a cloud
-il est soupçonné

5-after black clouds,clear weather
-après la pluie,le beau temps

clover

he's in clover
-il est comme un coq en pâte
-il a les doigts de pieds en éventail (*familier*)
-il est sous une bonne étoile

coal

to carry coal to Newcastle
-porter l'eau à la rivière

coast

the coast is clear
-le champ est libre

coat

1-it is not the gay coat that makes the gentleman
-l'habit ne fait pas le moine

2-turning one's coat for luck
-tourner sa veste

3-cut your coat according yo your cloth
-il faut aller selon sa bourse
-qui ne peut galoper,qu'il trotte

cobbler

every cobbler sticks to his last
-à chacun son métier,les vaches en sont mieux gardées

cobwebb

to blow away the cobwebb
-se rafraîchir les idées

cock

1-to live like fighting cocks
-vivre sur un grand pied

2-as the old cock crows,so does the young one
-l'aigle n'engendre pas la colombe
-les chiens ne font pas de chats

3-there is many a good cock come out of a tattered bag
-ce qu'il faut chercher à connaître,c'est le fond du panier
-il ne faut pas regarder la saleté du cochon pour en manger

4-to cock your eye
-faire un clin d'oeil

5-to cock a snook
-faire un pied de nez

6-cock and bull stories
-des contes à dormir debout

7-every cock crows on its one dunghill
-un coq est fort sur son fumier

cockles
> **to warm the cockles of one's heart**
> -réchauffer le coeur de quelqu'un

cod
> **you can't cod me**
> -tu ne peux pas me faire çà

coin
> **much coin,much care**
> -nul or sans écume

cold
> **to pour cold water on**
> -refroidir quelqu'un

collar
> **to get hot under the collar**
> -avoir les oreilles qui chauffent

colour
> **to come out in one's true colours**
> -se montrer sous son vrai jour

colt
> **1-young colts will canter**
> -il n'est feu que de bois vert

> **2-a ragged colt may make a good horse**
> -il faut que jeunesse se passe

combine
> **combine business with pleasure,the useful with the agreeable**
> -joindre l'utile à l'agréable

come
> **1-to come to an arrangement is better than to going law**
> -un mauvais arrangement vaut mieux qu'un bon procès
> -gagne assez qui sort de procès
> -il y a moins de mal à perdre sa vigne qu'à la plaider

> **2-come what may**
> -advienne que pourra
> -vienne qui plante

> **3-light come,light go**
> **-easy come,easy go**
> -ce qui vient de la flûte,s'en va par le tambour
> -cela va,cela vient
> -ce qui vient de fric,s'en va de frac

4-to come to the wrong shop
-frapper à la mauvaise porte

5-to come out in one's true colours
-se montrer sous son vrai jour

6-he that comes of a hen must scrape
-qui naît poule,aime à gratter

7-come hell or high water
-come rain or shine
-qu'il pleuve ou qu'il vente
-contre vents et marées

8-you came on his blind side
-vous avez touché son point faible

9-it will all come out in the wash
-nothing comes sooner to light than that has been long hid
-la vérité comme l'huile s'élève au dessus de tout

10-there comes nought of a sack but what was there
il ne sort du sac que ce qu'il y a

comforter
the comforter's head never aches
-les conseilleurs ne sont pas les payeurs

commit
he that commits a fault thinks everyboby speaks of it
-celui qui se sait coupable croit toujours qu'on parle de lui
-qui a mangé le lard,ronge l'os

commodity
every commodity has its discommodity
-toute médaille a son revers
-il n'y a pas de montagne sans vallée

communication
evil communications corrupt good manners
-argent fait perdre et prendre gens

companion
a merry companion is the waggon in the way
-quand les boeufs vont à deux,le labourage va mieux

company
1-good company on the road is the shortest cut
-quand les boeufs vont à deux,le labourage va mieux

2-the company makes the feast
-plus on est de fous plus on rit

3-low company taints the mind
-ceux qui touchent la poix se souillent les doigts

complain
he complains wrongfully of the sea that twice suffered shipwreck
-expérience est mère de science
-un âne ne trébuche pas deux fois sur la même pierre

condemn
>one must not condemn without hearing
>-juge hâtif est périlleux

confession
>open confession is good for the soul
>-péché avoué est à demi pardonné

conscience
>1-a good conscience is a soft pillow
>a good conscience is a sure card
>a clear conscience fears no false accusations
>a quiet conscience sleeps in thunder
>a good conscience makes an easy couch
>-une bonne conscience est un doux oreiller

>2-conscience does make cowards of us all
>-qui a mangé le lard ronge l'os

>3-a guilty conscience is a self accuser
>conscience is a thousand witnesses
>-celui qui se sait coupable croit toujours qu'on parle de lui

>4-a guilty conscience needs no accuser
>-aucun coupable n'est absous devant son propre tribunal

>5-a clean conscience laughs at false accusations
>-mains blanches sont assez lavées

constant
>a constant guest is never welcome
>-l'hôte et la pluie après trois jours ennuient

contempt
>contempt will sooner kill an injury than revenge
>-il n'est point de dette si tôt payée que le mépris

content
>1-content is more than a kingdom
>a contended mind is a continual feast
>-contentement passe richesse

>2-he who is content in his poverty,is wonderfully rich
>-suffisance fait richesse et convoitise fait pauvresse

cook
>1-the books have been cooked
>-les comptes ont été falsifiés

>2-what's cooking?
>-qu'est-ce qui se prépare?

>3-too many cooks spoil the broth
>-les étourneaux sont maigres parce qu'ils vont en troupe
>-deux chiens à l'os ne s'accordent

cord
>the cord breaks at last by the weakest pull
>-c'est la goutte d'eau qui fait déborder le vase

corner
> to be driven into a corner
> -être acculé au mur

corruption
> corruption of the best becomes the worst
> -mauvaises compagnies corrompent les bonnes moeurs
> -plus on remue la boue,plus elle pue

cost
> 1-there is nothing that costs less than civility
> -la politesse ne coûte rien
>
> 2-to cost a mint
> -coûter les yeux de la tête

counsel
> 1-good counsel never comes amiss
> if the counsel be good,no matter who gave it
> -un bon avis vaut un oeil dans la main
> -à quelque chose malheur est bon
>
> 2-counsel is irksome when the matter is past remedy
> -à chose faite,conseil pris
>
> 3-give neither counsel nor salt till you are asked for it
> -ne donne pas de conseil à moins qu'on ne t'en prie
>
> 4-counsel is no command
> -à parti pris,point de conseil

counsellors
> the land is never void of counsellors
> -rien ne se donne si libéralement que des conseils

count
> 1-count not four,except you have them in your wallet
> -il ne faut pas chômer les fêtes avant qu'elles soient venues
>
> 2-don't count your chicken before they are hatched
> -il ne faut pas compter les oeufs dans le derrière de la poule
> -il ne faut pas vendre la peau de l'ours avant de l'avoir tué

country
> 1-so many countries,so many customs
> every country has its costoms
> -autant de pays,autant de guises
>
> 2-in every country the sun rises in the morning
> -demain,il fera jour

couple
> every couple is not a pair
> -autant de mariages,autant de ménages

course
> the course of true love never did run smooth
> -amour a de coutume d'entremêler ses plaisirs d'amertume

courtesy
>**full of courtesy,full of craft**
>-tel vous semble applaudir qui vous raille et vous joue

cousin
>**I wouldn't call the king my cousin**
>-le roi n'est pas son cousin

cover
>**cover yourself with honey and you'll have plenty of flies**
>-compter les ruches à miel porte malheur
>-faites-vous miel,les mouches vous mangeront

covet
>**all covet,all lose**
>-qui trop embrasse,mal étreint

covetousness
>**1-covetousness bursts the sack**
>-jamais chiche ne fut riche
>-l'avarice perd tout en voulant tout gagner
>
>**2-covetousness is always filling a bottomless vessel**
>-les avares font nécessité de tout
>-on tirerait plutôt de l'huile d'un mur
>-on tirerait plutôt un pet d'un âne mort qu'un sou de sa bourse
>-un avare est toujours gueux

cow
>**1-bring a cow to the hall and she'll return to the byre**
>-chassez le naturel,il revient au galop,
>chassez le par la porte,il rentrera par la fenêtre
>
>**2-curst cows have curt horns**
>-on crie toujours le loup plus grand qu'il n'est
>
>**3-not until the cows come home**
>-quand les poules auront des dents
>
>**4-the cow knows not the worth of her tail till she loses it**
>-il vient un temps où les vaches ont besoin de leur queue
>
>**5-better a good cow than a cow of a good kind**
>-mieux vaut moineau en cage que poule d'eau qui nage
>
>**6-a bellowing cow soon forgets her calf**
>-rien ne sèche aussi vite que les larmes

coward
>**1-it is better to be a coward for a minute than dead for the rest of your life**
>-il vaut mieux être poltron et vivre plus longtemps
>
>**2-cowards die many times before their death**
>-qui craint de souffrir,il souffre déjà de ce qu'il craint
>
>**3-many would be cowards if they had courage enough**
>-mal est caché à qui l'on voit le dos

cowl

it's not the cowl that makes the friar
-la robe ne fait pas le médecin
-l'habit ne fait pas le moine

crack

1-in a crack
-à la seconde

2-cracked pipkins are discovered by their sound
-c'est la profonde ignorance qui inspire le ton dogmatique

credit

give credit where credit is due
-à tout seigneur,tout honneur

creditor

creditors have better memories than debtors
-prêter de l'argent fait perdre la mémoire

criticism

criticism is easy and art is difficult
-la critique est aisée mais l'art est difficile

crook

1-timely crooks the tree,that good cammock be
-jamais bon cheval ne devint rosse

2-there is a crook in the lot of every one
-au chaudron des douleurs,chacun porte son écuelle
-nulle rose sans épines

3-as crooked as a cammock
-tordu

cross

1-don't cross the bridge till you come to it
-il ne faut pas chanter triomphe avant la victoire

2-everyone must bear his own cross
-à chacun sa croix

3-to cross will learn to howl swords
-croiser le fer

4-to cross one's path
-trouver sur son chemin

5-I have neither cross nor pile
-je n'ai ni croix ni pile

6-cross the stream where it is shallowest
-là où la barrière est basse,le boeuf est en jambe
-on passe la haie où elle est la plus basse
-le plat le plus bas est toujours vide

7-no cross,no crown
-les mains noires font manger le pain blanc

crow

1-of an evil crow,an evil egg
-de mauvais corbeau,mauvais oeuf
-tel père,tel fils

2-I must pluck a crow with you
-il faut qu l'on s'explique

3-as the crow flies
-à vol d'oiseau

4-crow doesn't pick up crow's eye
-les loups ne se mangent pas entre eux

5-the crow's feet
-les pattes d'oie (rides au coin des yeux)

crust

a crust is better than no bread
-quand on n'a pas ce que l'on aime,il faut aimer ce que l'on a
-faute de grives,on se contente de merles

cry

1-to cry for the moon
-demander la lune

2-don't cry over the spilt milk
-quand la jument est sortie il n'est plus temps de fermer l'étable
-ce qui est fait est fait

3-much cry and little wool
-beaucoup de bruit pour rien

4-to be a far cry from
-être à cent lieues de

5-don't cry before you are hurt
-il ne faut pas pleurer avant d'être battu
-il est comme les anguilles de Melun qui crient avant qu'on les écorche
-il ne faut jamais trembler qu'on ne voit sa tête à ses pieds

6-to cry (or proclaim) from the housetop
-clamer à tous vents

7-to cry from the housetop
-clamer à tous vents

8-don't cry stinking fish
-avoir les chevilles qui enflent (*familier*)
-crâner
-le monde est bossu quand il se baisse

9-don't cry till you are out of the wood
-il ne faut pas chanter triomphe avant la victoire

cuckold

who is a cuckold and conceals it,carries coals in his bosom
-on ne pardonne point à qui nous fait rougir

cunning
too much cunning undoes
-homme rusé.tard abusé

cup
1-it's not my cup of tea
-ce n'est pas mon genre

2-that's another cup of tea
-c'est une autre paire de manches

cur
a snappish cur is ever in woe
-chien hargneux a toujours l'oreille déchirée

curb
to curb one's tongue
-mesurer ses paroles

cure
what can't be cured must be endured
-il faut souffrir ce qu'on ne peut empêcher
-quand il n'y a pas de remède.il faut se résigner
-il faut souffrir patiemment ce qu'on ne peut amender sainement
-il faut laisser courir le vent par dessus les tuiles
-ce qu'on ne peut empêcher.il faut le vouloir

curiosity
too much curiosity lost paradise
-la mouche se brûle à la chandelle

curtain
it'll be curtain for you if...
-vous y laisserez votre peau si...

custom
1-custom is a second nature
-l'habitude est une seconde nature
-vieil arbre d'un coup ne s'arrache
-le chien détaché traine encore son lien

2-custom makes all things easy
-le lendemain s'instruit aux leçons de la veille
-cent fois sur le métier remettez votre ouvrage

customer
the customer is always right
-le client a toujours raison

cut
1-it doesn't cut any ice
-celà ne casse rien

2-the short cut is often the longest way round
-rien ne sert de courir il faut partir à point

3-do not cut the tree that gives you shade
don't cut the bough you are standing on
-il ne faut pas scier la branche sur laquelle on est assis

4-to cut the hair
-couper les cheveux en quatre

5-to cut a feather
-faire de la dentelle

6-don't cut your nose to spite your face
-to cut one's throat
-travailler à sa propre perte
-fou est qui s'oublie

7-to cut the grass from under a person feet
-couper l'herbe sous le pied de quelqu'un

8-cut the cackleand come to the "osses"
-revenons à nos moutons

9-cut off a dog's tail and he will be a dog still
-un singe vêtu de pourpre est toujours un singe

D

dainty

    the dainties of the great are the tears of the poor
    -de tout temps,les petits ont pâti des sottises des grands

daisy

    he's been pushing up daisies for a long time
    to be food for worms
    -il y a longtemps qu'il mange les pissenlits par la racine

dance

    1-I'll lead you a pretty dance
    -donner le bal à quelqu'un

    2-they that dance must pay the fiddler
    -qui fait la faute aussi la boive
    -qui casse les verres,les paie
    -on ne va pas aux noces sans manger

danger

    1-danger itself the best remedy for danger
    -un clou chasse l'autre

    2-danger is next neighbour to security
    -la crainte de DIeu est le commencement de la sagesse

    3-danger makes man devout
    -quand le diable devient vieux,il se fait ermite

    4-the danger past and God forgotten
    -c'est le mal joli pas plutôt fini qu'on en rit (pour parler d'une femme qui vient
    d'accoucher)
    -tambour lointain n'a pas de son

dangerous

    it is dangerous to play with edged tools
    -on ne joue pas avec le feu

dare

    don't dare to darken my door again!
    -passez votre chemin!

day

    1-other days,other ways
    -autres temps,autres moeurs

    2-I have had my day
    -j'ai eu mon compte

    3-lay something for a rainy day
    -garder une poire pour la soif
    -il est bon avoir aucune chose sous le mortier

    4-dog days
    -canicule

5-everyday comes night
-les meilleures choses ont une fin
-demain,il fera jour
-après la pluie,le beau temps

6-every day is holiday with sluggards
-au paresseux,le poil lui pousse dans la main

7-not a long day,but a good heart rids work
-besogne qui plaît est à moitié faite

8-one of these days
-one day or another
-un de ces quatre matins

9-the longest day must have an end
-après la pluie le beau temps

10-one of these days is none of these days
-il ne faut jamais remettre à plius tard ce que l'on peut faire le jour même

11-no day so clear but has dark clouds
-nulle rose sans épines

dead

1-dead as a dodo
dead as a door nail
-mort et enterré
-raide mort
-mort et bien mort

2-to dead men and absent there are no friends left
-un homme mort n'a ni parents ni amis
-l'éloge des absents se fait sans flatterie

3-dead men tell no tales
-dead dogs don't bite
-morte la bête,morte le venin

4-half dead with fright
-plus mort que vif

5-dead on the hour
-à l'heure juste

6-I am at dead lift
-je suis au bout du rouleau

7-let the dead bury the dead
-à tout péché,miséricorde

8-I'm a dead duck,a dead pigeon
-je suis perdu
-je suis un homme mort

deaf

1-deaf as a white cat
-deaf as a post
-sourd comme un pot

2-none so deaf as those who won't hear
-il n'y a de pire sourd que celui qui ne veut pas entendre

deal

1-always deal with the top man
-il vaut mieux avoir affaire au bon Dieu qu'à ses saints

2-he that deals in dirt has aye foul fingers
-ceux qui touchent la poix,se souillent les doigts

3-if you deal with a fox,think of his tricks
-à trompeur,trompeur et demi

dear

dear bought is the honey that is licked from the horn
-trop cher achète le miel qui le lèche sur les épines

dearth

dearths foreseen come not
-plus on désire une chose,plus elle se fait attendre

death

1-death warmed up
-un cadavre ambulant

2-after death,doctor
-après la mort,le médecin

3-death combs us all with the same comb
death is a great leveller
-six pieds de terre suffisent au plus grand homme
-le plus riche en mourant n'emporte qu'un drap
-autant meurt veau que vache

4-death pays all debts
-au mort et à l'absent injure ni tourment

5-nothing is certain but death and taxes
-contre la mort,point de remède

6-death keeps no calendar
-on ne sait ni qui meurt ni qui vit

debt

1-speak not of my debts unless you mean to pay them
-ne me parlez pas de mes dettes à moins que vous ne vouliez les payer

2-an hundred pounds of sorrow pays not one ounce of debt
-cent livres de mélancolie ne payent un sou de dettes

3-a man in debt is caught in a net
-qui doit n'a rien à soi

4-out of debt,out of danger
-qui paye ses dettes s'enrichit

December

a December and May marriage is seldom a happy one
-vieux mari et jeune épouse font rarement un heureux mariage

deed

1-every deed is to be judged by the doer's intention
-c'est l'intention qui compte
-l'intention vaut le fait

2-the deed comes back upon the doer
-qui fera bien,bien trouvera
-au bon joueur,la balle
-les méchants portent leur enfer en eux

**3-deeds are fruits,words are but leaves
deeds but not words**
-mieux vaut donner sans promettre que promettre sans tenir
-ce ne sont pas les mots qui comptent mais les actions

4-one good deed is never lost
-un bienfait n'est jamais perdu

delay

delay is the antidote of anger
-rien ne gagne à un retardement si ce n'est la colère

Denmark

something is rotten in the state of Denmark
-il y a quelque chose de pourri au royaume des cieux

depend

he who depends on another dines ill and sups worse
-le pain d'autrui est amer
-mieux vaut ta propre morue que le dindon des autres

desert

desert and reward seldom keep company
-jamais à un bon chien il ne vient un bon os
-ce ne sont pas les chevaux qui tirent le plus fort qui mangent l'avoine

deserve

first deserve then desire
-le mérite se cache,il faut l'aller trouver
-la nature fait le mérite,et la fortune le met en oeuvre

desire

he that desires but little has no need of much
-je suis riche des biens dont je sais me passer

despair

despair gives courage to a coward
-le désespoir comble non seulement notre misère mais notre faiblesse

desperate

desperate diseases must have desperate remedies
-aux grands maux les grands remèdes

deuce

1-the deuce is in you
-vous avez le diable dans la peau

289

2-it played the deuce with me and my belongings
-cela m'a donné du fil à retordre

devil

1-the devil is not so black as he is painted
-on crie toujours le loup plus grand qu'il n'est
-un diable n'est pas toujours aussi diable qu'il est noir

2-when the devil is blind
-quand les poules auront des dents
-le trente-six du mois

3-the devil rides on a fiddlestick
-beaucoup de bruit pour rien

4-give the devil his due
-à tout seigneur tout honneur
-il faut rendre à César ce qui est à César

5-between the devil and the deep blue sea
-entre la peste et le choléra

6-needs must when the devil drives
-il faut marcher quand le diable est aux trousses

7-talk of the devil and he's sure to appear
talk of the angels and you will hear the flutter of their wings
-quand on parle du loup on en voit la queue
-quand on parle du soleil on en voit les rayons

8-the devil finds work for idle hands to do
the devil tempts all,but the idle man tempts the devil
-le diable s'empare des personnes oisives
-l'oisiveté est la mère de tous les vices
-les conseils de l'ennui sont les conseils du diable

9-to be full of the devil
-avoir le diable au corps

10-the devil dances in an empty pocket
-il ne faut pas tenter le diable

11-he who sups with the devil should have a long spoon
-à manger avec le diable,la fourchette n'est jamais trop longue

12-the devil sick would be a monk
-la crainte de Dieu est le commencement de la sagesse

13-what is got over the devil's back is spent under his belly
-ce qui vient du diable retourne au diable

14-better the devil you know than the devil you don't know
-il vaut mieux tenir que courir
-changer et trouver mieux sont deux
-on sait ce que l'on perd,on ne sait pas ce que l'on gagne

15-here's the very devil to pay
-nous sommes dans de beaux draps

16-the devil to pay and pitch hot
-cela va être difficile de s'en remettre

17-no devil so load as a she-devil
-femme sait un art avant le diable

18-the devil catch the hindmost
-lâcher la proie pour l'ombre

19-as the devil loves holy water
-pas du tout

20-the devil goes up the belfry by the vicar's skirts
-le diable chante la grand'messe

diamond
1-he's a diamond in the rough
-c'est un coeur d'or sous une rude écorce

2-diamond cut diamond
-à malin,malin et demi
-à bon chat,bon rat

dice
the dice are loaded
-les dés ont pipés
-les cartes sont truquées

die
1-to die in harness
to die with one's boots on
-mourir debout

2-he that dies this year is excused for the next
he that died half a year ago is as dead as Adam
-on ne meurt qu'une fois

3-the die is cast
-les dés sont jetés

4-dying is as natural as living
-contre la mort,point de remède

5-better to die in glory than live in dishonor
-mieux vaut mourir selon les règles que de réchapper contre les règles

6-to die by inches
-mourir à petit feu

7-to die in the last ditch
-luitter jusqu'à la dernière extrêmité

8-they die well that live well
-he dies like a beast who has done no good when he lived
-de telle vie,telle fin

difference
1-there is no difference of blood in a basin
-Dieu nous a tous pétris du même limon

2-there is a great difference between words and deeds
-dire et faire sont deux

dig

that dig was meant for you
-c'est une pierre dans votre jardin

diligence

diligence is the mother of good fortune
-prudence est mère de sûreté

diligent

1-for the diligent the week has seven todays,for the slothful seven tomorrows
-ne remetez pas au lendemain ce que vous pouvez faire le jour même

2-the diligent spinner has a large shift
-qui sème en pleurs,recueille en heur

dint

by dint of doing blacksmith work,one becomes blacksmith
-c'est en forgeant qu'on devient forgeron

dip

you can't dip into the future
-nous ne savons pas ce que l'avenir nous reserve

discontent

discontent is the first step in progress
-de la discussion jaillit la lumière
-nécessité est mère d'industrie

discretion

discretion is the better part of valour
-il vaut mieux tendre la main que le cou
-il vaut mieux se dédire que se détruire

dish

1-no dish pleases not all palates alike
-tous les goûts sont dans la nature
-tous les ânes ne portent pas de sac

2-many dishes make many diseases
-la gourmandise tue plus de monde que l'épée

dispute

there is no disputing about tastes
-tous les goûts sont dans la nature

distance

distance lends enchantment to the view
-loin des yeux,près du coeur

distress

two in distress make sorrow less
-chagrin partagé est moins lourd à porter

ditch

a last ditch struggle
-to fight up to the last ditch
-lutter jusqu'à la dernière extrêmité

divide

divide and rule (conquer)
-diviser pour régner

do

1-in doing we learn
-c'est en forgeant qu'on devient forgeron

2-do right and fear no man
-une bonne conscience est n doux oreiller

3-do well and have well
-qui fera bien,bein trouvera

4-doing is better than saying
-better to do well than to say well
-mieux vaut donner sans promettre que promettre sans tenir
-le dire c'est bien mais le faire c'est mieux

5-he that has done ill once will do it again
-qui a bu,boira
-qui a fait un panier fera bien une hotte
-qui vole un oeuf,vole un boeuf

6-do unto others as you would have them do unto you
do as you would be done by
-ne fais pas à autrui ce que tu ne voudrais pas qu'on te fît

7-one cannot do two things at one time
-on ne peut être à la fois au four et au moulin
-on ne peut sonner les cloches et aller à la procession

8-you would do little for God if the devil were dead
-le diable parle toujours en l'évangile

9-what is done cannot be undone
-ce qui est fait est fait

10-it's do or die
-marche ou crève (familier)
-c'est à prendre ou à laisser

11-do as I say,not as I do
-fais ce que je dis et non ce que je fais

12-do your duty,come what may
-fais ce que tu dois,advienne que pourra

13-he does ill hates the light
-rarement de sa faute on aime le témoin

14-do as most men do,then most men will speak well of you
-you must do as others do
-il faut hurler avec les loups

15-to be done brown
-être marron

16-do what you ought and come what can
-quand nous serons morts,fouira la vigne qui pourra

17-he that has to do with what is foul,never somes away clean
-ceux qui touchent la poix,se souillent les doigts

18-what may be done at any time may be done at no time
-il ne faut jamais remettre à plus tard ce que l'on peut faire le jour même

19-he that may not do as he would,must do as he may
-il faut souffri ce qu'on ne peut empêcher
-il faut souffrir patiemment ce qu'on ne peut amender sainement

20-you must do as others do
-il faut se tenir au gros de l'arbre

21-he that does evil,never was good
-de telle vie, telle fin

dog

1-every dog is valiant at its own door
every dog is a lion at home
-un chien est fort à la porte de son maître

2-a well-bred dog hunts by nature
-bon chien chasse de race

3-you can never scare a dog away from a greasy hide
-quand le camelot a pris son pli,c'est pour toujours

4-a black dog for a white monkey
-les affaires sont les affaires

5-better to have a dog fawn on you than bite you
-un maître familier nourrit un valet impertinent

6-the dog return to its vomit
-l'assassin revient toujours sur le lieu de son crime
-le lièvre retourne toujours au lancer
-toujours il souvient à Robin de ses flûtes

7-dead dogs don't bite
-un chien mort ne mord plus

8-to a mischievous dog a heavy clog
-à méchant chien court lien

9-the dog in the manger would neither eat the hay himself, nor let the ox eat it
-le chien du jardinier ne veut ni manger les choux ni permettre au lapin de les manger

10-give a dog a bad name and hang him
he that would hang his dog,gives out first that he is mad
if you want a pretence to whip a dog,say he ate the frying pan
any stick will do to beat a dog with

10-give a dog a bad name and hang him (suite)
he who has a mind to beat his dog will easily find a stick
there are more ways to kill a dog than hang him
-qui veut noyer son chien,l'accuse de la rage

11-a live dog is better than a dead lion
-chien en vie vaut mieux que lion mort
-mieux vaut goujat debout qu'empereur enterré

12-hungry dogs will eat dirty pudding
-à qui a faim,tout est pain

13-a bad dog never sees the wolf
-à mauvais chien on ne peut montrer le loup

14-it is an ill dog that deserves not a crust
-à chair de loup,sauce de chien

15-to dog someone footsteps
-être toujours sur les talons de quelqu'un

16-if the old dog barks,he gives counsel
-l'aboi d'un vieux chien doit-on croire
-en conseil écoute le vieil

17-it's dogged that does it
-cent fois sur le métier remettez votre ouvrage

18-barking dogs seldom bite
chien qui aboie ne mord pas
il ne pleut pas comme quand il tonne

19-dog doesn't eat dog
-les loups ne se mangent pas entre eux

20-every dog has his day
-tout vient à point à qui sait atttendre

21-in dog's age
-cela fait une paye,un bail

22-it is a poor dog that is not worth the whistling
-viendra un temps où la vache aura besoin de sa queue

donkey
1-to ride the black donkey
-être têtu comme un âne

2-the donkey means one thing and the driver another
-ce que pense l'âne ne pense l'ânier

door
1-the door must be either shut or open
-une porte doit être ouverte ou fermée

2-to meet behind closed doors
-se réunir à huis clos

3-when one door shuts,another opens
-ce que vous avez perdu dans le feu,vous le retrouverez dans la cendre
-autant de trous,autant de chevilles
-on a perdu une bataille mais on n'a pas perdu la guerre

4-every door may be shut but death's door
-contre la mort,point de remède

5-an open door may tempt a saint
-at open doors dogs come in
-il ne faut pas tenter le diable
-il ne faut pas mettre dans la cave un ivrogne qui a renoncé au vin

dose

a dose of one's own medicine
-rendre la monnaie de sa pièce

dot

to dot the i's and cross the t's
-être méticuleux
-mettre les points sur les "i"

double

double or quits
-quitte ou double

doubt

1-when in doubt do nothing
-dans le doute,abstiens toi

2-doubt is the key of knowledge
-le doute est le commencement de la sagesse

draw

1-to draw a blank
-faire chou blanc (familier)

2-one must draw a line somewhere
-l'excès en tout nuit
-il faut savoir s'arrêter
-il y a limite à tout

3-to draw in one's horns
-mettre de l'eau dans son vin

4-draw not your bow until your arrow is fixed
-il ne faut pas chanter triomphe avant la victoire

5-to draw a red herring across the path
-noyer le poisson (familier)

6-drawn from the wood
-à la pression (pour la bière)
-au tonneau (pour le vin)

7-one must draw back in order to leap better
-il faut reculer pour mieux sauter

8-to draw straws
-tirer à la courte paille

9-don't draw water with a sieve
-c'est le tonneau des Danaïdes

dream
dreams are lies
-tous songes sont mensonges

dress
dressed up like a dog's dinner
-tiré à quatre épingles

drink
1-to drink the cup of sorrow
-boire la coupe jusqu'à la lie

2-one cannot drink and whistle at once
-on ne peut être à la fois au four et au moulin
-on ne peut souffler et humer ensemble
-on ne peut sonner les cloches et aller à la procession

3-one must drink as one brew
-quand le vin est tiré il faut le boire

drip
constant dripping wears away a stone
-à force de coups,on abat un chêne

drive
1-who drive fat oxen shall himself be fat
-quand on veut gouverner les hommes,il ne faut pas les chasser devant soi,il faut les suivre

2-you can drive out nature with a pitchfork,but she keeps on coming back
-chassez le naturel il revient au galop

3-to drive a nail into one's coffin
-pousser quelqu'un dans la tombe

4-to drive someone up the wall
-to be driven round the bend
-rendre fou
-faire grimper aux arbres

5-driving a red herring across the path
noyer le poisson (familier)

drop
1-one drop of poison infects the whole tun of wine
-une cuillerée de goudron gâte un tonneau de miel
-il suffit d'une pomme pourrie pour gâter tout le tas

2-at the drop of a hat
-tout de go
-de but en blanc

3-to get the drop on someone
-avoir quelqu'un sous sa coupe

4-the last drop makes the cup run over
-c'est la goutte d'eau qui fait déborder le vase

5-the falling drops hollow the stone
constant dropping wears away a stone
-goutte à goutte, l'eau creuse la pierre

6-to drop a brick
-jeter un pavé dans la mare

7-many drops make an ocean
-many drops make a shower
-les petits ruisseaux font les grandes rivières

drowning
 a drowning man will catch a straw
 -un noyé s'accroche à un brin d'herbe

drum
 to be drummed out
 -être jeté dehors tambour battant

drunken
 a drunken man is a mad man
 -bon vin,mauvaise tête
 -le vin entre et la raison sort

dry
 1-he 's not even dry behind the ears
 -si on lui presse le nez,il en sort encore du lait
 -il tête encore sa mère

 2-I am dry with talking
 -je n'ai plus de salive

 3-nothing dries sooner than tears
 -rien ne sèche aussi vite que les larmes

Dutchman
 if not I'm a Dutchman
 -j'en mettrais ma main au feu (ma main à couper)

duck
 1-I'm a dead duck,a dead pigeon
 -je suis perdu
 -les carottes sont cuites (*familier*)

 2-don't make ducks and drakes of your money
 -ne jetez pas votre argent par les fenêtres

 3-to get one's ducks in a row
 -il ne manque pas un bouton de guêtre

dusk
 in the dusk
 -entre chien et loup

dust
 to through dust (speck) in his eyes
 -jeter de la poudre aux yeux

dustman
> **the dustman has arrived**
> -le marchand de sable est passé

duty
> **do your duty,come what may**
> -fais ce que dois,advienne que pourra

dwarf
> **a dwarf on a giant's shoulders sees the farthest of the two**
> -un nain sur les épaules d'un géant voit plus loin que celui qui le porte

dwell
> **he that dwells next door to a cripple,will learn to halt**
> -avec les loups,on apprend à hurler

dye
> **dyed in the wool**
> -pur sang
> -à tous crins

E

each

1-to each let it be given according to his deserts
-à chacun selon ses mérites

2-to each his own
-chaque âge a ses plaisirs
-à chaque fou sa marotte
-à chacun son goût

eagle

1-eagles don't breed doves
-l'aigle n'engendre pas la colombe
-une source salée ne peut donner d'eau douce

2-an eagle doesn't hawk at flies
-un aigle ne chasse point aux mouches

ear

1-his ears must be burning
-avoir les oreilles qui chauffent

2-in one ear and out of the other
-entré par une oreille,sorti par l'autre

3-over head and ears,up to the ears
-par dessus les oreilles

4-to have one's ear to the ground
-avoir les oreilles qui traînent

5-to turn a deaf ear
-faire la sourde oreille

6-to get a thick ear
-recevoir une gifle

7-to play it by ear
-aller au pifomètre

8-to be up to the ears in debt
-être endetté jusqu'au cou

9-if your ear glow,someone is talking of you
-ses oreilles doivent lui siffler

early

1-early to bed and early to rise makes a man healthy wealthy and wise
-coucher de poule et lever de corbeau éloignent l'homme du tombeau
-l'avenir appartient à ceux qui se lèvent tôt

2-it early pricks that will be a thorn
-on ne s'amende pas de vieillir

earth

1-earth is the best shelter
-au mort et à l'absent injure ni tourment

2-six feet of earth make all men equal
-six pieds de terre suffisent au plus grand homme

earthen

the earthen pot must keep clear of the brass kettle
-le pot de terre contre le pot de fer

east

1-east or west home is best
-un petit chez-soi est mieux qu'un grand chez les autres

2-too far east is west
-the longer east,the shorter west
-les extrêmes se touchent

easy

1-easier said than done
-plus facile à dire qu'à faire

2-it is easy to bear the misfortune of others
-nous avons tous assez de force pour supporter les maux d'autrui
-le boeuf de la vallée ne connaît pas les souffrances du boeuf de la colline
-le mal d'autrui est un songe
-la misère du boeuf n'est pas une peine pour le cheval

3-it is easy to do what one's own self wills
-besogne qui plaît est à moitié faite

4-it is easier to descend than to ascend
-it is easier to pull down than to build
-il est plus facile de descendre que de monter

5-it is easy as pie
-c'est du gâteau

6-it is easy to be wise after the event
-tout le monde sait être sage après coup

eat

1-to eat humble pie
-aller à Canossa

2-he that will eat the kernel,must crack the nut
-he who would eat the nut,must first crack the shell
-il faut casser le noyau pour en avoir l'amende
-celui qui laboure le champ,le mange

3-go away and eat coke
-va au diable

4-I could eat a horse
-j'ai une faim de loup
-je mange comme quatre

5-eat to live,not live to eat
-il faut manger pour vivre et non vivre pour manger

6-don't eat the calf on the coco's belly
-il ne faut pas vendre la peau de l'ours avant de l'avoir tué

7-to eat high off the hog
-se tailler la part du lion

8-to eat someone out of house and home
-il vaudrait mieux le tuer que le nourrir

9-eaten bread is soon forgotten
-à ventre soul.cerises amères

10-he that never ate flesh,thinks a pudding a dainty
-ce que les yeux ne voient pas ne fait pas mal au coeur

edge

he has a lot of rough edges
-c'est un ours mal léché

education

education begins a gentleman,conversation completes him
-beau parler n'écorche pas la langue

effect

the effect speaks,the tongue needs not
-ce ne sont pas les mots qui comptent mais les actions
-les faits sont là

egg

1-to take eggs for money
-prendre les enfants du Bon Dieu pour des canards sauvages

2-as sure as eggs is eggs
-aussi sûr que deux et deux font quatre

3-I have eggs on the spit
-j'ai des oeufs sur le feu

4-don't put all your eggs in one basket
-il ne faut pas mettre tous ses oeufs dans le même panier

5-better an egg today than a hen tomorrow
-un oeuf aujourd'hui vaut mieux qu'un poulet pour demain

6-he that would have eggs must endure the cackling of hens
-veux-tu des oeufs,souffre le caquetage des poules

elephant

1-to use an elephant to crack a nut
-faire d'une mouche un éléphant
-en faire une montagne

2-only an elephant can bear an elephant's load
-à l'impossible,nul n'est tenu

emperor

he is the meperor of China
-le roi n'est pas son cousin

302

empty

    1-an empty belly bears no body
    -la faim est mauvaise conseillère

    2-empty vessels make the greatest sound
    -ce sont les tonneaux vides qui font le plus de bruit

end

    1-at the end of the game you'll see the winner
    -qui n'entend qu'une cloche n'entend qu'un son
    -rira bien qui rira le dernier

    2-one end is sure to be boned
    -tout ce qui brille n'est pas d'or
    -on sait ce que parler veut dire

    3-the end makes all equal
    -le plus riche en mourrant n'emporte qu'un drap

    4-think of the end before you begin
    -rien n'est plus difficile à écorcher que la queue
    -à la queue gît la difficulté

    5-the end justifies the means
    -la fin justifie les moyens

    6-the end crowns the work
    -tout est bien qui finit bien
    -rien n'est plus difficile à écorcher que la queue
    -en la queue gît la difficulté

    7-in the end things will mend
    -après la pluie,le beau temps

ending

    the ending rounds off the whole
    -à la fin saura-t-on qui a mangé le lard

endure

    he that will not endure labour in this world,let him not be born
    -qui veut durer,doit endurer

enemy

    1-there is no little enemy
    -il n'est si petit buisson qui ne porte son ombre
    -il n'est si petit chat qui n'égratigne
    -il n'est nuls petits ennemis
    -il n'est si petit ennemi qui ne puisse faire tort
    -ce sont les petites pluies qui gâtent les grands chemins

    2-never tell an enemy that your foot aches
    -le chien attaque toujours celui qui a les pantalons déchirés

    3-better an open enemy than a false friend
    -mieux vaut ami grondeur que flatteur
    -mieux vaut un sage ennemi qu'un ignorant ami

English

    -an Englishman's house is his castle
    -la familiarité engendre le mépris

enjoy

if you would enjoy the fire,you must put up with the smoke
-qui ne risque rien,n'a rien

enough

1-more than enough is too much
-la sursomme abât l'âne
-le surplus rompt le couvercle
-la dernière goutte est celle qui fait déborder le vase
-l'excès d'un très grand bien devient un mal très grand
-quand on serre trop l'anguille,on la laisse partir
-entre trop et trop peu est la juste mesure

2-enough is as good as a feast
enough is enough
-contentement passe richesse
-trop et trop peu n'est pas mesure
-il y a deux sortes de trop le trop et le trop peu
-il faut lier le sac avant qu'il soit plein

3-enough to make a cat laugh
-ridicule

4-enough to make a cat speak
-de quoi ne pas avoir sa langue dans sa poche

enter

when you enter in a house,leave anger ever at the door
-à cheval hargneux,il faut une écurie à part
-il faut faire coucher la colère à la porte

entertain

to entertain an angel unaware
-faire diverson

entreprise

in every entreprise consider where you would come out
-en toutes choses il faut considérer la fin

envy

1-envy shoots at others and wounds herself
-quand on crache en l'air,cela vous retombe sur le nez

2-better be envied than pitied
-mieux vaut faire envie que pitié

err

to err is human,to forgive divine
-l'erreur est humaine,le pardon divin

escape

he escaped by the skin of his teeth
-il l'a échappé belle

evening

1-the evening crowns the day
-tout est bien qui finit bien
-à la fin saura-t-on qui a mangé le lard

2-evening red and morning grey stes the traveller on his way
-rouge au soir,blanc au matin,c'est la journée du pélerin

event
coming events cast their shadow before them
-l'évènement à venir projette son ombre

everybody
1-everybody slanders everybody else
-chacun médit du tiers comme du quart

2-what is everybody's business is nobody's business
-affaire à tout le monde,affaire à personne
-il n'y a pas d'âne plus mal bâté que celui du commun

everyone
1-everyone to his taste
-à chacun selon son goût
-chacun prend son plaisir où il se trouve

2-everyone who was anyone was there
-toute la haute volée était venue

everything
1-everything comes to him who waits
-tout vient à point à qui sait attendre
-avec le temps et la paille les nèfles mûrissent

2-everything has its seed
-il faut un commencement à tout

3-everything has its day
-chaque chose en son temps

4-everything is good in its season
-de saison tout est bon

5-everything has an end
-les meilleures choses ont une fin

evil
1-of two evils,choose the less
-entre deux maux il faut choisir le moindre

2-evil communications corrupt good manners
-argent fait perdre et prendre gens
-argent fait perdre et prendre gens

3-the evil that man do lives after them,the good is oft interred with their bones
-les bienfaits s'écrivent sur le sable et les injures sur l'airain

4-evil to him that evil thinks
-honni soit qui mal y pense

5-evil does not always come to injure
-à quelque chose malheur est bon

6-of an evil crow,an evil egg
-toujours le vin sent son terroir

example

1-example is better than precept
-nous avons d'assez bons préceptes mais peu de maîtres
-a beau parler qui n'a cure de bien faire

2-a good example is the best sermon
-le sermon édifie,l'exemple détruit
-a beau parler qui n'a cure de bien faire

exception

the exception proves the rule
-l'exception confirme la règle

excess

if in excess,even nectar is poison
-trop tranchant ne coupe pas,trop pointu ne perce pas
-l'excès en tout nuit
-le surplus rompt le couvercle

exchange

a fair exchange is no robbery
-les affaires sont les affaires

excuse

1-a bad excuse is better than none
-"pardon" ne guérit pas la bosse

2-he who excuses himself accuses himself
-qui s'excuse,s'accuse

expect

1-what can you expect from a pig but a grunt?
-les coucous ne font pas les merles
-le vin sent toujours son terroir
-on ne peut faire d'une buse un épervier
-on a tiré un feu d'artifice à sa naissance

2-we may not expect a good whelp from an ill dog
la plus belle fille du monde ne peut donner que ce qu'elle a

3-no one is expected to do the impossible
-à l'impossible nul n'est tenu
-qui ne peut galoper,qu'il trotte

expectation

expectation is better than realization
-il vaut mieux arriver en retard qu'arriver en corbillard
-l'espoir fait vivre

experience

1-experience without learning is better than learning without experience
-les ans ont beaucoup plus vu que les livres n'en ont connu
-une once d'esprit vaut mieux qu'une livre de science

2-experience must be bought
-apprenti n'est pas maître

3-experience is the best teacher
-de jeune avocat,héritage perdu

4-experience is good if not bought too dear
-qui trébuche et ne tombe pas avance son chemin

extreme

extremes meet
-les extrêmes se touchent

eye

1-in the eyes of the lover,pock-marks are dimples
-ce qu'on aime est toujours beau

2-better eye sore than be blind altogether
-quand on n'a pas ce que l'on aime,il faut aimer ce que l'on a

3-an eye for an eye,a tooth for a tooth
-oeil pour oeil,dent pour dent

4-to see eye to eye with someone
-voir du même oeil que quelqu'un

5-one eye-witness is better than ten ear-witness
-un seul témoin oculaire en vaut dix qui ont entendu

6-four eyes see more than two
-quatre yeux voient mieux que deux

7-the eye of a needle
-le chat d'une aiguille

8-to have eyes like a hawk
-avoir des yeux de lynx

9-all my eye and Betty Martin!
-mon oeil!

10-far from eye,far from mind
-far from eye,far from heart
-loin des yeux,loin du coeur
-l'absence est l'ennemie de l'amour

11-the eye that sees all things else sees not itself
-oeil un autre oeil voit mais pas le sien

12-better eye out than always ache
-il faut perdre un vairon pour gagner un saumon

13-sharp eye and steady hand
-bon pied,bon oeil

14-the eye of the master will do more work than both his hands
-one eye of the master sees more than ten of the servants
-il n'est pour voir que l'oeil du maître

15-eyes are bigger than the belly
-avoir les yeux plus gros que le ventre

16-the eye is the window of the heart (mind)
-les yeux sont le miroir de l'âme

17-what the eye doesn't see,the heart doesn't grieve over
-ce que les yeux ne voient pas ne fait pas mal au coeur

F

face

1-fair face,foul heart
-a fair face may hide a fool heart
-beau boucaut,mauvaise morue

2-a good face is a letter of recommandation
-rien n'agrée sans bonne mine

3-to keep two faces under one hood
to be doubled-faced(or two faced)
-être un Tartuffe
-il ne faut pas se fier à qui entend deux messes

4-a straight faced man
-un pince sans rire

5-she has a face that would stop a clock
-elle a une gueule de raie

6-to face the music
-affronter l'orage (sens figuré)
-payer les pots cassés

7-the face is no index to the heart
-quand on regarde quelqu'un,on n'en voit que la moitié
-qui peint la fleur,n'en peut peindre l'odeur
-qui ferme la bouche ne montre pas les dents

8-to be doubled-faced
-être un tartuffe

fact

facts are stubborn things
-les faits sont là

failure

every failure one meets will add to experience
-un âne ne trébuche pas deux fois sur la même pierre
-expérience est mère de science

faint

faint heart never won fair lady
-jamais honteux n'eut belle amie
-il ne faut pas laisser de semer par crainte des pigeons
-à coquin honteux,plate besace
-le chien peureux n'a jamais son soûl de lard

fair

1-fair without,fale within
-belle chère et coeur arrière
-en belle gaine d'or,couteau de plomb gît et dort
-serpent qui change de peau est toujours serpent

2-fair and soft go far in the day
-qui va doucement va sûrement
-plus fait douceur que violence
-patience et longueur de temps font plus que force et rage
-qui veut voyager loin,ménage sa monture

308

3-all is fair in love and war
-tous les coups sont permis
-à la guerre comme à la guerre

4-the fair and the foul by dark are like store
-la nuit,tous les chats sont gris

faith

1-faith is everything
-il n'y a que la foi qui sauve

2-faith will move mountains
-la foi transporte les montagnes

fall

1-to fall on one's lap
-tomber du ciel

2-to fall two dogs with one stone
-faire d'une pierre deux coups

3-to fall into sin is human,to remain in sin is devilish
-il n'y a de damnés que les obstinés
-errare humanum est,sed perseverare diabolicum
-se tromper est humain,persévérer dans son erreur estr diabolique

4-it fell off the back of a lorry
-c'est tombé du ciel

5-he that falls today may rise tomorrow
-ce que vous avez perdu dans le feu,vous le retrouverez dans la cendre

6-to fall short of one's expectations
-répondre à ses espérances

false

on efalse move may lose the game
-faute d'un point,Martin perdit son âne

falsehood

falsehood never made a fair hinder end
-homme rusé,tard abusé

fame

a good fame is better than a good face
-bonne renommée vaut mieux que ceinture dorée

familiarity

familiarity brings contempt
-la familiarité engendre le mépris

family

every family has a skeleton in the cupboard
-nulle rose sans épines

fan

to fan the flames
-mettre de l'huile sur le feu
-attiser le feu

far

1-far folk fare best
-au mort et à l'absent,injure ni tourment
-un peu d'absence fait grand bien

2-far from Jupiter,far from the thunder
-la crainte de Dieu est le commencement de la sagesse
-la crainte du gendarme est le commencement de la sagesse

3-far from court,far from care
-far from eye,far from heart
-loin des yeux,loin du coeur
-les os sont pour les absents

4-far shooting never killed birds
-tambour lointain n'a pas de son

farmer

a good farmer makes a good farm
-tant vaut l'homme,tant vaut la terre

fasten

eveyone fastens where there is gain
-espoir de gain diminue la peine

fat

1-the fat is in the fire
-jeter de l'huile sur le feu

2-a bit of fat
-un coup de chance

father

1-like father,like son
-tel père,tel fils

2-whatsoeverwas the father of the disease,an ill diet was the mother
-la gourmandise tue plus de monde que l'épée

3-niggard father,spendthrift son
-à père avare,fils prodigue

fault

like fault,like punishment
-méchanceté porte sa peine

faute

fautes are thick when love is thin
-on pardonne tant que l'on aime

fear

1-all fear is bondage
-la peur ne guérit de rien

2-he that fears leaves let him not go into the woods
-n'aille au bois qui a peur des feuilles

3-he that fears every bush must not go abirding
he that fears every grass must not walk in a meadow
-qui craint le danger ne doit pas aller en mer

4-who fears to suffer,suffers from fear
-qui craint de souffrir,il souffre déjà de ce qu'il craint

5-fear gives wings
-la peur a bon pas

6-it is better to fear than to trust too far
-puce en l'oreille,l'homme réveille

feather
1-it's a feather in his cap
-c'est un titre de gloire

2-fine feathers make fine birds
-c'est la plume qui fait l'oiseau

3-a broken feather in one's wing
-avoir du plomb dans l'aile

4-to make the feathers fly
-voler dans les plumes de quelqu'un (familier)

5-feather by feather the goose is plucked
-petit à petit,l'oiseau fait son nid

feed
to feed a fly
-remplir une dent creuse

feel
1-he felt that the hour for the upturning of his glass was at hand
-il sentit sa dernière heure arriver

2-to feel under the weather
-se sentir "chose"

3-he feels like a fish out of the water
-il est dans ses petits souliers

fence
1-he didn't want anyone to fence him in
-il ne voulait pas qu'on entrave sa liberté

2-good fences make good neighbours
-les bons comptes font les bons amis

few
the fewer his years,the fewer his tears
-petits enfants,petits soucis,grands enfants,grands soucis

field
fields have eyes,and woods have ears
-les murs ont des oreilles

fight
1-he that fights and runs away may live to fight another day
-il vaut mieux se dédire que se détruire

2-fight fire with fire
-l'épée est la meilleure langue pour répondre à l'outrage

3-to fight tooth and nail
-se défendre peid à pied

filth

the filth under the white snow the sun discovers
-qui est âne et veut être cerf se connaît au saut du fossé
-on doit plaire par moeurs et non par robe de couleur
-sous la crasse,la beauté s'y cache
-il ne faut pas regarder la saleté d'un cochon pour en manger
-il faut déshabiller un maïs pour voir sa bonté

find

1-you have found an elephant in the moon
-tu te fourres le doigt dans l'oeil jusqu'au coude (*familier*)

2-to find a silver lining in every cloud
-faire contre mauvaise fortune bon coeur

-he has found the bean in the cake
-il a gagné le gros lot

finder

finders,keepers;loosers weepers
-tout ce qui tombe dans le fossé est pour le soldat

finding

findings is keeping
-ce qui tombe dans le fossé est pour le soldat
-l'habit fait le moine
-l'oiseau doit beaucoup à son plumage

fine

fine as five pence
-belle comme un sous neuf

finger

1-his fingers are all thumbs
-il est maladroit

2-not to lift a finger
-ne pas lever le petit doigt

3-my little finger told me that
-c'est mon petit doigt qui me l'a dit

4-to be finger and glove with another
they are finger and thumb
-être comme les deux doigts de la main
-être comme deux frères
-ils sont comme cul et chemise (*familier*)
-quand l'un dit "tue!" l'autre dit "assomme!"

5-to have it at one's fingers'ends
-le connaître sur le bout du doight

6-fingers were made before forks
-les mains sont faites avant les couteaux
-où il y a de la gêne,il n'y a pas de plaisir

7-to keep one's finger crossed
-se tenir les pouces

8-to slip through one's finger
-glisser entre les doigts

9-to have a finger in the pie
-avoir sa part du gâteau
-avoir un droit de regard

10-with a wet finger
-facilement

11-to have a finger in every pie
-mettre son nez partout
-être un touche à tout
12-to have a finger in the pie
-avoir sa part du gâteau

13-better a finger off than always aching
-il faut perdre un vairon pour gagner un saumon

-the finger that touches rouge will be red
-ceux qui touchent la poix se souillent les doigts

fingertip
at my fingertips
-à ma disposition

finish
to finish Aladdin's window
-le génie commence les beaux ouvrages mais le travail les achève

fire
1-a little fire burns up a great deal of corn
-faute d'un point,Martin perdit son âne
-petites causes,grands effets

2-one fire drives another's burning
-un clou chasse l'autre

3-he never stops hurling fire and brimstone at his enemies
-il ne cesse de brandir l'anathème contre ses ennemis

4-no smoke without fire
the fire is never without heat
-pas de fumée sans feu
-on ne dit guère Martin qu'il n'y ait d'âne
-il n'y a pas de plume tombée sans oiseau plumé

5-a soft fire makes sweet malt
-plus fait douceur que violence
-hâtez-vous lentement

6-if you play with the fire,you get burnt
-il ne faut pas jouer avec le feu

313

7-fire that's closest kept burns most of all
-le feu le plus couvert est le plus ardent

8-fire cannot be hidden in flax
-la plus belle fille du monde ne peut donner que ce qu'elle a
-rage d'amour est pire que le mal de dents
-le feu le plus couvert est le plus ardent

first

1-first in,first served
-first come,first served
-le premier venu engrène
-premier levé,premier chaussé
-l'avenir appartient à ceux qui se lèvent tôt

2-I am not the first and I shall not be the last
-je n'en apporterai pas la mode

3-the first blow is half the battle
-c'est la première impression qui compte

4-it is first rate
-c'est du cousu main

5-if at first you don't succeed,then try,try,and try again
-cent fois sur le métier remettez votre ouvrage

6-first creep then walk
-rien ne sert de courir, il faut partir à point

fish

1-I have other fish to fry
-j'ai d'autres chats à fouetter

2-neither fish,flesh or fowl
-neither fish,flesh nor good herring
-mi-chair,mi-poisson
-mi figue,mi raisin

3-a big fish in a little pound
-au royaume des aveugles,le borgne est roi

4-there are as good fish in the seas as ever came out of it
-there is more fish where that came from
-sea has fish for every man
-there are more fish for every man
-il n'y a plus d'un âne à la foire qui s'appelle Martin
-personne n'est irremplaçable
-un de perdu,dix de retrouvés

5-that fish will soon be caught that nibbles at every bait
-souris qui n'a qu'un trou est bientôt prise
-si vous n'avez pas d'autre sifflet,votre chien est perdu
-la mouche va si souvent au lait qu'elle y demeure

6-all is fish that comes to my net
-il n'y a pas de petit profit
-tout fait farine à bon moulin

7-fish begins to stink at the head
-c'est par la tête que le poisson commence à sentir

8-better are small fish than an empty dish
-quand n'a pas ce que l'aime,il faut aimer ce que l'on a

9-it is a silly fish that is caught twicce at the same bait
-un âne ne trébuche pas deux fois sur la même pierre
-expérience est mère de science

10-there is more fish for every man
-il y a plus d'un âne à la foire qui s'appelle Martin

11-he is a regular flat fish
-il est bête comme ses pieds

12-old fish,old oil,and an old friend are the best
-les vieux amis et les vieux écus sont les meilleurs

13-it's ill fishing before the net
-ne criez pas "des moules" avant qu'elles ne soient au bord

14-little fish slip through net,but great ones are taken
-quand on n'est pas le plus fort,il faut être le plus fin

15-you must not make fish of one and flesh of the other
-il n'y a pas deux poids,deux mesures

16-the best fish swim near the bottom
-les meilleurs poissons nagent près du fond

17-great fish eat up the small
-les gros poissons mangent les petits
-les grands voleurs pendent les petits

fishing

1-it is good fishing in trouble waters
-l'eau trouble fait le gain du pêcheur

2-it's ill fishing before the net
-ne criez pas "des moules" avant qu'elles ne soient au bord

fist

-he is close-fisted
-il est près de ses sous

fit

1-to be fit as a fiddle
-se porter comme le Pont-Neuf
-se porter comme un charme
-avoir bon pied,bon oeil

2-by fits and starts
-par à-coups
-d'une façon décousue

flag

the flag protects the cargo
-le pavillon couvre la marchandise

flash

a flash in the pan
-un feu de paille

flea

1-to send someone away with a flea in his ear
-renvoyer quelqu'un avec un refus catégorique

2-great fleas have lesser fleas
-on a toujours besoin d'un plus petit que soi

flesh

flesh is frail
-la chair est faible

flint

in the coldest flint there is a hot fire
-il n'y a pas de montagnes sans vallée
-mains froides,coeur chaud

flock

it si a sorry flock where the ewe bears the bell
-ce n'est pas à la poule de chanter devant le coq

flog

it is useless to flog a dead horse
-les longs propos font les courts jours

flow

1-a flow will have an ebb
-après le flux,le reflux

2-flow of words is not always flow of wisdom
-parler de quelque chose comme un aveugle des couleurs

flower

1-the fairest flowers soonest fade
-la beauté est une fleur éphémère

2-give flowers make friends
-les petits présents entretiennent l'amitié

3-no flowers by request
-ni fleurs,ni couronnes

fly

1-there's fly in the ointment
-il y a une ombre au tableau

2-no flying without wings
-oiseau ne peut voler sans ailes

3-to fly off the handle
-sortir de ses gonds

4-don't fly in the face of providence
-rien ne sert de courir,il faut partir à point

5-to fly in one's face
-voler dans les plumes de quelqu'un (familier)

6-no flying from fate
-on ne peut rien changer à son destin

7-the fly that plays too long in the candle,singes his wings at last
-qui s'y frotte,s'y pique

8-to be the fly on the coachwheel
-faire la mouche du coche

9-to change a fly into an elephant
-faire d'une mouche un éléphant

foal

how can the foal amble if the horse and mare trot?
-les chiens ne font pas de chats
-tel père,tel fils

foe

no foes to a flatterer
-tout flatteur vit aux dépens de celui qui l'écoute de celui qui l'écoute

fog

a fog cannot be dispelled by a fan
-aux grands maux les grands remèdes

folk

1-rich folk have many friends
-à bourse pleine,amis nombreux

2-short folk are soon angry
-quand les brebis enragent elles sont pires que les loups

3-far folk,far best
-un peu d'absence fait grand bien

4-young folks think old folks to be fools but old folks know young folks to be fools
-le vieux n'y voit pas assez pour marteler la faux et le jeune ne sait pas l'affiler

follow

1-follow the river and you'll get to the sea
-on va de tout vent à un même endroit

2-he who follows truth too closely will have dirt kicked in his face
-rien n'est si dangereux que trop de bonne foi

3-he that follows two hares at a time is sure to catch neither
-il ne faut pas courir deux lièvres à la fois

4-to follow one's nose
-ne pas voir plus loin que le bout de son nez

folly

1-folly grows without watering
-tête de fou ne blanchit pas

2-folly is the product of all countries and ages
-il y a plus de fous que de sages

2-folly is the product of all countries and ages (suite)
-d'âge en âge on ne fait que changer de folie
-il est des sots de tout pays

3-the folly of one man is the fortune of another
-le malheur des uns fait le bonheur des autres

food

1-there is nothing like plain food
-la soupe fait le soldat

2-to be food for worms
-il y a longtemps qu'il mange les pissenlits par la racine

fool

1-one fool praises another
-un âne gratte l'autre

2-a fool should never hold a bauble in his hand
-if the fool knew how to be silent he could sit amongst the wise
-fools are wise as long as silent
-fol semble sage quand il se tait
-fou qui se tait passe pour sage

3-if all fools wore feathers,we should seem a flock of geese
-quand le soleil est couché,il y a bien des bêtes à l'ombre

4-to live in a fool's paradise
-se bercer d'illusions

5-a fool may give a wise man counsel
-fool rush in where angels fear to tread
-un fou avise bien un sage
-les fous inventent les modes et les sages les suivent
-ce sont les fous qui troublent l'eau et ce sont les sages qui pèchent
-les fols font les banquets et les sages les mangent

6-fools live poor to die rich
-un avare est toujours gueux
-fol et avoir ne se peuvent entr'avoir

7-to be a fool for one's pains
-travailler pour la gloire
-travailler pour le grand turc
-travailler pour le roi de Prusse

8-fools never know when they are well off
-quand le puits est à sec,on sait ce que vaut l'eau

9-a fool's bolt is soon shot
-la flèche d'un sot file vite

10-fools will be fools still
-tête de fou ne blanchit pas

11-there is no fool like an old fool
-les vieux fous sont plus fous que le jeunes

12-fools bite one another,but wise men agree
-il n'y a que les fous qui ne changent pas d'avis

13-he that has to do with a fool,never comes away clean
-si on met la main à la pâte,il en reste toujours aux doigts

14-a fool's tongue is long enough to cut his own throat
-la parole est d'argent mais le silence est d'or

15-a fool always rushes to the fore
-à la presse vont les fous

16-a fool and his money are soon parted
-ce qui vient de la flute s'en va par le tambour

17-to fool about
-faire le zouave

foolish

**1-one cannot do a foolish thing once in one's life but one must hear
of it a hundred times**
-qui mange la vache du roi,à cent ans de là en paye les os

**2-it is a foolish bird that soils its own nest
it is a foolish sheep that makes the wolf his confessor**
-de fol folie,de cuir courroie
-il ne faut pas scier la branche sur laquelle on est assis

3-from a foolish judge,a quick sentence
-de fou juge,brève sentence

foot

**1-one foot is better than two crutches
better a bad foot than none**
-quand on n'a pas ce que l'on aime,il faut aimer ce que l'on a

**2-to put your best foot forward
-to put the best foot foremost**
-celui qui n'a pas bon pied,part avant
-paraître sous un meilleur jour

3-to have feet of clay
-avoir un caractère faible

4-the foot knows where the shoe pinches
-la langue va où la dent fait mal

5-all feet tread not in one shoe
-tous les goûts sont dans la nature

6-six feet of earth make all men equal
-six pieds de terre suffisent au plus grand homme

7-to have a foot in several camps
-manger à plusieurs rateliers

footing

1-he is on good footing with the world
-il est bien dans sa peau

319

2-to be on good footing with someone
-être en bons termes avec quelqu'un

footloose
it's a footloose and fancy free
-c'est un individu sans feu ni lieu

footprint
footprints on the sands of time are made by sitting down
-qui fuit la meule fuit la farine

forbidden
forbidden fruit is sweetest
-nous défendre quelque chose,c'est nous en donner envie

forebearance
forebearance is no acquittance
-"pardon" ne guérit pas la bosse

forehead
in the forehead and the eye,the lecture of the mind doth lie
-les yeux sont le miroir de l'âme

forest
we cannot see the forest for the trees
-l'arbre ne doit pas nous cacher la forêt

forewarned
forewarned is forearned
-un homme averti en vaut deux

forgive
1-if we are bound to forgive an enemy,we are not bound to trust him
-de notre ennemi réconcilié,il faut se garder

2-forgive and forget
-à tout péché,miséricorde

fortune
1-fortune is made of glass
-la Fortune est de verre;au moment où elle brille le plus, elle se brise

2-fortune is good to him who knows to make good use of her
-quand le puits est à sec,on sait ce que vaut l'eau

3-fortune to one is mother,to another is stepmother
-la fortune tourne à l'avantage de ceux qu'elle favorise

4-fortune favours fools
-aux innocents les mains pleines

5-fortune favours brave
fortune favours the bold
-la fortune sourit aux audacieux

6-when fortune smiles,embrace her
-une occasion perdue ne se rattrape jamais
-quand on tient la poule,il faut la plumer

7-fortune knocks once at least at every man's gate
-tout vient à point à qui sait attendre

8-fortune is blind
-la fortune est aveugle

foul

he that has to do with a foul,never comes away clean
-quand on met la main à la pâte,il en reste toujours aux doigts

fowl

far fowl have far feathers
-vache qui vient de loin a gros pis

fowler

the fowler's pipe sounds sweet till the bird is caught
-l'air ne fait pas la chanson
-de beaux raisins,parfois pauvre vin

fox

1-when the fox preaches,then beware your geese
-quand le renard prêche,veillez sur vos oies

2-an old fox is not easily snared
-expérience est mère de science

3-the fox may grow grey but never good
-en sa peau mourra le renard

4-though the fox run,the chicken has wings
-at length the fox is brought to the furrier
-homme rusé,tard abusé

5-a fox shouldn't be one of the jury at a goose's trial
-on ne peut être juge et partie

6-to set the fox to mind the geeese
-mettre un loup dans la bergerie

7-the wise fox will never rob his neighbour's henroost
-un bon renard ne mange jamais les poules de son voisin

8-the sleepy fox has seldom feathered breakfasts
-renard qui dort la matinée n'a plus la gueule emplumée

free

to be free as a bird
-être libre comme l'air

freeze

he freezes who does not burn
-qui n'a suffisance,n'a rien
-il vaut mieux suer que grelotter

frequent

frequent and regular repetition is the principal factor of success
-cent fois sur le métier remettez votre ouvrage

321

friar

the friar preached against stealing and had a goose in his sleeve
-fais ce que je dis et non ce que je fais

Friday

when two Fridays come together
-la semaine des quatre jeudis
-le trente-six du mois

friend

1-short reckonings make long friends
-les bons comptes font les bons amis
-à tout bon compte,revenir

2-before you make a friend eat a bushel of salt with him
-pour bien connaître un homme,il faut avoir manger un muid de sel avec lui

3-all are not friends that speak us fair
-la main qui caresse est souvent la main qui tue

4-the best friens must part
-il n'est si bonne compagnie qu'on ne quitte

5-a friend in need is a friend indeed
-au besoin l'ami
-on connaît le véritable ami dans le besoin
-c'est dans le malheur qu'on connaît ses vrais amis

6-select your friend with a silk-gloved hand and hold him with an iron gauntlet
-croyez tout le monde honnête et vivez avec tous comme avec des fripons

7-your friends are your mirror,they show you yourself
-dis-moi qui tu hantes,je te dirai qui tu es

8-with friends like that,who needs enemy?
-mieux vaut ami grondeur que flatteur

9-friends are plenty when the purse is full
-à bourse pleine,amis nombreux
-riche homme ne sait qui ami lui est

10-a friend in court is better thatn a penny in purse
-mieux vaut ami en voie que denier en courroie

11-a friend in the market is better than a penny in the chest
-mieux vaut ami en place qu'argent en bourse

12-old friends and old wine and old gold are best
-les vieux amis et les vieux écus sont les meilleurs

13-treat your friend as he might become a foe
-ta chemise ne sache ta guise

14-a friend is not so soon gotten as lost
-un ami est long à trouver et prompt à perdre

322

15-love your friend with his fault
-si ton ami est borgne regarde de profil

16-when friends meet, hearts warm
-il n'y a que la main d'un ami qui arrache l'épine du coeur

17-friends agree best at distance
-loin des yeux,près du coeur

friendship
1-friendship is a plant which must be often watered
-sur le chemin de l'amitié,ne laissez pas croître d'herbe

2-sudden friendship,sudden repentance
-qui se marie à la hâte se repent à loisir

3-real friendship does not freeze in winter
-au besoin l'ami
-une main lave l'autre

frog
1-a frog in the throat
-un chat dans la gorge

2-the frog cannot out of her bog
-le naturel de la grenouille est qu'elle boit et souvent gazouille
-on ne peut faire d'une buse un épervier
-toujours le vin sent son terroir

fruit
1-when the fruit is ripe,it must fall off
-quand la poire est mûre,il faut qu'elle tombe
-il faut attendre à cueillir la poire qu'elle soit mûre

2-he that would have the fruit,must climb the tree
-veux-tu des oeufs,souffre le caquetage des poules
-pour avoir la moelle,il faut briser l'os
-au fond du taillis sont les mûres
-celui qui laboure le champ,le mange

3-by their fruits shall you know them
-on reconnaît l'arbre à ses fruits

4-fruit ripens not well in the shade
-enfant haï est toujours triste

frying-pan
he who has the frying-pan in his hand turns it at will
il n'y a point de si empêché que celui qui tient la queue de la poêle

fuel
adding fuel to the fire
-mettre de l'huile sur le feu

full
to be full of devil
-avoir le diable au corps

funeral
    one funeral makes many
    -un malheur n'arrive jamais seul

fussy
    as fussy as a hen with one chick
    -comme une poule qui a trouvé un couteau

future
    we can't dip into the future
    we don't know what the future has in store for us
    -nous ne savons pas ce que l'avenir nous réserve

G

gain

1-what you gain on the swings,you lose on the roundabouts
-à tout prendre on ne gagne ni ne perd

2-great gain makes work easy
-l'espoir de gain diminue la peine

3-light gains make a heavy purse
-il n'y a pas de petit profit

4-he gains enough whom fortune loses
-expérience est mère de science

5-no gain without pain
-les mains noires font manger le pain blanc

gambler

once a gambler,always a gambler
-qui a bu,boira

game

1-the game's a foot
-les dés sont jetés

2-the game is not worth the candle
-le jeu n'en vaut pas la chandelle

3-at the end of the game,we shall see who gains
-loue le beau jour au soir,et la vie à ta mort

gape

he that gapes until be fed,well may be gape until be dead
gape long enough,larks will fall into mouth
-il attend que les alouettes lui tombent toutes rôties dans le bec

garden

no garden without its weeds
-nulle rose sans épines

gasp

to be at your last gasp
-être aux abois

gate

1-a creaking gate hangs long
-les pots fêlés sont ceux qui durent le plus

2-make not the gate wider than the city
-il faut tailler son manteau selon son drap
-n'ayez pas les yeux plus gros que le ventre

gather

1-gather ye rosebuds while ye may
-il faut battre le fer pendant qu'il est chaud
-il faut tourner le moulin lorsque souffle le vent

2-one cannot gather grapes of thorns or figs or thistles
-la plus belle fille du monde ne peut donner que ce qu'elle a

gay
gay as the king' candle
-bariolé comme la chandelle des rois

gaze
he that gazes upon the sun,shall at last be blind
-de trop près se chauffe qui se brûle
-qui s'y frotte,s'y pique

general
one bad general is better than two good ones
-c'est raison que chacun soit maître en son logis

genius
genius is an infinite capacity for taking pains
-le génie est une longue patience
-on n'a rien sans rien

gentleman
a gentleman's agreement
-convention verbale entre gens de parole

get
1-you can't get too much of a good thing
-abondance de biens ne nuit pas

2-to get it in the neck
-l'avoir dans le baba (*familier*)
-se faire taper sur les doigts

3-get down to brasstack,to nitty-gritty
-venez en au fait
-revenons à nos moutons

4-you can't get blood out of a turnip
-you cannot get blood out of a stone
-on ne peut peigner un diable qui n'a pas de cheveu
-la plus belle fille du monde ne peut donner que ce qu'elle a

5-don't get the wrong saw by the ear
-don't get the wrong end of the stick
-tourner sept fois sa langue dans sa bouche

6-to get the needle
-to get the spike
-to get huffy
-prendre la mouche

7-he got a bead on the man in the lead
-il a pris l'homme de tête en point de mire

8-you don't get something for nothing
-pour avoir la moëlle il faut briser l'os
-on n'a rien sans rien
-au fond du taillis sont les mûres
-veux-tu des oeufs,souffre le caquetage des poules

9-he has gotten the boot and the better horse
-il a les deux oreilles et la queue

10-to get off the hook
-sortir du pétrin

11-to get in one's hair
-to get my goat
-taper sur les nerfs de quelqu'un

gift

1-don't look a gift horse in the mouth
-à cheval donné on ne regarde pas la bride

2-it's not the gift,it's the giver
-la manière de donner vaut mieux que ce que l'on donne

gilt

to take the gilt off the gingerbread
-détruire l'illusion

girl

-a naive young girl
-une oie blanche

give

1-to give up the goat
-mourir

2-he that gives fair words feeds you with an empty spoon
-la beauté ne sale pas la marmite
-la belle cage ne nourrit pas l'oiseau

3-to give someone a hand
-donner un coup de main à quelqu'un

4-who gives to all,denies all
-épouseur à toutes mains,épouseur du genre humain
-qui tout promet,rien ne promet

5-to give something up as lost
-faire son deuil de quelque chose

6-give him an inch and he'll take a mile
-accordez-lui long comme un doigt,il en prendra long comme un bras
-laissez le coq passer le seuil,vous le verrez bientôt sur le buffet

7-I'll give him beams
-s'il me donne des pois,je lui donnerai des fèves

8-to give one the cold shoulder
-battre froid quelqu'un

9-he that gives quickly,gives twice
-qui oblige promptement,oblige doublement

10-give and spend,and God will send
-he who gives to the poorlays up a treasure in heaven
-qui donne aux pauvres,prête à Dieu

11-give credit where credit is due
-give the devil his due
-il faut rendre à César ce qui est à César
-à tout seigneur,tout honneur

12-it's give and take
-à bon chat,bon rat
-à charge de revanche

13-he that gives thee a bone,woukd have not thee die
-la façon de donner vaut mieux que ce qu'on donne

14-to give a lark to catch a kite
-le jeu n'en vaut pas la chandelle

15-give her bells and let her fly
-ne jetez pas votre argent par les fenêtres

16-to give up the substance for the shadow
-lâcher la proie pour l'ombre

17-give it another brush
-mettre la dernière main

18-not to give a rap about anything
-se moquer du tiers comme du quart

19-give a lie a twenty four hours'start,and you can never overtake it
-à beau mensonge,longue mémoire

20-give us the tools and we will finish the job
-on ne peut faire d'omelette sans casser des oeufs

21-to give (pass) one's word
-donner sa parole

22-to be given a fair crack of the whip
-avoir sa part du gâteau

23-to give somebody a leg up
-aider quelqu'un à mettre un pied à l'étrier

24-to give one the mitten
-plaquer son amoureux

25-to give a silver bullet (pour se débarrasser de quelqu'un)
-faire un pont d'or

26-give flowers make friends
-les petits présents entretiennent l'amitié

27-to give the Cook's tour
-faire le tour du propriétaire

28-to give the shirt off one's back
se mettre en quatre

29-to give a dressing down
-passer un savon

glass

people who live in glass houses shouldn't throw stones
-qui sème le vent,récolte la tempête

glitter
> **all that glitter is not gold**
> -tout ce qui brille n'est pas d'or

glutton
> **the glutton commits suicide with his fork**
> -le gourmand creuse sa fosse avec ses dents

gluttony
> **gluttony kills more than the sword**
> -la gourmandise tue plus de monde que l'épée

go

> **1-what goes around,comes around**
> -tout ce qui tombe,arrive
> l'évènement à venir projette son ombre

> **2-to go at a snail gallop**
> -aller son train de sénateur

> **3-to go off his rocker**
> -déménager (*sens argotique*)

> **4-go to hell**
> **go to Halifax**
> **go away and eat coke**
> -va au diable

> **5-to go from bad to worse**
> -aller de mal en pis

> **6-he is gone to the bad**
> -il tourne mal

> **7-to go on all four**
> -marcher à quatre pattes

> **8-gone with the wind**
> -autant en emporte le vent

> **9-to go by the book**
> -être à cheval sur le règlement

> **10-you may go farther and far worse**
> -un "tiens" vaut mieux que "deux tu l'auras"

> **11-they went but a pair of shears between them**
> -quand l'un dit "tue!",l'autre dit "assomme!"

> **12-he that goes against the fashion is himself its slave**
> -il faut hurler avec les loups

> **13-gone to the bad for the shadow of an ass**
> -lâcher la proie pour l'ombre

> **14-to go up the creek without a paddle**
> -aller aux mûres sans crochet

15-many go out for wool and come home shorn
-tel entre pape au conclave qui en sort cardinal

16-to go west
-passer l'arme à gauche (familier)

17-he who goes into a mill comes out powdered
-qui entre dans un moulin,il convient de nécessité qu'il enfarine

18-I've gone and done it
-j'ai réussi!
-j'ai gagné ma journée

19-well goes the case when wisdom counsels
-tant vaut le seigneur,tant vaut la terre

20-to go by the board
-tomber à l'eau

goat

1-when the goat is tied,it must browse
-où la chèvre est liée,il faut qu'elle broute

2-we must separate the sheep from the goats
-il ne faut pas mélanger les torchons et les serviettes
-il faut séparer le bon grain de l'ivraie
-il y a fagots et fagots

3-a goat's hide buys a goat's hide and a gourd a gourd
-oeil pour oeil,dent pour dent

God

1-God's in heaven;all's right with the world
-autant de trous,autant de chevilles

2-may God defend me from my friends;I can defend myself from my enemies
-on n'est jamais trahi que par les siens

3-God tempers the wind to the shorn lamb
-Dieu mesure le froid à la brebis tondue
-Dieu donne le froid selon le drap

4-God sends nuts to those who have no teeth
-après le dîner,la moutarde
-quand ma fille est mariée,tout le monde la demande
-les meilleurs partent les premiers

5-God oft has a good share in a little house
-en petite maison la part de DIeu est grande
-jamais grand nez ne gâta beau visage

6-God sides with the strongest
God is always on the side of the big bataillons
-le bon dieu est toujours du côté des gros bataillons

7-God forgives sins,otherwise heaven would be empty
-Il y a un Dieu pour les ivrognes
-Dieu aide à trois personnes aux fous,aux enfants et aux ivrognes

8-before God and the bus conductor we are all equal
-Dieu nous a tous pétris du même limon

9-God helps them that help themselves
-aide toi,le ciel t'aidera
-à toile ourdie,Dieu envoie le fil

10-God send joy,for sorrow will come fast enough
-il n'y a pas de bonne fête sans lendemain

11-whom the gods love die young
-les meilleurs partent les premiers

12-God gives the milk but not the pail
-qui fuit la meule,fuit la farine

13-God works in mysterious ways
-les voies du Seigneur sont impénétrables

14-not God above gets all men's love
-on ne peut contenter tout le monde et son père

going
1-when the going gets tough,the tough gets going
-quand le malheur entre dans la maison,faut lui donner une chaise
-à navire brisé,yous vents sonts sont contraires

2-a going foot is aye getting
-qui sème en pleurs recueille en heur

gold
1-she is as good as gold
-elle est sage comme une image cf sage

2-all he touches turn to gold
-il a de la chance dans tous les domaines

golden
1-we must not look for a golden life in an iron age
-il faut laisser le vent courir par dessus les tuiles

2-the golden age was never the present age
-le temps passé est toujours le meilleur

good
1-they are aye good that are away
-au mort et à l'absent injure ni tourment
-lon des yeux,près du coeur

2-the good die young
-les meilleurs partent les premiers

3-the good is the enemy of the best
-le mieux est l'ennemi du bien

4-a good when lost is valued most
-bien perdu,bien connu
-quand le puits est à sec,on sait ce que vaut l'eau

331

5-ill gotten goods seldom prosper
ill gotten,ill spent .
-bien mal acquis ne profite jamais
-l'habit volé ne va pas au voleur
-ce qui vient du Diable retourne au Diable
-farine du diable retourne en son

6-take the goods God provide
-faute de souliers,on va nu-pieds

7-all his goods in the window
-pour la gallerie

8-good and quickly seldom meet
-plus me hâte et plus me gâte

9-what is the good of a sundial in the shade?
-il ne faut pas mettre la lampe sous le boisseau

10-as good as one's promise
-as good as one's word
-être de parole

11-he is as good as his word
-il n'a qu'une parole

12-not good is to harp on the frayed string
-les longs propos font les courts jours

13-he is as good as gold
-il est sage comme une image
-il est bon comme le pain

14-good to begin well,better to end well
-le sillon n'est pas le champ

goose
1-he that has a goose,will get a goose
-qui chapon mange,chapon lui vient

2-he killed the goose that laid the golden eggs
-il a tué la poule aux oeufs d'or

3-the goose is cooked
-son affaire est bonne
-les carottes sont cuites (*familier*)

4-all his geese are swans
-voir tout en rose

grace
grace will last,beauty will blast
-la beauté est une fleur éphémère

grain
1-of evil grain no good seed can come
-tel père,tel fils
-une source salée ne peut donner d'eau douce

2-grain by grain,and then the hen fills her belly
-petit à petit,l'oiseau fait son nid

3-one grain fills not a sack,but helps his fellow
-il n'y a pas de petites économies

grasp
grasp all,lose all
-bon à tout,propre à rien
-qui trop embrasse,mal étreint

grass
the grass is always greener on the other side of the fence
-l'herbe est toujours plus verte dans le pré du voisin

great
great minds think alike
-les grands esprits se rencontrent

greatest
the greatest crabs be not all the best meat
the greatest calf is not the sweatest veal
-les grands boeufs ne font pas les grands labours

greek
When Greek meet Greek,then comes the tug of war
-à bon chat,bon rat

green
do you see any green in my eye?
do I look greenhorn?
-pour qui me prenez-vous?

grief
1-grief is lessened when imparted to others
he grieves sore who grieves alone
grief pent up will break the heart
-chagrin partagé est moins lourd à porter

2-all griefs with bread are less
-la table est l'entremetteuse de l'amitié

3-the greater grief drives out the less
-un clou chasse l'autre
-la lance d'Achille blesse et guérit

grieve
1-he grieves sore who grieves alone
-chagrin partagé est moins lours à porter

2-never grieve for what you cannot help
-il faut souffrir ce qu'on ne peut empêcher
-il ne sert à rien de montrer les dents lorsqu'on est édenté

grist
1-all's grist that comes to my mill
-je fais profit de tout

2-all's grist to the mill
-apporter de l'eau au moulin

333

groom
>**every groom is a king at home**
>un chien est fort à la porte de son maître
>un coq est bien fort sur son fumier

ground
>**to have the ground cut from under one's feet**
>-couper l'herbe sous le pied de quelqu'un

Grundy
>**what will Mr.Grundy say?**
>-et le "qu'en dira-t-on?"

guard
>**he is from the old guard**
>-c'est un vieux de la vieille

guess
>**1-none can guess the jewel by the casket**
>-on ne peut juger le sac à l'étiquette
>-le lien ne fait pas le fagot

>**2-to guess in a thousand years**
>-donner en mille

gun
>**to give the gun**
>-main morte

gut
>**gut not your fish till you get them**
>-il ne faut pas vendre la peau de l'ours avant de l'avoir tué

H

hackle

    to make one's hackles rise
    -sortir de ses gonds

hair

    1-no hair so small but has his shadow
    -un cheveu même a son ombre

    2-to split hairs
    -couper les cheveux en quatre

    3-hair by hair you will pull out the horse's tail
    -petit à petit l'oiseau fait son nid

    4-to get in one's hair
    to get my goat
    -taper sur les nerfs de quelqu'un

    5-grey hairs are death's blossoms
    -qui voit ses veines,voit ses peines
    -lunettes et cheveux gris sont quittance d'amour

half

    1-half a loaf is better than no bread
    half an egg is better than an empty shell
    -quand on n'a pas ce que l'on aime,il faut aimer ce que l'on a
    -faute de grives on se contente de merles

    2-half is more than the whole
    -mieux vaut moineau en cage que poule d'eau qui nage

halloo

    don't halloo till you are out of the wood
    -il ne faut pas chanter triomphe avant la victoire

hammer

    1-they go at it hammer and tongue
    -le torchon brûle chez eux

    2-it is better to be the hammer than the anvil
    -il vaut mieux être cheval que charrette
    -il vaut mieux être maître,on est valet quand on veut

    3-to be hammering a point home
    -être sur la chanterelle

hand

    1-to be hand and glove with
    -être comme les deux doigts de la main
    -être comme deux frères

    2-good hand,good hire
    -qui fera bien,bien trouvera
    -au bon joueur,la balle

    3-put not thy hand between the bark and the tree
    -il ne faut pas mettre le doigt entre l'arbre et l'écorce

4-cold hands,warm heart
-froides mains,chaudes amours

5-he is my right hand
-il est mon bras droit

6-good hand,good hire
-qui bon maître a,bon loyer a

7-his hands are tied
-il a un fil à la patte

8-many hands make little work
-les étourneaux sont maigres parce qu'ils vont en troupe

9-the right hand does not know what the left hand does
-que ta main gauche ignore ce que fait ta main droite

10-one hand washes the other
-une main lave l'autre

11-to hand on by the eyelids
-tenir par un fil

12-many hands make light work
-l'union fait la force

handle
to handle with kid glove
-faire patte de velours

handsome
handsome is as handsome does
-quand on regarde quelqu'un on n'en voit que la moitié
-la beauté ne sale pas la marmite
-ce ne sont pas les mots qui comptent mais les actions

hang
1-he that one of his family hanged,may not say to his neighbour,hang up your fish
-il ne faut pas clocher devant les boiteux
-on ne parle pas de corde dans la maison d'un pendu

2-to hand on by the eyelids
-tenir par un fil

3-I'll not hang all my bells on one horse
-il ne faut pas mettre tous ses oeufs dans le même panier

4-hanging and wiving go by destiny
-les mariages sont écrits dans le ciel
-le mariage est une loterie

5-as well be hanged for a sheep as for a lamb
quand le vin est tiré,il faut le boire

hangdog
to be hangdog
-raser les murs

hankerchief
with hankerchief in one hand and sword in the other
-faire l'âne pour avoir du son
-prêcher le faux pour savoir le vrai

hard
1-it si harder to change human nature than to change rivers and mountains
-chassez le naturel il revient au galop
-on ne peut empêcher les chiens d'aboyer ni les menteurs de mentir

2-to be hard up
-tirer le diable par la queue

3-though hardship to the stars
-les mains noires font manger le pain blanc

hare
the hare alw ays return to her form
-toujours il souvient à Robin de ses flûtes

harp
don't take your harp to the party
-harp not for ever on the same string
-les plaisanteries les plus courtes sont les meilleures
-les longs propos font les courts jours

hash
to settle one's hash
-rabattre le caquet
-clouer le bec

haste
1-haste makes waste
more haste,less speed
-rien ne sert de courir,il faut partir à point

2-who has no haste in his business,mountains to him seems valleys
-à dure enclume,marteua de plume

3-make haste slowly
-haste makes waste
-hâtez-vous lentement

hat
to take off one's hat to someone
-tirer son chapeau à quelqu'un

hate
the greatest hate springs from the greatest love
-de forte couture,forte déchirure

hatred
hatred is blind as well as love
-on aime sans raison et sans raison l'on hait

have
1-I have had my day
-j'ai eu mon compte

337

2-you cannot have it both ways
-on ne peut avoir le beurre et l'argent du beurre

3-they that have no other meat,bread and butter are glad
-quand on n'a pas ce que l'on aime,il faut vouloir ce que l'on a

4-to have at one's fingers end
-connaître sur le bout du doigt
-connaître par coeur

5-you cannot have it both ways
-vouloir le beurre et l'argent du beurre

6-you can have too much of a good thing
-à colombe soule,les cerises sont amères
-il faut lier le sac avant qu'il soit plein

7-to someone over a barrel
-avoir quelqu'un à sa merci

8-to have one on the hip
-avoir quelqu'un dans sa poche

9-he has nothing that is not contented
-suffisance fait richesse et convoitise fait pauvresse

hay

to make hay while the sun shines
-battre le fer pendant qu'il est chaud
-il faut tourner le moulin lorsque souffle le vent

head

1-to heads together
-de concert

2-better be the head of an ass than the tail of a horse
better to reign in Hell than serve in Heaven
better be the head of a pike than the tail of a sturgeon
better be the head of a dog than the tail of a lion
better be the head of a yeomanry than the tail of a gentry
-mieux vaut être premier dans son village que second à Rome

3-two heads are better than one
-deux avis valent mieux qu'un

4-heads or tails
what's yours is mine,and what's mine is my own
-pile ou face

5-over head and ears,up to the ears
-par dessus les oreilles

6-his head is screwed on the right way
-il a la tête sur les épaules

health
1-he that has good health,is young;and he is rich who owes nothing
-l'âge n'est fait que pour les chevaux

2-health is great riches
c'est une belle baronie que la santé

3-health and wealth create beauty
-la gaité,la santé changent l'hiver en été

4-health is not valued till sickness comes
-quand le puits est à sec,on sait ce que vaut l'eau

5-health is better than wealth
-celui qui a la santé est riche
-qui a la santé a tout,qui n'a pas la santé n'a rien

hear

1-hear all parties
-qui n'entend qu'une cloche n'entend qu'un son
-toute la sagesse n'est pas enfermée dans une tête

2-to hear through the grapevine
-apprendre par le bouche à oreille

3-to hear as a hog in harvest
-n'écouter que d'une oreille
-entré par une oreille,sorti par l'autre

hearing

from hearing,comes wisdom;from speaking repentance
-qui parle sème,qui écoute récolte
-il est bon de parler et meilleur de se taire

heart

**1-when the heart is in fir,some sparks will fly out of the mouth
what the heart thinks,the tongue speaks**
-coeur qui soupire n'a pas ce qu'il désire

2-his heart is in the right place
-il a du coeur
-il a un bon fond

3-his heart sank into his boots
-avoir la peur au ventre

4-when the heart is full of lust,the mouth's full of leasings
-la bouche parle de l'abondance du coeur

5-kind hearts are more than coronets
-amis valent mieux qu'argent

6-in one's heart of heart
-au fin fond de soi-même

7-who has no a heart,let him have legs
-quand on n'a pas de tête,il faut avoir des jambes

heaven

1-when Heaven appoints,man must obey
-l'homme propose et Dieu dispose

339

2-to be in the ninth heaven
to be in heaven's heaven
-être au septième ciel

3-heaven suits the back to the burden
-Dieu mesure le froid à la brebis tondue
-après la pluie,le beau temps
-Dieu donne le froid selon le drap

4-Heaven's vengeance is slow but sure
-la vengeance est un plat qui se mange froid

hedge

1-a hedge between keeps friendship green
-ta chemise ne sache ta guise
-la familiarité engendre le mépris

2-a low hedge is easily leaped over
-where the hedge is lowest men may soonest over
-le chien attaque toujours celui qui a les pantalons déchirés

heed

take heed of the snake in the grass
-il faut regarder à ses mains plutôt qu'à ses pieds

heel

1-to show a clean pair of heels
-avoir des ailes au talon

2-one pair of heels is often worth two pairs of hands
-il vaut mieux se dédire que se détruire

Hell

when Hell freezes over
-quand les poules auront des dents
-renvoyer aux calendes grecques

help

1-a little help is worth a great deal of pity
-ce ne sont pas les mots qui comptent mais les actions

2-he must need help,that is held by the chin
-il est plus facile de nager quand on vous tient le menton

helve

to throw the helve after the hatchet
-jeter le manche après la cognée

hen

1-he that comes of a hen,mut scrape
-qui naît poule,aime à gratter

2-a hen on a hot griddle
-un chat sur une pelote d'épingles

3-a black hen lays a white egg
-une poule noire pond un oeuf blanc

4-like hen,like chicken
-tel père,tel fils
-tel pain,tel soupe

5-henscratching
-écriture de pattes de mouche

herb
no herb will cure love
-rage d'amour fait passer le mal de dents

hero
1-to a real hero life is a mere straw
-il n'y a pas d'heure pour les braves

2-no man is a hero to his valet
-il n'y a pas de grand homme pour son valet de chambre

herring
1-every herring must hang on its own gill
-qui peut et empêche,pèche
-chacun est l'artisan de son sort

2-a herring barrel alwways smell of fish
-la caque sent toujours le hareng
-qui se frotte à l'aïl ne peut sentir la giroflée
-on ne peut rester dans la boutique d'un parfumeur sans en emporter l'odeur
-le mortier sent toujours l'aîl

3-to draw (to drive) a red herring across the path (track)
-faire diversion
-noyer le poisson

hesitate
he who hesitates is lost
-il ne faut pas aller par quatre chemins
-entre deux sièges on tombe à terre
-à force de choisir on prend le pire
-tel refuse qui après muse
-le chien peureux n'a jamais son soûl de lard
-à coquin honteux plate besace
-il faut pas laisser de semer par crainte des pigeons

hew
hew not too high lest the chips fall in thine eye
-ne forcez pas votre talent
-il ne faut pas ourdir plus qu'on ne peut tisser

hide
don't hide your lamp under a bushel
-il ne faut pas mettre la lampe sous le boisseau

high
1-not too high for the pie,not too low for the crow
-entre trop et trop peu est la juste mesure

2-the highest branch is not the safest roost
-quand les ailes poussent à la fourmi,c'est pour sa perte

3-the higher the ape goes,the more he shows his tail
plus le singe monte,plus on lui voit la queue

4-the higher the mountain,the greater the descent
les tours les plus hautes font les plus hautes chutes

5-the higher the plum-tree,the riper the plum,the richer the cobbler,the blacker his thumb
-qui fuit la meule,fuit la farine

hip
to have one on the hip
-avoir quelqu'un dans sa poche

history
history repeats itself
-l'histoire est un perpétuel recomencement

hit
1-he hit pay dirt (langage minier)
-il allait son petit bonhomme de chemin

2-to hit the nail on the head
to hit the bull's eye
to hit the axe on the helve
-frapper au but
-taper dans le mille
-faire mouche

hitch
hitch your wagon to a star
-le but n'est pas toujours placé pour être atteint mais pour servir de point de mire

hog
1-a hog that's bemired endeavours to bemire others
-il ne faut qu'une brebis galeuse pour infester le troupeau

2-the worst hog often gets the best pear
-tel en pâtit qui n'en peut mais
-les bons pâtissent pour les mauvais
-on frappe sur le sac pour que l'âne le sente

3-better my hog dirty than no hog at all
-quand on n'a pas ce que l'on aime,il faut aimer ce que l'on a

4-a hog that's bemired endeavours to bemire others
-il suffit d'une pomme pourrie pour gâter le tas

hoist
hoist your sail when the wind is fair
-il faut tourner le moulin lorsque souffle le vent

hold
1-he can't hold a candle to you
-il ne vous arrive pas à la cheville

2-don't hold a candle in the sun!
-ne donnez pas de coups d'épée dans l'eau!

3-he who holds the thread,holds the ball
-il n'y a point de si empêché que celui qui tient la queue de la poële

4-to hold the bag
-payer les pots cassés
-porter le chapeau

5-that won't hold water
cela ne tient pas la route (familier)

hollyer

don't take hollyer than thou
-il se prend pour un puits de science
-il se croit sorti de la cuisse de Jupiter
-il fait le matamore
-il a les chevilles qui enflent

home

1-there is no place like home
-à chaque oiseau,son nid est beau
-il n'y a pas de petit chez-soi
-un petit chez-soi vaut mieux qu'un grand chez les autres

2-dry bread at home is better than roast meet abroad
-le pain d'autrui est amer
-une tartine de sirop chez nous est parfois meilleure qu'un banquet ailleurs

homely

she is as homely as a mud fence
-une femme comme ça,c'est un remède contre l'amour

homer

homer sometimes nod
-l'erreur est humaine

homo

homo is a common name to all men
-Dieu nous a tous pétris du même limon

honesty

honesty is the best policy
-à tous bons comptes revenir

honey

1-too much honey cloys the stomach
-l'excès en tout nuit
-le surplus rompt le couvercle

2-cover yourself with honey and you'll have plenty of flies
-make yourself all honey and the flies will eat you
-brebis comptées,le loup les mange
-compter les ruches à miel porte malheur
-faites-vous miel,les mouches vous mangeront

3-a honeyed tongue,a heart of gall
he has honey in his mouth,and a razor at the girdle
-miel sur la bouche,fiel sur le coeur

4-honey catches more flies than vinegar
-qui manie le miel,s'en lèche les doigts

5-honey is sweet but the bees stings
-nulle rose sans épines

honeymoon
it is but honeymoon
-ça n'a qu'un temps

honor
1-there is honor among thieves
-les loups ne se mangent pas entre eux

2-honor to whom honor is due
-il faut rendre à César ce qui est à César
-à tout seigneur tout honneur

3-honour to whom honour is due
-à tout seigneur,tout honneur

hood
it's not the hood that makes the monk
-l'habit ne fait pas le moine
-la robe ne fait pas le médecin

hook
1-to get off the hook
-sortir du pétrin

2-to be on tenter hooks
-être sur les charbons ardents

3-a hook's well lost to catch a salmon
-il faut perdre un vairon pour gagner un saumon
-il faut toujours tendre un ver pour avoir une truite

hope
1-hope for the best and prepare the worst
-si tu veux la paix,prepare la guerre

2-a ray of hope
-une lueur d'espoir

3-hope deferred makes the heart sick
hope is a good breakfast but a bad supper
-l'espoir différé rend le coeur malade,mais le désir accompli est un arbre
de vie

4-hope is the dream of a man awake
-tout bonheur que la main n'atteint pas est un rêve
-l'espérance est le songe d'un homme éveillé

5-who that lives in hope dances to an ill tune
-qui vit en espérance danse sans tambourin

6-in the land of hope,there is never any winter
-qui vit en espérance danse sans tambourin

7-hope is the poor man bread
-hope is the bread of the unhappy
-l'espérance est le pain des malheureux

8-hope is the dream of those that wake
-l'espérance est le songe d'un homme éveillé
-tout bonheur que la main n'atteint pas est un rêve

9-hope springs eternal in the human breast
-l'espoir a la vie dure

10-hope keeps man alive
-if it were no hope,the heart would break
-none so old that he hopes not for a year of life
l'espoir fait vivre

11-they hope to catch the fox in his den
-ils espèrent trouver la pie au nid

horn

1-you cannot make a horn of a pig's tail
-quiconque est loup agisse en loup

2-to the horns of the altar
-contre vents et marées

horse

1-it's a good horse that never stumbles
a horse stumbles that has four legs
-il n'est si bon cheval qui ne bronche

2-every horse thinks its own pack heaviest
-chacun se plaint que son grenier n'est pas plein

3-don't spur the willing horse
-trop piquer le cheval le fait rétif

4-a good horse oft needs a good spur
-tout cheval a besoin d'éperon

5-straight from the horse's mouth
-je le tiens de la bouche du cheval

6-wild horses cannot make him admit
-il se ferait hacher plutôt que d'avouer

7-you can take a horse to the water but you cannot make him drink
one man may lead an ass to the pond's brink out twenty men cannot
make him drink
-on a beau mené le boeuf à l'eau,s'il n'a pas soif

8-no horseplay
-jeu de mains,jeu de vilains

9-that is a horse of another color
-c'est une autre paire de manches

10-to be on one's high horse
-monter sur ses grands chevaux

11-the best horse needs breaking and the aptest child needs training
-nul ne naît appris et instruit
-qui veut voyager loin,ménage sa monture

hour

1-an hour in the morning is worth two in the evening
-mieux vaut plus tôt que plus tard
-qui perd sa matinée,perd les trois quarts de sa journée

2-the darkest hour is that before dawn
-après la pluie,le beau temps

3-one hour today is worth two tomorrow
-il ne faut jamais remettre à plus tard ce que l'on peut faire le jour même

house

1-a house divided against itself cannot stand
-l'union fait la force

2-a house well furnished makes a woman wise
-vides chambres font dames folles

3-it is a sad house where the hen crows louder than the cock
-le ménage va mal quand la poule chante plus haut que le coq

hover

he is hovering between heaven and earth
-il est entre la vie et la mort

howl

one must howl with the wolves
-il faut hurler avec les loups

hundred

a hundred pounds of sorrow pays not one ounce of debt
-cent livres de mélancolie ne paient pas un sou de dette

hunger

1-hunger is the best sauce
hunger is good kitchen meat
-il n'est sauce que d'appétit

2-hunger makes hard beans sweet
-dents aigües et ventre plat trouve tout bon qu'est au plat

3-hunger will break through sonte walls
-hunger drives the wolf out of the wood
-la faim fait sortir le loup du bois

hungry

1-to a hungry soul every bitter thing is sweet
hungry dogs will eat dirty pudding
-à qui a faim,tout est pain

2-a hungry man will not listen to reason
a hungry man ,an angry man
-ventre affamé n'a pas d'oreille

346

3-to be hungry enough to eat a horse
-avoir l'estomac dans les talons

4-I'm as hungry as a bear
-j'ai une faim de loup

hunter
all ae not hunters that blow the horn
-tous ne sont pas chevaliers qui à cheval montent

hurrah
his last hurrah
-ses derniers feux

hurt
nothing hurts like the truth
-il n'y a que la vérité qui blesse

husband
1-it is too late to husband when all is spent
-qui épouse la femme,épouse les dettes

2-a prince of husband
-la crème des maris
-un mari en or

hypocrisy
hypocrisy is a homage that vice pays to virtue
-l'hypocrisie est un hommage que le vice rend à la vertu

I

idle

1-an idle brain is the devil workshop
-idle people have the least leisure
-an idle person is the devil's cushion
-an idle head is a box for the wind
-le diable s'empare des personnes oisives
-l'oisiveté est la mère de tous les vices

2-an idle youth,a needy age
-idleness is the key of beggary
-jeunesse oiseuse,vieillesse disetteuse

idleness

1-idleness turns the edge of wit
of idleness comes no goodness
idleness is the root of all evil
-ceux qui n'ont point d'affaires s'en font
-l'oisiveté est la mère de tous les vices

2-idleness must thank itself if it go barefoot
-si tu manges ton pain blanc le premier,tu manges ton pain noir plus t
ard

if

if ifs and ands were pots and pans,there'd be no work for tinkers'hand
-avec des si et des mais on mettrait Paris en bouteille

ignorance

1-there is no blindness like ignorance
-gardez vous d'un homme qui ne connaît qu'un livre

2-ignorance of the law excuses no man
-nul n'est censé ignorer la loi

3-ignorance and incuriosity are two very soft pilllows
-l'igborance et l'incuriosité font un doux oreiller

4-ignorance is bliss
-ignorance is the peace of life
-qui rien ne sait de rien ne doute

5-ignorance is the peace of life
-il fait bon vivre et ne rien savoir

6-where igborance is bliss,'tis folly to be wise
-ce que les yeux ne voient pas ne fait pas mal au coeur

ill

1-of one ill come many
ill (news) comes often on the back of worse
-un malheur n'arrive jamais seul
-jamais deux sans trois

2-ill may the kiln call the oven burnt-house
-c'est l'hôpital qui se moque de la charité
-c'est la pelle qui se moque du fourgon

3-ill comes in ells and goes out by inches
-les maladies viennent à cheval et s'en retournent à pied

4-ill ware never cheap
-on n'a jamais bon marché de mauvaises marchandises
-bon marché fait argent débourser

5-he is ill at ease
-il est dans ses petits souliers

imitation
imitation is the sincerest form of flattery
-il faut gratter les gens où il leur démange

impression
first impressions are the most lasting
-on revient toujours à ses premières amours

inch
an inch is as good as an ell
-de toutes tailles bons lévriers
-dans les petites boîtes,les bons onguents

injury
injuries are written in brass
injuries don't use to be written on ice
-les bienfaits sont écrits sur le sable et les injures dans l'airain

inspiration
ninety percent of inspiration is perspiration
-gens de lettres,gens de peine

intention
the good intention excuses the bad action
-c'est l'intention qui compte

invest
to invest in blue chip stock
-placement de père de famille

invite
who invited you to the roast?
-l'on ne doit pas aller à la noce sans y être convié

iron
1-to have several irons in the fire
-avoir plusieurs cordes à son arc

2-don't have too many irons in the fire
-il ne faut pas courir deux lièvres à la fois

3-the iron fist,or hand in the velvet glove
-une main de fer dans un gant de velours

4-to iron out the difficulties
-aplanir les difficultés

J

Jack

1-Jack's as good as his master
-les bons maîtres font les bons valets

2-there are more Jack than one at the fair
-il y a plus d'un âne à la foire qui s'appelle Martin

3-if Jack's in love,he's no judge of Jill's beauty
-ce qu'on aime est toujours beau

4-Jack of all trades,master of none
-bon à tout,propre à rien
-qui trop embrasse,mal étreint
-la trop grande abondance ne parvient pas à maturité

jade

better a lean jade than an empty halter
-quand on n'a pas ce que l'on aime,il faut aimer ce que l'on a

jam

jam tomorrow and jam yesterday but never jam today
-le temps passé est toujours le meilleur

jest

1-long jesting was never good
-la raillerie ne doit pas passer le jeu

2-it is ill jesting with edged tools
-on ne joue pas avec le feu

3-let your jest when it is at the best
-long jesting was never good
-les plaisanteries les plus courtes sont les meilleures

John

to be a John-a-dreams
-être dans la lune

Johnny

to be Johnny-on-the-spot
-être un vrai Saint-Bernard

journey

1-the longest journey starts with a single step
-il faut un commencement à tout

2-in a long journey,straw weighs
-au long aller le fardeau pèse

joy

1-joy and sorrow are next door neighbours
-trop rire fait pleurer
-tel qui rit vendredi,dimanche pleurera

2-the joy of the heart makes the fair face
-la gaîté,la santé changent l'hiver en été

judge

> **1-you cannot judge a tree (dog) by its bark**
> -beau noyau gît sous piètre écorce
> -on ne peut juger le sac à l'étiquette
> -une oreille coupée a toujours son conduit
>
> **2-never judge from appearances**
> -il ne faut pas juger un paquet d'après ses ficelles
> -être et paraître sont deux
>
> **3-no one should be judge in his own cause**
> -ne mesurez pas autrui à votre aulne

jump

> **to jump from the frying pan into the fire**
> -troquer son chevel borgne pour un aveugle
> -aller de mal en pis

K

ka

ka me,ka thy
-passez-moi la rhubarbe et je vous passerai le séné

keep

1-keep your eye open a sale is a sale
-que l'acheteur prenne garde
-le commerce est l'école de la tromperie

2-keep(or save) your breath to cool your porridge
-occupe-toi de tes affaires
-les affaires du cabri ne sont pas celles du mouton
-chacun son métier et les vaches seront bien gardées

3-to keep someone under one's thumb
-mener quelqu'un à la baguette

4-to keep at arm's length
-tenir à l'écart
-tenir à distance

5-better keep the devil at the door than turn him out of the house
-il ne faut pas mettre dans une cave un ivrogne qui a renoncé au vin

6-to keep one's fingers crossed
-se tenir les pouces
-toucher du bois

7-who keeps company with a wolf will learn to howl
-keep not ill men company,lest you increase the number
-qui entre dans un moulin,il convient de nécesité qu'il enfarine
-ceux qui touchent la poix,se souillent les doigts
-qui suit les poules,apprend à gratter

8-why keep a dog and bark yourself?
-on n'est jamais aussi bien servi que par soi-même

9-keep no more cats than will catch mice
-selon ta bourse,gouverne ta bouche

10-keep your pecker up
-ne jetez pas le manche après la cognée
-haut les coeurs!

11-easy to keep the castle that was never besieged
-tout le monde sait être sage après la bataille

12-to keep a stiff upper lip
-faire contre mauvaise fortune bon coeur

13-he kept an ace in his sleeve
-il a gardé un atout dans sa manche
-il a plus d'un tour dans son sac

14-to keep one's eyes peeled
-to keep one's weather eye open for trouble
-veiller au grain

15-keep your shop and your shop will you
-il vaut mieux aller au moulin qu'au médecin

16-keep something for the sorefoot
-il faut garder une poire pour la soif

17-keep your powder dry
-soyez fin prêts

18-keep your shop open and your shop will keep you
-qui sème en pleurs recueille en heur

19-he keeps a foot in both camps
-il mise sur les deux tableaux

20-to keep two faces under one hood
être un tartuffe

21-keep the golden mean
-trop et trop peu n'est pas mesure

19-keep a thing seven years and you'll always find a use for it
-viendra un temps où les vaches auront besoin de leur queue

Kettle
1-that's a pretty kettle of fish
-nous voilà dans de beaux draps
-c'est un bel embrouillamini

2-the kettle calls the pot burnt-arse
-la marmite dit au chaudron "tu as le derrière noir!"

key
a golden key can open any door
-la clé d'or ouvre toutes les portes

kick
1-to kick a man when he is down
-quand l'arbre est tombé,tout le monde court aux branches
-quand le loup est pris tous les chiens lui lardent les fesses

2-the kick of the mare hurts not the colt
-jamais coup de pied de jument ne fit mal à un cheval

3-why kick down the ladder by which you have climbed?
-il ne faut pas scier la branche sur laquelle on est assis
-brûler ses vaisseaux

4-to kick the bucket
-casser sa pipe (familier)
-passer l'arme à gauche (familier)

5-don't kick against the pricks
-quand il n'y a pas de remède,il faut se résigner
-il faut souffrir ce qu'on ne peut empêcher

6-he's kicking over the traces
-il rue dans les brancards

7-the kick of the mare hurts not the colt
-jamais coup de pied de jument ne fit de mal à un cheval

kill

1-to kill two birds with one stone
-to kill two flies with one flap
-faire d'une pierre deux coups

2-he killed the goose that laid the golden eggs
-il a tué la poule aux oeufs d'or

kindness

1-a forced kindness deserves no thanks
-petit présent trop attendu n'est point donné mais bien vendu

2-one kindness is the price of another
-un couteau aiguise l'autre

kindred

wheresoever you see your kindred,make much of your friend
-le sort fait les parents,le choix fait les amis

king

the king can do no wrong
-la loi dit ce que le roi veut

kiss

1-to kiss the hare's foot
-arriver après la bataille

2-you can kiss the money you lent them goodbye
-vous pouvez faire une croix sur l'argent que vous leur avez prêté

3-many kiss the hand they want to cut off
-tel vous semble applaudir qui vous raille et vous joue

kitten

wanton kittens make sober cats
-il faut que jeunesse se passe

knave

1-a crafty knave needs no broker
-le renard cache sa queue

2-once a knave,always a knave
-qui a bu,boira

knife

1-to be ready to knife one another
-être à couteaux tirés avec quelqu'un

2-the same knife cuts bread and fingers
-il n'est nuls petits ennemis

3-to knock on wood
-toucher du bois

know

1-I know him as well as if I had gone through with a lighted link
-je le connais aussi bien que si je l'avais fait

2-to know something like the palm of one's hand
-connaître quelque chose comme sa poche

3-he knows the water best who has waded through it
-il sait trop de chasse qui a été veneur

4-you are a know-it-all
-Monsieur je-sais-tout

5-you never know what you can do till you try
-nul ne sait ce qu'il peut faire avant d'avoir essayé

6-none knows what will happen to him before sunset
-on ne sait pas de quoi demain sera fait
-si tu ne vas pas à Mahomet,Mahomet viendra à toi

7-not to know someone from Adam
-ne connaître quelqu'un ni d'Eve ni d'Adam

8-to know a hawk from a handsaw
-to know the difference between chalk and cheese
-to know which side the bread is buttered
-connaître la musique (*sens figuré*)
-savoir ce que vaut l'aune

9-to know on which foot a man halts
-savoir sur quel pied danser

10-we never know the worth of water till the well is dry
-quand le puits est à sec,on sait ce que vaut l'eau

11-he that knows nothing,doubts nothing
-qui rien ne sait rien ne doute

12-he knows how many beans make five
-on sait ce que parler veut dire

13-to know downs and ups
-connaître des périodes de vaches maigres et de vaches grasses

14-you cannot know the wine by the barrel
-on ne connaît pas le vin au cercle

15-what you don't know can't hurt you
-il fait bon vivre et ne rien savoir
-ce que les yeux ne voient pas ne fait pas mal au coeur

16-the more one knows,the less one believes
-he that knows nothing,doubts nothing
-qui ne sait rien,de rien ne doute

knowledge
1-a little knowledge is a dangerous thing
-science sans conscience n'est que rine de l'âme

2-knowledge without practice makes but half an artist
-cent fois sur le métier remettez votre ouvrage
-une once d'esprit vaut mieux qu'une livre de science

3-knowledge is power
-savoir c'est pouvoir

L

labour

> **1-a little labour,much health**
> -il vaut mieux aller au moulin qu'au médecin
> -il n'est si petit métier qui ne nourrice son maître

> **2-he that labours and thrives,spins gold**
> -qui sème en pleurs,récolte en heur

labourer

> **the labourer is worthy of his hire**
> toute peine mérite salaire

lamb

> **1-make yourself a lamb and the wolf will eat you**
> -brebis comptées,le loup les mange
> -faites vous miel,les mouches vous mangeront

> **2-she took it like a lamb**
> -elle l'a bien pris

Lammas

> **at later Lammas**
> -renvoyer aux calendes grecques
> -quand les poules auront des dents

land

> **1-a land of milk and honey**
> -un pays de Cocagne

> **2-he that has land has trouble at hand**
> **he that has lands,has quarrels**
> -qui terre a,guerre a
> -bon pays,mauvais chemin
> -de grasse terre,méchant chemin
> -abondance engendre fâcherie
> -on ne jette de pierres qu'à l'arbre chargé de fruits

> **3-the land is never void of counsellors**
> -on ne donne rien si libéralement que des conseils

> **4-every land has its own law**
> -autant de pays,autant de guises

> **5-no land without stones,or meat without bones**
> -il n'y a pas de viande sans os

> **6-in the land of hope,there is never any winter**
> -tant qu'il y a de la vie,il y a de l'espoir

lane

> **it is a long lane that has no turning**
> -après la pluie,le beau temps

larder

> **no larder but has its mice**
> -chaque médaille a son revers

lark

1-to think that larks will fall into one's mouth ready roasted
-il attend que les alouettes lui tombent toutes rôties dans le bec

2-to give a lark to catch a kite
-le jeu n'en vaut pas la chandelle

late

1-it's too late too to call back yesterday
-une occasion perdue ne se rattrape jamais
-il ne faut pas regarder derrière soi

2-it is never too mate to learn
-on apprend à tout âge

3-it is too late to husband when all is spent
-qui épouse la femme,épouse les dettes

4-it is too late to lock the stable when the horse has been stolen
-quand la jument est sortie,il n'est plus temps de fermer l'étable

5-better late than never
-mieux vaut tard que jamais
-il vaut ùieux arriver en retard qu'arriver en corbillard

6-it is too late to grieve when the chance is past
-une occasion perdue ne se rattrappe jamais

7-it is too late to spare when the bottom is bare
-provision,profusion

8-it is never too late to mend
-it is never too late to do well
-il n'est jamais trop tard pour bien faire

9-at later Lammas
-le trente-six du mois

lather

a good lather is half the shave
-chose bien commencée est à demi achevée

laugh

1-he laughs best who laughs last
-rira bien qui rira le dernier

2-he who laughs on Friday will weep on Sunday
laugh before breakfast,you'll cry before supper
laugh at leisure,you may greet ere night
joy and sorrow are next door neighbour
God send you joy,for sorrow will come fast enough
if you sing before breakfast,you'll cry before night
-tel qui rit vendredi,dimanche pleurera
-il n'y a pas de bonne fête sans lendemain

2-to laugh on the wrong side
-rire jaune

3-to laugh on one's sleeve
-rire sous cape

4-to laugh one's head off
-rire à gorge déployée

5-laugh,and the world laughs with you;weep,and you weep alone
-qui chante ses maux épouvante

laughter
laughter is natural to man
-le rire est le propre de l'homme

law
1-there is one law for the rich,and another one for the poor
-selon que vous serez puissant ou misérable,les jugements de cour vous rendront blanc ou noir

2-every law has a loophole
-il n'est règle qui ne faille,on peut violer sans qu'elle crie

lawyer
1-he that is his own lawyer has a fool for a client
-chacun est l'ennemi de soi-même
-oeil un autre oeil voit et non soi

2-a good lawyer makes a bad neighbour
-bon avocat,mauvais voisin

lay
1-to lay something for a rainy day
-garder une poire pour la soif
-il est bon avoir aucune chose sous le mortier

2-lay your wame to your winning
-il faut aller selon sa bourse

3-all lay load on the willing horse
-accordez-lui long comme le doigt,il en prendra long comme un bras
-le chien attaque celui qui a les pantalons déchirés

4-nought lay down,nought take up
-qui ne risque rien,n'a rien

5-he lays odds both ways
-il mise sur les deux tableaux

law
1-every law has a loophole
-il n'est règle qui ne faille

2-much law,but little justice
-la force prime le droit

lawyer
a good lawyer makes a bad neighbour
-bon avocat,mauvais voisin
-pour une fois qu'un avocat est bon, il se retrouve contre vous

lead

1-it's a lead pipe cinch
-c'est l'enfance de l'art

2-I'll lead you a pretty dance
-donner le bal à quelqu'un

3-he lead me up the garden path
-il m'a monté un bâteau

4-lead a pig to the Rhine,it remains a pig
-qui bête va à Rome,tel en retourne

5-to lead somebody a merry chase
-donner du fil à retordre

6-to lead one by the ear (nose)
-mener quelqu'un par le bout du nez

leaf

to take a leaf out of someone's book
-imiter quelqu'un

leak

a little leak will sink a big ship
-petites causes,grands effets

leap

1-everyone leaps over the dyke where it is lowest
-le chien attaque toujours celui qui a les pantalons déchirés

2-there is no leaping from Deliah's lap into Abraham's bosom
-l'on ne peut servir ensemble Dieu et le diable

learn

1-it is never too late to learn
one is never too old to learn
-on apprend à tout âge

2-who so learns young,forgets not when he is old
learning in one's youth is engraving in stone
what's learnt in the craddle lasts till the tomb
-ce qu'on apprend au berceau dure jusqu'au tombeau

3-learn to walk before you run
-il faut commencer par le commencement

4-there is no learning,there is no art
-il n'est rien comme les vieux ciseaux pour couper la soie

5-learning makes a good man better and an ill man worse
-une once d'esprit vaut mieux qu'une livre de science

6-a little learning is a dangerous thing
-science sans conscience n'est que ruine de l'âme

least

least said,soonest mended
-plus on se découvre,plus on a froid

leave

1-he that leaves the highway to cut short,commonly goes about
-qui trop se hâte,reste en chemin

2-one cannot leave one's country without a tug
-partir c'est mourir un peu

3-to leave off with an appetite
-rester sur sa faim

4-leave off when the play is good
-les plaisanteries les plus courtes sont les meilleures

5-to leave no stone unturned
-remuer ciel et terre
-faire des pieds et des mains

lee

there are lees to everyone
-chaque vin a sa lie
-la perfection n'est pas de ce monde

left

to be left in the basket
-être laissé pour compte

leg

1-on its last leg
-moribond

2-to have pins and needles in one's legs
-avoir des fourmis dans les jambes

lend

lend your money and lose your friend
-when I lent I had a friend;when I asked he was unkind
-qui prête aux amis perd au double
-ami au prêter,ennemi au rendre

leopard

the leopard cannot change his spots
-chassez le naturel,il revient au galop
-la brebis bêle toujours d'une même sorte
-on ne voit cygne noir ni corbeau blanc
-on ne voit cygne noir,ni nulle neige noire
-nul lait noir,nul corbeau blanc

liar

1-a liar ought to have a good memory
one lie makes many
-il faut qu'un menteur ait une bonne mémoire

2-the liar and the murderer are children of the same village
-les menteurs sont les enfants du Diable

3-the liar is sooner caught than the cripple
-on attrappe plus unn menteur qu'un voleur

4-a liar is not believed when he speaks the truth
-à dire vérités et mensonges,les vérités seront crues les dernières

liberty

a lean liberty is better that fat slavery
-liberté et pain cuit

lick

1-a lick and a promise
-une toilette de chat

2-to take a licking
-ramasser une veste

lie

1-to lie at rack and manger
-être comme l'oiseau sur la branche
-vivre au jour le jour

2-if you lie down with dogs,you will get up with fleas
-qui se couche avec les chiens,se lève avec les puces
-ceux qui touchent la poix,se souillent les doigts

3-we shall lie all alike in our grave
-le plus riche en mourant n'emporte qu'un drap

4-we must not lie down and cry
-aide-toi,le ciel t'aidera

5-to lie in bed till meat falls into one's mouth
-il attend qur les alouettes lui tombent toutes rôties dans le bec

6-if you lie upon roses when young,you'll lie upon thorns when old
-jeunesse oiseuse,vieillesse disetteuse

7-to lie in one's throat
-mentir comme un arracheur de dents

8-better a lie that heals than a truth that wounds
-beaux mensonges aident
-toute vérité n'est pas bonne à dire

9-a lie has no legs
-qui dit un mensonge en dit cent

life

1-life is short and time is swift
-il faut battre le fer pendant qu'il est chaud
-l'occasion est chauve
-il n'y a rien qui aille aussi vite que le temps

2-our life is but a span
-il est bien près du temps des cerises le temps des cyprès
-la vie n'est qu'un songe

3-while there is life there is hope
-tant qu'il y a de la vie il y a de l'espoir

4-life is but a long journey to death
-aujourd'hui en chair,demain en bière
-ce qui vient avec le béguin,s'en retourne avec le suaire

5-life is not all cakes and ale
-life is not beer and skittles
-the life of a man is a winter's day and a winter's way
-il faut apprendre de la vie à souffrir la vie
-le lange l'a apporté,le linceul l'emportera
-la vie est un panier à rats

6-not on your life
-pas pour tout l'or du monde

7-a good life makes a good death
-such a life,such a death
-an ill life,an ill end
-de telle vie,telle fin
-quand on n'a pas su vivre,on doit encore moins savoir mourir

lifeless

he is lifeless that is faultless
-chacun est bossu quand il se baisse
-l'erreur est humaine
-il n'y a que ceux qui ne font rien qui ne se trompent pas

light

1-light come,light go
-ce qui vient de la flûte s'en va par le tambour
-le bien facilement acquis se dépense de même

2-light gains make a heavy purse
-il n'y a pas de petit profit

3-every light is not the sun
-tout ce qui brille n'est pas d'or

4-every light has its shadow
-toute médaille a son revers

5-the light is nought for sore eye
-ce que les yeux ne voient pas ne fait pas mal au coeur

6-the more light a torch gives,the shorter it lasts
-vie de cochon ,courte et bonne

lightning

lightning never strikes twice at the same place
-expérience est mère de science

like

1-like begets like
like cures like
like will to like
-un barbier rase l'autre
-dis moi qui tu hantes,je te dirai qui tu es
-à l'âne,l'âne semble beau

362

2-if you don't like it,you may lump it

-si cela ne vous plaît pas,n'en dégoûtez pas les autres
-si vous n'aimez pas ça,n'en dégoûtez pas les autres

3-like blood,like good,and like age makes the happiest marriage
-âne avec le cheval n'attèle

4-like breeds like
-les chiens ne font pas de chats
-on se ressemble de plus loin

line

1-to line up all a row
-se mettre en rang d'oignons

2-to line one's pockets
-se remplir les poches

lion

1-if the lion's skin cannot,the fox' shall
-coudre la peau du renard à celle du lion

2-a lion may be beholden to a mouse
-on a souvent besoin d'un plus petit que soi

3-to take the lion's share
-tirer la couverture à soi
-prendre la part du lion

4-a lion at home,a mouse abroad
-l'aigle d'une maison n'est qu'un sot dans une autre

lionize

to be lionized
-être porté aux nues
-être porté au pinacle

listen

to listen with half an ear
-n'écouter que d'une oreille

listener

listeners (eavesdroppers)never hear any good of themselves
-la mouche se brûle à la chandelle

litter

the litter is the like to the sire and dam
-les chiens ne font pas de chats

little

1-a little and good fills the trencher
-little things please little minds
-peu et bon
-mieux vaut moins mais mieux
-une abeille vaut mieux que mille mouches

2-little and often fill the purse
-petit à petit,l'oiseau fait son nid

3-every little helps
-many a little makes a muckle
-little gains make a heavy
-petit à petit,l'oiseau fait son nid
-il n'y a pas de petites économies

live

1-as we live,so shall we end
-he that lives wickedly can hardly die honestly
-de telle vie,telle fin
-quand on n'a pas su vivre,on doit encore moins savoir mourir

2-I have lived too near a wood to be frightened by owls
-il sait trop de chasse qui a été veneur

3-to live on knife's edge
-vivre sur le corde raide

4-to live from hand to mouth
-tirer le diable par la queue
-vivre d'expédients
-vivre au jour le jour

5-he lives unsafely that looks too near on things
-de trop près se chauffe qui se brûle

6-to live in a fool's paradise
-se bercer d'illusions

7-to live like two love birds
-filer le parfait amour

8-live and learn
-l'homme arrive novice à chaque âge de la vie
-qui vivra verra

9-to live in clover
-to live high off the hog
to live like fighting cocks
-vivre comme un coq en pâte
-vivre sur un grand pied

10-we can live without our friends,but not without our neighbours
-il n'est voisin qui ne voisine

11-who lives by hope,will die byhunger
-petite négligence accouche d'un grand mal

12-to live on borrowed time
-ses jours sont comptés

13-they that live longest should die at last
-contre la mort,point de remède

14-live and let live
il faut que tout le monde vive

15-he who lives with cats will get a taste of mice
-qui se couche avec les chiens,se lèvent avec les puces

16-he who lives by the sword dies by the sword
-quiconque se sert de l'épée périra par l'épée

17-if you would not live to be old,you must be hanged when you are young
-il faut vieillir ou mourir jeune

18-to live on a shoestring
-vivre d'amour et d'eau fraîche

19-who that lives in hope dances to an ill tune
-qui vit en espérance danse sans tambourin

20-he that lives most,dies most
-vie de cochon,courte et bonne

lock
no lock will hold against the power of gold
-la clé d'or ouvre toutes les portes

log
crooked logs make straight fires
-le bois tordu fait le feu droit

loneliness
loneliness is the ultimate poverty
-les malheureux sont seuls au monde

long
1-it is not how long,but how well we live
-une abeille vaut mieux que mille mouches
-mieux vaut moins mais mieux
-peu et bon

2-as long lives a merry man as a sad
-autant meurt veau que vache

3-the long and the short of the matter
-en deux mots

4-if he were as long as he is lither,he might thatch a house without a ladder
-avec des si et des mais,on mettrait Paris en bouteille

look
1-he that looks in a man's face knows not what money is in his pocket
-tout ce qui brille n'est pas d'or
-qui ferme la bouche ne montre pas les dents
-quand on regarde quelqu'un on n'en voit que la moitié

2-to look deep in thoughts
-avoir l'air pensif

3-we must not look for a golden life in an iron age
-quand on n'a pas ce que l'on aime,il faut vouloir ce que l'on a
-on mange bien des perdrix sans oranges-
-il faut laisser courir le vent par dessus les tuiles

4-he that looks not before,finds himself behind
-quand on n'avance pas,on recule

5-to look through blue glasses
-voir les choses en noir

6-long looked for comes at last
-tant crie-t-on Noël qu'il vient
-avec la paille et le temps,se mûrissent les nèfles et les glands
-la patience est amère mais son fruit est doux

7-looking for a needle in a bottle of hay (in a haystack)
-chercher une aiguille dans une botte de foin

8-don't look a gift horse in the mouth
-à cheval donné on ne regarde pas la bride

9-look after the pennies and the pounds will look after themselves
-il n'y a pas de petites économies

10-look before you leap
-il faut tourner sept fois sa langue dans sa bouche
-il faut reculer pour mieux sauter

11-he looks a bit of a mug
-il a une bonne poire (familier)

12-do I look greenhorn?
-pour qui me prenez-vous?

13-look to thyself when thy neighbour's house is on fire
-il y en a toujours qui aimeront mieux se sauver que passer les seaux

looker
    lookers-on see most of the game
    -il faut reculer pour mieux sauter
    -un lac réfléchit mieux les étoiles qu'une rivière

lord
    new lords,new laws
    -à nouvelles affaires,nouveaux conseils
    -tel roi,telle loi

lose
    1-to lose one's marbles
    -perdre la boule

    2-all is lost that is put into a riven dish
    -oignez vilain,il vous poindra
    -fais du bien à un cochon et il viendra chier sur ton balcon

    3-one never loses by doing a good turn
    -un bienfait n'est jamais perdu

    4-he loses his thanks who promises and delays
    -petit présent trop attendu n'est point donné mais bien vendu

    5-all is not lost that is in danger
    -tout ce qui branle ne tombe pas

5-all is not lost that is in danger (suite)
-la foudre ne tombe pas toutes les fois qu'il tonne
-on a perdu une bataille mais on n'a pas perdu la guerre

6-to lose one's bearings
-to lose one's grip
-perdre pied
-perdre le nord

7-you cannot lose what you never had
-on ne peut perdre ce que l'on n'a jamais eu

8-lose a leg rather thana life
-il faut perdre un vairon pour gagner un saumon

9-lost with all ahnds
-perdu corps et biens

10-one never loses anything by politeness
-la politesse ne coûte rien

11-for love nor money
-à quelque prix que ce soit
-à aucun prix

12-it is not lost that comes at last
-il n'est jamais trop tard pour bien faire
-mieux vaut tard que jamais

13-what you lose on the swingsyou gain on the roundabouts
-il faut perdre un vairon pour gagner un saumon

14-though lost to sight,to memory dear
-loin des yeux,près du coeur

lover

lovers are mad men
-fou est le prêtre qui blame ses reliques

loss

1-he who is not sensible to his loss has lost nothing
-qui perd le sien perd le sens

2-there is no great loss without some gain
-à quelque chose malheur est bon

3-one man's loss is another man's gain
-ce n'est pas perdu pour tout le monde

louse

better a louse in the pot than no flesh at all
-quand on n'a pas ce que l'o aime,il faut aimer ce que l'on a

love

1-love is blind
-l'amour est aveugle

2-love sees no fault
-affection aveugle raison

3-it is love that makes the world go around
-amour vainct tout sauf coeur de félon

4-love and lordship like no fellowship
-les rois et les juges n'ont point de parents

5-he that does not love a woman,sucked a saw
-une fille sans ami est un printemps sans rose

6-in love is no lack
-quand on aime,ventre affamé n'a pas faim

7-love me,love my dog
-qui m'aime,aime mon chien
-les amis de nos amis sont nos amis
-qui aime Martin,aime son chien

8-old love will not be forgotten
no love like the first love
-on revient toujours à ses premières amours

9-love covers many infirmities
-la rage d'amour fait passer le mal de dents

10-love begets love
love is the true reward of love
-enfant aime moult qui beau l'appelle

11-love makes all hearts gentle
-l'amour apprend aux ânes à danser

12-love is lawless
-l'amour ne connaît pas de loi

13-when love puts in,friendship is gone
-l'amour et l'amitié s'excluent l'un l'autre

14-love is the fruit of the idleness
-l'amour fait passer le temps et le temps fait passer l'amour

15-love and a cough cannot be hid
-amour,toux,fumée et argent ne se peuvent cacher longtemps

16-love will find a way
-love laughs at locksmiths
-love conquers all
-love will go through stone walls
-l'amour vainc tout sauf coeur de félon

17-love does much,money does everything
-amour peut moult,argent peut tout

18-no love is foul,nor prison fair
-il n'y a pas de belles prisons ni de laides amours

19-love without end has no end
-sound love is not soon forgotten
-le lierre meut où il s'attache
-qui aime bien,tard oublie

20-if you love the boll,you cannot hate the branches
-love your friend with his fault
-dans l'adversité de nos meilleurs amis,nous trouvons quelque chose qui ne nous déplaît pas

21-he that loves the tree loves the branch
-if you love the boll,you cannot hate the branches
-si ton ami est borgne,regarde de profil

22-next to love quietness
-un coeur tranquille est la vie du corps

23-love is without reason
one cannot love and be wise
-le coeur a ses raisons que la raison ignore
-la raison n'est pas ce qui règle l'amour

24-love your neighbour but pull not down thy edge (your fence)
-les bons comptes font les bons amis

25-they love dancing well that dance among thorns
-trop cher achète le miel qui le lèche sur les épines

26-love is never without jealousy
-la jalousie est la soeur de l'amour comme le diable est le frère des anges

27-when love is in,there is faith
-l'amour avidement croit tout ce qu'il souhaite

28-the love of money is the root of an evil
où il y a un écu,il y a le diable
-où il n'y en a pas il y en a deux

29-love lasts as long as money endures
-lorsque la faim est à la porte,l'amour s'en va par la fenêtre

lover

the lover is not where he lives but where he loves
-le lierre meurt où il s'attache

luck

1-shitten luck is good luck
-marcher du pied gauche dans la merde,ça porte bonheur

2-there is luck in odd numbers
-tierce fois.c'est droit

3-the worse luck now,the better another time
-après la pluie le beau temps
-tout vient à point à qui sait attendre

4-ill luck is good for something
-à quelque chose malheur est bon

lucky

1-lucky at cards,unlucky in love
-heureux au jeu,malheureux en amour

2-lucky men need no counsel
-aux innocents les mains pleines

lure

to lure into one's web
-attraper dans ses filets

M

maid

1-a maid oft seen and a gown oft worn,are desestemed and held in scorn
-jardin entamé n'est plus respecté

2-all are not maiden that wear bare hair
-tout ce qui brille n'est pas d'or

3-a maid that laughs is half taken
-fille et ville qui parlementent sont à demi rendues

4-maids say "nay" and take it
-fille et ville qui parlementent sont à demi rendues

Majesty

to her Majesty's expense
-aux frais de la princesse

make

1-make haste slowly
-hâtez-vous lentement

2-as you make your bed,so you must lie upon it
-comme on fait son lit on se couche

3-he makes no bones about it
-il ne s'en fait pas

4-to make one's teeth water
-to make one's mouth water
-mettre l'eau à la bouche

5-to make assurance doubly sure
-porter la ceinture et les bretelles

6-you cannot make a silk purse out of a sow's ear
-you cannot make a horn of a pig's tail
-you cannot make a Mercury of every log
-it's hard to make mutton of a sow
-on ne peut faire d'une buse un épervier
-la plus belle fille du monde ne peut donner que ce qu'elle a

7-you cannot make a crab walk straight
-bois tordu ne se redresse pas
-on ne peut faire de bois tordu droite flèche
-ce qui est courbé ne peut être redressé,et ce qui manque ne peut être compté

8-make the best of a bad bargain
make the best of a bad job
-faire contre mauvaise fortune bon coeur
-entre deux maux,il faut choisir le moindre

9-to make one's pile
-faire son beurre (*familier*)

10-you cannot make people honest by act of Parliament
-bon droit a besoin d'aide
-jamais cheval ni méchant homme,n'amenda pour aller à Rome

11-you must not make fish of one and flesh of the other
-il n'y a pas deux poids,deux mesures

12-you cannot make an omelet without breaking eggs
-la fin justifie les moyens
-on ne peut faire d'omelette sans casser les oeufs

13-to make a federal case
-faire toute une histoire,une affaire d'Etat

14-to make someone sing another tune
-faire changer de registre à quelqu'un

man

1-every man buckles his belt his ain gate
-chacun voit midi à sa pendu!e

2-rather a man without money than money without a man
-on fait tout avec de l'argent excepté les hommes

3-no man can play the fool so well as the wise man
-c'est être sage que de savoir feindre la folie
-il n'est si grande folie que de sage homme

4-a man is known by the company he keeps
a man is known by his friends
-as a man is,so is his company
-dis moi qui tu hantes je te dirai qui tu es

5-every man is the architect of his own fortune
every man is the son of his own work
every man should work out his own salvation
every man buckles his belt his ain gate
-chacun se fait fouetter à sa guise
-chacun est l'artisan de son sort

6-no man is his craft's master the first day
-le lendemain s'instruit aux leçons de la veille
-cent fois sur le métier remetez votre ouvrage

7-a man cannot do more than he can
-no living man all things can
-à l'impossible nul n'est tenu
-il faut tondre ses brebis et non les écorcher

8-a merry man makes a cheerful countenance
-ventre plein donne de l'assurance

9-one man's meat is another man's poison
-one man's loss is another man's gain
-le malheur des uns fait le bonheur des autres
-chacun prend son plaisir où il se trouve
-tout n'est qu'heur et malheur
-il faut que le vent soit bien mauvais pour n'être bon à personne

10-a man without religion is like a horse without a bridle
-la religion ne nous fait pas bons,mais elle nous empêche
-de devenir trop mauvais

11-a man of words and not of deeds, is like a garden full of weeds
-mieux vaut donner sans promettre que promettre sans tenir
-ce ne sont pas les mots qui comptent,mais les actions

12-every man a little beyond himself is a fool
-every man has a fool in his sleeve
-no man is wise at all times
-il n'est si sage qui ne foloie
-le juste pèche sept fois par jour

13-today a man,tomorrow a mouse
-aujourd'hui roi,demain rien

14-every man has the defects of his own virtues
-le bon blé porte bien l'ivraie

15-every man has his price
-chou pour chou,Aubervilliers vaut bien Paris

16-man cannot live by bread alone
-l'homme ne vit pas seulement de pain

17-a man is not always asleep when his eyes are shut
-tous ne sont pas chevaliers qui à cheval montent

18-a man must plough with such owen he has
-on doit souffrir patiemment ce qu'on ne peut amender sainement

19-every man likes his own thing best
-chacun aime le sien

20-if a man deceives me once,shame on him;if he deceives me twice,shame on me
-expérience est mère de science

21-a man were better to be half blind than both have his eyes out
-quand on n'a pas ce que l'on aime;il fut aimer ce que l'on a

22-a man's home is his castle
-charbonnier est maître chez soi
-il n'y a pas de petit chez-soi

23-every man for himself and God for us all
every man for himself and the devil takes the hindmost
-chacun pour soi et Dieu pour tous

24-a man without a smiling face must not open a shop
-ce n'est pas le tout que des choux,il faut du lard pour les cuire

25-a man in debt is caught in a net
-qui doit,n'a rien à soi

26-a man can die but once
-on ne meurt qu'une fois
-de toutes les douleurs on ne peut faire qu'une mort

27-to a crafty man,a crafty and a half
-à bon chat,bon rat
-à malin,malin et demi

28-a great man and a great river are often ill neighbours
-un grand chemin,une grande rivière et un grand seigneur sont trois mauvais voisins

29-every man is his own worst enemy
-chacun est l'ennemi de soi-même

30-whatever man has done,man may do
-qui fait un panier,fait bien une hotte
-qui peut le plus,peut le moins

31-every man cannot be a master
-la plus belle fille du monde ne peut donner que ce qu'elle a

32-man is the head,but woman turns it
-nul si fin que femme n'assote

33-no man is content with his lot
-de la fortune nul n'est content

34-every man is a fool sometimes and none at all times
-every man a little beyond himself is a fool
-every man has a fool in his sleeve
-no man is wise at all times
-il n'est si sage qui ne foloie
-qui ne sait être fou n'est pas sage

35-every man is his brother's keeper
-je ne suis pas le gardien de mon frère

36-no man is a hero to his valet
-il n'y a pas de grand homme pour son valet de chambre

37-man is wolf to man
-l'homme est un loup pour l'homme

38-a man is old as he feels and a woman as old as she looks
-homme aime quand il veut et femme quand elle peut

39-every man's censure is first moulded in his own nature
-c'est l'hôpital qui se moque de la charité
-c'est la morte qui se moque de la décapitée

40-if the young man would,and the old man could,there would be nothing
undo
-si jeunesse savait,si vieillesse pouvait

41-when all men say you are an ass,it is time to bray
-qui se sent morveux,qu'il se mouche

42-no man knows when he should die,although he knows he must die
-contre la mort, point de remède

43-the early man never borrows from the late man
-il vaut mieux être le premier de sa race que le dernier

44-one man may lead an ass to the pond's brink but twenty men cannot make him drink
-on a beau mené le boeuf à l'eau,s'il n'a soif

45-no man is born wise or learned
-nul ne naît appris et instruit

46-every man bows to the bush he gets bields of
-il est mon oncle qui mon ventre me comble

47-a man is not a horse because he was born in a stable
-à l'ongle,on connaît le lion

48-if a man is a miser,he will certainly have a prodigal son
-à père avare,fils prodigue

49-no man is indispensable
-no man so good but another may be as good as he
-personne n'est irremplaçable
-il n'est pas unique au monde

50-to a brave and faithful man nothing is difficult
-pluie du matin n'arrête pas le pélerin

51-every man bastes the dog
-on ne prête qu'aux riches

52-no man better knows what good is than he who endured evil
-quand le puits est à sec,on sait ce que vaut l'eau

53-when a man grows angry his reason rides out
-la raison qui s'emporte a le sort de l'erreur

54-where every man is a master,the world goes to wrack
-c'est raison que chacun soit maître en son logis

55-one man osws and another reaps
-l'un sème,l'autre récolte

56-no man can serve two masters
-nul ne peut servir deux maîtres

57-a man is a man to God
-le plus riche en mourant n'emporte qu'un drap
-le soleil luit pour tout le monde

58-where every man is a master,the world goes to wrack
-ce qui n'a pas de tête ne va pas;ce qui a deux têtes va moins bien encore

59-a man has no more goods than he gets good of
-tant vaut la chose comme elle peut être vendue

60-no man can be a good ruler unless he has first been ruled
-il n'y a point de plus sage abbé que celui qui a été moine

61-men make houses,women make homes
-selon l'oiseau le nid,selon la femme le logis

62-men leap where the hedge is lowest
-là où la barrière est basse,le boeuf emjambe
-on passe la haie par où elle est la plus basse

63-men are blind in their own cause
every man is his own worst enemy
-chacun est l'ennemi de soi-même
-l'oeil porte en soi l'image laquelle il ne voit
-oeil un autre oeil voit et non soi

64-men have greater faith in those things which they do not understand
-rien n'est cru si fermement que ce que l'on sait le moins

65-old men and travellers may lie by authority
-a beau mentir qui vient de loin

66-many men,many minds
-so many men,so many opinions
-autant de mariages,autant de ménages
-autant de têtes,autant d'avis
-chacun voit avec ses lunettes

67-the best of men are but men at best
-à l'impossible nul n'est tenu

68-men are not to be measured by inches
-on ne mesure pas les hommes à la toise

69-young men may die,but old men must die
-autant meurt veau que vache

70-men are best loved furthest off
-loin des yeux,près du coeur

71-men's years and their faults are always more than they are willing to own
-la vieillesse nous attache plus de rides en l'esprit qu'au visage

manner

1-manners know distance
-la familiarité engendre le mépris

2-manners make the man
-la manière fait tout

3-of ill manners,good laws
-les mauvaises moeurs engendrent les bonnes lois

many

1-many are called but few are chosen
-il y a beaucoup d'appelés mais peu d'élus

2-many men,many minds
-autant de ménages,autant de mariages
-autant de têtes,autant d'avis

March
  March comes like a lion and goes away like a lamb
  -si Mars commence en courroux,il finira tout doux,tout doux

mare
  the grey mare is the better horse
  -elle porte la culotte

mark
  to mark with a white stone
  -marque d'une pierre blanche

marriage
  1-marriage is a lotery
  -le mariage est une loterie
  -il faut chercher une femme avec les oreilles plutôt qu'avec les yeux

  2-marriage in haste and repent at leisure
  -l'on se marie promptement et puis l'on se repend à loisir

  3-marriages are made in Heaven
  -les mariages sont écrits dans le ciel

  4-at marriages and funerals,friends are discerned from kinsfolk
  -au mariage et à la mort,le diable fait son effort

marry
  1-marry your son when you will,and your daughter when you can
  -marie ton fils quand tu voudras et ta fille quand tu pourras

  2-marry first and love will follow
  -l'amour est souvent le fruit du mariage

  3-marry in haste,repent at leisure
  -fiançailles vont en selle et repentailles en croupe
  -l'on se marie promptement et puis l'on se repend à loisir

  4-who marries for love without money,has good nights and sorry days
  -qui se marie par amour,a de bonnes nuits et de mauvais jours

master
  1-the eye of the master will do more work than both his hands
  one eye of the master sees more than ten of the servants
  -il n'est pour voir que l'oeil du maître

  2-a good master,a good scholar
  -c'est le bon veneur qui fait la bonne meute
  -le moine répond comme l'abbé chante

  3-one master in a house is enough
  -c'est raison que chacun soit maître en son logis

  4-the master's eye makes the horse fat
  -l'oeil du maître engraisse le cheval

match
  he met his match
  -il a trouvé plus fort que lui

may be
>**every may be has a may not be**
>-"peut-être" garde les gens de mentir

may
>**1-he that may not as he would,must do as he may**
>-quand on n'a pas ce que l'on aime,il faut vouloir ce que l'on a
>
>**2-may this piece of bread choke me if what I say is not true**
>-j'en mettrais ma main au feu (à couper)

maybe
>**every maybe has a may not be**
>-"peut-être" garde les gens de mentir

mean
>**the mean is the best**
>**golden mean is best**
>**keep the golden mean**
>-entre trop et trop peu est la juste mesure

measure
>**1-measure is merry mean**
>**-measure is treasure**
>**-there is measure in all things**
>-trop et trop peu n'est pas mesure
>
>**2-measure is medicine**
>-la modération est la santé de l'âme
>
>**3-to measure other people's corn by one's own bushel**
>**-don't measure other's feet by your own last**
>-ne mesurez pas autrui à votre aulne

meat
>**1-new meat begets a new appetite**
>-changement de corbillon fait trouver le pain bon
>-changement de corbillon, appétit de pain béni
>
>**2-all meat pleases not all mouths**
>-tous les ânes ne portent pas de sac
>-tous les goûts sont dans la nature
>
>**3-all meats to be eaten,all amids to be wed**
>-chacun prend son plaisir où il se trouve
>
>**4-after meat,mustard**
>-après le dîner,la moutarde
>
>**5-they that have no other meat,bread and butter are glad**
>-quand on n'a pas ce que l'on aime,il faut vouloir ce que l'on a
>
>**6-when meat is in,anger is out**
>-quand le foin manque au ratelier,les chevaux se battent
>-nourriture passe nature
>
>**7-much meat,much malady**
>-la gourmandise tue plus de monde que l'épée

medal
> **every medal has two sides**
> **-every medal has its everse**
> -chaque médaille a son revers

meddle
> **meddle and smart for it**
> -qui s'y frotte,s'y pique

meet
> **1-don't meet trouble half way**
> -il ne faut pas pleurer avant d'être battu
>
> **2-to meet behind closed doors**
> -se réunir à huis clos
>
> **3-he met his match**
> -il a trouvé plus fort que lui

melt
> **to melt like butter before the sun**
> -fondre comme neige au soleil

merchant
> **a merchant that gains not loses**
> -marchand qui perd ne peut rire

mercury
> **you cannot make a mercury out of every log**
> -quiconque est loup agisse en loup
> -la plus belle fille du monde ne peut donner que ce qu'elle a

merry
> **1-merry as a cricket**
> **as merry as a lark**
> **merry as a pie**
> -gai comme un pinson
>
> **2-all are not merry that dance lightly**
> -tel chante qui ne rit pas

might
> **might makes right**
> -la force prime le droit
> -la raison du plus fort est toujours la meilleure

mildness
> **mildness does better than harshness**
> -plus fait douceur que violence
> -on prend plus de mouches avec du miel qu'avec du vinaigre
> -patience et longueur de temps font plus que force et que rage

milk
> **that accounts for the milk in the coconut**
> -et voilà pourquoi votre fille est muette

mill
> **1-the mill gets by going**
> -il vaut mieux aller au moulin qu'au médecin
> -qui sème en pleurs,récolte en heur

2-the mills of God grind slowly
-la vengeance est un plat qui se mange froid

miller

the miller got never better moulter than he took with his own hands
-on n'est jamais aussi bien servi que par soi-même
-on ne trouve jamais meilleur messager que soi-même

millstone

1-the lower millstone grounds as well as the upper
-le malheur n'est pas toujours à la porte du pauvre
-le diable n'est pas toujours à la porte du pauvre
-le pire n'est pas toujours sûr

2-to have a millstone around one's neck
-traîner un boulet

mince

to mince one's words
-ne pas mâcher ses mots

mind

1-mind and space are not commensurable
-comparaison n'est pas raison
-il ne faut pas confondre coco et abricot le coco a de l'eau,l'abricot un noyau

2-to have a mind like a cesspool
-avoir l'esprit mal tourné

3-mind your "P,s" and "Q,s"
-tenez vous sur vos gardes

4-great minds think alike
-les grands esprits se rencontrent

5-he who has a mind to beat his dog will easily find a stick
-occasion trouve qui son chat bat

minute

a minute gained,a lifetime lost
-qui trop se hâte reste en chemin

mitrh

mirth without measure is madness
-le surplus rompt le couvercle

mischief

1-he that mischief hatches mischief catches
-qui veut mal,mal lui vient
-qui mal cherche,mal trouve
-tel est pris qui croyait prendre

2-miscjhief comes by the pound and goes away by the ounce
-les maladies viennent à chaval et s'en retournent à pied

miser

a miser has no friends
-main serrée,coeur étroit

misery
misery loves company
-chagrin ârtagé est moins lourd à porter

misfortune
1-misfortune makes foes of friends
-l'or s'épure au feu,l'homme s'éprouve au creuset du malheur
-ami au prêter,ennemi au rendre

2-misfortunes never comes singly
-un malheur n'arrive jamais seul
-jamais deux sans trois

3-misfortune tells us what fortune is
-quand le puits est à sec,on sait ce que vaut l'eau
-bien perdu,bien connu

4-misfortune arrives on horseback but departs on foot
-le mal arrive d'un seul coup et se retire par parcelles

miss
1-a miss is as good as a mile
-faute d'un point,Martin perdit son âne

2-you never miss the water till the well runs dry
-quand le puits est à sec,on sait ce que vaut l'eau

Missouri
I'm from Missouri,you've got to show me
-mon oeil!
-je ne crois que ce que je vois

mistake
he who makes no mistakes,makes nothing
-il n'y a que ceux qui ne font rien qui ne se trompent pas

mitten
to get the mitten
-mettre un amoureux à la porte

moderation
moderation in all things
-trop et trop peu n'est pas mesure

money
1-money is the only monarch
-hors de l'église,point de salut
-la clé d'or ouvre toutes les portes
-la lune est à l'abri des loups

2-money for jam,money for old rope
-bien mal acquis ne profite jamais

3-money has no smell
money is welcome though it come in a dirty clout
money never comes out of season
-l'argent n'a pas d'odeur

4-money refused loses its brightness
-un bienfait reproché tient lieu d'offense

5-money will make the mare go
money is the sinews of war
-l'argent est le nerf de le guerre

6-money talks
-la clé d'or ouvre toutes les portes

7-to make money hand over fist
-faire des affaires en or

8-money isn't everything
-l'argent ne fait pas le bonheur
-plaie d'argent n'est pas mortelle

9-money is a good servant but a bad master
-l'argent est serviteur ou maître

10-it takes money to make money
-money would be gotten if there were money to get it with
-money makes money
money begets money
-l'eau va à la rivière
-l'argent va à l'argent
-les rivières retournent à la mer
-un sou amène l'autre

11-money is the root of all evil
-où il y a un écu,il y a un diable.
-où il n'y en a pas,il y en a deux

12-no money,no piper
no money,no Swiss
-pas d'argent,pas de suisse

13-money makes a man free everywhere
-richesse donne hardiesse

14-a moneyless man goes fast through the market
-nécessité fait trotter les vieilles

15-money burns a hole in his pocket
-il mange toujours son blé en herbe

16-money is round and rolls away
-ce que la mer apporte en montant,elle le remporte en descendant

17-he that has no money needs no purse
-il ne sort du sac que ce qu'il y a

18-too much money makes one mad
-le surplus rompt le couvercle

monk
a monk out of his cloister is loke a fish out of water
-hors de l'église,point de salut

monkey
> **1-to throw a monkey wrench into the work**
> -entraver les projets
>
> **2-the higher the monkey climbs,the more he shows his tail**
> -plus le singe s'élève plus il montre son cul pelé

moon
> **1-when the moon turns blue**
> -quand les poules auront des dents
> -le trente-six du mois
>
> **2-the moon is not seen where the sun shines**
> -il ne faut pas courir deux lièvres à la fois

moonlight
> **to do a moonlight flit**
> -déménager à la cloche de bois

moonshine
> **that's all moonshine**
> -autant en emporte le vent

more
> **1-the more,the merrier**
> -plus on est de fous,plus on rit
>
> **2-more than meets the eye**
> -quelque chose à la clé
>
> **3-the more one has,the more one desires (wants)**
> -quand on prend du galon,on n'en saurait trop prendre
> -plus on en a,plus on en veut
>
> **4-more than enough is too much**
> -trop et trop peu n'est pas mesure

morn
> **let the morn come,and the meat with it**
> -il ne faut pas pleurer avant d'être battu

morning
> **a foul morning may turn to a fair day**
> **-cloudy mornings turn to clear evenings**
> -après la pluie,le beau temps

mother
> **1-the mother's breast is aye sweet**
> -l'asile le plus sûr est le sein de sa mère
>
> **2-like mother,like daughter**
> **if the mother trot,how can the daughter amble?**
> -tel père,tel fils
> -tel pain,telle soupe
>
> **3-every mother's child is handsome**
> **-every mother has it**
> -une maman est un bon bol à couvercle

mountain
    1- make a mountain out of a molehill
    -en faire une montagne
    -se noyer dans un verre d'eau
    -faire d'une mouche un éléphant
    -en faire une pendule(familier)

    2-if the mountain does not come to Mahomet,Mahomet must go to the mountain
    -si tu ne vas pas à Mahomet,Mahomet viendra à toi

    3-the mountain has brought forth a mouse
    -la montagne a accouché d'une souris

mouse
    1-it a bold mouse that nestles in the cat's ear
    -c'est dans les grands dangers qu'on voit un grand courage
    -au danger, on connaît les braves

    2-a mouse may help a lion
    -on a toujours besoin d'un plus petit que soi

    3-the mouse that has but one hole is quickly taken
    -il ne faut pas mettre tous ses oeufs dans le même panier
    -il vaut mieux avoir plusieurs cordes à son arc

    4-the escaped mouse ever feels the taste of the bait
    -chat échaudé craint l'eau froide

    5-a mouse in time may bite in two a cable
    -à force de coups,on abat le chêne
    -au long aller,la lime mange le fer
    -la patience vient à bout de tout

    6-don't make yourself a mouse,or the cat will eat you
    -faites-vous miel,les mouches vous mangeront

mouth
    1-a closed mouth catches no flies
    -dans une bouche close il n'entre point de mouches
    -il ne ment jamais s'il n'ouvre la bouche
    -dans bouche fermée rien ne rentre
    -qui ferme la bouche ne montre pas les dents
    -bonnes sont les dents qui retiennent la langue
    -il vaut mieux se mordre la langue avant de parler qu'après avoir parlé

    2-to make one's mouth water
    to make one's teeth water
    -faire saliver
    -mettre l'eau à la bouche

    3-he has a large mouth and a small girdle
    -c'est un panier percé

move
    to move heaven and earth
    -remuer ciel et terre

much

    1-it is much of a muchness
    -c'est du pareil au même

    2-much would have more
    -qui plus a,plus convoite
    -plus a le diable,plus veut avoir

muck

    muck and money go together
    where there is muck,there is brass
    -on ne manie pas le beurre sans se graisser les doigts

murder

    murder will out
    -la colère des dieux est lente mais terrible

music

    1-music is the eye of the ear
    -la musique est le plus cher de tous les bruits

    2-to face the music
    -affronter l'orage

musket

    -take not a musket to kill a butterfly
    -pour un moine,l'abbaye ne se perd pas

must

    1-what must be,must be
    -ce qui doit être,sera
    -il faut souffrir ce qu'on ne peut empêcher

    2-you must grin and bear it
    -il faut souffrir patiemment ce qu'on ne peut amender sainement

    3-we must not look for a golden life in an iron age
    -il faut laisser le vent courir par dessus les tuiles

mute

    mute as a fish
    -mute as a mackerel
    -muet cimme une tombe
    -muet comme une carpe

mutton

    it is hard to make a mutton of a saw
    -jamais un corbeau n'a fait un canari

N

nail

1-on the nail
-sur le champ
-rubis sur l'ongle(*familier,pour un paiement*)

2-to nail down someone
-mettre quelqu'un au pied du mur

3-nail drives out nail
-un clou chasse l'autre

naked

1-naked as my nail
naked as a frog
-naked as a needle
naked as a worm
naked as a robin
-nu comme un ver

2-naked as he was born
-en costume d'Adam

name

1-a good name is better than a golden girdle
-il a beau se lever tard qui a bruit de se lever matin
-bonne renommée vaut mieux que ceinture dorée
-une fois en mauvais renom,jamais puits n'a été estimé bon

2-a good name is sooner lost than won
-une fois en mauvais renom,jamais un puits n'a été estimé bon
-il est plus facile de descendre que de monter

3-no names,no packdrill
-il faut laver son linge sale en famille
-c'est un vilain oiseau qui salit son nid

4-don't name him in the same breath with his father
-il n'arrive pas à la cheville de son père

5-name not a rope where one has hange himself
-il ne faut pas parler de corde dans la maison d'un pendu
-il ne faut pas parler latin devant les cordeliers

narrow

narrow gathered,widely spent
-il n'est festin que de gens chiches
-il n'est chère que de vilain

nature

1-you can drive out nature with a pitchfork but she keeps coming back
-chassez le naturel,il revient au galop(*cf naturel*)
-nature ne peut mentir

2-nature is the true law
nature does nothing in vain
-les seins ne sont jamais trop lourds pour la poitrine

3-nature will have her course
-chassez le naturel,il revient au galop
-nature ne peut mentir

4-nature is no botcher
-la nature fait bien les choses
-il ne pleut que sur la vendange

5-nature is content with a little
-la nature se contente de peu

6-the nature of a fish is to swim
-qui est né chat court après les souris

7-nature and the sin of Adam can ill be concealed by fig leaves
-la plus belle fille du monde ne peut donner que ce qu'elle a

8-nature abhors a vacuum
-la nature a horreur du vide

9-natuer is conquered by obeying her
-on ne commande à la nature qu'en lui obéissant

10-nature passes nurture
-nourriture passe nature

near

1-as near as bark to tree
-être comme deux frères

2-the nearer the church,the farther from God
-près de l'église,loin de Dieu

necessity

1-necessity is the mother of invention
-nécessité est mère d'industrie
-de tout s'avise à qui pain faut

2-necessity has no holiday
-nécessité n'a pas de jour férié

3-necessity and opportunity may make a coward valiant
-la nécessité fait du timide un brave

4-necessity knows no law
-nécessité n'a pas de loi

neck

1-neck and crop
-corps et âme

2-neck and neck
-au coude à coude

3-it is neck or nothing
-marche ou crève

need

1-need makes the old wife trot
need makes the naked man rucn
-nécessité fait trotter les vieilles

387

2-it needs more skill than I can tell to play the second fiddle well
-pour être grand il faut avoir été petit

3-needs must when the devil drives
-il faut marcher quand le diable est aux trousses

neglect

neglect will kill injuries sooner than revenge
-à sot compliment point de réponse

neighbour

1-love your neighbour,yet pull not down your fence
-ta chemise ne sache ta guise

2-no one is rich enough to do without his neighbours
-il n'est voisin qui ne voisine

3-a near neighbour is better than a far dwelling kinsman
-le sort fait les parents,le choix fait les amis

4-our neighbour's cow yields better milk than ours
-l'herbe est toujours plus verte dans le pré du voisin

5-our neighbour's ground yields better corn than ours
-moisson d'autrui plus belle que la sienne

6-a good neighbour,a good morrow
-qui a bon voisin,a bon matin

net

the net of the sleeper catches fish
-la fortune vient en dormant

never

1-it is never too late to learn
-on apprend à tout âge

2-never is a long day
-il ne faut jurer de rien

3-never say die
-il ne faut pas jeter le manche après la cognée

4-neve say never
-never is a long day
-il ne faut jamais dire "fontaine,je ne boirai pas de ton eau"

5-never never land
-pays de Cocagne

new

1-what is new cannot be true
-ferveur de novice ne dure pas longtemps

2-everything new is fine
-new things are fair things
-tout nouveau,tout beau

3-there is nothing new under the sun
-il n'y a rien de nouveau sous le soleil

4-what is new is not true and what is true is not new
-la vérité est un fruit qui ne doit être cueilli que s'il est tout à fait mûr

news

1-good news goes on crutches,bad news travel quickly, ill news travel apace
-les bonnes nouvelles sont toujours retardées et les mauvaises ont des ailes
-quand le malheur entre dans la maison,faut lui donner une chaise

2-no news is good news
-pas de nouvelles,bonnes nouvelles

nick

in the nick of time
-fort à propos
-à pic

niggard

niggard father,spendthrift son
-à femme avare galant escroc

night

1-night is the mother of counsel
-la nuit porte conseil

2-the longest night will have an end
-après la pluie,le beau temps

nineteen

nineteen nay-says of a maiden are half a grant
-fille et ville qui parlementent sont à demi rendues

ninety

ninety percent of inspiration is perspiration
-on n'a rien sans rien

nip

1-to nip the plot (brair) in the bud
-tuer (étouffer) le complot dans l'oeuf
-prendre le mal à la racine

2-it was nip and tuck as to which would win
la lutte était si serrée qu'on ne savait pas qui allait gagner

nit

to nit-pick
-chercher la petite bête

nobody

nobody ever admits they are to blame
-il se ferait hacher plutôt que d'avouer

nod

a nod is as good as a wink for a blind horse
-mange bien des mouches qui n'y voit pas

noise

　　the noise is greater than the nuts
　　-plus de peur que de mal

nose

　　1-don't cut off your nose to spite your face
　　-fou est qui s'oublie
　　-elle s'est punie elle-même
　　-elle boude contre son ventre

　　2-a nose of wax
　　-influençable

　　3-by a nose
　　-d'un cheveu

　　4-he that has a great nose thinks everybody is speaking of it
　　-celui qui se sait coupable croit toujours qu'on parle de lui

　　5-to have one's nose to the grindstone
　　-avoir les oreilles qui traînent

nothing

　　1-nothing venture,nothing have
　　nothing stake,nothing draw
　　-le succès est toujours un enfant de l'audace
　　-qui ne s'aventure pas n'a ni cheval,ni mule
　　-à coquin honteux,plate besace
　　-qui ne hasarde rien,n'a rien
　　-qui veut jouir d'aile,il lui faut lever la cuisse

　　2-nothing is certain but the unforeseen
　　-la seule certitude,c'est que rien n'est certain

　　3-nothing is impossible to the willing heart
　　-à cœur vaillant rien d'impossible

　　4-nothing is worse than care
　　-le mieux est l'ennemi du bien

　　5-out of nothing one can get nothing
　　-la plus belle fille du monde ne peut donner que ce qu'elle a

　　6-nothing must be done hastily but killing of fleas
　　-hâtez-vous lentement

　　7-nothing is certain
　　-il ne faut jurer de rien

　　8-nothing but is good for something
　　-à quelque chose malheur est bon

　　9-nothing is certain but death and taxes
　　-contre la mort,point de remède

　　10-nothing is as good as it seems before hand
　　-il faut garder une poire pour la soif

　　11-there is nothing like plain food
　　-la soupe fait le soldat

nought

1-nought lay down,nought take up
-on n'engraisse pas les cochons avec de l'eau claire
-point de pigeon pour une obole

2-of nought comes nought
-there comes nought out of the sack but what was there
la plus belle fille du monde ne peut donner que ce qu'elle a
-on n'a rien sans rien

novelty

novelty always appears handsome
-tout nouveau,tout beau
-de nouveau,tout m'est beau

now

that which is now shall not abide for ever
-les temps changent et nous changeons avec eux
-autres temps,autres moeurs

nowt

there is nowt so queer as folk
-il faut de tout pour faire un monde

number

1-I've got your number
-à bon chat,bon rat

2-to be a back number
être rétro

nutty

he is as nutty as a fruit cake
-il est fou à lier

O

oak
> every oak has been an acorn
> -mighty oaks from little acorns grow
> -il faut un commencement à tout

obedience
> through obedience learn to command
> -il faut apprendre à obéir pour savoir commander

obey
> he that cannot obey cannot command
> -pour être grand,il faut avoir été petit

object
> the object of words is to conceal thoughts
> -à mauvais jeu,bonne mine

odds
> 1-what's the odds?
> -qu'est-ce que ça fait?
>
> 2-the odds were against us
> -les chances étaient contre nous
>
> 3-it makes no odds
> -ça ne fait rien
>
> 4-what's the odds as long as you are happy?
> -il ne faut pas pleurer avant d'être battu

offer
> 1-never offer fish to swim
> -on n'apprend pas ua singe à faire la grimace
>
> 2-to offer the sun and the moon,the king ransom
> -faire un pont d'or

office
> 1-office will show the man
> -à l'oeuvre on connaît l'artisan
> -c'est au pied du mur qu'on reconnaît le maçon
>
> 2-out of office,out of danger
> -tambour lointain n'a pas de son

old
> 1-never too old to learn
> -il n'y a pas d'âge pour apprendre
>
> 2-as old as the hills
> -vieux comme le monde
>
> 3-old be,or yound die
> -il faut vieillir ou mourir jeune

omelet
> you can't make an omelet without breaking eggs
> -à bonne volonté ne vaut faculté
> -on ne peut faire d'omelette sans casser des oeufs

once

1-once a thief,always a thief
once a gambler,always a gambler
once a knave,always a knave
-qui a bu,boira

2-once doesn't make a habit
-once is no rule
-une fois n'est pas coutume

3-once a use,ever a custom
-il n'y a que le provisoire qui dure

4-once in a blue moon
-à la saint Glin-glin
-le trente-six du mois

one

one of these days is none of these days
one today is worth two tomorrows
one hour today is worth to morrow
-il ne faut jamais remettre au lendemain ce que l'on peut faire le jour
même

open

an open door may tempt a saint
-il ne faut pas tenter le diable

opera

the opera isn't over till the fat lady sings
rira bien qui rira le dernier

opportunity

1-opportunity never knocks twice
-une occasion perdue ne se rattrape jamais

2-opportunity makes the thief
-l'occasion fait le larron

ought

too much of ought is good for nought
-l'excès en tout nuit
-l'excès d'un très grand bien devient un mal très grand
-le surplus rompt le couvercle
-quand on serre trop l'anguille,on la laisse partir

ounce

1-an ounce of practice is worth a pound of theory
-ce ne sont pas les mots qui comptent mais les actions
-a beau parler qui n'a cure de bien faire

2-an ounce of discretion is worth a pound of wit
-il est bon de parler et meilleur de se taire

3-an ounce of prevention is worth a pound of cure
-mieux vaut prévenir que guérir

4-an ounce of good fortune is worth a pound of forecast
-il faut tourner le moulin lorsque souffle le vent

owl

the owl thinks her own young fairest
-ce qu'on aime est toujours beau
-à l'âne,l'âne semble beau

P

pack

1-he sends the pests packing
to send one packing
-il les a envoyés paître,sur les roses,promener

2-there is no pack of cards without a knave
-nulle rose sans épine

paddle

paddle your own canoe
-volez de vos propres ailes

pain

1-no pains,no gains
-nul pain sans peine
-qui a métier,a rente

2-pain is forgotten where gain follows
-espoir de gain diminue la peine

3-take a pain for a pleasure all wise men can
-les mains noires font manger le pain blanc

4-if you will not take pains,pains will take you
-qui ne risque rien,n'a rien

5-there is more pain to do nothing than something
-c'est proprement ne valoir rien que de n'être utile à personne

paint

don't paint the lily
-celui-là seul sait louer qui loue avec restriction

pass

to pass under the yolk
-passer sous les fourches caudines

pater

'pater noster' built churches,and 'our father' pulls them down
une religion peu à peu emporte une autre

path

every path has its puddle
-chaque vin a sa lie

patience

1-patience provoked turns to fury
-craignez la colère de la colombe

2-patience is a virtue
-la patience est la vertu des ânes

3-he that has patience,has fat thrushes for a farthing
-la patience est amère mais son fruit est doux
-à dure enclume,marteau de plume

4-patience and time run through the longest day
-patience is a plaster for all sores
-patience drives a snail to Jerusalem
-la patience vient à bout de tout

patient

patient waiters are no losers
-on ne perd pas à attendre
-on ne perd pas son temps quand on aiguise ses outils

pay

1-to pay in one's own coin
-to pay with the same dish you borrow
-rendre la monnaie de sa pièce

2-to pay on the barrelhead
-to pay cash on the nail
-payer rubis sur l'ongle

3-he who pays the piper calls the tune
you pays your money and you takes your choice
-qui a de l'argent a des pirouettes
-qui paie les violons choisit la musique

4-to pay in cold hard cash
-payer en espèces sonnantes et trébuchantes

5-to pay in promises
-to pay with wooden nickels
-payer en monnaie de singe

6-to pay the piper
-avaler la pilule

7-to pay through the nose
-coûter les yeux de la tête

peacock

the peacock has fair feathers,but foul feet
-tel a de beaux yeux qui ne voit goutte

peanut

1-to work for peanuts
-travailler pour des prunes

2-peanut gallery (*theatre*)
-poulailler

peddlar

let every peddlar carry his own burden
-on ne fait pas de procession pour tailler les vignes
-chacun se fait fouetter à sa guise

peep

he who peeps through a hole may see what wil vex him
-la mouche va si souvent au lait qu'elle y demeure

penny

1-the unrighteous penny corrupts the righteous pound
-il suffit d'une pomme pourrie pour infester tout le tas

2-he thinks his penny good silver
-chacun aime le sien

3-to be penny wise
to pinch pennies
-faire des économies de bouts de chandelle

4-a penny saved is a penny earned
-qui épargne,gagne

5-don't be penny wise and pound foolish
habit de velours,ventre de son

6-not to have a penny to bless oneself with
-être pauvre comme Job
-ne pas avoir un sou vaillant

7-a bad penny always turns up
-en sa peau mourra le loup

8-put two pennies in a purse and they will draw together
-penny and penny laid up will be many
-un sou amène l'autre

9-in for a penny,in for a pound
-quand le vin est tiré,il faut le boire

people
people who live in glass houses shouldn't throw stones
-qui sème le vent,récolte la tempête

permanent
there is nothing permanent except change
-on ne se baigne jamais deux fois dans le même fleuve
-autres temps,autres moeurs

perseverance
perseverance kills the game
-la persévérance vient à bout de tout

physician
physicians kill more than they cure
-a young physician fattens the churchyard
-les médecins font les cimetières bossus

pick
1-to pick up the threads
-revenons à nos moutons

2-pick and choose,and take the worst
-qui veut choisir prend souvent le pire

3-pick us and pieces
-ramasser à la petite cuiller

pie
a pie in the sky
-demander la lune

pig

1-when the pigs have wings
-quand les poules auront des dents

2-pigs might fly
-avec des si et des mais,on mettrait Paris en bouteille

pill

1-bitter pills may have whollesome effects
-à quelque chose malheur est bon

2-a bitter pill to swallow
avaler la pilule

pin

to have pins and needles on one's leg
-avoir des fourmis dans les jambes

piss

1-piss not against the stream
-à pisser contre le vent,on mouille sa chemise

2-a pin a day is a groat a year
-un sou amène l'autre

pitcher

1-little pitchers have great ears
-petit chaudron,grandes oreillles

2-the pitcher goes often to the well but is broken at last
-tant va la cruche à l'eau qu'elle se casse

3-whether the pitcher strikes the stone,or the stone the pithcher,it is bad for the pitcher
-le pot de terre contre le pot de fer

4-the pithcher went once too often to the wall
-c'est la goutte d'eau qui fait déborder le vase

place

1-there is no place like home
à chaque oiseau son nid est beau
-il n'y a pas de petit chez-soi

2-high places have their precipices
-il y a des lumières que l'on éteint en les plaçant sur des chandeliers

plain

it's as plain as the nose on your face
-c'est clair comme deux et deux font quatre
-c'est cousu de fil blanc
-cela se voit comme le nez au milieu de la figure
-cela saute aux yeux

plan

the best-laid plans may fall
-brebis comptées,le loup les mange

play
1-if you play with the fire,you get burnt
-don't play with matches
-de trop près se chauffe qui se brûle

2-they who play bowls must expect to meet with rubbers
-près des ânes, on attrape des coups de pied
-pas de fumée sans feu
-mangeant du foin,vous sentirez l'âne
-ceux qui touchent la poix,se souillent les doigts

3-it played the deuce with me and my belongings
-he played old gooseberry with me
-il m'a donné du fil à retordre

4-it is dangerous to pkay with edged tools
don't play with matches
-on ne joue pas avec le feu

5-you may play with a bull till you get his horn in your eye
-qui s'y frotte,s'y pique

6-to play cat and mouse
-jouer au chat et à la souris

7-to play one's last trump
-jouer sa dernière carte

8-to play by the ear
-aller au pifomètre

pleasant
pleasant hours fly fast
-nous ne comptons les heures que lorsqu'elles sont perdues

please
one cannot please everybody and his wife
you cannot please everyone
-on ne peut contenter tout el monde et son père
-on ne peut ménager la chèvre et le chou

pleasure
1-short pleasure,long lament
-pour un plaisir,mille douleurs

2-there is no pleasure without pain
-les mains noires font manger le pain blanc

3-the pleasures of the mighty are the tears of the poor
-de tout temps,les petits ont pâti des sottises des grands

plenty
1-plenty breeds pride
-sac plein dresse l'oreille
-richesse donne hardiesse
-il n'est orgueil que de pauvre enrichi
-ventre plein donne de l'assurance

2-plenty is not plague
-abondance de biens ne nuit pas

3-plenty makes dainty
plenty is no dainty
-chose accoutumée rarement prisée
-abondance engendre satiété

4-he tah has plenty of goods shall have more
-la pierre va toujours au tas

plough

plough deep,while sluggards smeep,and you will have corn to sell and to keep
-celui qui laboure le champ,le mange

plum

a black plum is as sweet as a white
-l'habit ne fait pas le moine
-sous la crasse,la beauté s'y cache

poach

to poach on other people's territory
-marcher sur les plates-bandes de quelqu'un

poacher

an old poacher makes the best keeper
-à malin,malin et demi

poet

poets are born not made
-on naît poète,artiste

poison

1-the poison drives another
-one poison drives out another
-un clou chasse l'autre
-les poils du chien guérissent la morsure du chien

2-one drop of poison infects the whole tun of wine
-une cuillerée de goudron gâte un tonneau de miel

3-poison is poison though it comes in a golden cup
-serpent qui change de peau est toujours serpent
-en belle gaine d'or,cuteau de plomb gît et dort
-un singe vêtu de pourpre est toujours un singe

poke

to poke fire with a sword
-jeter de l'huile sur le feu

pole

-they are poles apart
-elles (ils) sont comme le jour et la nuit

pomp

all our pomp the earth covers
-le plus riche en moiurant n'emporte qu'un drap

pool

    standing pools gather filth
    -c'est folie de vanner les plumes au vent
    -au paresseux,le poil lui pousse dans la main

poor

    1-the poor man pays for all
    the poor suffers all the wrong
    -à chevaux maigres vont les mouches
    -quand le loup est pris tous les chiens lui lardent les fesses

    2-he is not poor that has little,but he that desires much
    -un avare est toujours gueux
    -ne désirer que ce qu'on a, c'est avoir tout ce qu'on désire

    3-to be poor as a rat
    -être fauché comme les blés (familier)

    4-to be poor as Job's turkey
    -to be poor as a rat
    -to be as poor as a church mouse
    -être pauvre comme Job

port

    any port in a storm
    -nécessité est de raison la moitié
    -nécessité n'a pas de loi

possession

    1-possession is better than expectation
    -il vaut mieux tenir que courir
    -on sait ce que l'on perd,on ne sait pas ce que l'on gagne

    2-possession is nine points of the law
    -en fait de meuble,la possession vaut titre

pot

    1-a little pot is soon hot
    -quand les brebis enragent elles sont pires que les loups

    2-when the pot is full it will boil over
    -la coupe est pleine

    3-a watched pot never boils
    -plus on désire une chose,plus elle se fait attendre

    4-a pot that belongs to many is ill stired ans worse boiled
    -affaire à tout le monde,affaire à personne
    -à chemin battu il ne croît point d'herbe

    5-it is the pot calling the kettle black
    -c'est la pelle qui se moque du fourgon

potter

    1-one potter envies another
    -le potier au potier porte envie

    2-every potter praises his own pot
    -chaque mercier prise ses aiguilles et son panier

pound

>**a pound in the purse is worth two in the book**
>-mieux vaut tenir que courir
>-un tiens vaut mieux que deux tu l'auras

pour

>**to pour oil on trouble waters**
>-calmer le jeu

poverty

>**1-poverty is no crime**
>-la pauvreté n'est pas un pêché,mieux vaut cependant la cacher
>-pauvreté n'est pas vice

>**2-poverty is the mother of invention**
>**-poverty is the mother of all arts**
>-de tout s'avise à qui pain faut
>-l'infortune est la sage femme du génie

>**3-he who is content in his poverty,is wonderfully rich**
>-ne désirer que ce qu'on a,c'est avoir tout ce qu'on désire

>**4-when poverty comes in at the door,love flies out at the window**
>-lorsque la faim est à la prote,l'amour s'en va par la fenêtre

>**5-poverty and wealth are twin sisters**
>-quand il neige dans les montagnes,il fait froid dans les vallées

>**6-poverty parts fellowship**
>-pauvre hoimme n'a point d'amis

powder

>**he isn't worth the powder to blow him up with**
>-il ne vaut pas la corde pour le prendre

practice

>**1-practice makes perfect**
>-le lendemain s'instruit aux leçons de la veille
>-cent fois sur le métier remettez votre ouvrage

>**2-practice what you preach**
>fais ce que tu dis
>-a beau précher qui n'a cure de bien faire

praise

>**1-praise without profit puts little in the pot**
>-la beauté ne sale pas la marmite

>**2-after praising the wine,they sell us vinegar**
>-à la boucherie toues les vaches sont boeufs,à la tannerie-tous les boeufs sont vaches

>**3-he that praises himself,patters himself**
>-qui se loue s'emboue

>**4-to praise to the skies**
>-porter au pinacle

5-self praise stinks
-la vanité n'a pas de plus grand ennemi que la vanité

preservation
self preservation is the first law of nature
-chacun pour soi et DIeu pour tous
-un noyé s'accroche à un brin d'herbe

prettiness
prettiness dies first
-la beauté est une fleur éphémère

prevention
prevention is better than cure
-mieux vaut prévenir que guérir

price
prices have been skyrocketing
-les prix montent en flèche

prick
1-to prick up one's ears
-dresser l'oreille

2-it early pricks that will be a thorn
-jamais bon cheval ne devint rosse
-on ne s'amende pas de vieillir

pride
pride goes before and shame follows after
-quand orgueil chevauche devant,honte et dommage suivent de près

prince
of a new prince,new bondage
-à nouvelles affaires,nouveau conseil

prize
it's ill prizing of green barley
ۥc'est viande mal prête que viande en buisson
-il ne faut pas vendre la peau de l'ours avant de l'avoir tué

probability
one thousand probabilities does not make one truth
-mieux vaut une certitude qu'une promesse en l'air

proclaim
to proclaim from the housetop
-clamer à tous vents

procrastination
procrastination is the thief of time
-il ne faut jamais remettre à plus tard ce que l'on peut faire le jour même

prodigal
young prodigal in a coach,will be an old beggar barefoot
-grande chère,petit testament

promise
1-he that promise too much,means nothing
-qui tout promet rien ne promet
-longue langue,courte main

2-promises are like pie-crust,made to be broken
-promettre et tenir sont deux

3-many fair promises in marriage making,but few in totcher paying
-tel fiance qui n'épouse point

4-promise is debt
-le beau dire ne dispense pas du bien faire
-dire et faire sont deux
-ce n'est pas tout de vendre,il faut livrer

5-between promising and performing,a man may marry his daughter
-entre promettre et donner,doit-on sa fille marier?

6-a promise is a promise
-il y a loin de la coupe aux lèvres
-chose promise,chose due

proof
the proof of the pudding is in the eating
-ce ne sont pas les mots qui comptent mais les actions
-le fait juge l'homme

prophet
a prophet is not without honor except in his own country
-nul n'est prophète en son pays
-l'aigle d'une maison n'est qu'un sot dans une autre

procrastination
procrastination is the thief of time
-il ne faut jamais remettre à plus tard ce que l'on peut faire le jour même

prosperity
1-prosperity makes friends,adversity tries them
-c'est dans le malheur qu'on connaît ses vrais amis
-l'adversité est la pierre de touche de l'amitié

2-in time of prosperity,friends will be plenty;in time of adversity,not one amongst twenty
-pauvre homme n'a point d'amis

proud
as proud as a peacock
-fier comme Artaban

prove
that which proves too much,proves nothing
-qui prouve trop,ne prouve rien

provide
1-to provide grist to the mill
-apporter de l'eau au moulin

2-providing is preventing
-gouverner c'est prévoir

pudding
1-too much pudding will choke a dog
-l'excès en tout nuit
-le surplus rompt le couvercle

2-better some of the pudding than none of the pie
-quand on n'a pas ce que l'on aime,il faut vouloir ce que l'on a

pull

1-to pull the chesnuts out of the fire
-tirer les marrons du feu

2-to pull oneself together
-se secouer

3-to pull a face
-faire une grimace

4-to pull the rug out from under someone
-couper l'herbe sous le pied de quelqu'un

5-to pull one's weight
-mettre du sien

6-to pull the strings
-tirer sur les ficelles

punctuality

punctuality is the politness of kings
-l'exactitude est la politesse des rois

pure

1-to be as pure as the driven snow
-être blanc comme neige

2-to the pure all things are pure
-tout est pur aux purs

purse

1-let your purse be your master
-il faut aller selon sa bourse

2-he that has a full purse never wanted a friend
-la prospérité fait peu d'amis

3-a full purse makes the mouth speak
-sac plein fait dresser l'oreille

4-if you put nothing in your purse,you can take nothing out
-celui qui laboure le champ,le mange

push

he's been pushing up the daisies for a long time
-il y a longtemps qu'il mange les pissenlits par la racine

put

1-he is put to bed with a shovel
-enterré

2-not to put too fine an edge on it
-ne pas y aller avec le dos de la cuiller

3-to put someone in the picture
-tenir quelqu'un au courant

4-one cannot put back the clock
-le temps fuit sans retour
-le temps perdu ne se rattrappe jamais

5-put that in your pipe and smoke it
-croyez cela et buvez de l'eau
-mettez ça dans votre poche et votre mouchoir par dessus

6-put not the bucket too often in the well
-tant va la cruche à l'eau qu'elle se casse

7-put down in black and white
-écrit noir sur blanc

8-that puts a new face on the matter
-cela éclaire l'affaire d'un jour nouveau

9-to put a bolf or a good face on the matter
-you must put a good face on a bad business
-faire contre mauvaise fortune bon coeur

10-to put one's head in the lion's mouth
-se jeter dans la gueule du loup

11-to put all one's eggs in one basket
-to put one's shirt
-jouer quelque chose sur un coup de dés

12-to put up the prank
-tirer les marrons du feu

13-put not your hand between the bark and the tree
-il ne faut pas mettre le doigt entre l'arbre et l'écorce

14-he put something for a rainy day
-il a gardé une poire pour la soif

15-never put off till to morrow what you can do today
-il ne faut jamais remettre au lendemain ce que l'on peut faire le jour même

putty

he was putty in her hands
-elle le menait par le bout du nez

Q

quake
> **he quakes in his boots**
> -il est dans ses petits souliers

quality
> **quality speaks for itself**
> -au vin qui se vend bien,ne faut point de lierre

quarrel
> **1-to quarrel one's over bishop's cope,over goat's wool**
> -se manger la laine sur le dos
>
> **2-to quarrel with your bread and butter**
> -elle boude contre son ventre
> -elle s'est punie elle-même
> -fou est qui s'oublie
>
> **3-quarrels would not last so long if the fault was only on one side**
> -les querelles ne dureraient pas si longtemps,si le tort n'était que d'un côté

queen
> **Queen Anne is dead**
> -c'est vieux comme Erode

question
> **1-ask a silly question and you'll get a silly answer**
> **like question,like answer**
> -à question abstruse,abstruse réponse
>
> **2-a stupid question deserves no answer**
> -à sotte demande il ne faut point de réponse
>
> **3-is is not every question that deserves an answer**
> -à bon demandeur,bon refuseur

quey
> **quey calves are dead veal**
> -il a tué la poule aux oeufs d'or

quick
> **quick tempered but his heart is in the right place**
> -mauvaise tête mais bon coeur

quiet
> **1-the quiet life is the happy life**
> -pour vivre heureux,vivons cachés
>
> **2-as quiet as a mouse**
> -il est sage comme une image

R

rabbit
>to pull a rabbit out of the hat
>to pull teeth
>-trouver une solution miracle

rabbit food
>les légumes

race
>the race is got by running
>-on n'a rien sans rien

rain
>1-if it rains when the sun is shining,the devil is beating his wife
>-c'est le diable qui bat sa femme et marie sa fille

>2-small rain lays great dust
>-petite pluie abat grand vent

>3-it never rains,it pours
>-un malheur n'arrive jamais seul

>4-although it rain,throw not away your watering pot
>-il faut garder une poire pour la soif
>-il faut avoir deux cordes à son arc

>5-you'll get a raim check
>-c'est partie remise

>6-it is raining cats and dogs
>-il pleut des cordes
>-il pleut des hallebardes

>7-if it rains on St Swithin's day (15th of July),ther will be rain for fourty days
>-s'il pleut à la St Médard,il pleut quarante jours plus tard

>8-rain before seven,fine before eleven
>-pluie matinale n'est pas journale

rally
>to rally the occasion
>-se montrer à la hauteur des circonstances

rat
>1-a rat leaving a sinking ship
>-les rats désertent le navire qui coule

>2-it's an old rat that won't eat cheese
>-il ne mord pas à l'hameçon

reach
>to reach the point of no return
>-franchir le Rubicon

reaper
>there is a reaper whose name is death
>-la mort est un moissonneur qui ne fait pas la sieste

reason
> there is a reason in the roasting of eggs
> -en toutes choses,il faut considérer la fin
> -ce qu'il faut chercher à connaître,c'est le fond du panier

receiver
> the receiver is as bad as the thief
> -autant pèche celui qui tient le sac que celui qui l'emplit

reckon
> he that reckon without his host,must reckon again
> -qui compte sans son hôte,compte deux fois

reckoning
> even (short)reckoning make long friends
> -les bons comptes font les bons amis
> -à tout bon compte, revenir

reed
> where there are reeds,there is water
> -pas de fumée sans feu

reek
> where there is reek,there is heart
> -pas de fumée sans feu

refuse
> 1-to refuse and to give tardly is all the same
> -donner tard c'est refuser
>
> 2-never refuse a good offer
> -l'occasion est chauve
> -l'occasion n'a qu'un cheveu

remedy
> 1-the remedy may be worse than the disease
> -il vaut mieux laisser un enfant morveux que de lui arracher le nez
> -le remède est parfois pire que le mal
>
> 2-there is remedy for everything but death
> -contre la mort,point de remède

remember
> remember you are but a man
> -un de perdu,dix de retrouvés

remembrance
> the remembrance of past sorrow is joyful
> -le temps passé est toujours le meilleur

remorse
> remorse is lust's desert
> -après bon temps,on se repent

removal
> three removals are as bad as a fire
> -trois déménagements valent un incendie

render

>**render unto Caesar the things which are Caesar's**
>-il faut rendre à César ce qui est à César

repair

>**he that repairs not a part,builds all**
>-he that repairs not his gutters,repairs his whole house
>-petite négligence accouche d'un grand mal

repeat

>**I repeated it to him hundreds of time**
>-je le lui ai répété vingt fois

report

>**to report sick**
>-se faire porter pâle

reproach

>**when one has nothing to reproach one self with one aughs at the lies of the wicked**
>-une bonne conscience est un doux oreiller

respect

>**respect is better from a distance**
>-la familiarité engendre le mépris

return

>**1-to return home as wise as one went**
>-qui bête va à Rome,tel en retourne
>-jamais cheval ni méchant n'amenda pour aller à Rome
>
>**2-to return like for like**
>-rendre la monnaie de sa pièce

revenge

>**1-revenge is sweet**
>-la vengeance est plus douce que le miel
>-oeil pour oeil,dent pour dent
>
>**2-revenge is a dish that can be eaten cold**
>-revenge of a hundred year has still its sucking teeth
>-la vengeance est un plat qui se mange froid

revolution

>**revolutions are not made with rosewater**
>-on ne fait pas les révolutions avec de l'eau de rose

reward

>**no reward without toil**
>-nul pain sans peine

rich

>**1-a rich man's joke is always funny**
>-à bourse pleine,amis nombreux
>-les paroles des grands ne tombent jamais à terre
>-les sottises des grands sont des sentences
>
>**2-the rich knows not who is his friend**
>-riche homme ne sait qui ami lui est

3-he that will be rich before night,may be hanged before noon
la rivière ne grossit pas sans trouble

4-he is rich that has few wants
-je suis riche des biens dont je sais me passer

5-no one is rich enough to do without his nrighbours
-il n'est voisin qui ne voisine

rid

to rid with the beard on the shoulder
-savoir se tenir sur ses gardes

ride

1-if two ride a horse,one must ride behind
-jamais deux orgueilleux ne chevaucheront bien un âne

2-he rides this subject to death
-c'est son cheval de bataille

3-to ride the black donkey
-être têtu comme un âne

4-he who rides a tiger is afraid to dismount
-quand le vin est tiré,il faut le boire

5-don't ride your horse to death
-qui veut voyager loin,ménage sa monture

righteous

the righteous man sins before an open chest
-il ne faut pas tenter le diable
-il ne faut pas mettre dans la cave un ivrogne qui a renoncé au vin

ring

1-to ring up the curtain
-frapper les trois coups

2-to ring down the curtain
-sonner le glas d'une affaire

rise

1-he that rises first,is first dressed
-l'avenir appartient à ceux qui se lèvent tôt

2-though you rise early,yet the day comes at his time,and not till then
-avant l'heure,c'est pas l'heure;après l'heure,c'est plus l'heure

3-to ride the high horse
-monter sur se grands chevaux

river

1-rivers need a spring
-il faut un commencement à tout

2-all rivers run into the sea
-tous les chemins mènent à Rome

3-the river passed and God forgotten
-la fête passée,adieu le saint
-mal passé,adieu le saint

road

1-the road to hell is paved with good intentions
-l'enfer est pavé de bonnes intentions

2-all roads lead to Rome
-tous les chemins mènent à Rome

3-there is no royal road to learning
-nul ne naît appris et instruit
-science sans conscience n'est que ruine de l'âme

roast

roasted pigeons don't fly through the air
-si le ciel tombait,il y aurait bien des laouettes prises

rob

don't rob Peter to pay Paul
-il ne faut pas déshabiller Pierre pour habiller Paul

robin

a robin doesn't make spring
-une hirondelle ne fait pas le printemps

rod

to make a rod for one's own back
-du bâton que l'on tient on est souvent battu
-c'est la graisse du cochon qui a cuit le cochon

roland

-a roland for an oliver
-s'il me donne des pois,je lui donnerai des fèves

roll

1-roll my log and I'll roll yours
-passez moi la rhubarbe et je vous passerai le séné

2-to be rolling in money
-rouler sur l'or

Rome

when in Rome,do as romans do
-à Rome,il faut vivre comme à Rome

room

1-there is no room to swing a cat
-il n'y a pas de place pour se retourner

2-there is always room at the top
-tout soldat a dans son sac un bâton de maréchal

root

no root,no fruit
-qui sème,récolte
-il faut un commencement à tout

rope

1-name not a rope where one has hang himself
-il ne faut pas parler de corde dans la maison d'un pendu
-il ne faut pas clocher devant les boiteux
-il ne faut pas parler latin devant les cordeliers

2-the rope has never been made that binds thoughts
-les pensées ne paient point de douane

rose

1-his life was no bed of roses
-tout n'a pas été rose dans sa vie

2-under the rose
-sous le sceau du secret

3-a rose by any other name would still be a rose
-serpent qui change de peau est toujours serpent
-lavez chien,peignez chien,toutefois n'est chien que chien

4-the fairest rose at last is whithered
-il n'est si belle rose qui ne se flétrisse
-il n'est si beau soulier qui ne devienne savate
-la beauté est une fleur éphémère

5-no rose without a thorn
-nulle rose sans épine

rotten

he's rotten to the core
-il est pourri jusqu'à la racine
-il est mauvais comme la gale

rough

1-we shall have to rough it,that's all
-à la guerre comme à la guerre

2-the rough net is not the best catcher of birds
-qui manie le miel s'en lèche les doigts

rouse

it rouses my bile
-cela me fait grimper aux arbres

royet

royet lads make sober men
-il faut que jeunesse se passe

rub

here is the rub
-voilà le hic!

ruin

many have been ruined by buying good pennyworths
-bon marché fait argent débourser

rule

1-to rule the roost
-porter la culotte

2-to rule someone with a rod of iron
-faire marcher quelqu'un à la baguette

run

1-don't try to run before you walk
-il faut attendre à cueillir la poire qu'elle soit mûre
-il ne faut pas mettre la charrue avant les boeufs

2-to run away from one's own guns
-tourner casaque

3-to have a long run
-tenir l'affiche

4-he ran through quickly
-il n'a pas fait long feu

5-run with the hare and hunt with the hounds
-il faut ménager la chèvre et le chou

6-it is enough to run,one must set out on time
-rien en sert de courir.il faut partir à point

7-it runs in the blood
-c'est dans le sang

S

sack

    1-empty sacks will never stand upright
    -sac vide ne tient pas debout

    2-there comes nought of the sack but what was there
    -d'un sac à charbon ne peut sortir blanche farine
    -il ne sort du sac que ce qu'il y a

sadness

    sadness and gladness succeed each other
    -les jours se suivent et ne se ressemblent pas
    -les merles ne chantent pas comme les grives

safe

    1-it is best to be on the safe side
    deux précautions valent mieux qu'une

    2-safe find,safe bind
    -prudence est mère de sûreté

safety

    1-safety lies in the middle course
    -entre trop et trop peu est la juste mesure
    -il faut lier le sac avant qu'il soit plein

    2-there is safety in numbers
    -il faut hurler avec les loups
    -l'union fait la force

saint

    1-all are not saints that go to church
    -qui est près de l'église est souvent loin de Dieu
    -il ne faut point se fier à qui entend deux messes

    2-a saint in crape is twice a saint in lawn
    -jamais à un bon chien il ne vient un bon os
    -il est bien aisé d'aller à pied quand on tient son cheval par la bride

salad

    a good salad may be the prologue to a bad supper
    -le sillon n'est pas le champ

salesman

    every salesman boats of his own wares
    -il n'est bon maçon qui pierre refuse

same

    it will all be the same in a hundred years hence
    -il passera bien de l'eau sous le pont

sand

    many sands will sink a ship
    -grain à grain la poule remplit son ventre

sandman

    the sandman is about
    -le marchand de sable est passé

Satan
> it's Satan rebuking sin
> -c'est la pelle qui se moque du fourgon

sauce
> **1-the sauce was better than the fish**
> -la sauce vaut mieux que le poisson
>
> **2-what is sauce for the goose is sauce for the gander**
> -ce qui est bon pour l'un est bon pour l'autre
>
> **3-make not your sauce before you have caught your fish**
> -il ne faut pas mettre le lièvre en sauce avant de l'avoir attrapé

savage
> **as savage as a bear with a sorehead**
> -la mule du pape garde sept ans son coup de pied

save
> **save us from our friends**
> -on est aisément dupé par ce qu'on aime
> -on a peine à haîr ce qu'on a bien aimé

say
> **1-I say little but I think the more**
> -je ne dis rien mais je n'en pense pas moins
>
> **2-saying and doing are two things**
> **saying is one thing and doing another**
> -dire et faire sont deux
> -au parler ange,au faire change
>
> **3-better say nothing than not to the purpose**
> -arriver comme un chien dans un jeu de quille
>
> **4-least said,soonest mended**
> -moins on en dit,mieux on se porte
> -moins on parle,mieux celà vaut
> -plus on se découvre,plus on a froid
> -trop parler nuit
>
> **5-what will Mr.Grundy say?**
> -et le "qu'en-dira-t-on?"
>
> **6-don't say till you are asked**
> -ne donne pas de conseil à moins qu'on t'en prie
>
> **7-don't say "I'll never drink of this water how dirty so ever it be"**
> -il ne faut jamais dire "fontaine,je ne boirai pas de ton eau"
>
> **8-easier said than done**
> **-saying is one thing and doing another**
> -plus facile à dire qu'à faire
>
> **9-better say "here it is",than,"here it was"**
> -il vaut mieux être qu'avoir été
>
> **10-all that is said in the kitchen should not be heard in the hall**
> -un mot dit à l'oreille est entendu de loin

11-say no ill of the year till it be past
-on ne sait pas de quoi demain sera fait

scale
> **to type the scales**
> -faire pencher la balance

scapegoat
> **to be the scapegoat**
> -être la tête de turc

scare
> **1-you can never scare a dog away from a greay hide**
> -quand le camelot a pris son pli,c'est pour toujours
> -l'habitude est une seconde nature

> **2-she's scared to death**
> -elle a une peur bleue

science
> **much science,much sorrow**
> -ce que les yeux ne voient pas ne fait pas mal au coeur

scissor
> **I have my own scissors to grind**
> -j'ai d'autres chats à fouetter

score
> **score twice before you cut once**
> -deux précautions valent mieux qu'une
> -tourner sept fois sa langue dans sa bouche avant de parler

scratch
> **1-scratch a Russian and you find a Tartar**
> -grattez le Russe et vous trouvez le Tartare

> **2-you scratch my back and I'll scratch yours**
> -passez moi la casse (rhubarbe) et je vous passerai le séné

screech
> **to screech round the corner**
> -prendre un virage sur les chapeaux de roues

Scylla
> **between Scylla and Charybdis**
> -tomber de Charybde en Scylla

sea
> **in a calm sea every man is a pilot**
> -tout le monde sait être sage après la bataille

secret
> **1-three may keep a secret if two of them are dead**
> -secret de trois,secret de tous

> **2-where there is secret,there must be something wrong**
> -pas de fumée sans feu

secure

      secure is not safe
      -la crainte de DIeu est le commencement de la sagesse

see

      1-one may see day at a little hole
      -un cheveu même a son ombre

      2-we didn't see a soul
      -nous n'avons pas vu un chat

      3-we didn't see neither hide or hair of one
      -nous n'avons pas vu la queue d'un chat

      4-to see which way the cat jumps
      to see how the land lies
      to see how the wind blows
      -voir de quel côté le vent souffle
      -prendre le vent

      5-seeing is believing
      -je ne crois que ce que je vois

      6-to see stars
      -voir trente-six chandelles

      7-he can't the beam he has in his own eye
      -oeil un autre oeil voit mais pas le sien

      8-to see eye to eye
      -voir du même oeil

      9-and did you ever see an oyster walk upstairs?
      -mon oeil!

      10-do you see any green in my eye?
      -pour qui me prenez-vous?

      11-to see an inch before his nose
      ne pas voir plus loin que le bout de son nez

      12-he can't see the beam he has in his own eye
      -il voit la paille dans l'oeil du voisin mais pas la paille dans le sien

seed

      good seed makes a cgood crop
      -on récolte ce que l'on a semé

seek

      1-seeking for a knot in a rush
      -chercher une aiguille dans une meule de foin

      2-seek till you find,and you will not lose your labor
      -tant chauffe-t-on le fer qu'il rougit
      -cent fois sur le métier remettez votre ouvrage

      3-nothing seek,nothing find
      -on n'a rien sans rien

4-he that seeks trouble,never misses
-qui mal cherche,mal trouve
-qui veut mal,mal lui tourne

seldom

1-seldom does the hated man ends well
-homme haï est demi-mort

2-seldom seen,seldom heard
seldom seen,soon forgotten
-loin des yeux,loin du coeur

select

select your friend with a silk gloved hand and hold him with and iron gauntlet
-croyez tout le monde honnête et vivez avec tous comme avec des fripons

sell

1-you cannot sell the cow and sup the milk
-on ne peut avoir le drap et l'argent

2-don't sell the skin before you have caught the bear
-il ne faut pas vendre la peau de l'ours avant de l'avoir tué

3-it is selling like hot cakes
-cela se vend comme des petits pains

send

1-send a fool to the market and a fool will return again
-qui bête va à Rome,tel en retourne
-qui fol envoie,fol attend

2-to send up the river
-être envoyé au violon (familier)

3-to send one to the right about
-to send the pests packing
-to send one packing
-envoyer paître (promener,sur les roses)

sense

you should come to your senses
-vous devriez vous faire une raison

separate

1-we must separate the sheep from the goat
-il y a fagots et fagots

2-we must separate the sheep from the goats
-il ne faut pas mélanger les torchons et les serviettes

3-to separate the wheat from the chaff
-il faut séparer le bon grain de l'ivraie

separation

separation secures manifest friendship
-loin des yeux,près du coeur

serpent

    whom a serpent has bitten,a lizard alarms
    -chat échaudé craint l'eau froide

servant

    1-a servant is known by his master absence
    -en l'absence du valet se connaît le serviteur

    2-one must be a servant before one can be a master
    -pour devenir le maître il faut agir en esclave

    3-so many servants,so many enemies
    -autant de valets,autant d'ennemis

serve

    1-they also serve who only stand and wait
    -la patience est amère mais son fruit est doux
    -plus fait douceur que violence

    2-if you want to be well served,serve yourself
    -on n'est jamais aussi bien servi que par soi-même
    -on ne trouve jamais meilleur messager que soi-même

    3-serve a great man and you will know what sorrow is
    -le gentilhomme croit sincèrement que la chasse est un plaisir
    royal,mais son piqueur n'est pas de ce sentiment

    4-no man can serve two masters
    -nul ne peut servir deux maîtres

    5-to serve someone hand and foot
    -être à la merci de quelqu'un

    6-he that serves God for money,will serve the devil for better wages
    -plus a le diable,plus veut en avoir

    7-you cannot serve God and Mammon
    -l'on ne peut servir ensemble Dieu et le Diable

service

    service is no inheritance
    service d'autrui n'est pas héritage

set

    1-he won't set the world on fire
    -il n'a pas inventé le fil à couper le beurre

    2-set a beggar on horseback and he'll ride to the devil
    -donnez le pied à un nègre,il prend la main
    -graissez les bottes d'un vilain,il dira qu'on les lui brûle

    3-set not your loaf in till the oven is hot
    -il ne faut vendre la peau de l'ours avant de l'avoir tué

settle

    to settle one's hash
    -clouer le bec de quelqu'un (*familier*)
    rabattre le caquet

sew

    it's all sewed up
    -c'est l'enfance de l'art
    -cousu de fil blanc

shake

    1-in two shakes of a lamb's tail
    in a brace of shakes
    -en deux temps,trois mouvements
    -à la seconde
    -tambour battant
    -en trois coups de cuiller à pot

    2-all that shakes falls not
    -tout ce qui branle ne tombe pas

    3-to shake one's sides
    -se tenir les côtes

    4-to shake in one's shoes
    -trembler comme une feuille
    -trembler dans sa culotte(*familier*)

    5-to shake a loose leg
    -mener une vie de bâton de chaise

    6-to shake a leg
    -mettre su sien

shame

    1-he that shames shall be shent
    -honni soit qui mal y pense

    2-it is a shame to steal but worse to carry home
    -se tromper est humain,persévérer dans son erreur est diabolique

    3-past shame,past amendment
    -on ne pardonne pas à qui nous fait rougir

sharp

    1-the sharper the point,the better the needle
    -il n'y a que la vérité qui blesse

    2-the sharper the storm,the sooner it's over
    -all that is sharp,is short
    -les oeuvres de la violence ne sont pas durables

shave

    1-it's ill shaving against the wool
    -il faut hurler avec les loups

    2-it is very hard to shave an egg
    -on ne peut tondre un oeuf

shearer

    a bad shearer never had a good sickle
    -mauvais ouvrier ne trouve jamais bon outil

sheep

1-the lone sheep is in danger of the wolf
-poule égarée est bonne pour le renard
-homme seul est viande à loups

2-one scabbed sheep infests the whole flock
-il ne faut qu'une brebis galeuse pour infester le troupeau

3-the black sheep
-la brebis galeuse
-le vilain petit canard

4-the black sheep of the family
-le vilain petit canard

5-if one sheep leaps over the ditch,all the rest will follow
-un chien qui pisse fait pisser l'autre
-un bon bailleur en fait bailler sept

6-let every sheep hang on its own shank
-qui peut et empêche,pêche
-chacun se fait fouetter à sa guise
-chacun est l'artisan de son sort

7-a bleating sheep loses a bite
-brebis qui bêle perd sa goulée
-qui va à la chasse perd sa place
-qui quitte la partie la perd

8-there is a black sheep in every flock
-chaque vin a sa lie

9-he that makes himself a sheep,shall be eaten by the wolf
-faites-vous miel,les mouches vous mangeront

sheet

that is my sheet anchor
-c'était ma bouée de sauvetage

shelter

it is good sheltering under an old hedge
-en conseil écoute le vieil

shilly

no more shilly-shallying
-cesser de tourner et de virer

shirt

to give the shirt off one's back
-se mettre en quatre
-donner sa chemise

shoe

1-another pair of shoes
-une autre paire de manches

2-the shoe will hold with the sole
-qui hante chien,puces remporte
-tel père,tel fils

3-a shoe too large trips one up
-trop de profit crève la poche
-les branches des arbres trop chargées de fruit rompent

4-if the shoe fits,wear it
-trouver chaussure à son pied
-il n'est si méchant pot qui ne trouve son couvercle
-il n'est pas de grenouille qui ne trouve son crapaud
-à tel pot,telle cuiller

5-where the shoe pinches
-où le bât blesse

6-to die in one's shoes
-mourir debout

7-every shoe fits not every foot
-à chacun son goût

8-to shoe the goose
-aller aux fraises (familier)

9-over shoes,over boots
-quand le vin est tiré,il faut le boire

shoemaker
the shoemaker's chidren never have shoes
who is worse shod than the shoemaker's wife?
none is more bare than the shoemaker's wife and the smith's mare
-les cordonniers sont les plus mal chaussés

shoestring
to live on a shoestring
-vivre d'amour et d'eau fraîche

shoot
1-to shoot down in flames
-descendre en flèches

2-to shoot a line
-en mettre plein la vue

3-to shoot a second arrow to find the first
-courir à sa perte

4-to shoot one's linen
-faire étalage

5-to shoot the cat
-rendre tripes et boyaux

shop
you have come to the wrong shop
-vous avez frappé à la mauvaise porte

short
cut it short!
-cut the cackle and come to the "osses"
-revenons à nos moutons!

shoulder
> **1-to work shoulder to shoulder**
> -travailler au coude à coude

> **2-to put one's shoulder to the wheel**
> -mettre du sien

show
> **1-to show a clean pair of heels**
> -avoir des ailes au talon

> **2-the show must go on**
> -faire contre mauvaise fortune bon coeur

> **3-to show your credentials**
> -montrer patte blanche

> **4-to show the bull-horn**
> -faire sa tête de cochon

shower
> **to shower money**
> -faire un pont d'or

shroud
> **shrouds have no pockets**
> -la chemise du mort n'a pas de poches

shunning
> **shunning the smoke they fall into the fire**
> -troquer son cheval borgne pour un aveugle
> -tomber de Charybde en Scylla

shut
> **to shut the door to someone's face**
> -fermer la porte au nez de quelqu'un

sickness
> **sickness shows us what we are**
> -l'adversité est l'épreuve du courage

side
> **1-to be on the right (wrong) side of the hedge**
> -être du bon (mauvaos) côté de la barrière

> **2-there are two sides to every question**
> -qui n'entend qu'une cloche n'entend qu'un son

sight
> **out of sight,out of languor**
> **-out of sight,out of mind**
> -loin des yeux,loin du coeur

sign
> **it's an ill sign to see a fox lick a lamb**
> -quand le renard pêche,veillez sur vos oies

silence
> **1-silence gives consent**
> -qui ne dit mot consent

2-silence never makes any blunder
-bouche en coeur au sage,coeur en bouche au fou

3-silence catches a mouse
-on n'atrape pas de lièvre aveec un tambour

silent

as silent as a grave
-muet comme une tombe

silk

the fairest silk is soonest stained
-il n'est si beau soulier qui ne devienne savate

silver

1-white silver draws black lines
-une poule noire pond un oeuf blanc

2-to give a silver bullet
-faire un pont d'or à quelqu'un pour s'en débarrasser

3-he that hath not silver in his purse should have silk in his tongue
-qui n'a pas d'argent en bourse,qu'il ait du miel en bouche

4-no silver without its dross
-nulle rose sans épine

sin

1-there is a sin of omission as well as commission
-qui ne dit mot consent

2-who swims in sin shall sink in sorrow
-every sin brings its punishment with it
-on est souvent puni par où l'on a peché

3-old sins cast long shadows
-vieux péché fait nouvelle honte
-les bienfaits s'écrivent sur le sable et les injures sur l'airain

4-it is no sin for a man to labour in his vocation
-il n'y a pas de sot métier,il n'y a que de sottes gens

5-there is no such a thing as unforgiveable sin
-no sin but should find mercy
-à tout péché miséricorde

6-sin plucks on sin
-qui vole un oeuf,vole un boeuf

sing

1-to make someone sing another tune
-faire changer de registre à quelqu'un

2-sing a different tune
-retourné comme une crêpe

3-if you sing before breakfast,you will cry before night
-tel qui rit vendredi,dimanche pleurera

sink

>**sink or swimm**
>-marche ou crève

sit

>**1-he sits not sure that sits too high**
>-les tours les plus hautes font les plus hautes chutes

>**2-to sit on the fence**
>-on ne peut ménager la chèvre et le chou

>**3-it is best to sit near the fire when the chimney smokes**
>-une occasion perdue ne se rattrappe jamais

>**4-to sit on somebody**
>-serrer la vis à quelqu'un

>**5-it is ill sitting at Rome and striving against the Pope**
>-qui veut vivre à Rome ne doit pas se quereller avec le Pape

>**6-sit in your place and none can make you rise**
>-il y a des lumières que l'on éteint en les plaçant sur des chandeliers

six

>**1-it is six of one and half a dozen of the other**
>-c'est bonnet blanc et blanc bonnet

>**2-to be at sixes and sevens**
>-s'en moquer comme de l'an quarante
>-s'en moquer comme de sa première chemise

sizzle

>**all that sizzles may not be meat**
>-tout ce qui brille n'est pas d'or

Skiddaw

>**whenever Skiddaw hath a cap,Scruffel wots full of that**
>-il y en a toujours qui aimeront mieux sauver que passer les seaux

skill

>**it needs more skill than I can tell to play the second fiddle well**
>-l'obéissance est un métier bien rude

skin

>**1-don't skin an eel by the tail**
>-il est comme le chien de Jean de Nivelle,il fuit quand on l'appelle

>**2-that's no skin off my nose**
>-ce ne sont pas mes oignons

>**3-to skin a flint**
>-tondre un oeuf

skip

>**to skip from one subject to another**
>-sauter du coq à l'âne

sky

a red sky at night is the sheperd's delight;a red sky in the morning is the pilgrim's warning
-ciel rouge le soir,blanc le matin,c'est le souhait du pélerin
-rouge au soir,blanc au matin,c'est la journée du pélerin

slander

1-everybody slanders everybody else
-chacun médit du tiers comme du quart

2-slander leaves a sore behind
-on n'est jamais sali que par la boue

slave

we are all slaves of opinion
-et le "qu'en dira-t-on?"

sleep

1-he that will sleep all the morning may go a beging all the day after
-l'avenir appartient à ceux qui se lèvent tôt

2-let sleeping dogs lie
wake not a sleeping lion
-n'éveillez pas le chat qui dort

3-who sleeps,dine
when a man sleeps,his head is in his stomach
the sleeping fox catches no poultry
-qui dort dîne

4-to sleep like a log
-dormir comme un loir
-dormir comme une souche

5-in sleep all passes away
-le sommeil est l'enfance de la raison

6-sleep on it
-la nuit porte conseil

7-not to sleep a wink
-ne pas fermer l'oeil

slip

there's many a slip'twixt the cup and the lip
-il y a loin de la coupe aux lèvres

slow

slow but sure wins the race
-doucement mais sûrement
-rien ne sert de courir il faut partir à point
-qui va doucement,va sûrement
-petit à petit,l'oiseau fait son nid

sluggard

the sluggard's convenient season never comes
-il attend que les alouettes lui tombent toutes rôties dans le bec

sly

to be sly minx
-être une fine mouche

small

many small make a great
-il n'y a pas de petites économies

smell

1-the smell of garlic takes away the smell of onion
-un clou chasse l'autre

2-I smell a rat
-il y a anguille sous roche
-mettre la puce à l'oreille

3-one is not smelt wwhere all stink
-plus on remue la boue,plus elle pue

smoke

1-much smoke,little fire
-beaucoup de bruit pour rien
-crier comme un aveugle qui a perdu son bâton

2-where there is smoke,there is fire
-il n'y a pas de fumée sans feu

3-to smoke like a chimney
-fumer comme un pompier

smooth

to smooth things over
-arrondir les angles

snail

the snail slides up the tower at last,though the swallow mounteth it sooner
-doucement mais sûrement
-rien ne sert de courir il faut partir à point

snap

not worth a snap of the fingers
-ça ne vaut pas un clou
-ça ne vaut pas un pet de lapin (familier)

sneak

-to sneak in through the back door
-entrer par la petite porte

snow

just because there is snow on the roof doesn't mean there's no fire in the heart
-there's snow on the roof but there is fire in the furnace
-se méfier du feu qui couve

snug

as snug as the the bug in the rug
-bien au chaud
-tranquille comme Baptiste

sober

> **sober as a judge**
> -sobre comme un chameau

soberness

> **what soberness conceals,drunkenness reveals**
> -in vino veritas
> -bon vin,mauvaise tête
> -le vin entre et la raison sort

soft

> **1-a soft answer turneth away wrath**
> -soft fire makes sweet malt
> -soft pace goes far
> -plus fait douceur que violence
>
> **2-soft wax will take any impression**
> -poussin chante comme le coq lui apprend

solitary

> **a solitary man is either a beast or an angel**
> -il n'y a que le méchant qui soit seul

solitude

> **solitude is often the best societty**
> -mieux vaut être seul que mal accompagné

something

> **1-something must be left to chance**
> -il faut laisser quelque chose au hasard
>
> **2-something is better than nothing**
> -quand on n'a pas ce que l'on aime,il faut vouloir ce que l'on a
> -faute de grives on se contente de merles
>
> **3-something is rotten in the state of Denmark**
> -il y a quelque chose de pourri au royaume des cieux

song

> **no song,no supper**
> -pas d'argent,pas de suisse

soon

> **1-sooner or later**
> -un jour ou l'autre
>
> **2-no sooner said than done**
> -aussitôt dit,aussitôt fait
>
> **3-soon enough to cry "chuck" when it is out of the shell**
> -il ne faut pas chanter triomphe avant la victoire
>
> **4-one may sooner fall than rise**
> -il est plus facile de descendre que de monter
>
> **5-sooner or later merit will come to the front**
> -le bon grain finit toujours par lever
>
> **6-soon enough is well enough**
> -avant l'heure,c'est pas l'heure;après l'heure,c'est plus l'heure

7-the sooner,the better
-le plus tôt sera le mieux

8-soon ripe,soon rotten
-soon learnt,soon forgotten
-soon gotten,soon spent
-soon hot,soon cold
-soon up,soon down
-ce qui vient de la flute,s'en va par le tambour
-cela va,cela vient

sore

sore upon sore is not salve
-mal sur mal n'est pas santé

sorrow

1-make not two sorrows of one
-l'affliction ne guérit pas le mal

2-small sorrows speak;great ones are silent
-sorrow makes silent her best orator
-la douleur qui se tait n'en est que plus funeste
-les grandes douleurs sont muettes

3-when sorrow is asleep,wake it not
-n'éveillez pas le chat qui dort
-ne remuez pas le fer dans la plaie

4-sorrow is always dry
-assez boit qui a deuil

5-sorrow will pay no debt
-a hundred pouns of sorrow pays not one ounce of debt
-cent livres de mélancolie ne paient pas un sou de dette

6-sorrow and evil life make soon an old wife
-l'écurie use plus le cheval que la course

7-sorrow is soon enough when it comes
-il ne faut pas pleurer avant d'être battu

sort

1-to be out of sorts
-ne pas être dans son assiette

2-it takes all sorts to make a world
-il faut de tout pour faire un monde
-vin versé n'est pas avalé

soul

1-the soul needs few things,the body many
-il faut entretenir la vigueur du corps pour conserver celle de l'esprit

2-not to have a soul above buttons
-être au ras des pâquerettes

3-the soul is not where it lives,but where it loves
-loin des yeux,près du coeur

sound

    a sound mind in a sound body
    -un esprit sain dans un corps sain

sow

    1-the still sow eats up all the draff
    -il n'est pire eau que l'eau qui dort
    -méfiez-vous de l'eau qui dort

    2-as you sow,so shall you reap
    -he that sows thorns must not expect corn
    -on récolte ce que l'on a semé

    3-to sow beans in the wind
    -travailler pour des prunes

    4-he who sows the wind reaps the whirlwind
    -qui sème le vent,récolte la tempête

spare

    1-spare the rod and spoil the child
    qui aime bien,châtie bien

    2-sparing is a great revenue
    -sparing is the first gaining
    -il n'y a pas de petites économies
    -l'épargne est un grand revenu

    3-don't spare out the spigot and spill at the bung
    -il ne faut pas économiser le son et gaspiller la farine

spark

    1-a single spark can start a prairie fire
    -c'est l'étincelle qui a mis le feu aux poudres
    -il suffit d'une étincelle pour allumer un incendie

    2-of a small spark ,a great fire
    -faute d'un point,Martin perdit son âne
    -petites causes,grands effets

sparrow

    1-two sparrows on one ear of corn make an ill agreement
    -deux chiens à l'os ne s'accordent

    2-one sparrow doesn't make a summer
    -une hirondelle ne fait pas le printemps
    -une fois n'est pas coutume

speak

    1-he that speaks ill of the mare would buy her
    -qui dit du mal de l'âne le voudrait à la maison

    2-many speak much who cannot speak well
    -on parle toujours mal quand on n'a rien à dire -

    3-he cannot speak well that cannot hold his tongue
    -celui qui ne sait pas se taire sait rarement bien parler

4-don't speak to a man at the wheel
-jamais deux orgueilleux ne chevaucheront bien un âne

5-everyone speaks well of the bridge which carries him over
-il est mon oncle qui mon ventre me comble

6-speak not of my debts unless you mean to pay them
-ne me parlez de mes dettes à moins que vous ne vouliez les payer

7-there is a time to speak and a time to be silent
-qui parle sème,qui écoute récolte

speech

1-speech is silver but silence is golden
-la parole est d'argent mais le silence est d'or

2-speech is the picture of the mind
-juge l'oiseau à la plume et au chant et au parler l'homme bon ou méchant

spend

1-spend as you get
-il faut aller selon sa bourse

2-much spends the traveller more than the abider
-on ne gagne pas beaucoup à courir le monde

3-never spend your money until you have it
-il ne faut pas vendre la peau de l'ours avant de l'avoir tué

spill

to spill the beans
-cracher le morceau (familier)
-vendre la mèche

spindle

one by one the spindles are made
-maille à maille est fait le haubergeon

spit

1-he that spits against the wind,spits in his own face
-qui crache au ciel,il lui retombe sur le visage

2-spit on a stone and it will wet ay last
-à force de coups,on abat le chêne
-petit à petit,l'oiseau fait son nid

spite

to do something out of sheer spite
-agir par pure méchanceté

split

to split hairs
-couper les cheveux en quatre

spoke

to put a spoke in one's wheel
-mettre des bâtons dans les roues

sponge
> **to sponge on someone**
> -vivre au crochet de quelqu'un

spot
> **there are spots even in the sun**
> -nulle rose sans épine

sprat
> **1-don't use a sprat to catch a whale**
> -d'un veau on espère un boeuf et d'une poule un oeuf
>
> **2-it takes a sprat to catch a mackerel**
> -on a rien sans rien

spread
> **1-spread the table,and contention will cease**
> -la table est l'entremetteuse de l'amitié
> -quand le foin manque au ratelier,les chevaux se battent
>
> **2-don't qpread the cloth till the pot begins to boil**
> -il ne faut pas vendre la peau de l'ours avant de l'avoir tué
>
> **3-she put on a big spread**
> -elle avait mis les petits plats dans les grands

spur
> **don't spur the willing horse**
> -trop piquer le cheval le fait rétif

squeaking
> **the squeaking wheel gets the grease**
> -Dieu lui-même a besoin de cloches
> -qui ne prie,ne prend
> -le roi n'est pas servi sans qu'il parle
> -qui ne demande rien n'a rien

squeeze
> **if you squeeze a cork,you will get but little juice**
> -d'un âne on ne peut demander de la viande de boeuf

stack
> **an ill stack stands longest**
> -les pots félés sont ceux qui durent le plus
> -une santé délicate est parfois un brevet de longue vie

stake
> **1-to stake everything on a single cast of dice**
> -jouer quelque chose sur un coups de dés
>
> **2-nothing stake,nothing draw**
> -qui ne risque rien,n'a rien

stand
> **1-to stand on one's own two feet**
> **-every tub should stand on its own bottom**
> -se débrouiller
> -voler de ses propres ailes

2-it stands to reason
-celà va sans dire

3-to stand someone up
-faire faux bond à quelqu'un

4-standing pools gather filth
-petite négligence accouche d'un grand mal
-au paresseux,le poil lui pousse dans la main

stare

to stare like a stuck pig
-on dirait une vache qui regarde passer un train

start

to be off to a good start
-bon pied,bon oeil

stay

1-let's stay out of the limelight
-pour vivre heureux,vivons cachés

2-he that stays in the valley,shall never get over the hill
-qui ne risque rien,n'a rien

steal

1-if you steal for others,you shall be hang for yourself
-autant pêche celui qui tient le sac que celui qui l'emplit

2-he that will steal a pin,will steal a better thing
-he that steal an egg,will steal an ox
-he that steal a pin,will steal a pound
-he that steal a pin,will steal a better thing
-qui vole in oeuf,vole un boeuf
-toujours pèche qui en prend un

3-to steal one's thunder
-couper ses effets

4-he that steals honey,should beware of the sting
-qui s'y frotte,s'y pique

5-he would steal from his grandmother
-il vendrait père et mère

step

1-step after step the ladder is ascended
-petit à petit l'oiseau fait son nid
-il faut un commencement à tout

2-the greatest step is that out of doors
- qui entre en nef n'a pas vent à gré
-personne ne veut attacher la sonnette au cou du chat
-c'est le premier pas qui coûte

3-it's the first step that is difficult
-the first step is the hardest
-c'est le premier pas qui coûte

stick

1-to stick to one's guns
-camper sur ses positions

2-the stick is the surest pacemaker
-la crainte du gendarme est le commencement de la sagesse

3-sticks and stones may break my bones,but words will never hurt me
-la bave du crapaud n'atteint pas la blanche colombe
-bien faire et laisser dire

4-a straight stick is crooked in the water
-le bois tordu fait le feu droit

5-any stick will do to beat a dog with
-qui veut noyer son chien,l'accuse de la rage

sting

1-the sting is in the tail
-en la queue et en la fin gît de coutume le venin

2-it is better to be stung by a nettle than pricked by a rose
-mieux vaut un sage ennemi qu'un ignorant ami

3-the sting of a reproach is the truth of it
-il n'y a que la vérité qui blesse

stir

1-the more you stir,the more it stinks
-plus on remue la boue,plus elle pue

2-to stir up a hornet's nest
-soulever un lièvre

stitch

a stitch in time saves nine
-petite négligence accouche d'un grand mal
-prudence est mère de sûreté

stocking

to have a long stocking
-avoir un gros bas de laine

stone

1-the stone that lies not in your gate breaks not your toes
-va bien au moulin qui y envoie son âne
-le mal d'autrui est un songe
-nous avons tous assez de force pour supporter les maux d'autrui

2-a little stone in the way overturns a great wain
-petites causes,grands effets

3-a rolling stone
-l'oiseau sur la branche

4-a rolling stone gathers no moss
-pierre qui roule n'amasse pas mousse

stoop

> **he must stoop who has a low door**
> -qui n'a pas d'argent en bourse,qu'il ait du miel en bouche

stop

> **1-he never stops hurling fire and brimstone at his enemies**
> -il ne cesse de brandir l'anathème contre ses ennemis

> **2-stop hemming and having**
> -cessez de tourner et de virer

store

> **store is no sore**
> -abondance de biens ne nuit pas

storm

> **1-a storm in a tea cup**
> -beaucoup de bruit pour rien
> -faire d'une mouche un éléphant

> **2-after a storm comes a calm**
> -après le calme,la tempête

story

> **1-his story is a mixture of fact and fancy**
> -il y a à boire et à manger dans son histoire

> **2-it was the story of the dog and the shadow**
> -c'est l'histoire du corbeau et du renard

straight

> **1-as straight as a cedar**
> -droit comme un "i"

> **2-a straight faced man**
> -un pince sans rire

straighten

> **to straighten everything out**
> -arrondir les angles

strain

> **1-to strain a rope to breaking point**
> -il ne faut pas trop tirer sur la corde

> **2-don't strain at a gnat and swallow a camel**
> -ne cherchez pas midi à quatorze heures

strait

> **to be in sad straits**
> -être dans de beaux draps

straw

> **1-a straw shows which way the wind blows**
> -on connaît le cerf aux abattues
> -l'évènement à venir projette son ombre

2-that's the last straw
-that's the straw that broke the camel's back
-c'est la goutte d'eau qui fait déborder le vase
-le surplus rompt le couvercle

3-to draw straws
-tirer à la courte paille

stream
1-the stream cannot rise above its source
-à petit mercier,petit panier
-péter plus haut que son cul (familier)

2-the stream stopped swells the higher
-le feu le plus couvert est le plus ardent

street
by the street of by and by one arrives at the house of never
-il ne faut jamais remettre à plus tard ce que l'on peut faire le jour même

strength
in unity there is strength
-l'union fait la force

stretch
1-everyone stretches his legs according to the length of his coverlet
-n'étendez vos jambes qu'à la longueur du tapis

2-stretch your arm no further than your sleeve will reach
-everyone stretches his legs according to the length of the coverlet
-ne forcez pas votre talent
-il ne faut pas ourdir plus qu'on ne peut tisser
-on ne saurait péter plus haut que son cul (familier)
-il ne faut pas être plus royaliste que le roi
-il faut aller selon sa bourse
-n'étend les jambes qu'à la longueur du tapis

strike
1-to strike while the iron is hot
-battre le fer pendant qu'il est chaud

2-without striking a blow
-pas un mot plus haut que l'autre
-sans souffler mot

3-he that strikes with the sword,shall be beaten with the scabbard
-quiconque se sert de l'épée périra par l'épée

string
1-strings high streched either soon crack or quickly grow out of tune
-tant va la cruche à l'eau qu'elle se casse

2-to pull the strings
-donner un coup de pouce
-tirer les ficelles

3-to put a string on your finger
-faire un noeud à son mouchoir

4-to have two strings to one's bow
-avoir plusieurs cordes à son arc

strive

1-it is ill stiving against the stream
-il faut hurler avec les loups

2-striving the better oft we mar what's well
-le mieux est l'ennemi du bien

stroke

little strokes fell great oaks
-il n'y a si petit buisson qui ne porte son ombre
-il n'y a si petit ennemi qui ne puisse faire tort
-il n'est si petit chat qui n'égratigne
-un poil fait ombre
-à force de coups,on abat le chêne

strong

1-the strong prey upon the the weak
-on a toujours besoin d'un plus petit que soi

2-a strong town is not won in one hour
-Paris ne s'est pas fait en un jour

Stuart

all Stuarts are not sib to the king
-tout ce qui brille n'est pas d'or
-être et paraître sont deux

studies

a man's studies pass into his character
-les études deviennent des habitudes

study

study without thought is vain,thought without study is dangerous
-science sans conscience n'est que ruine de l'âme

stumble

he that stumbles twice over one stone,deserves to break his shins
-un âne ne trébuche pas deux fois sur la même pierre

style

the style is the man
-le style c'est l'homme

sublime

from the sublime to the ridiculous is only a step
-tout ce qui est exagéré est insignifiant

success

1-nothing succeeds like success
-rien ne réussit comme le succès

2-success has many friends
-à bourse pleine,amis nombreux

suffer

it is better to suffer wrong than do it
-il est plus malheureux de commettre une injustice que de la souffrir

sufficient
>   **-sufficient unto the day is the evil thereof**
>   -plus on remue la boue,plus elle pue
>   -du bâton que l'on tient,on est souvent battu
>   -à chaque jour suffit sa peine

suit
>   **that suits me down to the ground**
>   -cela ma va comme un gant

sulk
>   **to sulk in one's tent**
>   -se retirer sous sa tente

summer
>   **no summer but has its winter**
>   -nulle rose sans épine

sun
>   **1-the sun belongs to everyone**
>   **-the sun loses nothing by shining into a puddle**
>   - le soleil luit pour tout le monde
>
>   **2-let not the sun go down on your wrath**
>   -il faut coucher la colère à la porte
>
>   **3-two suns cannot shine in one sphere**
>   -les chiens ne chassent pas ensemble
>   -il n'y a pas deux crabes mâles dans un même trou
>
>   **4-although th sin shines,leave not your cloak at home**
>   -il faut garder une poire pour la soif
>
>   **5-no sun without its shadow**
>   -nulle rose sans épine

sup
>   **1-it is better to sup with a cutty than want a spoon**
>   -quand on n'a pas ce que l'on aime,il faut vouloir ce que l'on a
>
>   **2-he who sups with the devil should have a long spoon**
>   -à manger avec le diable,la fourchette n'est jamais trop longue

supper
>   **after supper walk a mile**
>   -un bon verre de vin enlève l'écu au médecin

sure
>   **1-better be sure than sorry**
>   -il vaut mieux arriver en retard qu'arriver en corbillard
>   -il vaut mieux arriver au moulin qu'au médecin
>
>   **2-as sure as eggs is eggs**
>   -aussi sûr que deux et deux font quatre

surprise
>   **he that is surprised with the first frost,feels it all winter**
>   -c'est la première impression qui compte

swallow

1-to swallow an ox ,and be choked with the tail
-quand on a avalé un boeuf,il ne faut pas s'arrêter à la queue

2-if you have swallowed the devil,you may swallow his horns
-quand le vin est tiré,il faut le boire

swan

all my swans are turned to geese
-l'affaire est dans le lac

swear

1-he that will swear,will lie
-un menteur est toujours prodigue de serments

2-to swear up and down
-jurer ses grands dieux

3-to swear like a trooper
-jurer comme un charretier

4-to swear on a stack of bibles
-mettre sa main au feu

sweep

1-to sweep someone under the rug
-laisser tomber quelqu'un

2-if each would sweep before his own door,we should have a clean street
-ne vous mêlez pas de ce qui ne vous regarde pas
-qu'il balaye d'abord devant sa porte

sweet

1-sweet is the nut,but bitter is the shell
-beau noyau gît sous piètre écorce

2-what is sweet in the mouth is often bitter in the stomach
-tout ce qui brille n'est pas d'or
-ce qu'il faut chercher à connaître c'est le fond du panier

3-sweet are the uses of adversity
-à quelque chose malheur est bon

4-no sweet without sweat
-on n'a rien sans rien
-qui ne risque rien,n'a rien
-il faut semer pour récolter

5-every sweet has its sour
-nulle rose sans épine

6-from the sweetest wine,the tartest vinegar
-de bon vin,bon vinaigre

swift

be swift to hear,slow to speak
-la nature nous a donné deux oreilles et seulement une
langue afin de pouvoir écouter davantage et parler moins
-tourner sept fois sa langue dans sa bouche avant de parler

swim

> **1-he must need swim,that is held up by the chin**
> -il est plus facile de nager quand on vous tient le menton

> **2-it is often better to swin with the stream**
> -il faut hurler avec les loups
> -il vaut être fou avec tous que sage tout seul
> -contre le tonnerre ne pète

> **3-to swim like a cork**
> **-to swim like a fish**
> **-to swim like a duck**
> -être comme un poisson dans l'eau

> **4-who swims in sin shall sink in sorrow**
> -on est souvent puni par où l'on a péché

swimmer

> **good swimmers at length are drowned**
> -bon nageurs sont à la fin noyés

swine

> **swine,women,and bees cannot be turned**
> -ce que femme veut,Dieu le veut

sword

> **he who lives by the sword dies by the sword**
> **-he that strikes with the sword,shall be beaten with the scabbard**
> -quiconque se sert de l'épée périra par l'épée

T

table

> **the tables are turned**
> -tel est pris qui croyait prendre

tailor

> **the tailor makes the man**
> -l'oiseau doit beaucoup à son plumage
> -l'habit fait l'homme
> -c'est la robe qu'on salue

take

> **1-take away the cause,and the effect must cease**
> -il n'y a pas d'effet sans cause
>
> **2-she that takes gifts,herself she sells,and she that gives,does not else**
> -femme qui prend,elle se vend;femme qui donne,s'abandonne
>
> **3-take the goods the gods provide**
> -quand on n'a pas ce que l'on aime,il faut vouloir ce que l'on a
> -faute de souliers,on va nu-pieds
>
> **4-to be taken to the cleaners**
> -recevoir le coup de fusil
>
> **5-it takes two to tango**
> **-it takes two to make a quarrel**
> -les querelles ne dureraient jamais longtemps si les torts n'étaient que d'un côté
> -qui n'entend qu'une cloche,n'entend qu'un son
>
> **6-to take the rough with the smooth**
> -prendre les choses comme elles viennent
>
> **7-take not a musket to kill a butterfly**
> -l'excès en tout nuit
>
> **8-it takes one to know one**
> -vous en êtes un autre
>
> **9-take it out in sleep**
> -qui dort, dîne
>
> **10-to take a load off one's minds**
> -tirer une épine du pied
>
> **11-don't take things at their face value**
> -il ne faut pas se fier aux apparences
> -serpent qui change de peau est toujours serpent
>
> **12-you can't take the breecks of a Highlander**
> -la plus belle fille du monde ne peut donner que ce qu'elle a
>
> **13-to take a French leave**
> -filer à l'anglaise
>
> **14-to take the bear by the tooth**
> -se jeter dans la gueule du loup

15-to take the wind out of one's sails
-couper l'herbe sous le pied

16-take no more on you than you are able to bear
-à l'impossible nul n'est tenu

17-to take a lot of coaxing
-se faire tirer l'oreille

18-to take the lion's share
-prendre la part du lion

19-she took it like a lamb
-elle l'a bien pris

tale

1-one tale is good till another is told
-qui n'entend qu'une cloche n'entend qu'un son

2-a tale never loses in telling
-a good tale none the worse for being told twice
-on crie toujours le loup plus grand qu'il n'est

talk

1-you are talking through your hat
-tu travailles du chapeau

2-there is more talk than trouble
-beaucoup de bruit pour rien
-plus de peur que de mal

3-talk of the angels and you will hear the flutter of their wings
-talk of the devil and he is sure to appear
-quand on parle du loup on en voit la queue
-quand on parle du soleil on en voit les rayons

4-to talk the hind leg off a donkey
-tenir la jambe

5-to talk nineteen to the dozen
-parler comme une mitraillette

6-to talk a person's head off
-soûler quelqu'un de paroles

7-to talk until you are blue in the face
-se tuer à la dire

8-I talk to him like a Dutch uncle
-je lui ai dit ses quatre vérités
-je lui ai vidé mon sac

9-he that talks much of his happiness summons grief
-pour vivre heureux,vivons cachés

talker

the greatest talkers are the least doers
-les grands diseurs ne sont pas les grands faiseurs
-de grands vanteurs petits faiseurs

talking
> **talking pays no toll**
> -les belles paroles ne donnent pas à manger

tape
> **to cut the red tape**
> -abandonner les chinoiseries

tapster
> **the tapster is undone by chalk**
> -crédit est mort,les mauvais payeurs l'ont tué

tare
> **they are just tared with the same brush**
> -ils sont tous à mettre dans le même panier

tarry
> **long tarrying takes all the thanks away**
> petit présent trop attendu n'est point donné mais bien vendu

taste
> **1-there is no disputing about tastes**
> -des goûts et des couleurs on ne discute pas
>
> **2-that doesn't taste half bad**
> -cela se laisse manger

tailor
> **the tailor makes the man**
> -l'habit fait l'homme

tarry
> **long tarrying takes all the thanks away**
> -petit présent trop attendu n'est point donné mais bien vendu

taste
> **to him that has lost his taste,sweet is sour**
> -il faut de l'âme pour avoir du goût

tea
> **1-a tea-kettle broth**
> -une soupe maigre
>
> **2-not for all the tea in China**
> -pas pour tout l'or du monde
>
> **3-for all the tea in China**
> -pour un boulet de canon
> -pour tout l'or du monde
>
> **4-that's another cup of tea**
> -c'est une autre paire de manches

teach
> **1-you cannot teach an old dog new tricks**
> **-you cannot teach your grandmother to suck eggs**
> **-never offer to teach fish to swim**
> -on n'apprend pas au singe à faire la grimace
> -il veut montrer à son père à faire des enfants
> -il n'est pas né de la dernière pluie

2-better untaught than ill taught
-si tu donnes un poisson à un enfant,c'est bien;si tu lui apprends à pêcher,c'est mieux

3-he who teaches,learns
-en enseignant,on apprend

tell

1-you can't tell a book by its cover
-l'habit ne fait pas le moine
-parois blanches,parois fendues

2-don't tell tales out of school
-il faut laver son linge sale en famille
-c'est un vilain oiseau qui salit son nid

3-they told him dozens of times
-on le lui a dit trente-six fois

4-tell me with whom thou goest,and I'll tell thee what thou doest
-dis-moi qui tu fréquentes,je te dirai qui tu es

5-tell the truth and shame the devil
-il ne faut pas mettre la lampe sous le boisseau

6-none can tell the jewel by the casket
-le lien ne fait pas le fagot
-on ne connaît pas le sac à l'étiquette

7-I told him off straight to his face
-je lui ai dit ses quatre vérités

temptation
all temptations are found in hope or fear
-tout est tentation à qui la craint

tent
to sulk in one's tent
-se retirer sous sa tente

tenter
to be on tenter hooks
-être sur des charbons ardents

thick

1-as thick as a door post
-bête comme ses pieds

2-through thick and thin
-contre vents et marées

thief

1-set a thief to catch a thief
- à malin,malin et demi

2-the thief is sorry to be hanged,but not that he is a thief
-notre repentir n'est pas tant un regret du mal que nous avons fait qu'une crainte de celui qui nous en peut arriver

3-they are thick as thieves
-ils s'entendent comme larrons en foire

4-thieves'handsel ever lucky
-bien mal acquis ne profite jamais

5-all are not thieves that dogs bark at
-tous ne sont pas chevaliers qui à cheval montent

6-once a thief,always a thief
-qui a bu,boira

7-little thieves are hanged,but great ones escape
-les grands voleurs pendent les petits

thing

1-things passed cannot be recalled
-le plus beau lendemain ne nous rend pas la veille

2-things like that don't grow on trees
-cela ne se trouve pas sous le pied d'un cheval

3-one thing brings up another thing
-une chose en entraîne une autre

4-to take things as they come
-prendre les choses comme elles viennent
-ce qu'on ne peut empêcher,il faut le vouloir

5-many things happen unlooked for
-on rencontre sa destinée souvent par des chemins qu'on
-prend pour l'éviter

6-all things are difficult before they are easy
-c'est le premier pas qui coûte
-cent fois sur le métier remettez votre ouvrage
-le lendemain s'instruit aux leçons de la veille
-il faut un commencement à tout

7-things are seldom what they seem
-tel a de beaux yeux qui ne voit goutte
-de beaux raisins parfois pauvre vin
-les grands boeufs ne font pas les grands labours
-être et paraître sont deux

8-there is many a fair thing,full false
-les grands boeufs ne font pas les grands labours
-grosse tête,peu de sens
-parois blanches,parois fendues
-il faut déshabiller un maïs pour voir sa bonté

9-when things are at the worst they begin to mend
-après la pluie,le beau temps

10-however things are,we must accept them as they are
-à la guerre comme à la guerre
-il faut souffrir ce qu'on ne peut empêcher

11-things thought difficult and hard usually become quite simple when faced
-il n'y a que le premier pas qui coûte

12-all things fit not all persons
-chacun prend son plaisir où il se trouve

13-all good things must come to an end
-les meilleures choses ont une fin

14-all things are obedient to money
-la clé d'or ouvre toutes les portes

15-all things thrive at thrice
-tierce fois.c'est droit

16-the best things come in small packages
-dans les petites boîtes,les bons onguents

17-when a thing is done,advice comes too late
-quand la folie est faite, le conseil en est pris
-à parti pris,point de conseil

18-if a thing is worth doing,it's worth doing well
-labeurs sans soin,labeurs de rien
-mal fait qui ne parfait
-ce qui vaut la peine d'être fait,vaut la peine d'être bien fait

19-it's a good thing to eat your brown bread first
-si tu manges ton pain blanc le premier.tu manges ton pain noir plus tard

20-that thing which is rare is dear
-il n'y eut jamais peau de lion bon marché
-point de pigeon pour une obole

21-some things are better left unsaid
-la parole est d'argent mais le silence est d'or
-il n'y a que la vérité qui blesse

22-there is no such a thing as unforgiveable sin
-à tout péché miséricorde

23-most things have two handles
-après la pluie,le beau temps

24-there is no such a thing as a free lunch
-on n'a rien pour rien

25-two things a man should never be angry at   what he can help and what he cannot help
-il faut vouloir ce qu'on ne peut empêcher
-il ne sert à rien de montrer les dents lorqu'on est édenté

26-all things in their being are good for something
-à quelque chose malheur est bon
-il faut prendre le temps comme il vient,les gens pour ce qu'ils sont,l'argent pour ce qu'il vaut
-viendra le temps où la vache aura besoin de sa queue

27-all things come to those who wait
-avec le temps et la paille,les nèfles mûrissent
-tout vient à point à qui sait attendre

think

    1-think of the end before you begin
    -rien n'est plus difficile à écorcher que la queue
    -à la queue gît la difficulté

    2-he thinks the moon is made of green cheese
    -il croit au père Noël

    3-he thinks no small beer of himself (familier)
    -il ne se mouche pas du pied

    4-he thinks he is the cat's whiskers
    -il se croit quelqu'un
    -il se croit sorti de la cuisse de Jupiter

    5-one may think that dares not speak
    -il ne dit rien mais il n'en pense pas moins

    6-think twice before you speak
    -first think,then speak
    -tourner sept fois sa langue dans sa bouche avant de parler

    7-he thinks he is a know-it-all
    -il se prend pour un puits de science

    8-first think,then speak
    -réfléchissez avant de parler

    9-to think better of the matter
    -y regarder de plus près

    10-think of ease,but work on
    -on n'a rien sans rien

third

    third time's lucky
    -tierce fois,c'est droit

thorn

    1-thorns live and roses die
    -les meilleurs partent les premiers cf meilleur
    -bon grain périt,paille demeure

    2-of a thorn springs not a fig
    -une source salée ne peut donner d'eau douce

    3-a thorn in the flesh
    -une épine dans le pied

    4-the thorn comes forth with the point forwards
    -l'épine en naissant va la pointe en avant

thought

    1-thought is free
    -la pensée est libre

    2-second thoughts are best
    -il faut tourner sept fois sa langue dans sa bouche avant de parler
    -pesez vos paroles

thousand

 a thousand probabilities do not make one truth
 -un tiens vaut mieux que deux tu l'auras

thread

 the thread breaks where it is weakest
 -c'est le talon d'Achille

threat

 1-all threats are not carried out
 -tout ce qui branle ne tombe pas
 -la foudre ne tombe pas toutes les fois qu'il tonne

 2-never make threats you cannot carry out
 -il ne sert à rien de montrer les dents lorsqu'on est édenté

three

 when three people know,the whole world knows
 -three may keep a secret if two of them are dead
 -secret de trois,secret de tous

thrift

 thrift is a great revenue
 -les petits ruisseaux font les grandes rivières
 -un sou amène l'autre

thrive

 1-he that will thrive must rise at five
 -l'avenir appartient à ceux qu se lèvent tôt

 2-first thrive then wive
 -lorsque la faim est à la porte,l'amour s'en va par la fenêtre
 -mariage de gueux,la faim épouse la soif

throat

 to cut one's throat
 travailler à sa propre perte

throw

 1-to throw a spanner in the works
 -mettre des bâtons dans les roues

 2-to throw good money after bad
 -courir à sa perte
 -jeter son argent par les fenêtres

 3-don't throw your dirty water until you get fresh
 -il ne faut pas chanter triomphe avant la victoire

 4-to throw a tub to the whale
 -faire diversion

 5-don't throw the baby with the bath
 -il ne faut pas jeter le bébé avec l'eau du bain
 -ne faites pas de mal par excès de zèle
 -ne maniez pas le pavé de l'ours

 6-to throw you off the scent
 -donner le change

7-to throw the rope after the bucket
-jeter le manche après la cognée

8-to throw the towel
-jeter l'éponge

9-to throw dust (speck) in his eyes
-jeter de la poudre aux yeux

10-to throw (send)the axe after the helve
-don't throw the helve after the hatchet
-jeter le manche aprèsnla cognée

11-don't throw straw against the wind
-il faut laisser le vent courir par dessus les tuiles
-il faut laisser couler l'eau

12-throw plenty of dirt,some will sure to stick
-quand on met la main à la pâte,il en reste toujours aux doigts

13-throw out a sprat to catch a makerel
-il faut perdre un vairon pour gagner un saumon

14-to throw the house out of the window
-une poule n'y retrouverait pas ses poussins

15-throw no gift againat the giver's head
-à petit présent,petit merci

16-to throw cold water on a scheme
-refroidir quelqu'un (sens figuré)

thumb
1-to twiddle one's thumbs
-se tourner les pouces

2-to have a green thumb
-avoir la main verte

3-to thumb your nose
-faire un pied de nez

thunder
1-while the thunder lasted,two bad men were friends
-l'aigle quand il est malheureux,appelle le hibou son frère

2-when it thunders,the thief becomes honest
-la crainte du Seigneur est le commencement de la sagesse
-quand il tonne le voleur devient honnête homme

tide
1-there is a tide in the affairs of men
-il y a des hauts et des bas

2-the tide must be taken when it comes
-une occasion perdue ne se rattrappe jamais
-il faut puiser quand la corde est au puits

tie

1-he has tied a knot with his tongue that he cannot untie with his teeth
-il s'est passé la corde au cou (familier il s'est marié)

2-tied to one's mother's apron strings
-être dans les jupons de sa mère

tile

to have a tile loose
-avoir une case qui manque (familier)

time

1-those that make the best thing of their time,have none to spare
-le temps est comme l'argent,n'en perdez pas et vous en aurez assez

2-lost time is never found again
-le temps perdu ne se rattrape jamais

3-times have changed
-other times,other manners
-other times,other ways
-autres temps autres moeurs

4-times change and we with them
-les temps changent et nous changeons avec eux

5-there is time for everything
-chaque chose en son temps

6-there is a time for all things
-il y a un temps pour tout

7-the times are out of joint
-tout va de travers

8-time is money
-le temps c'est de l'argent

9-time is a great healer
-time with his balm heals all wounds
-le temps est le meilleur remède

10-time works wonders
-le temps fait des merveilles

11-he that has time,has life
-qui a temps,a vie

12-time flies
-le temps passe

13-the time to come is no more than the time past
-on ne sait ni qui vit,ni qui meurt

14-it is time to lay our nuts aside
-il est temps d'être sérieux

15-a time for everything and everything in its proper place
-une place pour chaque chose et chaque chose à sa place
-après vêpres,complies

16-we must take time by the forelock
-il faut saisir l'occasion aux cheveux

17-time and tide wait for no man
-il ne faut jamais remettre au lendemain ce que l'on peut faire le jour même

18-no time like the present
-l'occasion est chauve

19-time is the father of truth
le gibet ne perd jamais ses droits
-la vérité comme l'huile vient au dessus

20-to have a hard time
-manger de la vache enragée

21-there is a time to speak and a time to be silent
-qui parle sème,qui écoute récolte

22-time out!
-pouce!

23-time devours all things
-time is a file that wears and makes no noise
-le temps dévore tout

24-time slips away when one is busy
-il n'y a rien qui aille aussi vite que le temps

-those that make the best thing of their time,have none to spare
-le temps c'est comme l'argent,n'en perdez pas et vous en aurez assez

tit

tit for tat
-s'il me donne des pois,je lui donnerai des fèves
-c'est un prêté pour un rendu

toad

1-the toad's bairns are ill to tame
-les chiens ne font pas de chats

2-the toad,ugly and venomous,wears yet a precious jewel in his head
-mauvaise tête et bon coeur
-beau noyau gît sous piètre écorce

today

1-today a man,tomorrow a mouse
-aujourd'hui roi,demain rien

2-if today will not,tomorrow may
-ce qui est différé n'est pas perdu
-la punition boîte mais elle arrive

3-one today is worth two twomorrows
-il ne faut jamais remettre à plus tard ce que l'on peut faire le jour même

toe
to toe the line
-marcher droit,au pas

tomboy
she is a tomboy
-c'est un garçon manqué

tomorrow
1-tomorrow is another (a new) day
-les jours se suivent et ne se ressemblent pas
-l'an qui vient est un brave homme
-demain,il fera jour

2-never put off till to morrow what you can do today
-tomorrow never comes
-"tomorrow" leads to the dead end of "never"
-il ne faut jamais remettre à plus tard ce que l'on peut faire le jour même

tongue
1-the tongue is sharper than any word
-the tongue is mightier than the sword
-the tongue is not steel,yet it cuts
-la langue est un bon bâton
-un coup de langue est pire qu'un coup de lance

2-the tongue is the rudder of our ship
-salive d'homme tous serpents dompte

3-let not thy tongue run away with thy brains
-let not your tongue run at rover
-little can a long tongue lein
-il faut tourner sa langue sept fois dans sa bouche
-il dit cela de bouche mais le coeur n'y touche

4-a still tongue makes a wise head
-moins on en dit,mieux on se porte

5-one tongue is enough for a woman
-il y a bien de la différence entre une femme et un fagot

6-a long tongue is a sign of short hand
-longue langue,courte main

7-to have a long tongue
-avoir la langue bien pendue

8-to have something on the tip of the tongue
-avoir quelque chose sur le bout de la langue

9-tongue and cheek
-mon oeil!

10-the tongue is the rudder of our ship
-salive d'homme tous serpents dompte

too

    too-too will in two
    -tant va la cruche à l'eau qu'elle se casse

tooth

    tooth and nail
    -pied à pied

tortoise

    the tortoise wins the race while the hare is sleeping
    -rien ne sert de courir,il faut partir à point
    -petit à petit,l'oiseau fait son nid

touch

    1-he that touches pitch shall be defiled
    -de trop près se chauffe qui se brûle
    -qui s'y frotte,s'y pique
    -on ne joue pas avec le feu

    2-he touches rouge,will be red
    -quand on met la main à ma pâte,il en reste toujours aux doigts

    3-one cannot touch pitch without being defiled
    -ceux qui touchent la poix,se souillent les doigts

tough

    a tough customer
    -une peau de vache (familier)

towel

    to throw the towel
    -jeter l'éponge

town

    there was never a good town but has a mire at one end of it
    -nulle rose sans épine

track

    1-to be on the wrong tack
    -faire fausse route

    2-to be on the right tack
    -être sur la bonne voie

trade

    1-trade is the mother of money
    -les affaires,c'est l'argent des autres

    2-a trade is better than service
    -mieux vaut acheter qu'emprunter

tradesmen

    tradesmen live upon lack
    -quand on est seul on devient nécessaire

travel

    1-travel broaders the mind
    -he that travels far knows much
    -les voyages forment la jeunesse

2-he travels fastest who travels alone
-les chiens ne chassent pas ensemble

3-it is better to travel hopefully than to arrive
-l'espoir fait vivre
-il vaut mieux arriver en retard qu'arriver en corbillard

traveller

1-travellers change climate not conditions
-qui bête va à Rome,tel en retourne

2-travellers tale fine tales
-travellers may lie with authority
-a beau mentir qui vient de loin

treat

to treat like dirt
-traiter par dessus la jambe

tree

1-a tree often transplanted,bears not much fruit
-arbre trop souvent transplanté,rarement fait fruit à planter

2-as the tree,so the fruit
-like tree,like fruit
-tel arbre,tle fruit

3-a straight tree may have crooked roots
-nous aurions souvent honte de nos plus belles actions, si le monde voyait tous les motifs qui les produisent
-le bois tordu fait le feu droit

4-a tree must be bent while it is young
-ce que le poulain prend en jeunesse,il le continue en vieillesse
-ce qu'on apprend au berceau dure jusqu'au tombeau

5-as a tree falls,so shall it lie
-de telle vie,telle fin

6-as the tree is bent,so is the tree inclined
-bon fruit vient de bonne semence

7-it is only at the tree loaded with fruit,that people throw stones
-on ne jette de pierres qu'à l'arbre chargé de fruits

8-the highest tree has the greatest fall
-de grande montée,grande chute

9-great trees are good for nothing but shades
-grosse tête,peu de sens

10-the whole tree or not a cherry on it
-tout ou rien

11-there is no tree but bare some fruit
-viendra le temps où la vache aura besoin de sa queue

trick

1-there are tricks in every trade
-le commerce est l'école de la tromperie

2-he has more than one trick up his sleeve
-il a plus d'un tour dans son sac

tricky
he is as tricky as they come
-il est malin comme un singe

trifle
do not trifle with love
-on ne badine pas avec l'amour

trim
trim your sails to the wind
-selon le vent,la voile

triton
a triton among the minnows
-faire diversion
-noyer le poisson (familier)

triumph
don't triumph before the victory
-il ne faut pas chanter triomphe avant la victoire

trouble
1-don't trouble trouble until trouble troubles you
-don't meet trouble half-way
-plus on remue la boue,plus elle pue
-du bâton que l'on tient on est souvent battu
-un renard ne se laisse pas prendre deux fois à un piège

2-trouble brings experience and experience brings wisdom
-un âne ne trébuche pas deux fois sur la même pierre
-expérience est mère de science
-qui trébuche et ne tombe pas,avance son chemin

3-let your trouble tarry till its own day comes
-never trouble trouble till trouble troubles you
-il ne faut pas pleurer avant d'être battu

true
many a true word is spoken in jest
-toute vérité n'est pas bonne à dire
-la fable est la soeur aînée de l'histoire

trump
to play one's last trump
-jouer sa dernière carte

trust
1-he who trusts not,is not deceived
-in trust is treason
-la confiance est mère de dépit

2-who trust to rotten boughs,may fall
-mauvaises compagnies corrompent les bonnes moeurs

3-trust not a new friend nor an old enemy
-aujourd'hui ami,demain ennemi

4-trust is dead,ill payment killed it
-crédit est mort,les mauvais payeurs l'ont tué

5-trust not a woman when she weeps
-à toute heure chien pisse et femme pleure

truth

1-the truth is between the two
-entre trop et trop peu est la juste mesure

2-truth has a good face but bad clothes
-l'habit ne fait pas le moine
-face d'homme porte vertu
-mauvaise tête mais bon coeur

3-the greater the truth,the greater the libel
-il n'y a que la vérité qui blesse

4-truth is stranger than fiction
-le vrai peut quelquefois n'être pas vraisemblable

5-truth lies at the bottom of the well
-la vérité est cachée au fond du puits

6-truth will come to light
-ce qui se fait de nuit paraît au grand jour

7-truth will out
-le gibet ne perd jamais ses droits

8-truth and oil are ever above
-truth is time's daughter
-la vérité comme l'huile vient au dessus

9-some truths are better left unsaid
-all truths are not to be told
-toute vérité n'est pas bonne à dire

10-truth and roses have thorns about them
-à vouloir connaître la vérité à tout prix,on risque de se brûler soi-même

11-there is truth in wine
-in vino verita

try

1-don't try to put a square peg in a round hole
-it's no use trying to put a quart into a pint pot
-à petit trou,petit cheville
2-don't try to do two things at once
-fais ce que tu fais

3-he tried another tack
-il a changé son fusil d'épaule

4-don't try to sweep back the Atlantic with a besom
-il faut laisser couler l'eau sous le pont

5-to try two things at once
-courir deux lièvres à la fois

tub

every tub should stand on its own bottom
-qui peut et n'empêche,pèche
-chacun est l'artisan de son sort
-chacun se fait fouetter à sa guise
-on ne fait pas de procession pour tailler les vignes

turf

on the turf all men are equal and under it
-le plus riche en mourant n'emporte su'un drap

turn

1-turn about is fair play
-c'est juste de te rendre la pareille

2-a turn of the wheel
-un coup de dés

3-ten good turns lie dead and one ill deed report abroad does spread
-mauvaise réputation va jusqu'à la mer;bonne réputation reste au seuil de la maison
-les bienfaits s'écrivent sur le sable et les injures sur l'airain

4-turns lie dead,ten good
-qui mange la vache du roi,à cent ans de là en pye les os*

5-to turn a deaf ear
-faire la sourde oreille

6-one good turn deserves another
-à charge de revenche
-passe moi la rhubarbe,je te passerai le séné

7-turning one's coat for luck
-tourner sa veste

tweedledum

it's tweedledum and tweedledee
-c'est jus vert et vert jus
-c'est bonnet blanc et blanc bonnet

twelfth

at Twelfth Day the days are lengthened a cock-stride
-à la fête des rois,le jour croît d'un pas de roi

twiddle

to twiddle one's thumbs
-se tourner les pouces

twist

to twist someone around one's little finger
-faire ce que l'on veut de quelqu'un

two

1-two of a trade never agree
-le péché pénètre entre la vente et l'achat

2-two is company but three is none
-les étourneaux sont maigres parce qu'ils vont en troupe

type

to type the scale
-faire pencher la balance

U

umbrella
> **under the umbrella of so and so**
> -sous sa coupe

uneasy
> **uneasy lies the head that wears a crown**
> -le plus empêché est celui qui tient la queue de la poêle
> -quand les ailes poussent à la fourmi c'est pour sa perte

unexpected
> **the unespected always happens**
> -il pleut à tout vent

unhappy
> **an unhappy man's cart is eith to tumble**
> -quand un chien se noie tout le monde lui offre à boire
> -un malheur n'arrive jamais seul

union
> **union is strength**
> **-in unity there is strength**
> **-united we stand,divided we fall**
> -l'union fait la force

unkissed
> **unkissed,unkind**
> -enfant aime moult qui beau l'appelle

unminded
> **unminded,unmoaned**
> -loin des yeux,loin du coeur

unrighteous
> **the unrighteous penny corrupts the righteous pound**
> -il suffit d'une pomme pourrie pour gâter le tas

unseen
> **unseen,unrued**
> -loin des yeux,loin du coeur

unstring
> **to unstring the bow will not heal the wound**
> -débander l'arc ne guérit pas la plaie

up
> **up and running**
> -bon pied,bon oeil!

upset
> **he upset the applecart**
> -il a tout gâché

use
> **1-once a use and ever a custom**
> -il n'y a que le provisoire qui dure

2-don't use the swing-it-till-Monday basket
-il ne faut jamais remettre à demain ce que l'on peut faire le jour même

3-use makes mastery
-usage rend maître
-le temps est un grand maître

4-use is a second nature
-l'habitude est une seconde nature

5-it's no use trying to put a quart into a pint pot
-à l'impossible nul n'est tenu

6-it is no use crying over spilt milk
-une occasion perdue ne se rattrappe jamais

7-those who make the best use of their time,have none to spare
-le travail est souvent le père du plaisir

8-don't use a sprat to catch a mackerel
-d'un veau on espère un boeuf et d'une poule un oeuf

V

vain

    it is in vain to cast your net where there is no fish
    -se battre contre des moulins à vent

vanish

    to vanish into the air
    -disparaître sans laisser de traces

variety

    variety is the spice of life
    -variety takes away satiety
    -la plus universelle qualité des esprits est la diversité
    -l'ennui naquit un jour de l'uniformité
    -ferveur de novice ne dure pas longtemps

veal

    veal will be dear,because there are no calves
    -il a des jambes de coq

vengeance

    vengeance does not spoil with keeping
    -la vengeance est un plat qui se mange froid

venom

    the venom is in the tail
    -en la queue et en la fin gît de coutume le venin

venture

    1-take your venture as many a good ship has done
    -nothing venture,nothing have
    -qui ne s'aventure pas n'a ni cheval ni mule
    -qui trop regarde quel vent vente,jamais ne sème ni ne plante
    -qui ne risque rien,n'a rien
    -il ne faut pas laisser de semer par crainte des pigeons
    -le suucès fut toujours un enfant de l'audace

    2-never venture all in one bottom
    -il ne faut pas mettre tous ses oeufs dans le même panier

    3-don't venture the saddle after the horse
    -il ne faut pas jeter le manche parès la cognée

vice

    vice is often clothed in virtue's habit
    -belle chère et coeur arrière
    -un singe vêtu de pourpre est toujours un singe

victory

    he gets a double victory,who conquers himself
    -qui se vainc une fois peut se vaincre toujours

violent

    nothing that is violent is permanent
    -les oeuvres de la violence ne sont pas durables

viper

    no viper so little,but has its venom
    -il n'est si petit buisson qui ne porte son ombre

virtue
> **1-virtue never grows old**
> -tout passera,sauf le bien que tu as fait

> **2-virtue is its own reward**
> -la vertu a cela d'heureux qu'elle se suffit à elle-même
> -la vertu est sa propre récompense

> **3-virtue is the only nobility**
> -la naissance n'est rien où la vertu n'est pas

> **4-there is no virtue that poverty destroys not**
> -en grande pauvreté ne gît pas grande loyauté

voice
> **the voice is the best music**
> -c'est le ton qui fait la chanson

volunteer
> **one volunteer is worth two pressed men**
> -un homme averti en vaut deux

vow
> **vows made in storms are forgotten in calms**
> -selon le vent,la voile

voyage
> **that voyage never has luck where each one has a vote**
> -les chiens ne chassent pas ensemble

W

wagon

the wagon must go whither the horses draw it
-quand nous serons morts,fouira la vigne qui pourra

wait

1-everything comes to him who waits
-tout vient à point à qui sait attendre

2-he that waits for a dead man's shoes is in danger of going barefoot
-en attendant les souliers des morts,on peut aller longtemps à pied
-qui court après les souliers d'un mort risque souvent d'aller nu-pieds

wake

1-to wake the sleeping dog
-remuer le fer dans la plaie
-réveiller le chat qui dort

2-wake not a sleeping lion
-n'éveillez pas le chat qui dort

walk

learn to walk before you run
-il faut commencer par le commencement

wall

1-walls have ears
-les murs ont des oreilles

2-to be a wallflower
-faire tapisserie

wame

lay your wame to your winning
selon le bras,la saignée

want

1-one does not wash one's dirty clothes in public
-il faut laver son linge sale en famille

2-if you want a thing done well,do it yourself
-if you want to be well served,serve yourself
-he who wants a mule without fault,must walk on foot
-on n'est jamais aussi bien servi que par soi-même

3-for want of a nail,the shoe was lost
-faute d'un point,Martin perdit son âne

4-want makes a strife between man and wife
-quand le foin manque au ratelier,les chevaux se battent

5-if you want a pretence to whip a dog,say he ate the frying pan
-qui veut noyer son chien,l'accuse de la rage

6-if you want peace,prepare for war
-si tu veux la paix,prépare la guerre

war

1-of all wars,peace is in the end
-après la pluie,le beau temps

2-war is sweet to them that knows it not
-nul ne sait ce qu'est la guerre s'il n'y a son fils

3-there are more ways of killing a cat than by chocking it with cream
-qui veut noyer son chien,l'accuse de la rage

4-a just war is better than an unjust peace
-une méchante paix est pire que la guerre

ware

ill ware never cheap
-on n'a jamais bon marché de mauvaises marchandises

warm

1-he warms too near that burns
-de trop près se chauffe qui se brûle

2-to warm the cockles of one's heart
-réchauffer le coeur de quelqu'un

wash

1-there is no washing a blackamoor white
- à vouloir blanchir un nègre,on y perd sa lessive

2-wash your hands often,your feet seldom,and your head never
-netteté nourrit santé

waste

1-waste not want not
-qui épargne gagne

2-to waste one's breath talking
-prêcher dans le désert

water

1-still waters run deep
-il n'est pire eau que l'eau qui dort
-craignez la colère de la colombe

2-that won't hold water
-cela ne tient pas la route

3-don't go near the water until you learn how to swim
-il ne faut pas chanter triomphe avant la victoire
-qui s'y frotte,s'y pique
-de trop près se chauffe qui se brûle

4-water drinkers bring forth nothing good
-les buveurs d'eau sont méchants

5-don't draw water with a sieve
-c'est le tonneau des Danaïdes

6-where the water is shallow,no vessel will ride
-le plat le plus bas est toujours vide

465

7-to be in deep water
-être dans de beaux draps
-être dans un mauvais pas

8-you cannot get water out of a stone
-la plus belle fille du monde ne peut donner que ce qu'elle a
-on tirerait plutôt de l'huile d'un mur

9-there was aye some water where the stirk drowned
-pas de fumée sans feu

10-water is boon in the desert but the drowning man curses it
-quand le puits est à sec on sait ce que vaut l'eau

11-too much water drowned the miller
-le surplus rompt le couvercle

12-salt water and absence wash away love
-loin des yeux,loin du coeur

way

1-the way to man's heart is through his stomach
-ventre affamé n'a pas d'oreille

2-there is but one way to enter this life but the gates of death are without number
-on ne sait ni qui meurt ni qui vit

3-there are many ways of dressing a calf's head
-there are more ways to the wood than one
-there is more than one way to skin a cat
-there are more ways to kill a cat than choke it with cream
-there are more ways to kill a dog than hang it
-tous les chemins mènent à Rome

4-the way to be safe is never to be secure
-prudence est mère de sûreté

5-there are more than two ways of doing it
-il y a trente-six façons de le faire

weaker

the weaker has the worse
-le chien attaque toujours celui qui a les pantalons déchirés
-au pauvre la besace

wealth

the greatest wealth is content with a little
-je suis riche des biens dont je sais me passer

weapon

the weapon of the brave is in his heart
-à vaillant homme,courte épée

wear

1-better to wear out than to rust out
-'tis better to wear out shoes than sheets
-mieux vaut suer que grelotter
-mieux vaut user des souliers que des draps

weep

2-to wear one's heart upon one's sleeve
ouvrir son coeur à tout le monde
-avoir un coeur d'artichaut

3-she is the one who wears the trousers
-elle porte la culotte

4-do not wear out your welcome
-l'hôte et la pluie après trois jours ennuient

5-never wear a brown hat in Friesland
-il faut hurler avec les loups

6-she wears the breeches
-elle porte la culotte

weather
1-the weather is so foul not even a Caper would venture out
-c'est un temps à ne pas mettre un chien dehors

2-don't make heavy weather of something
-n'en faites pas une montagne!
-ne vous noyez pas dans un verre d'eau
-ne faites pas d'une mouche un éléphant
-n'en faites pas une pendule (familier)

3-in fair weather,prepare for foul
-si tu veux la paix,prépare la guerre

web
for a web begun God sends the thread
-à toile ourdie,Dieu envoie le fil

wed
better wed over the mixen than over the moor
-qui trop loin va se marier,sera trompé ou veut tromper

wedlock
wedlock is padlock
se passer la corde au cou
-le mariage est une loterie

weed
1-one ill weed mars a whole pot of pottage
- peu de fiel gâte beaucoup de miel
-il suffit d'une pomme pourrie pour gâter le tas

2-ill weeds grow apace
-weeds want no sowing
-mauvaise herbe croît soudain
-les mauvaises herbes poussent toujours
-il n'est si dur fruit et acerbe qui ne mûrisse

3-the weeds overgrow the corn
-il y a plus de paille que de grain

weep
to weep millstones
-pleurer des larmes de crocodile

467

well

1-well is that well done
-mal fait qui ne parfait

2-when the well is full,it will run over
-tant va la cruche à l'eau qu'elle se casse

3-where it is well with me,there si my country
où l'on est bien,là est la patrie

4-let well enough alone
-le mieux est l'ennemi du bien

west

to go west
-passer l'arme à gauche (familier)

wet

1-with a wet finger
-les doigts dans le nez

2-he is wet behind the ears
-he's pretty wet
-don't talk wet
-c'est un blanc-bec
-si on lui presse le nez,il en sort encore du lait

whale

to throw a tub to the whale
-faire diversion
-noyer le poisson

wheat

to separate the wheat from the chaff
-séparer le bon grain de l'ivraie

wheel

1-to put a spoke in one's wheel
-mettre des bâtons dans les roues

2-he's a big wheel,a V.I.P.
-c'est une huile,c'est un ponte,une grosse légume

3-the wheel has come full circle
-on récolte ce que l'on a semé

whelp

we may not expect a good whelp from an ill dog
-la plus belle fille du monde ne peut donner que ce qu'elle a

which

which way to turn
-à quel saint se vouer

whisker

he came within a whisker (hair's breath,to a cow's thumb)
-il s'en est fallu d'un cheveu

whistle

to whistle down the wind
-comme si on chantait
-pisser dans un violon (familier)

white

1-a white boy
-un chouchou

2-she is white with fear
-elle est verte de peur

whore

a whore in a fine dress is like a clean entry to a durty house
-joli dessus,vilaine doublure
-on doit plaire par moeurs et non par robe de couleur

why

every why has a wherefore
-il n'y a pas de fumée sans feu
-les rivières ne deviennent jamais grosses qu'il n'y entre de l'eau

wicked

a wicked man is his own hell
-brebis trop apprivoisée de trop d'agneaux est tétée

wicker

the wicker has the worst
au pauvre, la besace

widow

widows are always rich
-on ne jette pas le coffre au feu parce que la clé en est perdue

wife

1-who has a fair wife,needs more than two eyes
-une femme honnête et jolie est deux fois honnête

2-old wives were aye good maidens
-le diable était beau quand il était jeune

3-who has a wife has a master
-contre femme point ne débattre

4-the wife is the key of the house
-les femmes font et défont les maisons

5-he that has no wife,beats her oft
-médecin,guéris-toi,toi-même

wile

-wiles help weak folk
-la haine,c'est la colère des faibles

will

1-he who will the end,will the means
-la fin justifie les moyens
-qui veut la fin,veut les moyens
-à bonne volonté ne vaut faculté
-on ne va pas aux mûres sans crochet

2-where there is a will,there is a way
-a wilful man will have his way
-when your will is ready,your feet are light
-quand on veut,on peut
-vouloir c'est pouvoir
-à coeur vaillant rien d'impossible

3-if one will not,another will
-chacun prend son plaisir où il se trouve
-le malhaur des uns fait le bonheur des autres

4-he that will not when he may,when he will he shall have nay
-tel refuse qui après muse
-une occasion perdue ne se rattrappe jamais

5-take the will for the deed
-l'intention vaut le fait

willow

willows are weak,yet they bind other wood
-on a toujours besoin d'un plus petit que soi
-viendra le temps où la vache aura besoin de sa queue

win

win a few,loose a few
-you can't win them all
-on ne peut pas toujours gagner

2-win at first and lose at last
-faire le lièvre

3-he won hands down
-il est arrivé dans un fauteuil
-il y est arrivé haut la main

4-I will win the horse or lose the saddle
quiite ou double

wind

1-a wind egg
-un oeuf clair

2-the wind in one's face makes one wise
-vent au visage rend l'homme sage
-la crainte de Dieu est le commencement de la sagesse

3-it's an ill wind that blows no good
-c'est un mauvais vent

4-a little wind kindles,much puts out the fire
-le surplus rompt le couvercle

window

all his goods in the window
-window dressing
-pour la galerie

wine

1-you cannot know the wine by the barrel
-on ne connaît pas le vin au cercle

2-there is truth in wine
-what soberness conceals,drunkenness reveals
-in vino veritas

3-the best wine comes out of an old vessel
-l'aboi d'un vieux chien doit on croire

4-there are lees to every wine
-chaque vin a sa lie

5-wine is a turncoat
-à ventre soul,cerises amères
-le vin entre et la raison sort

6-wine is old men's milk
-le vin est le lait des vieillards

7-when the wine is drawn,one has to drink it
-quand le vin est tiré,il faut le boire

8-good wine needs no bush
-à bon vin,point d'enseigne

winter
in the dead of winter
-au plus fort de l'hiver

wisdom
wisdom is better than strength
-plus fait douceur que violence

wise
1-a wise man changes his mind,a fool never
-il n'y a que les fous qui ne changent pas d'avis

2-it is easy to be wise after the event
-tout le monde sait être sage après coup

3-a word to the wise is enough
-à bon entendeur salut
-à bon entendeur demi-mot suffit
-qui se sent galeux se gratte

4-a wise man can learn from a fool
-un fou avise bien un sage
-les fous inventent les modes et les sages les suivent
-ce sont les fous qui troublent l'eau et ce sont les sages qui pèchent

5-wise men esteem every place
-là où l'on est bien,là est la patrie

6-as wise as an owl
-il est sage comme une image

7-a wise man is never less alone than when he is alone
-je ne suis jamais moins seul que dans la solitude (Cicéron)

wish

1-if wishes were horses,beggars would ride
-mere wishes are silly fishes
-if wishes were thrushes,then beggars would eat birds
-if wishes were butter-cakes,beggars might bite
-si souhaits fussent vrais,pastoureaux seraient rois
-si la mer bouillait,il y aurait des poissons cuits
-avec des si et des mais,on mettrait Paris en bouteille

2-the wish is father of the thought
-de tout s'avise à qui pain faut

3-wishes never can fill a sack
-oncques souhait n'emplit le sac

wit

1-let not your wits go wool-gathering
-mal fait qui ne parfait

2-at one's wit's end
-à quel saint se vouer

witness

one eye witness is better than ten ear-witness
un seul témoin oculaire en vaut dix qui ont entendu

woe

woes unite foes
-l'aigle quand il est malheureux appelle le hibou son frère

wolf

1-the wolf may lose his teeth but never his nature
-en sa peau mourra le loup
-le loup change de poil mais non de naturel

2-when the wolf comes at the door,love creeps out of the window
-lorque la faim est à la porte,l'amour s'en va par la fenêtre

3-it is a wolf in sheep's clothing
-c'est un loup déguisé en brebis

woman

1-a woman's tongue wags like a lamb's tail
-elle est bavarde comme une pie

2-a woman is a weathercock
-women are fickle
-a woman's mind and a winter wind change oft
-women are as wavering as the wind
-souvent femme varie,bien fol est qui s'y fie
-ciel pommelé et femme fardée ne sont pas de longue durée

3-a woman's sword is her tongue,and she does not let it rust
- langue des femmes est leur épée,elles ne la laissent pas rouiller

4-a woman without virtue is like palled wine
-beauté sans bonté est comme vin éventé

5-women will have their wills
-once a woman's mind is made up,there is no changing it
-ce que femme veut,Dieu le veut

6-the woman wears the trousers
-elle porte la culotte

7-a woman,a dog,and a walnut tree,the more you beat them the better they be
-les femmes sont comme les omelettes,elles ne sont jamais assez battues

8-a woman and a ship ever want mending
-à une femme et une vieille maison,il y a toujours à refaire

9-women laugh when they can and weep when they will
-femme rit quand elle peut et pleure quand elle veut

10-a woman that parleys is half gotten
-a woman kissed is half won
-women resist in order to be conquered
-fille et ville qui parlementent sont à demi rendues

11-a woman's sword is her tongue,and she does not let it rust
-la langue des femmes est leur épée,elles ne la laissent pas rouiller

12-his words carry no weight
-il n'est que la cinquième roue du carosse

wonder

1-wonders will never cease
-l'ignorance est toujours prête à admirer

2-wonder is ths daughter of ignorance
-l'admiration est la fille de l'ignorance
-l'ignorance est toujours prête à s'admirer

3-a wonder lasts but nine days
-un feu de paille

wood

1-to be out of the woods
-être sorti de l'auberge

2-to knock on wood
-toucher du bois

3-drawn from the wood (for beer or wine)
-bière à la pression
-vin au tonneau

4-green wood makes a hot fire
-il n'est feu que de bois vert

wool

1-to be wool gathering
-être dans la lune

2-no wool so white than a dyer cannot blacken it
-la fumée s'attache au blanc

word

1-good words without deeds are rushes and reeds
-fine words butter no parsnips
-le fait juge l'homme

2-upon my word (or of honour)
-parole d'honneur

3-from word to deed is a great space
-dire et faire sont deux

4-words are but wind,but blows unkind
-méchante parole jetée va partout à la volée

5-many words will not fill a bushel
-la beauté ne sale pas la marmite

6-to give or pass one's word
-donner sa parole

7-soft words butter no parsnips
-la belle cage ne nourrit pas l'oiseau
-la beauté ne sale pas la marmite
-beauté de femme n'enrichit l'homme
-il dit cela de bouche,mais le coeur n'y touche

8-in many words,the truth goes by
-on sait ce que parler veut dire

9-a word spoken is an arrow let fly
-la langue est un bon bâton

10-a word to the wise is enough
-à bon entendeur.salut
-à bon entendeur.demi-mot suffit

11-a word spoken is past recalling
-a word and a stone let go cannot be recalled
-tourner sept fois sa langue dans sa bouche avant de parler

12-in many words the truth goes by
-on sait ce que parler veut dire

13-to take words for gospel
-prendre des paroles pour argent comptant
-prendre des paroles pour paroles d'évangile

14-words fly,writings remain
-les paroles s'envolent mais les écrits restent

15-words bind men
-l'usage est le tyran des langues

work

1-a work ill done must be done twice
-jamais deux sans trois
-cent fois sur le métier remettez votre ouvrage
-labeurs sans soin,labeurs de rien

2-it is not work that kills but sorrow
-l'écurie use plus le cheval que la course

3-if you don't work,you shan't eat
-chaque poule vit de ce qu'elle gratte
-nul pain sans peine
-les mains noires font manger le pain blanc
-si tu manges ton pain blanc le premier,tu manges ton pain noir plus tard
-celui qui laboure le champ,le mange

4-to work like the devil
-travailler à tour de bras

5-to work a dead horse
-to work tooth and nail
-mettre les bouchées doubles
-travailler sans se soustraire à la tâche

6-all work and no play makes Jack a dull boy
-l'arc ne peut toujours être tendu
-l'ennui naquit un jour de l'uniformité

7-work expands as to fill the time available
-l'homme naquit pour travailler comme l'oiseau pour voler
-on n'a jamais fini de faire son devoir

8-it worked like a charm
-cela s'est passé comme une fleur

9-all work is honorable
-il n'y a pas de sot métier,il n'y a que de sottes gens

10-to have the work cut out for
-avoir du pain sur la planche

11-to work for peanuts
-travailler pour des prunes

12-to work shoulder to shoulder
-travailler au coude à coude

workman

1-the workman is known by his work
-as the workman so is the work
-c'est au pied du mur qu'on reconnait le maçon
-à l'oeuvre on connaît l'artisan
-à la griffe on reconnaît le lion
-tant vaut l'homme,tant vaut la terre

2-what is a workman without his tools?
-on ne peut faire d'omelette sans casser des oeufs

3-a bad workman blames his tools
-mauvais artisan ne trouve jamais bon outil

world

1-one half of the world does not know how the other lives
-la moitié du monde ne sait comment l'autre vit

2-let the world wag
-le monde est un spectacle à regarder et non un problème à résoudre

3-it's a small world
-seules les montagnes ne se rencontrent jamais

4-it is a wicked world and we make part of it
-que celui qui n'a jamais péché jette la première pierre

5-the world is full of fools
-il est des sots de tout pays

worm

one day the worm will turn
-il arrive que l'agneau devienne enragé

worry

not to worry
-dormir sur ses deux oreilles

worship

more worship the rising than the setting sun
-rien ne réussit comme le succès

worst

the worst hog gets the best pear
-les bons pâtissent pour les mauvais

worth

1-no worth a rap
-not worth a snap of the fingers
-cela ne vaut pas un pet de lapin (familier)
-cela ne vaut pas un clou
-cela ne vaut pas un sous

2-the worth of a thing is what it will bring
-tant vaut la chose comme elle peut être vendue

wound

though the wound be healed,yet a scar remains
-chat échaudé craint l'eau froide

wrangle

-wrangle for an ass shadow
-lâcher la proie pour l'ombre

wrap

to wrap up in clean linen
-envelopper dans du papier de soie

wrath

when wrath speaks,wisdom veils her face
-la raison qui s'emporte a le sort de l'erreur

write

never write what you dare not sign
-les paroles s'envolent,les écrits restent
-ce qui est écrit est écrit

wrong

1-do wrong once and you'll never hear the end of it
-qui mange la vache du roi,à cent de là en paye les os

2-wrong never comes right
-il n'y a pas de prescription contre la vérité les erreurs pour être vieilles n'en sont pas meilleures

Y

yawn

to yawn one's head off
-bâiller à se décrocher la mâchoire

year

1-from year's end to years end
-d'un bout de l'année à l'autre

2-it will all be the same in a hundred year hence
-il passera bien de l'eau sous le pont

3-years know more than books
-il n'est rien comme les vieux ciseaux pour couper la soie

yes

a yes-man
-un béni oui-oui

young

young colts will canter
-il n'est feu que de bois vert

youth

1-youth will have its fling
-youth will have its swing
-youth must be served
-il faut que jeunesse se passe

2-what youth is used to,age remmbers
-l'habitude est une seconde nature
-ce qu'on apprend au berceau,dure jusqu'au tombeau
-ce que le poulain prend en jeunesse,il le continue en vieillesse

3-if youth but knew,if age but could
-if youth knew what age could crave,it would both get and save
-si jeunesse savait,si vieillesse pouvait

Z

zeal

zeal without knowledge is a runaway horse
-science sans conscience n'est que ruine de l'âme

Cet ouvrage a été achevé d'imprimer en octobre 1997
dans les ateliers de Normandie Roto Impression s.a.
61250 Lonrai
N° d'impression : 972107
Dépôt légal : octobre 1997

Imprimé en France